The *Paterik* of the Kievan Caves Monastery

HARVARD LIBRARY OF EARLY UKRAINIAN LITERATURE

English Translations   Volume I

Editorial Board

    Omeljan Pritsak, *Editor-in-Chief*
    Ihor Ševčenko, *Associate Editor-in-Chief*
    Paul Hollingsworth, *Managing Editor*
    Roman Koropeckyj, *Associate Managing Editor*
    George G. Grabowicz
    Edward L. Keenan
    Horace G. Lunt

Associate Editors

    Lubomyr Hajda
    Frank E. Sysyn

Consulting Editors

    Olexa Horbatsch (Frankfurt am Main)
    Jaroslav Isajevych (L'viv)
    Ryszard Łużny (Cracow)
    Oleksa Mišanič (Kiev)
    Riccardo Picchio (Naples)
    Hans Rothe (Bonn)
    George Y. Shevelov (New York)
    William R. Veder (Amsterdam)

Production Editor

    Thomas M. Kearney

ГАРВАРДСЬКА БІБЛІОТЕКА ДАВНЬОГО УКРАЇНСЬКОГО ПИСЬМЕНСТВА

Корпус Англійських Перекладів   Том I

The *Paterik* of the Kievan Caves Monastery

Translated by Muriel Heppell

with a Preface by Sir Dimitri Obolensky

Millennium Rus'-Ucrainae Sacrum

Distributed by the Harvard University Press
for the
Ukrainian Research Institute of Harvard University

© 1989 by the President and Fellows of Harvard College
All rights reserved
ISBN: 978-1-932650-07-5
Library of Congress Catalog Number 88-82377
Printed in the United States of America

*The preparation of this volume was made possible in part
by a grant from the National Endowment for the Humanities,
an independent federal agency.*

The Harvard Ukrainian Research Institute was established in 1973 as an integral part of Harvard University. It supports research associates and visiting scholars who are engaged in projects concerned with all aspects of Ukrainian studies. The Institute also works in close cooperation with the Committee on Ukrainian Studies, which supervises, and coordinates the teaching of Ukrainian history, language, and literature at Harvard University.

Printed by
Harvard University
Cambridge, Massachusetts
Office of the University Publisher

Publication of this volume was made possible through the generous support of Wolodymyr and Victoria Klos

Цей том появляється завдяки щедрій підтримці
Панства Володимира і Вікторії Клосів

*Dedicated to the memory of Hugh Seton-Watson,
with gratitude and affection*

Contents

Editorial Statement	xiii
Preface by Sir Dimitri Obolensky	xv
Abbreviations	xvi
Introduction by Muriel Heppell	xvii
Map	liii

The *Paterik* of the Kievan Caves Monastery

Discourse 1
Concerning the building of the church — 1

Discourse 2
Arrival of the craftsmen from Constantinople — 6

Discourse 3
When the church of the Caves Monastery was founded — 9

Discourse 4
The coming of the church-painters — 11

Discourse 5
A miracle concerning Ioann and Sergij — 14

Discourse 6
The holy table and the consecration of the great Church — 15

Discourse 7
An account of why the Caves Monastery is so called — 18

Discourse 8
The Life of our venerable father Feodosij — 24

Discourse 9
The translation of the relics of Feodosij — 89

Discourse 10
    The decoration of Feodosij's coffin   95

Discourse 11
    An encomium to our venerable father Feodosij   99

Discourse 12
    The first monks of the Caves Monastery   108

Discourse 13
    How Nifont saw Feodosij in a divine revelation   110

Discourse 14
    An epistle from the bishop Simon to Polikarp   113

Discourse 15
    Simon's narrative about the holy monks   120

Discourse 16
    Blessed Evstratij the Faster   123

Discourse 17
    The meek and long-suffering monk Nikon   125

Discourse 18
    The holy martyr Kukša and Pimin the Faster   128

Discourse 19
    Holy Afanasij the Solitary   129

Discourse 20
    The venerable Svjatoša   131

Discourse 21
    The monk Erazm   137

Discourse 22
    The monk Arefa   139

Discourse 23
    The priest Tit and the deacon Evagrij   140

Discourse 24
    A second epistle, to Archimandrite Akindin   142

Discourse 25
    Nikita the Solitary   143

Discourse 26
    Lavrentij the Solitary   146

Discourse 27
    The holy and blessed Agapit   147

Discourse 28
    Holy Grigorij the Miracle-worker   153

Discourse 29
    The much-suffering Ioann the Solitary   158

Discourse 30
    Venerable Moisej the Hungarian   162

Discourse 31
    The monk Proxor   169

Discourse 32
    Venerable Marko the Cave-dweller   175

Discourse 33
    The holy venerable fathers Feodor and Vasilij   181

Discourse 34
    Spiridon the baker and Alimpij the Icon-painter   190

Discourse 35
    The venerable and long-suffering father Pimin   200

Discourse 36
    Venerable Isaakij the Cave-dweller   205

Discourse 37
    The pious prince Izjaslav's inquiry   211

Discourse 38
    The death of Polikarp, and the priest Vasilij   215

Appendix I
    The Sources of Discourse 7   218

Appendix II
    Letter of Patriarch Nicholas Mouzalon to Nifont   223

Appendix III
    Suggested Reconstruction of Polikarp's Dedicatory Letter   224

Appendix IV
    Isaakij the Cave-dweller and the "Jurodstvo" Tradition   228

Bibliography   231

Index of Biblical References   242

Index of Greek Terms   245

Index of Slavonic Terms   246

Index   247

Editorial Statement

The *Harvard Library of Early Ukrainian Literature* is one portion of the Harvard Project in Commemoration of the Millennium of Christianity in Rus'-Ukraine, which is being carried out by the Ukrainian Research Institute of Harvard University with the financial support of the Ukrainian community.

The *Library* encompasses literary activity in Rus'-Ukraine from its beginning in the mid-eleventh century through the end of the eighteenth century, and primarily contains original works, although exceptions are made for such seminally important translations as the Ostroh Bible of 1581. Included are ecclesiastical and secular works written in a variety of languages, such as Church Slavonic, Old Rus', Ruthenian (Middle Ukrainian), Polish, and Latin. This linguistic diversity reflects the cultural pluralism of Ukrainian intellectual activity in the medieval and early-modern periods.

The *Library* consists of three parts. The *Texts* series publishes the original works, in facsimile whenever appropriate. Texts from the medieval period are offered either in the best available scholarly edition or in one specially prepared for the *Library*, while those from the later periods are reproduced from manuscripts or early printed editions. Two other series—*English Translations* and *Ukrainian Translations*—contain translations of the original works.

Each volume begins with an introductory essay by a specialist. The two translation series also include indices, as well as a concordance table to the companion volume in the texts series. A cumulative index to the entire *Library* will be issued.

Forty volumes are planned for each of the series, although the total may be greater as additional works are accommodated. Volumes within each series are numbered and published in the order in which they are prepared.

The introductions and translations reflect the linguistic and terminological diversity of the original works. Thus, for example, appellations such as Rus', Rusija, Rossija, Mala Rossija, Malaja Rossija, Malorossija, Ruthenia, Malorossijskaja Ukrajina, Ukrajina, and so on, are presented according to their actual use in the given text. All of these terms have historically been used to designate "Ukraine" and "Ukrainian." In addition, the word Ruthenian is employed to translate early-modern nomenclature for "Ukraine" and "Ukrainian" and early-modern terminology describing common Ukrainian and Belorussian culture, language, and identity. For much of the period covered by the *Library* Ukrainian and Belorussian cultural figures were active in a shared social, intellectual, and religious milieu. Since the *Library* selects authors and works important to the Ukrainian part of this sphere, their names are rendered in Ukrainian form, even though at times they may also have been of significance in Belorussian territory.

Use of the definite article with "Ukraine" is left to the discretion of the author or translator of each volume.

With the exception of toponyms with already-established English forms, place-names are usually given in accordance with the official language of the state or, in the case of the Soviet Union, of the republic that holds the territory; pre-modern or alternative modern forms are indicated in the indices.

The *Library* uses the International System of transliteration for Church Slavonic, Old Rus', and the modern languages using the Cyrillic alphabet; this system has been adapted to transliterate Ruthenian (Middle Ukrainian) texts as well.

For the present volume, all citations from the Old Testament are rendered by Charles L. Brenton's 1851 translation of the Septuagint, and those from the New Testament by the King James version.

PREFACE

The *Paterik* of the Kievan Caves Monastery is a collection of stories, mostly stemming from the eleventh and early twelfth century, about monks who lived in the Kievan Caves Monastery, the leading monastic house in early medieval Rus'. For the most part they were written down in the early thirteenth century by a bishop who had formerly belonged to the community, and by one of its resident monks. These various writings were later collected and edited, and in 1462 one of its editors gave to this miscellany the title *Pečerskij Paterik*.

The *Paterik* is a document of great value to the student of medieval Rus' and of Byzantium. It illustrates the early phases of Kievan monasticism by providing first-hand information on its ideals, organization, and relation with secular society; it contains a detailed and vivid biography of one of the monastery's founders, St. Theodosius (Feodosij), a charismatic leader who exerted a great influence on church and society in medieval Rus'; it reflects the tension, never fully resolved in medieval Christian monasticism, between the contemplative calling and life in the community; and it reveals, often strikingly, the capacity for adapting Byzantine models to local conditions and needs which we find in other fields of medieval Rus' culture.

Dr. Muriel Heppell, drawing on a long and close acquaintance with the *Paterik*, has provided the first full-length English translation of this work. Students of the medieval history of Eastern Europe, of the Christian monastic tradition, and of the Orthodox Church of more recent times, will be greatly in her debt.

Dimitri Obolensky
Oxford, England

ABBREVIATIONS

Abramovyč, *Pateryk*. *Kyjevo-Pečers'kij Pateryk*, ed. D. I. Abramovyč. Kiev, 1930. Reprint, ed. D. Čyževs'kyj. Slavische Propyläen, 2. Munich, 1964.

Ἀνδρῶν ἁγίων βίβλος [The Book of Holy Men]. *The Old Church Slavonic Translation of the* Ἀνδρῶν ἁγίων βίβλος, *in the edition of Nicolaas van Wijk*. Ed. D. Armstrong et al. The Hague, 1975.

Cas. I. *Kievo-Pečerskij Paterik*, First Cassian Redaction (1460).

Cas. II. *Kievo-Pečerskij Paterik*, Second Cassian Redaction (1462).

Čtenija. *Čtenija v Imperatorskom Obščestve istorii i drevnostej rossijskix pri Moskovskom universitete*.

IORJAS. *Izvestija Otdelenija russkogo jazyka i slovesnosti Imperatorskoj akademii nauk*.

OLDP. *Obščestvo ljubitelej drevnej pismennosti*.

PG. *Patrologia Graeca*, ed. J. P. Migne.

PL. *Patrologia Latina*, ed. J. P. Migne.

PSRL. *Polnoe sobranie russkix letopisej*.

PVL. *Povest' vremennyx let*. Ed. D. S. Lixačev. Moscow-Leningrad, 1950.

TODRL. *Trudy Otdela drevnerusskoj literatury*.

UspSb. *Uspenskij sbornik*.

ŽMNP. *Žurnal Ministerstva narodnogo prosveščenija*.

INTRODUCTION

No single institution was more important for the development of a Christian society among the East Slavs than the Monastery of the Dormition of the Theotokos in Kiev, more commonly known by its traditional name—the Kievan Caves Monastery (*Kievo-pečer'skaja lavra*). It was not the oldest formal monastic community of medieval Rus'. According to a twelfth-century chronicle, during his reign Prince Jaroslav Volodimerovič of Kiev (1019–54) endowed two monasteries, one dedicated to St. George and another to St. Irene.[1] Yet even then a small monastic community was coalescing on the southern outskirts of Kiev around the figure of Antonij, a native of Rus' who had lived on Mount Athos but had returned to Kiev and taken up residence in a cave above the Dnieper. By the end of the century, thanks largely to the organizational ability of a series of dynamic superiors and the patronage of several generous Kievan princes, the Caves Monastery had become the leading monastery of the Middle Dnieper region.[2]

The Caves Monastery deserves the prominent role in the medieval East Slavic world which modern scholars attribute to it. Not only was it a leading center of intellectual and spiritual activity, but its superiors and monks also exerted a strong influence on the social and political life of the Kievan region. Moreover, its reputation and prestige were extended throughout Rus' by the many bishops who came from the monastery's ranks. Yet perhaps the most important reason why the Caves Monastery

---

[1] They are mentioned in the entry for the year 1037 in the *Povĕst' vremennyx lĕt* ("Tale of Bygone Years," hereafter PVL), a compilation made ca. 1115 probably at the Caves Monastery and the most important literary source for early Rus' history. Because the PVL lacks an authoritative critical edition (see D. Ostrowski, "Textual Criticism and the *Povest' vremennykh let*," *Harvard Ukrainian Studies* 5 [1981]:11–31), all subsequent references will cite its two basic witnesses: the copy contained in the fourteenth-century *Laurentian Chronicle* (hereafter *Laur.*), *Polnoe sobranie russkix letopisej* (hereafter PSRL), vol. 1, 2nd. ed. (Leningrad, 1926), and the copy in the fifteenth-century *Hypatian Chronicle* (hereafter *Hyp.*), PSRL, vol. 2, 2nd. ed. (St. Petersburg, 1908). Unless otherwise noted, all references to volumes in the PSRL will refer to second editions. For the reference to Jaroslav's monastic foundations, see PVL 1037, PSRL 1:151, 2:139. St. George was his patron saint, and St. Irene was the patron of his wife, Ingigerd of Sweden.

[2] The history of monasticism in medieval Rus' still awaits a comprehensive study. Two brief surveys in English on the earliest period are R. Casey, "Early Russian Monasticism," *Orientalia Christiana Periodica* 19 (1953):372–423, and A. P. Vlasto, *The Entry of the Slavs into Christendom* (Cambridge, Eng., 1970), 301–7.

looms so large in our conception of medieval Rus' is, quite simply, that it is the only monastery from the pre-Mongol period about which detailed information has survived. By one scholar's reckoning, at least seventy monasteries had been founded in Rus' before the Mongol invasion of 1238–40,[3] but in most cases only the monastery's name, the date of its foundation, and sometimes the identity of its founder are known. For the Caves Monastery, however, we possess the *Paterik*, a thirteenth-century work drawing on both contemporary and ancient sources to narrate the monastery's origins and to relate the exploits of its holy men.[4] Concerned mainly with the spiritual struggles and aspirations of the monastery's inhabitants, the *Paterik* provides a wealth of details about the monastery as a religious institution, but because its monks were intimately involved in the political and social life of the city of Kiev, it also furnishes interesting glimpses of life beyond the monastery's walls. As such, it is one of the most crucial sources for reconstructing medieval Rus' history.

1. *The Literary Form of the* Paterik

In its most typical form—that of the *Second Cassian* redaction compiled in 1462, on which the present translation is based—the *Paterik* consists of 38 discourses (*slova*):

Discourses 1–6 describe the foundation, building, decoration, and consecration of the monastery's Church of the Dormition of the Theotokos, which was begun in 1073 and consecrated in 1089. These discourses were written early in the thirteenth century by Simon, bishop of Vladimir and Suzdal', himself a former member of the Caves Monastery.

Discourse 7 is an anonymous *Account of why the Caves Monastery is so called*, which introduces the principal figures in the monastery's early history: the hermit Antonij, its founder; Prince Izjaslav Jaroslavič of Kiev, its friend and benefactor; and the superior Feodosij, who laid the foundations of its cenobitic organization.

Discourses 8–11 concern Feodosij: his Life, written by Nestor, a monk of the monastery (Discourse 8); the translation of Feodosij's remains from the cave where he was buried to the stone church in 1091

---

[3] See E. E. Golubinskij, *Istorija russkoj cerkvi*, 2nd ed., vol. 1, pt. 2 (Moscow 1904), 746–76.

[4] The essential critical edition, the one from which this English translation was made, is D. Abramovyč, ed., *Kyjevo-Pečers'kyj pateryk* (Kiev, 1930) (hereafter abbreviated as Abramovyč, *Pateryk*).

(Discourse 9); an account of the decoration of his tomb there by a boyar named Georgij Simonovič around 1129 (Discourse 10); and a commemorative eulogy preached on his feast day many years after his death (Discourse 11).

Discourse 12 consists of short accounts of three contemporaries of Feodosij: the monks Damian, Ieremej, and Matfej; it is entitled, somewhat inaccurately, *The first monks of the Caves Monastery*.

Discourse 13 describes a visit to the monastery by Nifont, bishop of Novgorod, in 1156, just before his death; he was a former member of the monastery, and a great admirer of Feodosij, so that this discourse may also be considered as part of the "Feodosian" section of the *Paterik*.

Discourse 14 strikes a new, vivid, and personal note: it is a long letter from Simon, bishop of Vladimir and Suzdal' (the author of Discourses 1–6), to his spiritual son Polikarp, then a monk in the Caves Monastery.

Discourses 15–23 are nine accounts of former monks, most of them quite short, also written by Bishop Simon. The subjects of these discourses are either monks of outstanding achievement in the monastic life or individuals whose lives provided a warning against slackness and backsliding in the pursuit of the monastic ideal. Discourses 17–23 all end with personal messages to Polikarp, in which Simon points out the lesson to be learned from each narrative.

Simon's narratives in this part of the *Paterik* read as though they were hurriedly written without much thought for literary elegance; his main concern is didactic, namely to convey his message as effectively as possible and to emphasize and illustrate the points made in his letter to Polikarp.

Discourses 24–35 were written by Polikarp. Apart from a brief dedicatory letter to his superior, Archimandrite Akindin (Discourse 24), they are all narratives about monks who were in the monastery in the late eleventh century or earlier.

In contrast to Simon's material, Polikarp's narratives indicate a careful reworking of his sources and a desire to present them according to the accepted conventions of hagiographical writing. He includes numerous miracle stories, many of which have counterparts in earlier works, sometimes adapting them to suit his particular theme. He also introduces a psychological element by trying to depict, sometimes very successfully, the inner struggles and experiences of some of his subjects. He writes well, and some of his anecdotes, such as the story of the two bowls of tears at the end of Discourse 32, are masterpieces of vivid story telling.[5] Polikarp's narratives are followed by an anonymous account of a monk named Isaakij the Cave-dweller (Discourse 36). He was also a contemporary of the superior Feodosij and of the monks described in Discourse 12; an account of these four monks is included in the 1074 entry of the PVL, so it is curious that Isaakij's story got separated from the others in the *Paterik*.

Discourse 37 is a polemical treatise against the "Latins" attributed to the superior Feodosij; it is not found in earlier redactions of the *Paterik*, and its inclusion in the *Second Cassian* redaction in 1462 may well reflect the strong anti-Latin sentiment in the Orthodox Church after the Council of Florence in 1439.

Finally, Discourse 38 is a brief anonymous account of the election of a secular priest named Vasilij as superior of the monastery in 1182.

As a literary genre the *Paterik* is not easy to define. It is not a collection of *vitae*, though it does contain one good example of this kind of work, the Life of Feodosij, and most of the narrative discourses are written in the hagiographical style; nor is it a history of the Caves Monastery, though it contains a considerable amount of information from which the origins and early history of the monastery can be reconstructed. Its closest structural affinity is with such works of early monastic literature as the *Lausiac History* of Palladius and the *Historia monachorum in Aegypto* by Rufinus. These and other similar works from Late Antiquity were already known in Church Slavonic translations by the time the Kievan *Paterik* was written.

Indeed, the term *paterik* is taken from the translated literature, and when used alone almost always denoted the Church Slavonic translation of a Greek work described by Patriarch Photios as Ἀνδρῶν ἁγίων βίβλος (The Book of Holy Men).[6] The fullest and best known version of this work is the Latin translation of Pelagius and John the Deacon, which forms Books V and VI of Rosweyd's *Vitae Patrum*.[7] There are numerous Church Slavonic manuscripts containing different redactions of this work, and during the past twenty years several studies of these have

---

[5] Discourse 29 differs from the others in that most of it is related in the first person, which suggests that it might have been based on a "spiritual testament" composed by Ioann the Solitary himself.

[6] It is listed as No. 98 in the contents of Photios's library. See PG 103:664–65.

[7] See PL 73:858–1022. Parts I–XVII have been translated into English under the title "The Sayings of the Fathers." See W. O. Chadwick, *Western Asceticism*, Library of Christian Classics, 12 (London, 1958), 37–189.

appeared,[8] along with one edition of the text by the late Professor N. van Wijk,[9] who did much pioneer work in this field. In Church Slavonic translations of similar works the generic word *paterik* is accompanied by an adjective denoting the place to which the material refers.[10] For example, the *Egipetskij Paterik* contains most of the *Historia monachorum* and extracts from the *Lausiac History*,[11] while the Slavonic version of the *Pratum Spirituale* is called the *Sinajskij Paterik*.[12]

Yet despite a basic structural resemblance, the Kievan *Paterik* has distinctive features not found in the earlier works. The unity of place is much more limited, since it is confined to a single monastery, while the period of time covered is much greater—from the return of Moisej the Hungarian to Kiev around 1025[13] up to Bishop Simon's letter to Polikarp written early in the thirteenth century. Moreover, all of Polikarp's narratives and most of Simon's were based not on personal observation or oral tradition, but on written sources. Thus, the *Paterik* differs from the *Historia monachorum* and the *Lausiac History* in much the same way as history differs from memoirs. Whether by accident or design, the authors and editors of the *Paterik* succeeded in creating a literary medium admirably suited to their material: the predominance of the short narrative gives it a firm literary structure lacking in most early monastic writings of this type, while the variety of the subject matter and its treatment

---

[8] For bibliography, see G. Podskalsky, *Christentum und theologische Literatur in der Kiever Rus' (988–1237)* (Munich, 1982), 59–61.

[9] N. van Wijk, ed., *The Old Church Slavonic Translation of the* Ἀνδρῶν ἁγίων βίβλος, edited and prepared for publication by D. Armstrong, R. Pope, and C. H. van Schoonveld (The Hague, 1975).

[10] The descriptive epithet is not always accurate. For example, the material in the collection known as the *Ierusalimskij Paterik* refers more to Egypt than to Palestine and appears to be another version of the Ἀνδρῶν ἁγίων βίβλος. See N. van Wijk, "Podrobnyj obzor cerkovno-slavjanskogo perevoda Bol'šogo Limonarija," *Byzantinoslavica* 7 (1935–6):62–81, who provides a detailed description of the text of the *Ierusalimskij Paterik* contained in *Cod. Berol. Wuk. 40*.

[11] See N. van Wijk, "O proisxoždenii Egipetskogo Paterika," *Sbornik v čest na Prof. L. Miletič* (Sofia, 1933), 361–69, and I. P. Eremin, "K istorii drevnerusskoj perevodnoj povesti," TODRL 3 (1936):37–57.

[12] Parts of the *Sinajskij Paterik* were published over a century ago by I. I. Sreznevskij, *Svedenija i zametki o maloizvestnyx i neizvestnyx pamjatnikax*, vol. 4 (St. Petersburg, 1879), 49–110. For the complete text, see *Sinajskij Paterik*, ed. V. S. Golyšenko and V. F. Dubrovina (Moscow, 1967).

[13] See Discourse 30, n. 538.

prevents it from becoming monotonous.[14] Throughout the whole work it is the monastery that dominates, transcending even the most illustrious of its individual members.

2. *The Life of Feodosij*

Although the Life of Feodosij forms part of all extant redactions of the *Paterik*, it existed as an independent text long before the *Paterik* was composed,[15] having been written in the late eleventh century by the monk Nestor, who also wrote a *vita* and *passio* about SS. Boris and Glěb.[16] In both structure and style it shows the influence of earlier *vitae*, a number of which had been translated into Church Slavonic before the Life of Feodosij was written, in particular that of the Life of Sabbas the Sanctified by Cyril of Scythopolis.[17] Nestor was also familiar with the Life of St. Antony the Great (d. 356) by St. Athanasios, which he cites directly.[18] He had probably also read the Life of Euthymios the Great by Cyril of Scythopolis.[19] Thus he had ample sources on which to base his literary technique.

Nestor adheres closely to traditional hagiographic patterns, both in the presentation of his material and in his mode of expression, e.g., in the conventional introductory passage, in which he confesses his inadequacy for the task he has undertaken; in his account of Feodosij's childhood; in the numerous miracle stories woven into the texture of the narrative; and in the detailed description of Feodosij's death and post-mortem miracles. Yet Nestor was no slavish imitator, and his work has a pleasing

---

[14] See F. Bubner, *Das Kiever Paterikon; eine Untersuchung zu seiner Struktur und den literarischen Quellen* (Augsburg, 1969).

[15] The date of the composition of the Life of Feodosij can be approximately calculated from the text itself, since Nestor mentions the death of Prince Izjaslav, which occurred in 1078, and at the end of his work he writes as though Nikon were still superior. Nikon died in 1088, so Nestor must have written his work between 1078 and 1088. The issue is discussed in detail by A. Poppe, "Chronologia utworów Nestora hagiografa," *Slavia Orientalis* 14 (1965):297.

[16] See Discourse 7, n. 72; Discourse 8, p. 24.

[17] The textual resemblances between the Life of Feodosij and the Life of Sabbas have been tabulated by A. A. Šaxmatov "Neskol'ko slov o Nestorovom Žitii Feodosija," IORJAS 1 (1896):46–65.

[18] See Discourse 8, p. 46.

[19] There are some manuscripts in which the Lives of Antony, Euthymios, and Sabbas are found together (see Šaxmatov, "Neskol'ko slov," 64). There was probably one of these in the Caves Monastery when Nestor was writing, since Feodosij refers to these saints as a group in a Lenten address to his monks which is preserved in PVL 1074, PSRL 1:185, 2:175.

spontaneity. His description of Feodosij's struggles with a possessive mother shows a wealth of detail and liveliness of characterization which not only suggests some basis in fact (although the saint-versus-parent motif is a common hagiographic topos),[20] but also illustrates Nestor's ability to fit the material at his disposal into the established literary pattern. He shows himself to be a gifted storyteller, and some of his subsidiary characters are vividly drawn: the masterful priest and later superior Nikon, the humble and saintly Damian, the timorous brother in charge of the church lamps, and the disobedient cellarer. In the introductory *exordium* he constructs an image of Feodosij as the pastor and teacher of a newly converted land, thus giving his work a character specific to Rus'.[21] In short, the Life of Feodosij provides an example of that capacity for adaptation rather than imitation which is also apparent in other branches of creative activity in Rus', such as architecture and icon painting.

3. *The Authors of the* Paterik

(i) Nestor

Little is known about Nestor, apart from his own statement in the Life of Feodosij that he was received into the monastery and tonsured by the superior Stefan (1074–?1077), Feodosij's successor, and later ordained deacon by him.[22] Polikarp mentions a "Nestor the chronicler" in his list of the "devout fathers" of the monastery during the time of the superior Nikon (?1077–1088),[23] who was probably the same Nestor as the author of the Life of Feodosij. If he was also the Nestor who wrote the account of the translation of the relics of Feodosij,[24] then he was still in the monastery in 1091; it is not known when he died. As noted above,

---

[20] Nestor says he obtained this information about Feodosij's early life from the cellarer Feodor, who got it directly from Feodosij's mother. See Discourse 8, p. 35.

[21] See J. Børtnes, "Frame Technique in Nestor's Life of St. Theodosius," *Scando-Slavica* 13 (1967):6–9. For a more detailed analysis of the literary aspect of the Life of Feodosij, see idem., *Det gammelrussiske helgenvita. Dikterisk egenant og historisk betynding* (Oslo, 1975), and F. Siefkes, *Zur Form des Žitije Feodosija*, Frankfurter Abhandlungen zur Slavistik, 12 (Frankfurt, 1970).

[22] See Discourse 8, p. 88.

[23] See Discourse 25, p. 145. The issue of the connection between Nestor the hagiographer and Nestor who is linked by later tradition with early Kievan chronicle writing is one of the more disputed questions among specialists of Rus' history. For a balanced survey of the "Nestor question," see A. G. Kuz'min, *Načal'nye ètapy drevnerusskogo letopisanija* (Moscow, 1977), 133–54.

[24] See Discourse 9, p. 89.

he also wrote an account of the death of the princes Boris and Glěb, the object of the first and most widespread cult of saints in medieval Rus'.[25] His Life of Feodosij was evidently popular, and was both quoted and copied by later East Slavic hagiographers.[26]

(ii) Simon, Bishop of Vladimir and Suzdal'

Simon was bishop of Vladimir and Suzdal' from 1214 to 1226. The date of his birth and the circumstances of his early life are not known, nor is the date when he entered the Caves Monastery, but he was probably there before the end of the twelfth century.[27] By 1206 he had left Kiev and become superior of a monastery dedicated to the Nativity of the Theotokos in Vladimir-on-the-Kljazma,[28] and from there he was appointed bishop of Vladimir and Suzdal' in 1214.[29] This was a newly created see, carved out of the older diocese of Rostov.[30] The formation of this new see no doubt reflected the increasing importance of Suzdal' and the political aspirations of its Prince, Georgij Vsevolodovič (d. 1238), one of the numerous sons of prince Vsevolod "Great-Nest" of Vladimir (d. 1212). Simon's relations with Georgij appear to have been close and friendly throughout his period of office.[31] He died in 1226, and was buried in the "golden-domed" Cathedral of the Dormition in Vladimir.[32] Thus, the "ornament of Vladimir," as he himself described this cathedral, was his last earthly resting place, and not the "holy soil of the Caves Monastery," as he himself had so earnestly desired. Most of Simon's mature life was spent in Suzdalia, where as a bishop and friend of the prince he occupied a position of power and importance; possibly he was a member of one of the leading Suzdalian families. But throughout this time he longed to be back in the Caves Monastery.

---

[25] See above, p. xxii.

[26] See Discourse 3, p. 9; Discourse 11, *passim*; Discourse 27, p. 152. The *Žitie prepodobnogo Avraamija Smolenskogo i služby emu*, ed. S. F. Rozanov, Pamjatniki drevnerusskoj literatury, 1 (St. Petersburg, 1912), 1–24, contains a number of passages taken from the Life of Feodosij.

[27] This seems a reasonable assumption from the known facts of his later career; he left the monastery in 1206 in order to become a superior and appears to have spent several years there before then, judging by the way he talks about it.

[28] See *Laur.* 1206, PSRL 1:424. There is no indication of how long he had held this office.

[29] See *Laur.* 1214, PSRL 1:438.

[30] See the *Voskresenskij Chronicle* entry for 1214, PSRL 7:119.

[31] See PSRL 8:124–26.

[32] *Laur.* 1226, PSRL 1:448.

Away from it he felt an exile:

> Who does not know me, the sinful bishop Simon, [lord] of this cathedral church, the ornament of Vladimir, and the other church of Suzdal' which I founded myself? How many towns and villages they possess! And they collect tithes throughout this whole region, and I, unworthy as I am, am lord of all this. I would have left all this, but you know what important spiritual matters hold me back. I pray to the Lord that He will give me time to amend my life—and the Lord knows our secrets. I speak truly to you when I say that I would [swiftly] regard all this glory and honor as dirt! If I could be swept up with the dung in the Caves Monastery and be trampled by men, or if I could be one of the poor before the gates of that sacred *lavra*, and become a beggar, it would be better for me than this transitory glory.[33]

While in the monastery he had become very interested in its early history, and especially in the hermit Antonij and his earliest disciples; it was Simon who rescued from oblivion the long-neglected "Life of Antonij." He was well read too in translated ascetical literature, and by the standards of his time deserved the epithet "learned" applied to him in the brief notice of his death in the *Laurentian Chronicle*.[34] The combined influence of his reading and experience produced in him a profound conviction that in the Caves Monastery, and especially in the lives of its early members, the traditions of early monasticism had once more become a living reality. This conviction inspired all his writings and also, it would seem, communicated itself to Polikarp and to Archimandrite Akindin, who was superior of the Caves Monastery when he was writing.[35]

It has been suggested that Bishop Simon was not the author of those parts of the *Paterik* commonly attributed to him.[36] This assumption rests on a tradition that the Simon who contributed to the *Paterik* was in fact buried in the Caves Monastery. The only evidence to support this theory is a statement in an eighteenth-century monastic chronicle:

> In the year 1185 there died the holy bishop Simon, the first bishop of Vladimir, a member of the Kievan Caves

---

[33] Discourse 14, pp. 119–20.
[34] *Laur.* 1226, PSRL 1:448.
[35] See Discourse 24, p. 142.
[36] See V. A. Jakovlev, *Drevnekievskie religioznye skazanija* (Warsaw, 1875), 30–34, and the references there cited.

Monastery, who wrote part of the *Paterik* of the Caves Monastery. After his death he was buried in the Kievan caves, according to his own instruction.[37]

Although the evidence in favor of the bishop Simon who died in 1226 far outweighs the unsupported statement in this late source, the exact date of death given does suggest some sort of documentary basis.[38] The most reasonable explanation would seem to be that another Simon, perhaps also a bishop, was buried in the Caves Monastery in 1185, and that he was later confused with the bishop Simon who wrote part of the *Paterik*.[39]

(iii) Polikarp

Polikarp, unlike Simon, does not often use the first person, and when he does he says little about himself. But Simon says a great deal about him and draws a somewhat unflattering portrait. His chief criticism of Polikarp is that he has a false sense of values, since he cares more about advancement in the hierarchy of the church and the praise of men than about cultivating the virtues of meekness and humility. Polikarp, it seems, was of humble origin,[40] and by his own admission he was more concerned with ecclesiastical promotion than with his spiritual progress.[41] It was not that Simon doubted his capacity for a position of responsibility; he had in fact considered having him as his colleague in

---

[37] The quotation is from a chronicle written by a certain Aristarx, described as superior of the Bogoljub Monastery near Vladimir. See D. I. Abramovyč [Abramovič], *Issledovanie o Kievo-Pečerskom Paterike kak istoriko-literaturnom pamjatnike*, IORJAS 6, no. 3 (1901):230. Although this chronicle was written in the eighteenth century, it has been claimed, though not very convincingly, that it was a copy of an older work. See Jakovlev, *Drevnekievskie religioznye skazanija*, 36, n. 1.

[38] There can be little doubt that Simon's remains were buried in the Cathedral of the Dormition in Vladimir: the *Laurentian Chronicle* states that one of the tombs there has an inscription bearing his name and the date of his death. See A. Vinogradov, *Istorija Vladimirskogo katedral'nogo Uspenskogo sobora* (Vladimir, 1877), 4, and Bishop Sergij, *Polnyj mesjaceslov vostoka*, vol. 2, pt. 2 (Moscow, 1876), 177. There are no signs that his tomb was ever opened and his remains removed.

[39] The fact that bishop Simon's festival is celebrated on May 10 (Sergij, *Polnyj mesjaceslov*, 2, 2:138) and not on the anniversary of his death (May 22), also suggests that two monks with the same name might have been confused.

[40] See Discourse 20, p. 136.

[41] See Discourse 14, p. 116.

Suzdal'.⁴² Prince Georgij would have also liked to have him there, and the prince's sister, Verxoslavna,⁴³ was prepared to spend "a thousand pieces of silver" to secure his appointment to a suitable episcopal vacancy.⁴⁴ But Simon considered Polikarp unfit to be a bishop. He writes, "If he had remained in the monastery...keeping his conscience pure, obeying the superior and the brethren...then not only would he have been clothed in priestly garments, but would have been worthy of the higher [heavenly] kingdom."⁴⁵ Polikarp did not fulfill these conditions, and so he never had the ecclesiastical career he wanted so much. He seems to have found some compensation in writing his narratives and hoped that this would enhance both his reputation and his spiritual worth.⁴⁶

Simon's relationship with Polikarp gives us an interesting glimpse of the role of the spiritual father in the religious life of Rus', and shows how thoroughly the church in Rus' assimilated this important aspect of Byzantine religious practice (of course, probably not all spiritual fathers were as zealous as Bishop Simon in their concern for the welfare of their spiritual children). There can be little doubt that Simon was sincere in urging Polikarp to follow the path which he believed was best for him, and which he would have liked to follow himself. As he writes at the end of Discourse 19: "My son and brother...I give this advice to you: strengthen yourself in piety in the holy Caves Monastery, and do not desire power, or for the office of the superior or bishop; it will be sufficient for your salvation that you ended your life there."⁴⁷ It would be interesting to know how Polikarp reacted to these words, and whether

---

⁴² Ibid., pp. 117–18.
⁴³ See N. de Baumgarten, *Généalogies et mariages occidentaux des Rurikides russes du Xe au XIIIe siècle* (Rome, 1927) (=*Orientalia Christiana* 9), Table X, no. 7. The mother of this princess had been Simon's spiritual daughter (*Laur.* 1206, PSRL 1:424), and possibly the princess was also.
⁴⁴ See Discourse 14, p. 117.
⁴⁵ Ibid.
⁴⁶ In the long conclusion to the narrative about Agapit the Physician he writes: "It is a great thing for me to be adorned by such things, and I think that I shall conceal the shame of my deeds in this way: I shall simply call to mind the things I have heard, write them down, and think that it was I who sought out the marvelous deeds of these men." (Discourse 27, p. 153). See also T. H. Kopreeva, "Obraz inoka Polikarpa po pis'mam Simona i Polikarpa (opyt rekonstrukcii)," TODRL 24 (1969):114.
⁴⁷ Discourse 19, p. 130.

he was able to follow Simon's advice and profit from it; he gives no hint of this in his writings.[48]

Although distinctive in character, the narratives of Simon and Polikarp are integrally related since they both derive from Bishop Simon's interest in the early history of the monastery. Many remarks in their discourses give hints of the hours the two monks must have spent together, studying neglected manuscripts and discussing the "lives, deeds and miracles" of former monks which had, apparently, been almost forgotten.[49] These remarks raise a number of questions. What first aroused Simon's interest? Did he and Polikarp make copies of the works they read? Why does Polikarp always speak as though he were writing from memory?[50] What lay behind his insistence that the substance of his narratives was in danger of being forgotten?[51] Unfortunately, no clue as to how these questions might be answered is to be found in either the *Paterik* itself, or the scanty references to the Caves Monastery in Rus' chronicles relating to the time when Simon and Polikarp were writing.

Simon's letter to Polikarp and the biographical narratives which follow it can be dated by his reference to the cathedral of the Dormition of the Theotokos in Suzdal' which was founded in the year 1225.[52] They were written, therefore, towards the end of his life. The discourses about the church were probably written at the same time; although they appear separately in the *Second Cassian* redaction of the *Paterik*, in the earlier redactions they follow the biographical narratives. Polikarp's contribution is more difficult to date, in spite of two precise chronological statements: in the conclusion to his account of Agapit the Physician he says that he is writing in the fifteenth year of Archimandrite Akindin's period of office, and that the substance of what he is writing has been forgotten

---

[48] Kopreeva, "Obraz inoka Polikarpa," 112–14, regards Polikarp as a rebel against the monastic ethos of genuine humility and conventional self-denigration. This interesting interpretation is purely speculative; nothing in the texts suggests that Polikarp did not accept the ideas and practices of the milieu in which he lived. He simply wanted to be a superior or a bishop, not an ordinary monk.

[49] See Discourse 14, p. 120; Discourse 17, p. 127; Discourse 18, p. 128; Discourse 24, p. 142; Discourse 27, p. 152; Discourse 32, p. 175.

[50] See Discourse 32, p. 175, where Polikarp says that he is recording what he had heard from Bishop Simon, but does not mention a written source.

[51] See Discourse 26, p. 147; Discourse 27, p. 152.

[52] *Laur.* 1225, PSRL 1:447.

for 160 years.⁵³ Nothing can be deduced from the first statement, since the dates of Akindin's period of office are not known.⁵⁴ The second statement is more helpful, since Polikarp appears to be referring to the "Life of Antonij." This must have been written some time between Antonij's death in 1073 and the year 1097, by which time it was evidently well known in the monastery.⁵⁵ Taking these dates as outside limits, Polikarp must have written his discourses between 1233 and 1257. The latter date is unlikely, since by that time Kiev had been sacked by the Mongols and the Caves Monastery had been badly damaged, though not destroyed. The earlier date, 1233 (or thereabouts, since Polikarp's 160 years might not have been exactly calculated), is quite feasible.⁵⁶ This would mean that he was writing after Simon's death. Yet nothing indicates that Simon suggested that Polikarp should write about the earlier monks of the monastery. Polikarp himself says that he wrote his narratives because fear kept him from giving an adequate oral account of the material contained in them in the presence of Archimandrite Akindin.⁵⁷ Of course, this could well be a form of conventional self-denigration; the way Polikarp's narratives are written suggests that he wanted to write them and thoroughly enjoyed his task.

4. *The transmission of the text*

The *Paterik* is extant in numerous manuscripts, most of which belong to three main redactions: the *Arsenian* (1406), the *First Cassian* (1460), and the *Second Cassian* (1462). The oldest copy of the narratives of Simon and Polikarp, which form the core of the *Paterik*, is the *Arsenian* manuscript written in 1406 at the request of Arsenij, Bishop of Tver'.⁵⁸ In this text Simon's letter to Polikarp, Polikarp's letter to

---

53   Discourse 27, p. 152.
54   He is mentioned as superior of the Caves Monastery in 1231 (*Laur.* 1231, PSRL 1:456), but there is no indication of how long he had been in office.
55   The monk Feodor refers to it when talking to Prince M'stislav Svjatopolčič (see Discourse 33, p. 188) and he died in 1097 (PVL 1097, PSRL 1:272, 2:247).
56   See A. A. Šaxmatov, "Žitie Antonija i Pečerskaja Letopis'," ŽMNP 318 (1898):114, who suggests that Polikarp might have been thinking of the date of Antonij's death.
57   See Discourse 24, p. 142.
58   Described by Jakovlev, *Drevnekievskie religioznye skazanija*, 42–43, Abramovyč, *Issledovanie*, IORJAS 6, no. 4:68–71, and more briefly by Šaxmatov, "Kievo-Pečerskij Paterik i Pečerskaja Letopis'," 839. Arsenij, a former member of the Caves Monastery, was the protégé of Kiprian, metropolitan of all Rus' from 1390 to 1406, who spent several years as titular metropolitan of Kiev before that. Soon after Kiprian had esta-

Archimandrite Akindin, and his account of Alimpij the Icon-painter (Discourse 34 in the *Second Cassian* redaction) are omitted, along with Simon's exhortations to Polikarp at the end of Discourses 17–23 and the long conclusion to Polikarp's account of Agapit the Physician. Apart from the narrative about Alimpij (the exclusion of which is difficult to explain), all omitted passages are those in which the authors speak about themselves and the circumstances of their work; thus the personal element has been deliberately suppressed. This manuscript also includes the Life and Office of Feodosij, the sermon preached on his feast day, and the accounts of Ieremej and Damian; the latter are included among Polikarp's narratives, while those relating to Feodosij are placed at the beginning. This manuscript is the prototype of a group of texts which constitute the *Arsenian* redaction, the earliest surviving redaction of the *Paterik*.[59]

In 1460 and 1462 two new editions were produced, known respectively as the *First Cassian* (hereafter Cas. I) and the *Second Cassian* (Cas. II) redactions, from the name of the choirmaster (*klirošanin*) at whose request they were compiled.[60] The circumstances under which they appeared are of some interest. Little is known about the Caves Monastery between the time when Simon and Polikarp were writing and the second half of the fifteenth century; the scattered references to it in the chronicles do little more than testify to its continued existence,[61] in spite of damage inflicted by the Tatars.[62] But this in itself was an achievement, considering the state of Kiev and the surrounding area during the period of Mongol rule in Rus'. Subject first to the Tatars, then to the grand dukes of Lithuania, and finally to the Polish monarchy;

---

blished himself in Moscow (following a long struggle), he appointed Arsenij as bishop of Tver'. See M. Heppell, *The Ecclesiastical Career of Grigorij Camblak* (London, 1979), 38–43.

[59] Jakovlev, *Drevnekievskie religioznye skazanija*, 43–45, describes two other manuscripts of this redaction, and Abramovyč, *Issledovanie*, IORJAS 6, no. 4:71–93, eleven others.

[60] See Jakovlev, *Drevnekievskie religioznye skazanija*, 46, and Abramovyč, *Issledovanie*, IORJAS 7, no. 1 (1902):238, both of whom transcribe the colophon.

[61] See, e.g., the *Hustyn' Chronicle*, PSRL 2, 1st ed. (1843), *sub annibus* 1274 (345); 1289 (347); 1396 (352); and the *Voznesenskij Chronicle*, PSRL 7, 1385 (49); 1389 (60); 1392 (62); *Nov.* PSRL 4, 1399 (104); 1408 (111).

[62] The monastery is not mentioned in the account of the sack of Kiev by the Mongol general Batu in 1240 (*Hyp.* 1240, PSRL 2:784–91), but the stone church apparently was damaged (*Hustyn' Chronicle* 1470, PSRL 2, 1st ed., 358). In 1399 it had to pay an indemnity of 30 rubles after a Tatar raid (PSRL 3:101; PSRL 4:104), and in 1406 its buildings were burned (PSRL 2, 1st ed., 354; 4:111, 5:260, 6:140, 8:88).

enjoying at times a virtually independent administration under an elected council or an autonomous prince, but at others controlled by governors appointed by the Crown; abandoned by the metropolitans; its economic life ruined by the Tatars[63] —such was the city which Adam of Bremen in the early eleventh century had described as "aemula sceptri Constantinopoli, clarissimum decus Graeciae."[64] However, it seems that by the middle of the fifteenth century the situation had improved. No serious Tatar raids are mentioned between 1453[65] and the attacks of the Crimean Horde towards the end of the century.[66] From 1461 to 1471 Kiev and the surrounding area were ruled as a separate sub-kingdom under the suzerainty of the dukes of Lithuania, who were on the whole well-disposed towards Orthodoxy and what remained of Rus'-Byzantine culture.[67] It was at the instigation of Grand Duke Vytautas, himself a Catholic, that a separate metropolitan was established in Kiev in 1415.[68] In 1470 the stone church of the Caves Monastery was restored to something resembling its former splendor after a long period of neglect,[69] and presumably the buildings which had been destroyed by fire in 1416 were restored as well. The preparation of the two new editions of the *Paterik* not long before these structural renovations suggests that the conditions of the mid-fifteenth century were favorable to a revival of interest in the earlier history of the monastery.

The Cas. I's redaction of the *Paterik* contains 39 discourses arranged as follows:[70]

(i) Bishop Simon's narratives about the church;

(ii) The *Account of why the Caves Monastery is so called*;[71]

(iii) Four discourses relating to Feodosij: his Life, the translation of his relics, the decoration of his tomb, and the commemorative sermon;

---

[63] See M. Hruševs'kyj [Hrushevsky], *History of the Ukraine*, trans. C. J. Frederiksen (New Haven, 1941), Chapters 6–7.
[64] PL 146:514.
[65] See PSRL 2, 1st ed., 354.
[66] PSRL 2, 1st ed., 360; see also Hruševs'kyj, *History*, 150 ff.
[67] Though the Lithuanian rulers remained pagan until the Union of Krevo in 1386 (when they converted to Catholicism), they were tolerant towards their Orthodox subjects. There were a number of individual conversions to Orthodoxy among highly placed Lithuanians.
[68] See Heppell, *The Ecclesiastical Career*, Chapter 5.
[69] See PSRL 2, 1st ed., 358, and Discourse 3, n. 33.
[70] See Abramovyč, *Issledovanie*, IORJAS 7, no. 1:234–38.
[71] The Cas. I version of the *Account* appears in Jakovlev's edition of the *Paterik*; it is practically identical with the 1051 entry of the PVL, except that the latter does not mention Nestor.

(iv) Simon's letter to Polikarp, followed by his biographical narratives;

(v) Polikarp's letter to Archimandrite Akindin, followed by his narratives, including Alimpij the Icon-painter;

(vi) A number of items which have corresponding entries in the PVL or the *Hypatian Chronicle*: accounts of Damian, Ieremej, Matfej, and Isaakij;[72] the tonsuring of Prince Svjatoša, a member of the princely family which ruled the Černihiv land;[73] the entry of Feodosij's name into the *sinodik*;[74] the vision of Nifont, bishop of Novgorod;[75] and the death of Archimandrite Polikarp.[76]

Not many "pure" Cas. I manuscripts have survived,[77] but this redaction was the basis of a version of the *Paterik* included in the *Velikij Čet'i Minei* (Great Menologion) compiled in the sixteenth century, although with the order of the discourses altered, the most important change being that the items relating to Feodosij were placed first.[78] A. A. Šaxmatov and D. Abramovyč have suggested that the Cas. I redaction was based on an earlier cne which has not survived, inferring this from a group of later manuscripts (mostly from the seventeenth and eighteenth centuries) in which the narratives of Simon and Polikarp and the accounts of Damian, Ieremej, and Matfej appear in a form very similar to that of Cas. I, but the language of these manuscripts suggests that they were copied from a much older work. Apart from this basic core of the *Paterik*, they do not resemble Cas. I.[79] However, the existence of a lost primitive redaction remains hypothetical; there is no documentary evidence for any earlier redaction than the *Arsenian*.

The Cas. II redaction is very similar to Cas. I in substance and arrangement, and the small changes made in the order of the items are not important. For example, in Cas. II the positions of Discourses 2 and 3 are reversed; the entry of Feodosij's name into the *sinodik* is included

---

[72] Cf. PVL 1074, PSRL 1:188–91, 2:179–82. In Cas. II the account of Isaakij forms a separate narrative (Discourse 36).

[73] Cf. PVL 1106, PSRL 1:281; 2:258.

[74] Cf. PVL 1108, PSRL 1:283, 2:259.

[75] Cf. *Hyp*. 1156, PSRL 2:483–84.

[76] *Hyp*. 1182, PSRL 2:626.

[77] See Abramovyč, *Issledovanie*, IORJAS 7, no. 1:233.

[78] Ibid., 247–50. Abramovyč, 252–53, also describes briefly a group of MSS derived from the *Menologion* version, though not identical with it. One of these was used by Jakovlev for his edition.

[79] Šaxmatov, "Kievo-Pečerskij Paterik i Pečerskaja Letopis'," 798–800; Abramovyč, *Issledovanie*, IORJAS 6, no. 4:37–68.

in the account of the translation of Feodosij's relics; and the accounts of Damian, Ieremej, and Matfej, and the vision of Nifont are placed before Simon's letter to Polikarp. As a result, there is rather more emphasis on the chronological order of the contents of the *Paterik*. One new item is added: *An Inquiry by the pious prince Izjaslav concerning the Latins* (Discourse 37).

The important differences between the Cas. I and Cas. II redactions are those in the text of some of the items:

(i) Introductions, written in a somewhat rhetorical style, are added to the account of the translation of Feodosij's relics and to the narrative about Isaakij the Cave-dweller (Discourse 26).

(ii) The vision of Nifont, although substantially the same as in Cas. I, appears to be taken from an older text.[80]

(iii) The author of the account of the translation of Feodosij's relics is called "Nestor" in the title as well as in the text.

(iv) The Cas. II version of the *Account of why the Caves Monastery is so called* is longer, and contains the following additions: 1) two visits to Mount Athos are ascribed to Antonij, the first in the reign of Prince Volodimer I (d. 1015); 2) it is stated that Antonij personally received Feodosij when he arrived in Kiev; 3) and at the end of the text the name "Nestor" is given as the author.

The introductions to Discourse 9 (the translation of Feodosij's relics) and Discourse 36 (Isaakij the Cave-dweller) were probably composed by the editor, and he also probably inserted the name of "Nestor" into the title of Discourse 9, since it was present in the text. But the different version of the vision of Nifont and the additional material in the *Account of why the Caves Monastery is so called* suggest that a written source might have been used; in the opinion of Šaxmatov, this was a private monastic chronicle kept in the Caves Monastery, which was later lost.[81]

Two other redactions of the *Paterik* must be mentioned, though they are less important than those described above: the *Theodosian* redaction compiled in the fifteenth century, and the *Josif Trizna* redaction compiled in the seventeenth. The *Theodosian* redaction is

---

[80] Šaxmatov, "Kievo-Pečerskij Paterik i Pečerskaja Letopis'," 813.
[81] Ibid., 820. Abramovyč, IORJAS 7, no. 1:261, however, proposed that the additional elements in the *Account* might have been composed by Cassian himself, based on oral traditions then current on Mount Athos.

represented by only one manuscript.[82] Both Šaxmatov and Abramovyč thought that it was based on the lost primitive redaction.[83] However, the traditional order of the material is completely changed, even to the extent of mixing the narratives of Simon and Polikarp, and two irrelevant extracts from the PVL were added.[84] In the *Josif Trizna* redaction[85] the order of the items is further altered, and even more extracts from chronicles are added. This version also includes short biographies of the superiors Stefan, Nikon, and Varlaam, and of the monks Efrem and Isaia, all manufactured from material in other parts of the *Paterik*, mostly from the Life of Feodosij; there is also a short biography of Bishop Simon, placed after his narrative about Arefa (Discourse 22 in the Cas. II redaction). Dates are inserted into some of the narratives; for example, the date of the tonsuring of Alimpij the Icon-painter is given as 1083. Finally, the Cas. II version of the *Account of why the Caves Monastery is so called* is entitled *Žitie Antonija* (The Life of Antonij).

The significance of the *Josif Trizna* redaction lies in its connection with the version known as the "Printed *Paterik*."[86] The *Paterik* was first printed in Syl'vestr Kosov's Polish translation in 1635,[87] then again in its original language in 1661, both times on the private press of the Caves Monastery. Early in the seventeenth century Kiev had become the scene of a vigorous revival of interest in Orthodox culture, which owed much to the military protection of the Cossacks, especially Hetman Sahajdačnyj, and also to the financial resources of the Caves Monastery.

---

[82] See Metropolitan Makarij, "Obzor redakcij Kievo-Pečerskogo Paterika preimuščestvenno drevnix," *Istoričeskie čtenija o jazyke i slovesnosti v zasedanijax Vtorogo otdelenija IAN*, 1856–57, 52–62, who describes this redaction as "most unsatisfactory." See also Abramovyč, *Issledovanie*, IORJAS 6, no. 4:97–100. Abramovyč also describes a second manuscript belonging to this redaction (pp. 100–102), but although this has some features in common with the first, the order of the items is very different.

[83] Šaxmatov, "Kievo-Pečerskij Paterik i Pečerskaja Letopis'," 842; Abramovyč, *Issledovanie*, IORJAS 6, no. 4:95–96.

[84] I.e., the baptisms of Princess Ol'ga (PVL 955, PSRL 1:61; 2:49) and Volodimer (PVL 988, PSRL 1:111, 2:96–97).

[85] Described by Abramovyč, *Issledovanie*, IORJAS 7, no. 1:264–75.

[86] Abramovyč, ibid., 274–75, quotes passages from the unpublished *Josif Trizna* MS, together with corresponding ones from the "Printed *Paterik*."

[87] See Jakovlev, *Drevnekievskie religioznye skazanija*, 62–72, and V. N. Peretc, "Kievo-Pečerskij Paterik v pols'kom i ukrainskom perevode," *Slavjanskaja filologija* 3 (1968):74–210. A facsimile edition of Kosov's translation is now available in the *Harvard Library of Early Ukrainian Literature: Texts*, vol. IV (Cambridge, Mass., 1987), 3–118.

The printing press was purchased in 1615, and with it the monks published a number of works intended to strengthen the loyalty of the Orthodox population of the Ukraine to their own faith.[88] Thus it is not surprising that the edition of 1661 contains a "Preface to the Orthodox Reader," which is in fact a polemical treatise against those who think that Orthodox Christians should be in communion with Rome. The text of this "Printed *Paterik*" is arranged in four sections:

I

(i) "The Life of our venerable and devout father Antonij" (in fact the Cas. II version of the *Account of why the Caves Monastery is so called*).

(ii) The items relating to Feodosij.

(iii) Bishop Simon's narratives about the church.

(iv) "Lives" of Stefan, Nikon, Varlaam, Efrem, and Isaia, and accounts of Damian, Ieremej, Matfej, and Isaakij.

II

(i) Polikarp's narratives, arranged in the following order: Nikita the Solitary, Lavrentij the Solitary, Alimpij the Icon-painter, Agapit the Physician, Grigorij the Miracle-worker, Moisej the Hungarian, Ioann the Solitary, Proxor Lobednik, Marko the Cave-dweller, Feodor and Vasilij, Spiridon the Wafer-baker, and Pimin the Sufferer.

(ii) Polikarp's letter to Archimandrite Akindin.

III

(i) Simon's biographical narratives, in the same order as in Cas. I.[89]

(ii) The vision of Nifont.

(iii) Simon's letter to Polikarp.

IV

(i) Biographies of Nestor, Simon, and Polikarp.

(ii) Accounts of miracles which had occurred in the caves of the monastery since 1462.

---

[88] See Hruševs'kyj, *History*, 238 ff.
[89] Simon's narratives are placed after Polikarp's in the *Josif Trizna* redaction; see Abramovyč, *Issledovanie*, IORJAS 7, no. 1:270.

Judged by the standards current in western Europe at that time the "Printed Paterik" was a very unsatisfactory edition. Even a cursory examination of available manuscripts would have shown that the *Josif Trizna* redaction, which appears to have formed the basis of the printed edition, was a corruption of the original text, overloaded with far too much additional material, to the extent that the basic form of the work was distorted. No distinction is made between the original contributions of Nestor, Simon, and Polikarp and the "Lives" composed by later editors. In any case, these are worthless, since they do not even assemble the main facts correctly. For example, Polikarp, the contemporary of Bishop Simon, is identified with the archimandrite Polikarp who died in 1182, and the Nestor who wrote the Life of Feodosij is confused with the Nestor mentioned as the author of the *Account of why the Caves Monastery is so called*. Yet this was the only published version of the *Paterik* available until the appearance of Jakovlev's edition in 1872,[90] and it remained virtually unchanged, apart from the suppression or alteration of certain passages by the order of the Holy Synod.[91] The large number of reprints bears witness to the popularity of the work,[92] and to the absence of any critical study of the text until the middle of the nineteenth century.[93]

---

[90] V. A. Jakovlev, ed., *Pamjatniki russkoj-literatury XII i XIII vekov* (St. Petersburg, 1872). This edition is flawed. The basic manuscript was not a very wise choice, and Jakovlev made certain changes in the arrangement of the material (though not in the wording of the text) and introduced some additional items. There are few variant readings and no notes; the typography is poor and abbreviations are retained in the text, which makes reading difficult. But Jakovlev did at least provide an authentic text of the *Paterik*.

[91] See Abramovyč, *Issledovanie*, IORJAS 7, no. 2:210–20.

[92] The British Library Catalog notes seventeen reprints between 1661 and 1813.

[93] Serious study of the *Paterik* began when A. Kubarev published an article describing some versions of the text based on an examination of twelve manuscripts and of the 1661 Printed *Paterik*: "O Paterike Pečerskom," ŽMNP 20 (1838):1–34. Kubarev's classification was later criticized and amplified by Makarij, "Obzor redakcii Kievo-Pečerskogo Paterika." This was followed by a somewhat querulous reply from Kubarev, "O redakcijax Paterika Pečerskogo," *Čtenija*, 1858, no. 3:96–128. Meanwhile V. Undolskij had published a description of the *Josif Trizna* redaction: "Josif Trizna, redaktor Paterika Pečerskogo," *Čtenija*, 1846, no. 4:5–10, and Evgenij's *Opisanie Kievo-Pečerskoj Lavry* appeared in the same year. Finally, an article on the *Paterik*'s authors appeared in 1871: M. Viktorova and I. Nekrasov, "Sostaviteli Kievo-Pečerskogo Paterika i pozdnejšaja ego sud'ba," *Filologičeskije zapiski* (1871). This was the last study to appear before Jakovlev's edition of the text in 1872. The work of Šaxmatov and Abramovyč in the late nineteenth century inaugurated a new era in the study of the *Paterik*.

5. *The Life of Feodosij*

The textual history of the Life of Feodosij must be considered separately, since it is older than the rest of the *Paterik*. The earliest manuscript containing it is a miscellany (*sbornik*), which was formerly preserved in the Cathedral of the Dormition (*Uspenie*) in Moscow[94] and therefore is traditionally known as the *Uspenskij sbornik* (hereafter UspSb) copy. Its most recent editors attribute it to the late twelfth or early thirteenth century.[95] There are no other manuscripts apart from those included in the different redactions of the *Paterik*. A comparison of these with the UspSb shows a number of editorial insertions in the later versions:

(i) In the *Arsenian* redaction:
   a) in the opening paragraph Feodosij is described as "archimandrite and superior of all Rus'."[96]
   b) Feodosij is compared with his Palestinian namesake, Theodosios the Cenobiarch, archimandrite of Jerusalem;[97]
   c) Feodosij's birthplace is identified as Vasil'ev (Vasyl'kiv).[98]

(ii) In both *Cassian* redactions, in addition to the above:
   a) the date of the tonsuring of Feodosij is given as 1032;[99]
   b) a farewell speech by Feodosij on his deathbed to Prince Svjatoslav of Kiev is inserted.[100]

The first of these insertions was no doubt made by a copyist after it had become customary to give the superiors of the Caves Monastery the title of archimandrite; the first superior to have this title was Archimandrite Polikarp, who died in 1182.[101] The second also was probably added by a scribe: the fact that the interpolated passage is several lines long makes it unlikely that it was accidentally removed from the UspSb, and, there is no evidence that Nestor was familiar with the Life of Theodosios

---

[94] In 1895 this collection was transferred to the Moscow Synodal Library. It is now in the Lenin State Library.
[95] The UspSb was partly edited by A. A. Šaxmatov and P. A. Lavrov, *Sbornik XII veka Moskovskogo Uspenskogo Sobora*, pt. 1 (Moscow, 1899), but the only full edition is O. A. Knjazevskaja et al., *Uspenskij Sbornik XII–XIII vv.* (Moscow, 1971), with the Life of Feodosij on pp. 71–135.
[96] See Discourse 8, p. 24 and Abramovyč, *Paterik*, 20, nn. 34 and 35 (variant readings from UspSb).
[97] See Discourse 8, p. 25, and Abramovyč, *Pateryk*, 21, n. 34.
[98] See Discourse 8, p. 26, and Abramovyč, *Pateryk*, 22, n. 13.
[99] See Discourse 8, p. 33, and Abramovyč, *Pateryk*, 29, n. 15.
[100] See Discourse 8, pp. 80–81, and Abramovyč, *Pateryk*, 72, n. 3.
[101] This title first appears in *Hyp.* 1174, PSRL 2:568. Cf. Discourse 38, n. 676.

the Cenobiarch.[102] On the other hand, it is reasonable to assume that the omission of the name of Feodosij's birthplace from the UspSb was a mistake, since it is unlikely that Nestor's detailed information about the early life of Feodosij, derived from a monk who had talked with his mother, would not include it.

The interpolations in the *Cassian* redactions are less easy to explain. The date of the tonsuring of Feodosij is clearly an editorial addition, since it is at variance with the context of the narrative at this point, from which it is clear that Feodosij cannot have come to Kiev earlier than 1050.[103] The same is true of Feodosij's dying speech to Prince Svjatoslav, since this implies a hostile relationship between the Caves Monastery and the metropolitan of Kiev in the late eleventh century, for which there is no real evidence either in the Life of Feodosij or in other contemporary sources.[104] But it fits well enough with the ecclesiastical situation in Kiev in the middle of the fifteenth century. In 1460, the metropolitan of Kiev was Gregory, the friend and supporter of Metropolitan Isidore of Kiev and All Rus', whose support of the Union with the Roman Catholic Church concluded at the Council of Florence in 1439 was extremely unpopular in Moscow.[105] It also seems that there was strong opposition in Kiev to the appointment of Metropolitan Gregory, though it was not openly expressed.[106] As a result, this dying speech of Feodosij might well have been composed by Cassian himself. This is the opinion of A. Kubarev, one of the earliest students of the *Paterik*, who suggested that this speech was an elaboration of the statement in the PVL that Feodosij committed the monastery to Svjatoslav's care just before his death.[107]

---

[102] See *Leben des Theodosios*, ed. E. Schwartz, *Kyrillos von Skythopolis*, Texte und Untersuchungen zur Geschichte der altchristlichen Literatur, 49, 2 (Leipzig, 1939), 237–38.

[103] See Discourse 8, n. 118.

[104] There is perhaps some indirect evidence of strained relations between Kiev and Constantinople about the time when Feodosij died. See S. H. Cross and O. P. Sherbowitz-Wetzor, trans., *The Russian Primary Chronicle. Laurentian Text.* (Cambridge, Mass., 1953), 273, n. 265; this might explain why Feodosij committed the monastery to Prince Svjatoslav's care. See PVL 1074, PSRL 1:187, 2:177–78.

[105] See A. Kartašev, *Očerki po istorii russkoj cerkvi*, vol. 1 (Paris, 1959), 355–56.

[106] Ibid., 543–46. In 1469 Metropolitan Gregory renounced his allegiance to Rome and returned to Orthodoxy, but this was some years after the appearance of the Cas. II redaction of the *Paterik*.

[107] See Discourse 8, n. 225.

Thus we see that the history of the transmission of the text of the *Paterik* extends over nearly seven centuries, from the composition of the Life of Feodosij in the late eleventh century to the compilation of the *Josif Trizna* redaction in the seventeenth century. During this time the city of Kiev and its famous monastery suffered many calamities, but the text of the *Paterik* continued to be copied. The early monks of the Caves Monastery therefore escaped the oblivion feared by Polikarp, and the *Paterik*, though sadly neglected, survived to face the critical analysis of scholars in the late nineteenth and twentieth centuries.

6. *The Sources of the* Paterik

The value of the *Paterik* for reconstructing the lives of its subjects and the history of their society obviously depends on the extent to which its authors and compilers had access to firsthand information or reliable sources. From this point of view it will be convenient to consider separately the narratives of Simon and Polikarp, the Life of Feodosij, and the anonymous items.

(i) *The writings of Simon and Polikarp*

A few of Simon's narratives (Discourses 15, 21, 22, and 23) were based on personal observation or the reports of eyewitnesses;[108] others include comments which might have been based on firsthand knowledge[109] or on information preserved by the descendants of Prince Volodimer Monomax as part of their family tradition.[110] However, most of Simon's contribution, and all of Polikarp's, relate to the late eleventh and early twelfth centuries, that is to a period nearly a century and a half before the time when they were writing. It is clear that for these narratives they used written sources which were later lost, one of which was a work which they both call the "Life of Antonij." Simon refers to it four times: in Discourse 3, where he implies, though he does not explicitly state, that it was his main source for his account of the foundation of the "great church";[111] in his letter to Polikarp, where he ascribes to it the interesting detail that the monk Ilarion, later metropolitan of Rus', had

---

[108] See Discourse 15, p. 120; Discourse 21, p. 138; Discourse 22, p. 140; and Discourse 23, p. 141.
[109] See Discourse 3, p. 11; Discourse 4, p. 13.
[110] See Discourse 1, p. 5; Discourse 4, p. 13.
[111] Discourse 3, p. 9.

been tonsured by Antonij;[112] in his narrative about Evstratij the Faster;[113] and in his account of Afanasij the Solitary.[114] Polikarp refers to it three times: in his account of Agapit the Physician;[115] in his narrative about Moisej the Hungarian, which he says was based on material from the Life of Antonij;[116] and in his account of the monks Feodor and Vasilij, in which Vasilij says that the "Varangian Cave" is mentioned in the Life of Antonij.[117] It was probably also the source for the rather meager information about Antonij's early monastic life on Mount Athos which has been preserved in both extant versions of the *Account of why the Monastery of Caves is so called*,[118] and possibly for the reference to his flight to Černihiv included in the PVL.[119]

In spite of these explicit and precise references, doubts have been expressed as to whether the Life of Antonij ever did exist,[120] and the material derived from it is not usually considered historically trustworthy. However, the main problem seems to be the form of the work; no one has yet suggested that it was an invention of Simon and Polikarp. An analysis of the passages cited by them, together with the relevant parts of the *Account of why the Caves Monastery is so called*, indicates that while it apparently did not contain very many details about Antonij himself, it did include information about important events in the early history of the monastery (such as the building of the stone church) and about other early members of the monastery, especially those who had had some direct contact or connection with Antonij. There are, therefore, good grounds for assuming that it was not a conventional *žitie*, such as Nestor's Life of Feodosij, but a more diversified work about the origins of the monastery in which, of course, Antonij played an impor-

---

[112] Discourse 14, p. 118.
[113] Abramovyč, *Pateryk*, 106, n. 22, gives the variant *Arsenian* reading: "You will find other similar things, Brother Polikarp, in the Life of the holy Antonij. A certain man came to him from Kiev...."
[114] Discourse 19, p. 130.
[115] Discourse 27, p. 152.
[116] Discourse 30, p. 168.
[117] Discourse 33, p. 188.
[118] See Discourse 7, p. 18, and PVL 1051, PSRL 1:156, 2:144.
[119] PVL 1074, PSRL 1:193, 2:185.
[120] See Abramovyč, *Issledovanie*, IORJAS 7 (1902), no. 3:75; D. Čyževs'kyj [Čiževskij], *History of Russian Literature* (The Hague, 1960), 47; and R. Bosley, "A History of the Veneration of SS. Theodosij and Antonij of the Kievan Caves Monastery from the Eleventh to the Fifteenth Century." Ph. D. dissertation, Yale University, 1980, 33–43, 60–61.

tant role.[121] Since the text has disappeared, we will never know why Simon and Polikarp called it the "Life of Antonij"; possibly the words were used somewhere in the work, and they adopted them as a convenient form of reference.

The main reason why earlier students of the Caves Monastery attached little importance to the Life of Antonij as a historical source is that the material derived from it appears to contradict the Life of Feodosij, an extant source with good credentials.[122] In fact, the "Antonij" material often complements that in the Life of Feodosij, so that there is no reason why equal weight should not be given to both sources, especially because when material derived from the Life of Antonij is examined in relation to other available sources, foreign as well as East Slavic, it can be reasonably well authenticated. This is particularly true of Polikarp's account of Moisej the Hungarian, which is of vital importance in reconstructing the origins of the monastery.[123]

It would seem that Simon and Polikarp must have used another source (or sources), which subsequently disappeared but which provided material for Simon's last three discourses about the church, his detailed account of the monk Svjatoša (Discourse 20), and all of Polikarp's narratives except Moisej the Hungarian and, possibly, Ioann the Solitary. Simon himself mentions one such source in his letter to Polikarp, when he urges him to read the "old Rostov Chronicle,"[124] and Polikarp hints at the existence of another in the introduction to his account of Mark the Cave-dweller when he refers to a *Paterik Pečerskij*, though he gives no indication of its content.[125] It has generally been assumed by students of the early history of the Caves Monastery that there was at one time a private monastic chronicle, part of which was incorporated into the PVL

---

[121] See Čyževs'kyj, *History of Russian Literature*, 47: "...it is not improbable that the Life of Antonij was merely a chronicle of the monastery in the days of Antonij rather than a genuine Life of the saint himself." Bosley, "A History," 54, describes it as "a combination of history, adventure and miracles," and later (p. 58) says, "One could call it a patericon, but it was not a patericon like the *Lausiac History* of Palladius, or the *Verba Seniorum/Apophthegmata*." Both writers imply that the work is somehow inferior if it was not a *žitie*, but this does not affect its value as historical material.

[122] See, for example, Golubinskij, *Istorija russkoj cerkvi*, 1, 2:569–81; L. K. Goetz, *Das Kiever Höhlenkloster als Kulturzentrum des vormongolischen Russlands* (Passau, 1904), 14–33.

[123] See M. Heppell, "The *Vita Antonii*, a Lost Source of the *Paterikon* of the Monastery of Caves," *Byzantinoslavica* 13, no. 1 (1952):50–53.

[124] See Discourse 14, p. 119; also Kuz'min, *Načal'nye ètapy*, 175–76.

[125] See Discourse 32, p. 175.

and the *Hypatian Chronicle*, and that this was used by Simon and Polikarp. The main reason for this assumption is that Polikarp's narratives include a number of details not mentioned in the PVL, but connected with events described there.[126] Moreover, they contain numerous details not important enough to have been preserved in oral tradition for 150 years or more, nor are they part of the general stock-in-trade of the hagiographer, e.g., the remark that the monk Vasilij was sent away from the monastery on business and was absent for three months,[127] and the fact about Grigorij the Miracle-worker meeting Prince Rostislav Vsevolodovič when he was going down to the river to wash a vessel which had been defiled by an animal.[128]

The evidence relating to this hypothetical chronicle, known as the *Kievo-Pečerskaja Letopis'* ("Chronicle of the Caves Monastery") was minutely analyzed by Šaxmatov, though he was not the first person to deduce its existence, nor did he give it its name.[129] Yet it was he who developed the idea in considerable detail, attempted to reconstruct its content, and almost, as it were, re-wrote it.[130] He proposed that it was this lost chronicle, not the PVL, which Polikarp had in mind on the two occasions when he refers to "the chronicle,"[131] and that since he twice refers to the author as "Nestor," it can be assumed that at least part of it was written by the author of the Life of Feodosij, or else based on his

---

[126] He mentions, for example, that in the civil war among the princes that followed the blinding of Prince Vasil'ko of Terebovlja in 1097 there was an acute shortage of salt in Kiev, because salt merchants from Halyč had been forbidden to come to the city (Discourse 31, p. 172). But this fact is not mentioned in the long account of the war in PVL 1097, PSRL 1:262–73, 2:237–48.

[127] Discourse 33, p. 182, 185.

[128] Discourse 28, p. 156.

[129] See N. I. Kostomarov, *Lekcii po russkoj istorii* (St. Petersburg, 1861), 1:28.

[130] Šaxmatov, "Kievo-Pečerskij Paterik i Pečerskaja Letopis'," *passim*, suggests that it included all the items relating to the Caves Monastery preserved in the *Paterik* but not in the PVL, together with two items found only in the *Novgorod Fourth Chronicle*—the arrival of three "Greek singers" and their families in Kiev in 1051, and the death of Antonij in 1073 (PSRL 4:117, 133)—and all incidents mentioned by Polikarp which are connected with important historical events, apart from those derived from the "Life of Antonij." Since the first historical event to which Polikarp alludes is the death of Prince Glěb Svjatopolkovič in 1078, the *Pečerskaja Letopis'* could not have started earlier than this, and apparently was kept continuously until the appearance of the column (or columns) of fire above the refectory of the monastery in 1110, which is the last historical detail mentioned by Polikarp (see Discourse 35, p. 204). After this, it was no longer kept continuously, but intermittently during the twelfth century until the death of Archimandrite Polikarp in 1182.

[131] See Discourse 27, p. 152; Discourse 30, p. 168; Cf. Discourse 35, n. 650.

writings, though at some point the compiler also used the "Life of Antonij."

Šaxmatov presents his case persuasively, and his reconstruction of the chronicle's content is certainly ingenious. Yet the existence of such a chronicle, let alone the details of its content, remains a matter for conjecture. It is clear from the remarks made by Polikarp that he and Simon had access to some earlier sources which had been neglected, and that he felt that he had a duty to preserve their contents.[132] But the exact nature of these sources, together with the reasons for their neglect and ultimate disappearance, must remain an unsolved problem. Their historical value can be determined only by the extent to which those parts preserved by Simon and Polikarp can be checked against other sources.[133]

(ii) *The Life of Feodosij*

Unlike the narratives of Simon and Polikarp, the Life of Feodosij is virtually a contemporary source. Nestor had not known Feodosij personally, since he entered the monastery when his successor Stefan was superior.[134] But he wrote while the memory of his subject was fresh and he was still able to collect information from monks who had known Feodosij. Two of these he mentions by name: the cellarer Feodor and the monk Ilarion.[135] It was from Feodor that he obtained his detailed information about the superior's early life, which Feodor himself had obtained from Feodosij's mother; and he was presumably also the source for those incidents in which the cellarer is concerned. Parts of Nestor's work were almost certainly derived from the superior Nikon, who was probably still alive when Nestor was writing (he died in 1088), though he does not explicitly mention him as a source.[136] In general, Nestor shows a sound knowledge of contemporary political events, which is of some

---

[132] See Discourse 27, p. 152.
[133] These "checks" are referred to and discussed in notes throughout the text. On the whole, they do confirm the historical reliability of the material from the lost sources preserved in the writings of Simon and Polikarp.
[134] Discourse 8, p. 88.
[135] Ibid., p. 35 and p. 55.
[136] Probably for the tonsuring of Feodosij, Varlaam, and Efrem, all of whom were tonsured by Nikon (ibid., pp. 33, 36–37); and the quarrel with Prince Izjaslav which followed the tonsuring of Varlaam, in which Nikon played an important role (ibid., pp. 38 ff.).

interest in view of Šaxmatov's theory that the section of the PVL covering the years 1054 to 1073 was composed under Nikon's direction.[137]

The Life of Feodosij has a deservedly high reputation, both as a work of hagiography and as a historical source, but its value in this latter respect has perhaps been overestimated and insufficient attention paid to the gaps in Nestor's knowledge, or possibly his deliberate suppression of information. For example, he says little about Antonij and his connection with the monastery, and was almost certainly wrong in placing Antonij's withdrawal into solitude after Feodosij's arrival in Kiev.[138] Nor does he mention that the land on which the aboveground monastery was built was a gift from Prince Izjaslav.[139] He says nothing about the incidents connected with the foundation of the stone church, described in the first two discourses of the *Paterik*, in which Antonij played an important role.[140] Then in his account of the choice of Feodosij's successor, which took place just before the superior's death, he says that the choirmaster Stefan was chosen by the brotherhood and accepted by Feodosij without question,[141] whereas the PVL reports that Feodosij would have preferred a monk named Jakov.[142] Finally, he does not explain why Stefan was expelled from the monastery by the monks or a faction among them, although he had been chosen by the brotherhood; he merely says that this was due to the intrigues of the devil.[143] Yet he must have known why Stefan was expelled, since he himself was in the monastery at that time. These omissions do not seriously impair the value of the Life of Feodosij as a source, but they should be borne in mind so that it can be rightly appreciated in relation to other sources.

(iii) *The anonymous items*

Apart from the description of the decoration of Feodosij's tomb (Discourse 10) and the commemorative sermon (Discourse 11), all the

---

[137] A. A. Šaxmatov, *Razyskanija o drevnejšix russkix letopisnyx svodax* (St. Petersburg, 1908), Chapter 17.
[138] Discourse 8, p. 41.
[139] Discourse 7, p. 22.
[140] See below, pp. xlvi–xlviii, for a discussion of the authenticity of this material. It is, of course, possible that he knew these things but omitted them from a desire to play down Antonij's role in this stage of the monastery's history in order to enhance that of his subject, Feodosij.
[141] Discourse 8, p. 82.
[142] PVL 1074, PSRL 1:186–87, 2:177.
[143] Discourse 8, p. 87.

anonymous items in the *Paterik* have corresponding passages in the PVL or the *Hypatian Chronicle*. With the exception of the *Account of why the Caves Monastery is so called*, they are all straightforward narrative or descriptive texts, almost certainly based on personal observation or firsthand evidence.[144] Yet the *Account of why the Caves Monastery is so called*, both in structure and content, shows signs of being a conflation of different and sometimes contradictory sources, and it has probably been subject to so many re-workings and editorial additions that it is virtually impossible to disentangle its textual history.[145] But it is clear that basically the *Account of Why the Caves Monastery is so called* derives from two main sources: the Life of Antonij and the Life of Feodosij, or more probably a summary of the early history of the monastery written by Nestor or based on his work.[146] The *Account of why the Caves Monastery is so called*, therefore, is a derivative rather than an original source, and its historical value depends on that of its own principal sources, which have already been discussed.

So we see that the greater part of the *Paterik* was based on either firsthand evidence or on detailed and on the whole reliable contemporary sources, and that it can therefore itself be considered as a valuable source for the history of Rus', especially for the second half of the eleventh century.[147] Moreover, although the main emphasis is on the life of the monastery and the activities of the monks, the *Paterik* includes a considerable amount of information about political events and social conditions and also many vivid details from daily life which are not preserved in more formal records. While long disparaged as historical sources, hagiographic texts are now generally recognized as valuable for reconstructing medieval history. This is particularly important for a society such as Rus', about which relatively little documentary material has survived.

7. *Miracle stories in the* Paterik

In common with the Late Antique monastic literature which strongly influenced it, the *Paterik* contains numerous miracle stories.

---

[144] For example, the account of the translation of Feodosij's relics was written by a monk who claims that he played a leading part in this event (Discourse 9, p. 90).
[145] The indefatigable textologist Šaxmatov, "Žitie Antonija i Pečerskaja Letopis'," 130–34, makes some suggestions. See also Bosley, "The History," 43.
[146] See Appendix I.
[147] It is interesting to note that the *Paterik* is occasionally cited as the sole source for information not directly connected with its main theme, e.g., the presence of an Armenian colony in Kiev in the second half of the eleventh century. See Discourse 27, n. 470.

These include motifs found both in Scripture and in translated literature, which were grafted onto the incidents related in the *Paterik* in order to enhance Kievan figures or (as in the case of the foundation of the stone church) the spiritual significance of Kievan events. Yet the *Paterik* also includes some stories not found elsewhere, such as the one about the two bowls of tears at the end of the narrative about Marko the Cave-dweller (Discourse 32). Thus, the reader of the *Paterik* is confronted with a mixture of fact, legends partly based on fact, literary plagiarisms, and pure invention. These elements cannot be completely sifted and distinguished, but some attempt must be made to do this if the *Paterik* is to be correctly appreciated and fully used as a historical source. At the same time, the miracle stories should not be dismissed as being extraneous and unimportant to the modern reader, since they help us to understand the *Weltanschauung* of the authors of the *Paterik* and their audience.

The first six discourses, which describe the foundation, decoration, and consecration of the stone church of the monastery, written by Bishop Simon, provide a good example of the deliberate interweaving of fact and "legend." The miraculous element plays a large part in these narratives, but it can be shown that they also contain a substantial core of verifiable fact. Although little is known about his origins, there is no reason to doubt that the Varangian Šimon, who brought to Kiev the golden belt with which the foundations of the church were measured,[148] was a historical personage.[149] His son Georgij is mentioned as being chiliarch of Rostov both in the *Hypatian Chronicle* and in the *Paterik*.[150] The wooden crucifix from which Šimon says that he took the golden belt to provide the measurements of the monastery's stone church was of a type evidently popular in the Scandinavian lands in the eleventh century.[151] Moreover, it would be quite natural for a Varangian fleeing from his native land because of political troubles to seek and find a refuge in Kiev: up to at least the middle of the eleventh century the princes of Rus' were still conscious of their Varangian origin and maintained close

---

[148] Discourse 2, p. 8.
[149] A. Stender-Petersen, *Varangica*, vols. 1–2 (Aarhus, 1953), 147, suggests that Šimon's original name was Sigmundr, and that his father Afrikan was Alfrekr, "who, according to Swedish runic inscriptions, was a distant relative of Earl Hákon...."
[150] Discourse 1, p. 5, PSRL 2:293.
[151] See Discourse 1, n. 9.

and friendly links with Scandinavian rulers.[152] There is likewise no reason to doubt that the monastery's great stone church was actually built and decorated by Byzantine craftsmen.[153] When the surviving parts of the original walls of the church were uncovered in 1880, a piece of masonry bearing a Greek inscription was discovered, and two crosses of a design frequently found in Byzantine churches.[154] In addition, we have two precise factual statements made by Bishop Simon. Speaking of relics which the craftsmen had brought with them from Constantinople, he says, "The relics of holy martyrs were placed under all the walls, where they themselves are depicted on the walls above the relics";[155] and later, "Both the craftsmen and the painters did indeed live out their lives as monks in the Caves Monastery, and they are buried in their own chapel; their clothes are still now in the treasury and their Greek books have been preserved in memory of this miracle."[156]

The principal icon of the church also became a focus of miracles. The church was dedicated to the Dormition of the Theotokos, and the "special" icon (*naměstnaja ikona*) of the Theotokos brought from Constantinople by the mosaicists who decorated the church soon became an object of special veneration, as is illustrated in the story related in Discourse 5: a certain Kievan named Sergij (probably a merchant) was forced to recant his false statement about his deceased friend's property after swearing to it in front of the icon in the church of the Caves Monastery.[157]

Two passages in the narratives about the church have Biblical parallels: the one which describes how the Varangian Šimon measured with the golden belt the dimensions of a church which he had seen in a vision during a storm at sea,[158] and Antonij's prayer for a sign which

---

[152] See S. H. Cross, "Yaroslav the Wise in Norse Tradition," *Speculum* 4 (1929):177–97. The connection with the Scandinavian lands is also apparent in marriage alliances. See Baumgarten, *Généalogies*, Table I, nos. 8 and 27.

[153] This is accepted by I. Grabar', *Istorija russkogo isskustva* (Moscow, n. d.) 1:150; S. H. Cross, *Medieval Russian Churches*, ed. K. J. Conant (Cambridge, Mass., 1949), 17–18; G. H. Hamilton, *The Art and Architecture of Russia*, 2nd. ed. (London, 1975), 18.

[154] See Discourse 4, n. 40.

[155] Discourse 3, p. 9; cf. V. Puc'ko, "Kievskij xudožnik XI veka Alimpij Pečerskij," *Wiener slavistisches Jahrbuch* 25 (1979):70.

[156] Discourse 4, p. 12.

[157] Discourse 5, pp. 14–15.

[158] Discourse 1, p. 3.

would reveal the site of the church.[159] There are also more conventional hagiographical elements, such as the involuntary force which brought the mosaicists and icon-painters to Kiev.[160] However, quite apart from any factual basis, the miracle stories in these discourses are a vital part of the story: they both symbolize and emphasize the spiritual significance of every stage in the construction of the church, and testify to the truth of the statement at the beginning of the *Paterik* that the church was built "by the providence and will of the Lord Himself, and by the prayer and wish of His most holy Mother."[161] The real miracle was that the church was built at all, for at a time when the monastery sometimes lacked the means to supply its daily needs, a very large sum of money was made available, not only to build the church, but to adorn it lavishly with mosaics, the most expensive and luxurious form of church decoration.

Some incidents in the *Paterik* are presented as miracles, but can be otherwise explained, notably Polikarp's accounts of Pimin the Long-Suffering (Discourse 35) and Proxor Lobednik (Discourse 31). Pimin was brought to the monastery by his parents while he was still a child. He had suffered since birth from some kind of severe illness, and his parents, who wanted him to inherit their property, hoped that he would be cured by the prayers of the monks, but Pimin himself prayed for the continuance of his illness, as he wanted to stay in the monastery and become a monk. One night Pimin was visited, in a seemingly miraculous manner, by a host of angels who tonsured him as he lay on his sickbed. Yet there is nothing in the story as related by Polikarp incompatible with the fact that Pimin was secretly tonsured by the superior and the senior members of the community, who later pretended to have no knowledge of what had happened.[162] Such a deception would be justified, in their minds, by the need to carry out Pimin's wish, with which they no doubt sympathized, without angering his parents.

In Discourse 31 the transformation of cinders into salt is presented by Polikarp as evidence of the miracle-working powers of the monk Proxor Lobednik. Proxor derived his epithet from living on a kind of "bread" which he made from a plant called *lobeda* (atriplex, orach); during a period of famine in Kiev he supplied other people with this as well. He also supplied salt, apparently produced from cinders, when there was a shortage of this commodity in Kiev because the salt

---

[159] Discourse 2, p. 8.
[160] Discourse 4, p. 12.
[161] Discourse 1, p. 1.
[162] This is hinted at in a passage in the Arsenian text: Abramovyč, *Pateryk*, 181, n. 11.

merchants of Halyč had been excluded from the city during the interprincely war which followed the capture and blinding of Prince Vasil'ko of Terebovlja in 1097. It has been suggested that Proxor might have known of deposits of salt in the caves from which the monastery derived its name.[163] But botanical knowledge provides a simpler and more convincing explanation: the plant atriplex only grows in soil rich in salt, which it absorbs into its tissues, so that all Proxor had to do was to burn his customary source of food, and the ashes would contain and taste like salt.[164] The real point of the story is that the "miracle" made a deep impression on the violent and rapacious prince Svjatopolk II Izjaslavič, who became convinced that Proxor was indeed a "holy man," and that under Proxor's influence the prince's character changed for the better.[165]

However, there are other miraculous incidents in the *Paterik* which are less easy to interpret, such as the "translation" of the martyr Evstratij the Faster, the escape of his contemporary Nikon "the Dry" from his Cuman captors, the restoration of the dead body of Grigorij the Miracle-worker to his locked cell, and the painting of an icon for Alimpij the Icon-painter as he lay dying.[166] On the other hand, there are straightforward factual narratives in which there is very little of the miraculous element, such as Simon's accounts of the miserly monk Arefa (Discourse 21) and of the monk Erazm who regretted giving all his money to the church (Discourse 22), and Polikarp's accounts of Ioann the Solitary (Discourse 29), Moisej the Hungarian (Discourse 30), and the monks Feodor and Vasilij (Discourse 33). But the miracle stories, whatever their literary origin or their role in the narratives in which they are found, are an essential part of the *Paterik*, since they reveal to us a world in which people expected miracles to happen and where individuals were keenly aware of the influence of non-material forces: the assaults of demons, the constant vigilance of angels, the compassionate intercession of the Theotokos, the peculiar strength of a holy man, and above all the power of God to intervene at any time and in any way in human affairs. In this respect, the monks of the Caves Monastery showed themselves true heirs of the Byzantine monastic tradition.

---

[163] Goetz, *Das Kiever Höhlenkloster*, 176.
[164] A. H. Krappe, "L'arroche biblique et le *Paterik*," *Revue des études slaves* 13 (1933):244–45.
[165] See Discourse 31, pp. 173–74.
[166] See Discourse 16, p. 124; Discourse 17, p. 126; Discourse 28, p. 157; Discourse 34, p. 198.

8. *The Ascetical Life of the Caves Monastery*

Finally, we must consider what the *Paterik* tells us about the ascetical ideals and practices of the monks of the Caves Monastery, since the main reason the work was written was to encourage the members of the monastery in their spiritual progress along the hard road to "perfection." Bishop Simon reminds us of this goal in his letter to Polikarp (whom, in his opinion, had strayed from the path) when he says, "Perfection does not lie in being honored by all men, brother, but in amending your life and keeping yourself pure."[167]

One thing that emerges very clearly throughout the *Paterik* is the powerful belief that the monastery itself was a special vehicle of divine grace, so that to live in it afforded the best possible chance to grow in holiness, while to die there gave assurance of forgiveness of sins and salvation in the life to come. Yet as we read the narratives in the *Paterik* we see that many of the monks are depicted as lazy, avaricious, quarrelsome, disobedient, worldly (like Polikarp), and prone to spiritual pride. So it seems at first sight a strange paradox that descriptions of such conduct within the walls of a famous monastery could help others in their journey towards "perfection." In fact, the paradox contains an important spiritual truth, for one thing that nearly all the monks whose lives are recorded have in common is a steadfast determination to "try again" after every fall. There are two words, both difficult to translate adequately into English, which occur frequently in the *Paterik*: подвигъ (*podvig*) and исправление (*ispravlenie*). The former usually denotes the successful performance of a difficult task or progress achieved as a result of strenuous effort, while the latter, which means literally "correction," indicates the continual and indeed unending process of "amending one's life" and self-improvement which was the monk's primary task. This struggle was concerned not only with the outward observance of the monastic rule, the practice of self-denial and works of charity, but with improving one's inner life as well. Pride had to be rooted out completely and replaced by humility (as in the story of Isaakij the Cave-dweller); avarice must be conquered to the extent that even the existence of wealth was forgotten (as was the experience of the monk Feodor described in Discourse 33); enmity and hatred were to be replaced by love and forgiveness. The frank description of the sins and weakness of fallible human beings and the often dramatic narrative of the intense struggle waged by individuals to conquer their faults make the *Paterik* far more

---

[167] Discourse 14, p. 118.

convincing as a work designed to help those living the monastic life, than if it had presented only tales of virtue and sanctity. It is a chronicle of steadfast spiritual endeavor. As such, it has enduring validity, which no doubt explains why it continued to be read and copied throughout many troubled centuries.

The special grace of the monastery as an institution derived from the example, the continuing presence, and the intercessory prayers of those who had won the battle. Some of these, such as Feodosij, his contemporary Damian, and the prince-monk Svjatoša seem to have been naturally endowed with spiritual gifts, which they cultivated by strenuous effort and rigorous ascetic discipline; it was they who "shone forth like bright lights in the land of Rus'."[168] For others the road to "perfection" was clearly harder, but never impossible, and the special grace of the monastery was always there to help them.

Another impression which emerges from the *Paterik* is the individualism of the monks portrayed there. It is clear from the Life of Feodosij that his attempt to establish a strictly cenobitic way of life based on the rule of the Stoudios Monastery in Constantinople met with considerable resistance, and that its enforcement required constant vigilance. Soon after his death it appears to have broken down, and an unsuccessful effort to maintain it may well have been the reason for the expulsion of Feodosij's successor Stefan, about which Nestor is so reticent. Nikon, who succeeded Stefan, seems to have been a naturally authoritarian personality; while he was superior cenobitic discipline was probably largely restored, but after his death it was permanently weakened. However, this seems to have been compensated by the existence of strong personal friendships, in which individual monks helped each other in their spiritual struggles (there are several examples of this in the *Paterik*), and by the role of the spiritual father in the training of a young monk, which is so vividly portrayed in the relationship between Simon and Polikarp. Thus, from the late eleventh century onwards the Caves Monastery seems to have been more like a group of individuals linked together by the pursuit of a common goal than a community living a strictly common life. In this respect the monastery reflected the tension between the eremitic and cenobitic forms of monastic life which was always a feature of Byzantine monasticism; it also foreshadowed, to some extent, the divergence in ascetical ideals and practice which developed later in Muscovy, giving rise to the two groups known as the Possessors and the

---

[168] PVL 1074, PSRL 1:188, 2:179.

Non-Possessors. In fact, the Caves Monastery as depicted in the *Paterik* was in many ways a microcosm of monastic life in which we can see many of the characteristic trends of Orthodox spirituality, an institution in which the traditions of Byzantium, transplanted onto new soil, put down vigorous roots and ultimately produced a rich harvest over many centuries.

* * *

The present translation of the *Kievo-Pečerskij Paterik* is based on a thesis submitted for the degree of Ph. D. at the University of London in 1954, and I should like to express my thanks to my supervisor, Professor J. M. Hussey, and to Professor Sir Dimitri Obolensky for their advice and encouragement at that stage of the work. It was the approach of the Millennium of the conversion of Rus' that prompted me to return to the study of the *Paterik*. Updating the bibliography, after such a long interval and for a text with such diverse subject matter, was a formidable task, and I am most grateful to the Trustees of Dumbarton Oaks, who awarded me a Summer Fellowship for this purpose in 1986. I should like to express my special thanks to Professor Anthony Cutler, of Pennsylvania State University, who was working at Dumbarton Oaks at that time, both for his general encouragement and for his specialist advice on icons and icon painting, and also to Paul Hollingsworth, Thomas M. Kearney, and Roman Koropeckyj of the Harvard Ukrainian Research Institute for their assistance in preparing the manuscript for publication.

For several decades after the October Revolution the Caves Monastery was a secular museum. However, in June 1988, part of the present complex of buildings was turned over to the Ukrainian Exarchate of the Russian Orthodox Church in connection with the Millennial celebrations, and now the monastic tradition is alive once more in the Caves Monastery.

Muriel Heppell
London, England

Rus' in the Twelfth Century

THE PATERIK OF THE KIEVAN CAVES MONASTERY

Discourse 1. Concerning the building of the church, so that all may understand that it was by the providence and will of the Lord Himself and by the prayer and wish of His most holy Mother that a church dedicated to the Theotokos was erected and completed in the Caves Monastery, a church pleasing to God and like unto Heaven, the church of the archimandrite of the whole land of Rus', the lavra of our holy and great father Feodosij.

Give your blessing, father.

In the Varangian land there was a Prince Afrikan, the brother of Hakon the Blind who lost his gold surcoat in battle while fighting for Jaroslav against the fierce M'stislav.[1] This Afrikan had two sons, Friand and Šimon.[2] After the death of their father, Hakon expelled them from their provinces. Šimon came to our pious prince Jaroslav, who received him, treated him with honor,[3] and gave him to his son Vsevolod to be his elder, and he received considerable authority from Vsevolod. The reason for his deep love for this holy place was this:

---

[1] See PVL 1024, PSRL 1:148, 2:135–36. Hakon (Jakun) is not mentioned in any Old Norse saga, but is usually considered a historical personage. See Nora Chadwick, *The Beginnings of Russian History: an Enquiry into the Sources* (Cambridge, Eng., 1946), 101, and A. Stender-Petersen, *Varangica*, vols. 1–2 (Aarhus, 1953), 147. O. Pritsak, *The Origin of Rus'*, vol. 1 (Cambridge, Mass., 1981), 404–14, using the evidence of runic inscriptions, identifies Hakon with Hákon jarl Eriksson (d. 1029), a member of the Old Scandinavian Saemingar dynasty; he also suggests that the word сьлѣпъ ("blind") in the PVL should be read лѣпъ ("handsome"), since there is no tradition in Scandinavian sources of a blind ruler, but some evidence that Hákon jarl Eriksson's descendants were noted for their good looks. On Afrikan, see Pritsak, *The Origin of Rus'*, 1:417–19.

[2] A. F. Braun, "Friand i Simon, synov'ja Varjažkogo knjazja Afrikana," IORJAS 7, no. 1 (1902):359–65, has suggested that the name "Friand" is actually a corruption of an epithet applied to Simon, and that he had no brother. See also Pritsak, *The Origin of Rus'*, 1:418–19.

[3] On relations between the Rus' and Scandinavian courts in the eleventh century, see S. Cross, "Jaroslav the Wise in Norse Tradition," *Speculum* 4 (1929):177–97, and Stender-Petersen, *Varangica*, 1–2:147–48.

While the pious and great prince Izjaslav ruled in Kiev, the Cumans invaded the land of Rus' in the year 1068,[4] and the three sons of Jaroslav—Izjaslav, Svjatoslav, and Vsevolod—went out to meet them, taking Šimon with them. They came to the great and holy Antonij to receive his prayer and blessing.[5] The elder[6] opened his guileless lips and related clearly the disaster that would befall them. The Varangian prostrated himself at the elder's feet and begged that he might be preserved from such a misfortune. The blessed one said to him, "My son, many shall fall by the blade of the sword, and as you all flee from your enemies you will be trampled, wounded, and drowned in the water. But you will be saved and will be buried here in a church which is still to be built."

When they were at the Al'ta, both armies clashed and because of God's wrath the Christians were defeated.[7] As they were fleeing, the *voevodas* and a multitude of soldiers were killed. After the battle, Šimon lay wounded in their midst. Looking up to heaven, he saw an enormous church, as he had previously seen on the sea.[8] He recalled the Savior's words and said, "O Lord, deliver me from this bitter death through the prayers of Thy most pure Mother and of the venerable fathers Antonij and Feodosij." Immediately some power seized him from among the dead, and he immediately was healed from his wounds, and he found that all his limbs were whole and sound.

Then he returned home, came to the blessed Antonij, and told him of the marvelous incident, saying, "My father Afrikan made a cross and on it depicted the divine-human image of Christ in colors, in a new way, such as the Latins honor. It was large, ten cubits in height. To do Him honor, my father laid about His waist a belt weighing fifty *grivna* of

---

[4] See PVL 1068, PSRL 1:167, 2:156. The Cumans were nomads inhabiting the southern steppes of central Asia who frequently raided the land of Rus', especially in the second half of the eleventh century. The raid of 1068 is the first one mentioned in Rus' sources.

[5] By 1068 Antonij had retired from the Caves Monastery's community and was living as a recluse. But this did not prevent him from occasionally receiving visitors from both the monastery and the outside world, in keeping with the traditions of Orthodox monasticism. See M. Heppell, "The *Vita Antonii*, a Lost Source of the *Paterikon* of the Monastery of Caves," *Byzantinoslavica* 13, no. 2 (1952):54–55.

[6] *Starec* ("elder"), corresponding to the Greek γέρων, cannot be adequately translated into English; it means an experienced ascetic and a venerated holy man.

[7] See PVL 1068, PSRL 1:167, 2:156. The Al'ta is a tributary of the Trubež northwest of Perejaslav.

[8] See below, p. 3. Simon is almost certainly using material from the Life of Antonij, which would been have familiar to Polikarp. See the Introduction, p. xxxix–xliv ff.

gold, and a gold crown on His head.[9] When my uncle Hakon expelled me from my province, I took the belt from Jesus and the crown from His head, and I heard a voice from the image addressed to me, 'Never place this crown on your own head, but take it to the place prepared for it, where a church dedicated to my Mother is to be built by the venerable Feodosij. Give it into his hands, so that it may hang above my altar.' I fell down in terror, my limbs grew numb, and I lay like someone dead; then I got up and quickly went on board the boat.

"While we were at sea a great storm came up, so that we all despaired of our lives. I began to cry out, 'Lord, forgive me, for this day I am perishing on account of this belt, inasmuch as I took it from Thy noble and man-like image. Lo, up above I saw a church, and I wondered what church it could be. And a voice came to us from on high, 'It is the one which is to be built by the venerable one in the name of the Theotokos, in which you will be buried.' When we saw it in its height and magnitude, we measured it with the gold belt[10] —twenty cubits in breadth, thirty in length and height, and fifty for the walls with the dome. We all glorified God and took comfort in the great joy that we had been delivered from a bitter death. I had not known where that church which was revealed to me on the sea and at the Al'ta would be built until now, when I heard from your noble lips that I would be buried here, in a church still to be built."

Taking out the gold belt, he gave it to Antonij, saying, "See, the dimensions of the foundation, and let this crown be hung above the holy table." The elder praised God for this and said to the Varangian, "My son, from now on you will not be called Šimon, but Simon will be your name."[11] Then Antonij summoned the blessed Feodosij and said,

---

[9] Crucifixes of this type, with a metal crown on Christ's head, were popular in Scandinavia in the eleventh and twelfth centuries. There is a good example in the National Museum of Copenhagen, the Aaby Crucifix (Exhibit D. 629), though this is smaller than the one described by Simon. For a photograph, see R. W. Southern, *The Making of the Middle Ages* (London, 1953), Plate II (Plate III shows another Danish crucifix, also wearing a metal crown). The *grivna* was the basic monetary unit of Kievan Rus' and consisted of a bar of gold or silver. See G. Vernadsky, *Kievan Russia* (New Haven, 1948), 121–23.

[10] Cf. Rev. 21:15–17.

[11] V. Thomsen, *Samlede Afhandlinger*, vol. 1 (Copenhagen, 1919), 410, and Stender-Petersen, *Varangica*, 1–2:147–48, have proposed that here the name Šimon corresponds to the Scandinavian Sigmundr. Simon was a completely new name, in spite of its phonetic resemblance to Šimon. The significance of the change was, presumably, that a name with Biblical associations was more suitable for an instrument of divine providence than Sigmundr.

"Simon, this man will build such a church," and he gave him the belt and crown. From then on Simon had great love for holy Feodosij, and gave him many possessions towards the building of the monastery.

One day Simon came to the blessed one and after the usual conversation he said to the holy one, "Father, I ask one gift from you." Feodosij said to him, "My son, what can a man of your greatness ask of one in my humble position?" Simon said, "I seek from you a greater gift, beyond my power." Feodosij said, "My son, you know our poverty: often bread cannot be found for our daily meal. I do not know of anything else that I have." Simon said, "If you are willing, you will grant me it. For you have the ability through the grace given to you by the Lord, Who called you 'venerable.' For when I took the crown from the head of Jesus, He said to me, 'Take this to the place prepared for it and give it into the hands of the venerable one, who will build a church dedicated to my Mother.' And now I ask of you: give me your promise that your soul will bless me, even as in life, so also after your death and mine."

The holy one answered, "Simon, your request is beyond my power. But if, when I have departed this life, you see that this church has been built and that the traditional rules are performed in it after my death, let it be clear to you that I can approach God boldly.[12] Now I do not know whether my prayer will be accepted." Simon said, "The Lord has testified concerning you, for I myself heard of you from the immaculate lips of the holy image. For this reason I beg of you that, just as you pray for your monks, you will pray for me too, sinner that I am, and for my son Georgij, and for all the descendants of my family." The holy one as a promise said, "I pray not only for them, but for all who love this holy place for my sake."

Then Simon prostrated himself to the ground and said, "Father, I shall not leave you until you assure me of this in writing." Moved by love for him, the venerable one accordingly wrote the prayer, "In the name of the Father, the Son, and the Holy Spirit." To this day such a prayer is placed in the hands of the dying; from that time the custom became established to place such a written prayer in the hands of a dying person, but formerly no one had done such a thing in Rus'. These are the words he wrote in the prayer: "Remember me, O Lord, when Thou

---

[12] On the meaning of дръзновеніе (Greek παρρησία) see below, Discourse 8, n. 231.

comest into Thy Kingdom,[13] to render to each according to his deeds. Then, O Lord, vouchsafe that Thy servants Simon and Georgij may be worthy to stand at Thy right hand and in Thy glory and to hear Thy blessed voice saying, 'Come, ye blessed of my Father, inherit the Kingdom that was prepared for you from the foundation of the world.'"[14]

Simon said, "Add too, father, 'May the sins of my parents and kinsfolk be forgiven.'" Feodosij, lifting up his hands to heaven, said, "May the Lord bless thee out of Zion, and mayest thou see the prosperity of Jerusalem all the days of thy life even unto the last of thy generation."[15] Simon took the prayer and blessing from the holy one, like some pearl and gift of great price.[16] And he who had once been a Varangian became by Christ's grace a Christian, having been instructed by the holy Feodosij, having abandoned the folly of the Latins, and having come to believe truly in our Lord Jesus Christ, he and all his household, some three thousand, and his priests, on account of the miracles performed by the holy Antonij and Feodosij.[17]

Simon was indeed the first person to be buried in the church, and henceforth his son Georgij had a great love for the holy place.[18] Georgij was sent to the land of Suzdal' by Volodimer Monomax, who entrusted into his hands his own son Georgij. Many years later Georgij Volodimerovič resided in Kiev, and regarding his chiliarch Georgij as a father, he assigned to him the district of Suzdal'.[19]

---

[13] See Luke 23:42.
[14] Matt. 25:34. For further information about this prayer, see E. E. Golubinskij, *Istorija russkoj cerkvy*, 1, 1:839–40, and K. V. Xarlampovič, "O molitvax prep. Feodosija Pečerskogo," IORJAS 17 (1912):168–69, who point out that this formulation is not the same as those of the prayer of absolution in Orthodox service books.
[15] Ps. 127:5.
[16] Cf. Matt. 13:46.
[17] Šimon was of course already a Christian. The anti-Latin sentiment implicit in Simon's manner of expression is typical of the early thirteenth century rather than of the period of events described.
[18] See Discourse 10, p. 95. On Georgij Simonovič, see Pritsak, *The Origin of Rus'*, 1:420–21.
[19] Bishop Simon probably acquired this information from Prince Georgij (Jurij) Volodimerovič of Suzdal', a great-grandson of Volodimer Monomax.

Discourse 2. The account of the arrival of the craftsmen from Constantinople to Antonij and Feodosij.

Now, brethren, I shall tell you[20] of another wonderful and glorious miracle concerning this God-chosen Church of the Theotokos:

There came to the cave—to the great Antonij and Feodosij—four craftsmen[21] from Constantinople, very rich men, saying, "Where do you want to start on the church?" Antonij and Feodosij said to them, "Wherever the Lord designates." They said, "If you have foreseen your death, why did you give us gold without fixing the place?" Antonij and Feodosij, having summoned all the brethren, both questioned the Greeks, saying, "Tell the truth: what took place?"

The craftsmen said, "Early one morning when we were asleep in our houses, as the sun was rising, handsome eunuchs came to each of us, saying, 'The empress calls you to Blachernai.'[22] While we were on our way, we took with us our friends and kinsmen, and we found that we all had arrived at the same time and place. After talking among ourselves, we realized that we had heard the same message from the empress[23] and received the same messengers.

"We saw the empress and a multitude of soldiers around her. We prostrated ourselves before her, and she said to us, 'I want to build a church in Rus' for myself, in Kiev, and I bid you to take some gold for yourselves, enough for three years.'

"We prostrated ourselves and said to her, 'O empress and mistress, you are sending us to a foreign land. To whom shall we go there?' She said, 'I am sending you to these men, Antonij and Feodosij,' We said, 'Why, mistress, do you give us gold for three years? Tell them about us,

---

[20] As the narratives were originally addressed only to Polikarp, one would expect the singular братъ instead of the plural братїе here. The Arsenian MS has ти (the singular form of "you"): Abramovyč, *Pateryk*, 5, n. 25. Possibly the original text had the singular, which a later copyist replaced with the plural.

[21] The word used in the text—мастери—implies that they were designers and architects, not mere workmen.

[22] A reference to the Blachernai quarter of Constantinople, where there was an imperial palace and a Church of Our Lady of Blachernai. For the history and significance of this church, see R. Janin, *La géographie ecclésiastique de l'empire byzantin*, pt. 1, vol. 3, *Les églises et les monastères* (Paris, 1953), 169–79.

[23] The Cas. II reading here is Богородичину ("the same message from the Theotokos"), but other MSS have царицину ("the same message from the empress"): Abramovyč, *Pateryk*, 6, n. 5. This latter reading makes better sense, since it was not until they arrived in Kiev that the craftsmen realized that their audience with the "empress" was in fact a vision of the Theotokos.

about everything that we need for sustenance. You yourself know what to grant us.'[24]

"The empress said, 'Antonij will only give his blessing and then depart from this world to the eternal one; Feodosij will depart to the Lord two years after him.[25] Take as much gold as you need; as for paying due honor, no man can do this. I shall give you what the ear hath not heard, and hath not entered into the heart of man.[26] I myself will come to see the church, and I will dwell in it.' She then gave us the relics of the holy martyrs Artemios, Polyeuktos, Leontios, Akakios, Arethas, James, and Theodore, saying 'Put these in the foundation.' We took the gold, beyond what we needed. And she said to us, 'Go outside and behold its size.' We went outside and beheld a church in the sky. Then we entered, prostrated ourselves, and asked, 'Mistress, what is the name of this church?' She said, 'I will call it after myself.' But we dared not inquire after her name. She said, 'It will be called the Church of the Theotokos.' She gave us this icon and said, 'Let this be the special icon.'[27] We prostrated ourselves, then went back to our homes, carrying this icon which we had received from the hands of the empress."

Then they all glorified God and her who bore Him. Antonij said, "My sons, we never left this place." The Greeks swore, "But we received the gold from your hands in front of many witnesses, and in their company we accompanied you to the boat. After your departure we waited for one month, and then set off. It is now ten days since we left Constantinople. We asked the empress about the size of the church, and she said, 'I have sent as a measure the belt of my Son, in accordance with His bidding.'"

Antonij answered, "My sons, Christ has deemed you worthy of great grace, that you might accomplish His will. Those handsome eunuchs who summoned you were holy angels, and the empress at Blachernai who appeared to you in visible form was our most pure, holy and undefiled lady, the Theotokos and ever-virgin Mary, and the warriors standing about her were incorporeal angelic powers. As for the

---

[24] Evidently the Greeks thought that they had seen Antonij and Feodosij during their "audience"; presumably the "empress" indicated them when she mentioned their names.
[25] Feodosij died in 1074; hence Antonij died in 1072 or 1073. The *Novgorod Fourth Chronicle* (PSRL 4:133) gives the date of his death as 1073.
[26] 1 Cor. 2:9.
[27] The phrase намѣстная икона designates those icons placed on either side of the Royal Doors in the iconostasis. For a further note on these icons, see below, Discourse 34, n. 610.

semblance of us and the gift of gold to you, God Himself knows His work and His will for His servants. Blessed is your arrival, and you have had a good traveling companion, this noble icon of Our Lady. She will give you, even as she promised, what the ear hath not heard and hath not entered into the heart of man. No one can grant this but she herself and her Son, the Lord God, our Savior Jesus Christ, whose belt and crown were brought from the Varangians. And the dimensions of this holy church—the breadth, length, and height—were announced when a voice came from heaven from the exalted glory."

Awestruck, the Greeks prostrated themselves before the holy ones and said, "Where is this place? Let us see it." Antonij said, "We shall remain in prayer for three days, and the Lord will reveal it to us." That night, as he prayed, the Lord appeared to him, saying, "You have found favor in My sight." Antonij said, "Lord, if I have found favor in Thy sight, let there be dew upon all the earth, but that place which Thou desirest to sanctify, let it be dry." In the morning they found a dry place where the church now is, but dew upon all the earth. The next night he prayed, "Let it be dry upon all the earth, but let there be dew on the holy place." They went out and found that it was so. On the third day, standing on that very place, they prayed and blessed it, and measured the length and breadth with the gold belt. Lifting his hands to heaven, Antonij said with a great voice, "Hear me this day, O Lord, hear me with fire, so that all may understand that this is Thy will." At once fire fell from heaven, burned up all the thorns and briers, licked up the dew, and made a trench like a pit. Those who were with the holy ones fell down awestruck, as though dead. And this was the beginning of the divine church.[28]

---

[28] This whole passage is modelled on Judg. 6:21, 36–40. See also 3 Kings 18:36–38, and a corresponding passage in Ilarion's *Sermon on Law and Grace*, L. Müller, ed., *Des Metropoliten Ilarion Lobrede auf Vladimir den Heiligen und Glaubensbekenntnis* (Wiesbaden, 1962), 74, where Ilarion quotes Gideon's prayer to the Lord and then interprets it symbolically.

Discourse 3. When the church of the Caves Monastery was founded.[29]

The divine Church of the Theotokos was founded in the year 1073. They began to build the church in the days of the pious prince Svjatoslav, son of Jaroslav, who with his own hands began to dig the foundations.[30] The Christ-loving prince Svjatoslav also gave 100 gold *grivna* to assist the blessed one [Feodosij] and made the measurements with the gold belt in accordance with the voice from heaven which was heard on the sea. In the Life of St. Antonij you will find all these things described more fully.[31] In the Life of St. Feodosij they are made clear to everybody: how a pillar of fire appeared from the earth to heaven, sometimes as a cloud, sometimes as an arc from the dome of the other church to this place, and how the icon often could be seen crossing over, carried by angels, to the place where it was to be.[32]

What, brethren, is there more marvelous than this? Indeed, if you go through the books of the Old and New Testaments, nowhere will you find such miracles about holy churches as about this one. The crown came from the Varangians and from Our Lord Jesus Christ Himself, from His noble and divine and man-like image, from His sacred head. And from Christ's likeness we heard a divine voice commanding that it should be taken to the place prepared for it, and that the measurements should be made with His belt, in accordance with that voice which was heard before the beginning. So also from the Greeks came the icon with the craftsmen, and relics of holy martyrs were placed under all the walls, where they themselves are depicted on the walls above the relics.[33]

---

[29] This discourse falls into two sections: the first contains some further items of information about the foundation of the church, while the second, from the words "Therefore it is our duty...," appears to be a sermon, or part of one. This is clear from the more elevated style of the language, and the fact that the second person plural of the word "brethren" is used twice, though not in the Arsenian MS: see Abramovyč, *Pateryk*, 8, n. 23, 9, n. 12. As the sentiments are very similar to those of Bishop Simon's letter to Polikarp (see Discourse 14), this might be an extract from a sermon delivered by Simon while he was still in the Caves Monastery.

[30] For the church's history, see P. A. Rappoport, *Russkaja arxitektura X–XIII vv.* (Leningrad, 1982) (= *Arxeologija SSSR*, no. I-47), 23–25.

[31] This is Simon's first reference to the Life of Antonij, probably his principal source for his first two narratives about the church, since this material is not found in the Life of Feodosij.

[32] See Discourse 8, pp. 71–2.

[33] The 1470 entry in the *Hustyn' Chronicle*, PSRL, 1st ed., 2:358, states: "A long time after it had been damaged by Batu, the Church of the Theotokos in the Caves Monastery was restored at great expense by the pious prince Simeon Olel'kovič, or Aleksandrovič,

It is our duty first to praise the pious princes, Christ-loving boyars, venerable monks, and all Orthodox Christians [who have passed on before us.] Blessed and thrice-blessed is he who has been vouchsafed to be buried here; he has merited the grace and mercy of the Lord, through the prayers of the holy Theotokos and all the saints. Blessed and thrice-blessed is he who has been vouchsafed to be inscribed in its records, for he shall receive remission of his sins and will not lose his heavenly reward. For it is written, "Rejoice, and be glad, because your names are written in the heavens."[34] For God has loved this church as He loves heaven. It was the will of her who bore Him that this church should be built, as she promised the craftsmen at Blachernai, saying, "I shall go to see the church, and in it I will dwell." It is right and most fitting that she should reside in her holy and divine church. What glory and praise he receives who is buried there and whose name is inscribed in it into the Book of Life: he is forever remembered in her sight!

One more discourse I will set before you, beloved, for the strengthening of your soul. What is worse than turning aside from such light and loving darkness, cutting oneself off from the God-appointed church and leaving the church He founded, and seeking the human one wrought by robbery and violence, while the church herself cries out to her builder? For God was her architect and builder, her artist and creator; He by the fire of His Godhead consumed perishable things—trees and hills—and made level a way for the house of His Mother, so that His workmen might be transported thither. Consider, brethren, the church's foundation and origin: our Father from on high gave His blessing through the dew, the pillar of fire, and the translucent cloud; the Son gave the measurements with His belt (even if the cross seemed in substance to be of wood, it was nevertheless endued with divine power); and the Holy Spirit with immaterial fire dug a trench for laying the foundations. On this rock the Lord founded this church, and the gates of Hell

---

grandson of Volodimer Ol'gerdovič, of the princes of Sluck. He made it as fine and beautiful as possible, and also decorated the interior with iconography. Still, it was not like it had been before, for originally mosaics were set not only in the walls but in the floor. And he enriched it with gold and silver vessels, in the time of Archimandrite Ioann." N. de Baumgarten, *Généalogies des branches régnantes de Rurikides du XIII au XVIe siècle* (Rome, 1934) (=*Orientalia Christiana* 35), Table VI, no. 7, mentions a Princess Alessandra Olelkowicz, daughter of "Simeon, Prince of Kiev," as the wife of Prince Feodor Jaroslavič of Pinsk. Presumably her father was the Simeon Olel'kovič mentioned above.

[34] Matt. 5:12.

shall not prevail against it.[35] And what of the Theotokos? She gave the craftsmen gold for three years, and having given an icon of her own most holy image, she set up a substitute of herself, through which many miracles have been performed.

Discourse 4. Concerning the coming of the church painters from Constantinople to the superior Nikon.[36]

Here is a remarkable miracle which I shall tell you. Some icon painters came to the superior Nikon from the God-guarded city of Constantine and said, "Bring those two who contracted for our services. We want to dispute with them. They showed us a small church, and on that basis we agreed to decorate it in front of many witnesses, but this church is very large. Here, take back your gold, and we shall go to Constantinople." The superior replied, "What sort of people were they who made this agreement with you?" The painters described their likeness and appearance and mentioned the names Antonij and Feodosij. The superior said to them, "My sons, we cannot show you these men; they departed this world ten years ago.[37] They pray for us without ceasing and constantly keep watch over this church, and protect their monastery and take thought for those who are in it."

Hearing this reply, the Greeks were awestruck and brought many other merchants, Greeks and Abkhasians, who had made the trip with them. And they said, "We made an agreement in front of these people and took gold from the hands of those two men, and you do not want to show them to us. If they have died, show us their image, so that these people may see if they are the ones." Then in front of everybody the superior brought out their icons. When the Greeks and Abkhasians saw their image, they prostrated themselves and said, "They are indeed the ones, and we believe that they still live after death and that they can help and save and protect those who have recourse to them." Then they donated the mosaic which they had brought to sell and with it constructed the holy altar.

---

[35] See Matt. 16:18.
[36] Nikon was superior of the Caves Monastery from ca. 1077 to 1088. See Discourse 8, p. 87, and the entry for PVL 1088, PRSL 1:207–208, 2:199.
[37] Antonij died ca. 1072 and Feodosij in 1074. See above Discourse 2, n. 25.

Then the painters began to repent their sins. They said, "When we came to Kaniv[38] in our boats, we saw this church up on high. We asked those with us which church this was and they said, 'It is the church of the Caves Monastery, and you are its painters.' We became angry and wanted to go back downstream. That night there was a great storm on the river. When we arose in the morning we found ourselves near Trypillja,[39] and the boat was moving upstream of its own accord, as if some force were pulling it. We stopped it with some effort and stayed the whole day wondering what it could mean that in one night we had traversed so great a route without rowing, which others could scarcely manage with hard work in three days. The next night we saw this church and the wonderful special icon of the Theotokos, which said to us, 'Why are you confused for naught, and why do you not submit to the will of my Son and me? If you disobey me and desire to flee, I shall take you all, and with your boat I shall put you in my church. And know this: you will not depart from there, but in my monastery you will be tonsured and live out your lives, and I shall grant you mercy in the world to come for the sake of its builders, Antonij and Feodosij.' When we arose the next morning, we wanted to go back downstream. We rowed hard, but the boat went upstream against the current. Submitting to the will and power of God, we gave in, and soon the boat arrived by itself below the monastery."

Then together all the monks and the Greeks, the craftsmen and the painters, praised Almighty God, His most holy Mother, the marvelous icon, and the holy fathers Antonij and Feodosij. And so both the craftsmen and the painters did indeed live out their lives as monks in the Caves Monastery, and they are buried in their own chapel; their clothes are still now in the treasury and their Greek books have been preserved in memory of this miracle.[40]

---

[38] On Kaniv, an important ford on the Dnieper near the mouth of the Ros', see Abramovyč, *Pateryk*, 213, n. 9 (with references) and P. P. Toločko, "Kievskaja zemlja," *Drevnerusskie knjažestva X–XIII vv.*, ed. L. G. Beskrovnyj et al. (Moscow, 1975), 40–42.

[39] Trypillja was a fortress at the confluence of the Stuhna and Krasna rivers at the Dnieper. See Toločko, "Kievskaja zemlja," 34–35.

[40] When the oldest part of the church walls was uncovered in 1880, a piece of masonry bearing a Greek inscription and two crosses of a style frequently found in Byzantine churches were discovered in the fabric. See P. A. Laškarev, "Ostatki drevnix zdanij Kievo-Pečerskoj Lavry," *Trudy Kievskoj duxovnoj akademii*, 1883, no. 1:123–27. This corroborates the statements made about the Greek builders and icon painters in Discourses 2, 3 and 4. See also V. Puc'ko, "Kievskij xudožnik XI veka Alimpij Pečerskij," *Wiener slavistisches Jahrbuch* 25 (1979):70.

When the superior Stefan, formerly the choirmaster,[41] was expelled from the monastery he himself founded a church of Blachernai at Klov,[42] because he had witnessed these remarkable miracles: how the craftsmen came carrying the icon and had related their vision of the empress at Blachernai.

The pious prince Volodimer Vsevolodovič Monomax as a youth saw with his own eyes that remarkable miracle, when the fire fell from heaven and burned a trench where the foundation of the church was laid with the belt. And this was heard about throughout all the land of Rus'. For this reason Vsevolod and his son Volodimer came from Perejaslav to see the miracle.[43] At that time Volodimer was ill, and when the gold belt was put round him he immediately became well through the prayers of our holy fathers Antonij and Feodosij.[44] In his own principality, the Christ-loving Volodimer took the measurements of this divine church of the Caves Monastery and founded a church of exactly the same height, breadth, and length in the town of Rostov, and wrote a charter on parchment where every festival is written in its place,[45] and arranged all these things in imitation of this great God-appointed church. His son, Prince Georgij,[46] having heard from his father Volodimer what was done in that church, founded in his principality a church with the same dimensions in the town of Suzdal'. After some years all these churches fell into ruin, but this Church of the Theotokos alone abides forever.[47]

---

[41] Stefan succeeded Feodosij as superior in 1074. See below, Discourse 8, p. 86, PVL 1074, PSRL 1:188, 2:179. I. I. Sreznevskij, *Materialy dlja slovarja drevnerusskogo jazyka* (St. Petersburg, 1893), 1:652, equates деместьвьникъ with δομέστικος which in an ecclesiastical context apparently signifies the leader of a choir.

[42] See below, Discourse 8, p. 87.

[43] Vsevolod Jaroslavič (b. 1030) was prince in Perejaslav from ca. 1050 to 1078, when he moved to Kiev and ruled there until his death in 1093. Volodimer was born in 1052 and ruled first as prince in Perejaslav (1094–1113) and then in Kiev (1113–1125).

[44] Cf. below, Discourse 27, p. 149, which describes how Volodimer was cured of an illness by Agapit the Physician. Perhaps he did experience two miraculous cures; Simon's reference here may also be a "duplicate" of another recovery later in his life.

[45] This charter has not survived. At the time Rostov was part of the Perejaslav principality. Volodimer also founded a Church of the Theotokos in Smolensk, which was then dependent on Perejaslav.

[46] Georgij Volodimerovič (better known as Jurij Dolgorukij) ruled most of his life (ca. 1090–1157) as prince of Suzdal', although on three occasions (1149, 1151, 1155–57) he ruled also in Kiev. He maintained close contacts with the Caves Monastery.

[47] On the church in Suzdal' and its collapse and subsequent restoration, see Rappoport, *Russkaja arxitektura*, 59–60 (no. 84).

Discourse 5. An extraordinary miracle concerning Ioann and Sergij, which took place in the divine church of the Caves Monastery in front of the miraculous icon of the Theotokos.

Among the city's powerful men there were two named Ioann and Sergij, who were good friends. These two came to the God-appointed church and saw on the miraculous icon of the Theotokos a light brighter than the sun, and they entered into spiritual brotherhood with each other.[48] Many years later Ioann fell ill and died, leaving a son, Zaxarija, who was five years old. [Before his death] he summoned the superior Nikon and distributed his property to the poor, and his son's portion he entrusted to Sergij—1,000 silver *grivna* and 100 gold *grivna*.[49] He also left his son Zaxarija, who was then young, to the care of his friend, as to a faithful brother, and said to him, "When my son attains manhood, give him the gold and silver." When Zaxarija was fifteen years old, he wanted to take his father's gold and silver from Sergij. But the latter, goaded by the devil and reckoning that he could become rich, for which he was willing to destroy life and soul, said to the youth, "Your father gave all his property to God. Ask Him for the silver and gold. He is your debtor, if He will have mercy on you. I am obligated neither to you nor your father for a single piece of gold. This is what your father did for you by his folly: he distributed in almsgiving all that he had and left you a pauper and beggar."

Hearing this, the youth wept for his loss. He sent a message to Sergij, entreating him, "Give me half and keep the other half for yourself." But Sergij reviled him and his father in cruel words. Zaxarija then asked for a third part, and then a tenth. Seeing that he would be deprived of everything, he said to Sergij, "Come and swear to me in the church of the Caves Monastery, in front of the miracle-working icon of the Theotokos, where you made a pact of brotherhood with my father." Sergij went into the church and stood in front of the icon of the Theotokos and affirmed with an oath, "I did not receive 1,000 *grivna* of silver and 100

---

[48] See Golubinskij, *Istorija russkoj cerkvi*, 1, 2:461. Rus' adopted from Byzantium the custom whereby two people, usually of the same sex, made a church-based formal vow that they would help and cherish each other as though they were siblings. The relationship could be established for a limited time or permanently; in the latter case it was sanctified by a more elaborate ritual.

[49] We are told later in this discourse that double this sum was sufficient to build a small church, so its value must have been considerable; moreover, it represented only part of Ioann's fortune.

grivna of gold." He wanted to kiss the icon, but he could not approach it. As he was coming out of the church doors, he began to cry out, "O holy Antonij and Feodosij, do not bid this pitiless angel to destroy me! Pray to the holy Theotokos that she will drive away the many demons to which I am delivered! Take the gold and silver which is sealed up in my chamber." Fear fell on everybody, and henceforth no one was allowed to swear oaths in the name of the Theotokos.

They sent for the sealed vessel and found inside it 2,000 silver *grivna* and 200 gold *grivna*; for thus had the Lord, Who recompenses the charitable, doubled it. Zaxarija gave it all to the superior Ioann[50] for him to spend as he wished. He himself was tonsured and lived out his life there. The gold and silver were used to build the Church of St. John the Forerunner, just where you go into the sacristy, in memory of the boyar Ioann and his son Zaxarija, to whom the gold and silver belonged.[51]

Discourse 6. A story about the holy table and the consecration of the great Church of the Mother of God.

The church of the Caves Monastery was consecrated in the year 1089, Ioann's first year as superior. There was no stone slab[52] available for erecting the holy table. A prolonged inquiry was made about making a stone table, but not a single artisan could be found, so two wooden boards were made and set in position. But the metropolitan John[53] did not want to have a wooden table in such a great church, and on this account the superior was very distressed. So some days passed without the consecration taking place.

---

[50] Ioann was Nikon's successor and held office from 1088 to 1108. See PVL 1108, PSRL 1:283, 2:259, where the superior is mentioned as Feoktist.

[51] This church adjoined the northwest corner of the main church. As late as 1883 parts of its original fabric still remained. See Laškarev, "Ostatki drevnix zdanij," 119, and N. I. Petrov, *Istoriko-topografičeskie očerki drevnego Kieva* (Kiev, 1897), 75.

[52] доска: presumably a stone foundation for the holy table (altar in Western terminology).

[53] John II was metropolitan of Kiev from 1077 to 1089. He was evidently well-liked and is favorably eulogized in PVL 1089, PSRL 1:208, 2:199–200. For a summary of his career, see A. Poppe, "Die Metropoliten und Fürsten der Kiever Rus'," in: G. Podskalsky, *Christentum und theologische Literatur in der Kiever Rus' (988–1237)* (Munich, 1982), 286–87.

On August 13 the monks went into the church as usual to sing vespers,[54] and saw beside the altar's enclosure a stone slab with columns for placing the table. They quickly informed the metropolitan of this fact. He praised God and ordered that the consecration should take place, at vespers [on the next day].[55] They searched for a long time to find out where the slab had come from, who had brought it, and how it had been carried into the church, since it had been locked. Although they searched everywhere, both by land and by water, to find where it had come from, no trace was found of those who had carried it. They sent three silver *grivna* to the place where such things are made so that the artisan might take them for his work; orders went out in all directions, but the workman was not found. But this was the work of God, the author and creator of all things; He made it, set it in place, and made it firm with His priestly hands for the offering of His most pure Body and holy Blood. For it was His will that on this holy table which He Himself had given He should be sacrificed every day for the whole world.

The next day the bishops Ioann of Černihiv,[56] Isaia of Rostov,[57] Antonij of Jur'ev[58] and Luka of Bilhorod[59] came with Metropolitan John. Although no one had summoned them, they were present at the consecration. The blessed metropolitan asked them, "How have you

---

[54] The monks of the Caves Monastery followed the same canonical hours as the Stoudios monastery in Constantinople, since Feodosij introduced the Stoudite Rule soon after he became superior. See below, Discourse 8, pp. 44–5. On the Stoudite Rule, see A. P. Dobroklonskij, *Prep. Feodor, ispovednik i igumen Stoudijskij*, pt. 1 (Odessa 1913), 517–20.

[55] Though the date of the consecration is not explicitly stated here, the subsequent reference to August 14 clearly indicates that it was the day after the stone slab was found in position.

[56] Ioann is not mentioned in Bishop Simon's list of bishops (see Discourse 14, pp. 118–9). The see of Černihiv was probably established under Volodimer I. See Podskalsky, *Christentum*, 32.

[57] Isaia was probably the second bishop of Rostov (see Discourse 14, p. 118). He is mentioned elsewhere in the *Paterik* (Discourse 8, p. 51, Discourse 25, p. 145). The see of Rostov was probably carved out of the diocese of Perejaslav in the 1060s. See Podskalsky, *Christentum*, 33–34, and A. Poppe, *Pánstwo i kościół na Rusi w XI wieku* (Warsaw, 1968), 179–83.

[58] Antonij of Jur'ev is not mentioned in Bishop Simon's list (see Discourse 14, p. 117–8). The see of Jur'ev was founded before 1072, since Bishop Mixail of Jur'ev is mentioned at the translation of the relics of Boris and Glĕb (PVL 1072, PSRL 1:181, 2:171).

[59] The see of Bilhorod ranked next in importance after Kiev until the promotion of Novgorod to an archbishopric (Podskalsky, *Christentum*, 31). Luka is mentioned in Bishop Simon's list (see Discourse 14, p. 119).

come without being summoned?" The bishops answered, "Messengers came from your lordship yourself and told us that the church of the Caves Monastery would be consecrated on August 14, and that we must all be ready at the liturgy with you. We did not dare to disobey your instructions, and here we are." Bishop Antonij of Jur'ev replied, "I was ill, and that night a monk entered and told me, 'The church of the Caves Monastery will be consecrated tomorrow, and you must be there.' The moment I heard this I recovered, and here I am, in accordance with your command."

The metropolitan wanted to look for the men who had summoned them, and suddenly a voice was heard singing, "...them that seek to see...."[60] Then he stretched forth his hands to heaven and said, "O most holy Theotokos, as thou didst at the time of thy death summon the apostles from the ends of the earth in honour of thy burial,[61] so now thou hast summoned their successors, our servants, for the consecration of thy church." Everybody was awestruck by these miracles. They walked three times round the church and began to sing, "Lift up your gates, ye princes..." But there was no one in the church to sing in reply, "Who is this king of glory?"[62] For no one had stayed in the church; they were all marvelling at the arrival of the bishops. For a long time there was silence, and then a voice, as that of an angel, from inside the church sang, "Who is this king of glory?" They looked to see whose voices these could be and went into the church. All the doors were shut and there was not a soul in the church. It was clear to everybody that everything connected with this holy and divine church had been accomplished by God's providence. Therefore let us say, "O the depth of the riches both of the wisdom and knowledge [of God]! Who hath known the mind of the Lord? or who hath been His counsellor?"[63] May the Lord preserve and keep you all the days of your life through the prayers of the most holy Theotokos, our blessed fathers of the Caves Monastery, and the holy monks of this monastery. And may we receive with them mercy in

---

[60] Ps. 23:6: "This is the generation of them that seek the face of the God of Jacob."

[61] For a detailed survey of literature relating to the doctrine of the Dormition (Assumption) in Byzantine and East Slavic tradition, see M. Jugie, *La Mort et l'Assomption de la Sainte Vierge: étude historico-doctrinale*, Studi i Testi, 114 (Vatican City, 1944), 172–95, 214–70, 316–59.

[62] Ps. 23:7–8. It is clear that the pslams were sung antiphonally, but sometimes with unseemly haste. In his sermon on "Patience and Humility" Feodosij urged the monks "not to snatch the verses from each other." See I. P. Eremin, "Literaturnoe nasledie Feodosija Pečerskogo," TODRL 5 (1947):179.

[63] Rom. 11:33–34.

this life and in the one to come through Jesus Christ our Lord, to Whom be glory with the Father and the Holy Spirit now and forever, Amen.

Discourse 7. An account of why the Caves Monastery is so called, by Nestor, a monk of the Caves Monastery.[64]

In the reign of the pious great prince Volodimer Svjatoslavič, the sole ruler of the land of Rus', it pleased God to reveal for the land of Rus' a beacon and preceptor for those practicing the monastic life; our present account concerns him.[65]

There was a certain pious man from the town of Ljubeč[66] in whom the fear of God dwelt from his youth and who wished to be clothed in the monastic habit. Now the Lord, Who loves mankind, inspired him to go to the land of the Greeks and be tonsured there. He at once set out on his journey, and after traveling in the steps of our Lord, Who labored for our salvation,[67] he arrived at Constantinople.[68] Then he came to the Holy Mountain and went round the holy monasteries on Athos, and he saw the monasteries on the Holy Mountain and the manner of life of the fathers, higher than human nature; for while still in the flesh they imitated the life of the angels. An even stronger love for Christ burned in him, and he wished to emulate the life of those fathers. He came to one of the monasteries there and begged the superior to place on him the Angelic Habit of the monastic rank. The superior, foreseeing the virtues which would develop in him, acquiesced, and after teaching and instructing him about the monastic life, he tonsured him and gave him the name of Antonij.[69] Antonij pleased God in all things, laboring for others in meekness and humility so that all rejoiced in him. The superior said to him,

---

[64] The problems relating to the composition and textual history of the *Account* are dealt with in Appendix I.

[65] Volodimer I ruled in Kiev from ca. 980 to 1015. His baptism in 988 marked the decisive entry of Christianity into East Slavic territory.

[66] The PVL version of the *Account* also has the words именем мирскымь ("whose secular name was....") here (PSRL 1:156, 2:144). One would expect this to be followed by Antonij's secular name, but this has not survived in any version of the *Account*.

[67] These words suggest that Antonij might have made a pilgrimage to the Holy Land before going to Constantinople, but there is no firm evidence that he actually did so.

[68] Lit. "at the imperial city" (и достиже царствующаго града), a faithful rendering of the common Byzantine name for Constantinople (ἡ βασιλεύουσα πόλις).

[69] An extant source purporting to be a Life of Antonij states that he was tonsured at the Esphigmenou Monastery, but this seems to have been composed on Mount Athos in the nineteenth century and has no historical value. See Golubinskij, *Istorija russkoj cerkvi*, 1, 2:570, n. 1, and Abramovyč, "Issledovanija," IORJAS 7, no. 3 (1902):75, n. 114.

"Antonij, go back to Rus', so that you may strengthen others there by your success, and may the blessing of the Holy Mountain be with you."

Antonij came to the town of Kiev and considered where he should live. He went round the monasteries, but felt no desire to spend his life in any of them, for this was not God's will. He began to go everywhere round the woods and hills, and he came to Berestovo and found a cave which the Varangians had dug.[70] In this he settled and remained there, living in great austerity.

Some time after this the great prince Volodimer died, and the godless, accursed Svjatopolk settled in Kiev.[71] He began to kill off his brothers and murdered the holy Boris and Glěb.[72] Antonij, seeing what bloodshed the accursed Svjatopolk was causing, fled again to the Holy Mountain. When the pious prince Jaroslav defeated Svjatopolk and settled in Kiev, [he came back].[73]

The God-loving prince Jaroslav liked Berestovo and its Church of the Holy Apostles and had many priests under his care. In it there was a priest named Ilarion, a devout man, knowledgeable about the Scriptures and an ascetic. He used to go from Berestovo to a hill above the Dnieper, where the old Caves Monastery now is,[74] and pray, for there was a thick wood there. Here he dug a small cave, fourteen feet deep,[75]

---

[70] Cf. Discourse 33, pp. 183, 188, which also mentions a Varangian treasure hoard in a cave and explicitly states that this cave and its treasure are mentioned in the "Life of Antonij." Berestovo was a princely residence on Kiev's southern outskirts.

[71] Volodimer died at Berestovo on July 15, 1015.

[72] Svjatopolk, the oldest of Volodimer's surviving sons, was responsible for the murder of three of his half-brothers, Boris, Glěb, and Svjatoslav. The events of 1015 and the subsequent development of the cult of Boris and Glěb, the first canonized saints of the Rus' church, are narrated in PVL 1015, PSRL 1:130–41, 2:115–29, and two hagiographic works—Nestor's *Lesson concerning the Life and Murder of the Blessed Passion-sufferers Boris and Glěb* (ca. 1080) and the anonymous *Tale and Passion and Encomium of the Holy Martyrs Boris and Glěb*—published most authoritatively by D. I. Abramovyč, ed., *Žitija svjatyx mučenikov Borisa i Gleba i služby im* (Petrograd, 1916) [repr. L. Müller, *Die altrussischen hagiographischen Erzählungen und liturgischen Dichtungen über die Heiligen Boris und Gleb* (Munich, 1967)], and S. A. Buhoslavs'kyj, ed., *Ukrajino-rus'ki pam'jatky XI–XVIII v. v. pro knjaziv Borysa ta Hliba. Rozvidka i teksty* (Kiev, 1928).

[73] From this point the *Account* is almost identical with PVL 1051, PSRL 1:155–60, 2:144–49. Jaroslav finally overcame Svjatopolk in 1019 in a battle in which the latter was mortally wounded.

[74] A reference to the original aboveground monastery built shortly after Feodosij became superior in 1062. See Discourse 8, p. 44.

[75] The text here reads *dvu saženu* ("two *sažen*'s"). Sreznevskij, *Materialy*, 3:243, says that one *sažen* was approximately equivalent to three *aršin*, i.e., about seven feet.

and he used to come there from Berestovo and sing the Psalter and pray to God in secret. After some time it pleased God to inspire the pious great prince Jaroslav to assemble the bishops in the year 1051, and he appointed [Ilarion] metropolitan in St. Sophia, and he abandoned his cave.[76]

Antonij was then in the monastery on the Holy Mountain where he had been tonsured. The superior received a message from God, saying, "Send Antonij back to Rus', as I need him." The superior summoned Antonij and said to him, "Antonij, go back to Rus', for God wishes it, and may the blessing of the Holy Mountain be with you, for many shall become monks through you." He blessed him and dismissed him, saying, "Go in peace."

Antonij arrived in Kiev and came to the hill where Ilarion had dug his little cave, and as he liked the place he settled in it. He began to pray to God with tears, saying, "O Lord, strengthen me in this place, and may the blessing of the Holy Mountain and of my father who tonsured me rest upon it." And he began to live there, praying to God. His food was dry bread, and he drank water in moderation. He dug the cave, giving himself no rest day or night and continuing in labors, vigils, and prayers. After some time people learned of him and would come to him, bringing whatever he needed. He became famous, like the great Antony,[77] and those who came to him asked for his blessing.

After some time the great prince Jaroslav died, and his son Izjaslav assumed power and settled in Kiev.[78] Antonij was then renowned throughout the land of Rus'. When Prince Izjaslav learned of his life, he came to him with his retinue and asked for his blessing and prayers. The great Antonij became known and honored by everyone. Some God-

---

[76] There are no further references to Ilarion in Old Rus' sources after his appointment as metropolitan, but it would seem that he did not hold that office for long, since the 1055 entry of the *Novgorod Second Chronicle* gives the metropolitan's name as Efrem (PSRL 3:122). For a full discussion of the circumstances of Ilarion's appointment, see D. Obolensky, "Byzantium, Kiev and Moscow: a Study of Ecclesiastical Relations," *Dumbarton Oaks Papers* 11 (1957):60 ff. From a remark in Bishop Simon's letter to Polikarp, it seems that Ilarion was one of Antonij's first disciples (see below, Discourse 14, p. 118). M. D. Priselkov, *Očerki po cerkovno-političeskoj istorii Kievskoj Rusi X–XII vv.* (St. Petersburg, 1913), 181–82, suggested that he might be identical with the priest-monk Nikon, later superior of the Caves Monastery, who is mentioned several times in the Life of Feodosij. But no documentary evidence supports such a theory, and the circumstantial evidence adduced by Priselkov is not convincing.

[77] St. Antony of Egypt (ca. 250–356), whose Life by St. Athanasios had been translated into Church Slavonic by the late eleventh century.

[78] Jaroslav died in 1054. Izjaslav was the eldest surviving of his five sons.

loving people began to come to him to be tonsured, and he received and tonsured them.[79] A brotherhood gathered around him, twelve in number. Feodosij also came to him and was tonsured.[80] They dug a large cave, and a church and cells, which exist even to this day in the cave under the old monastery.

When the brothers had assembled [one day], Antonij said to them, "See, brethren, God has gathered us together, and I have tonsured you by the blessing of the Holy Mountain with which the superior on the Holy Mountain tonsured me. May there rest upon you first the blessing of God and the holy Theotokos, and second that of the Holy Mountain." And he said to them, "You live with each other, and I shall appoint you a superior. But I myself will go to yonder hill and settle there alone." As I said before, he was accustomed to live in solitude. He appointed them a superior named Varlaam and went himself to the hill, dug a cave, which is under the new monastery,[81] and ended his life in it, having lived virtuously for forty years without going out of the cave in which his noble relics lie, performing miracles to this day.[82]

The superior and the brethren continued to live in the cave. The brotherhood increased in numbers and could not be accommodated in the cave, and they decided to build a monastery outside the cave. The superior and the brethren came to the holy Antonij and said to him, "Father, the brotherhood has increased in numbers and cannot be accomodated in the cave. May God and the most pure Theotokos and your prayer ordain that we place a small church outside the cave." The venerable one so ordered them, and they prostrated themselves to the ground and departed. They placed above the cave a small church dedicated to the Dormition of the holy Theotokos.

Through the prayers of the most pure Theotokos and the venerable Antonij God began to increase the number of the monks, and the brethren discussed with the superior about building a monastery. Again they went to Antonij and said to him, "Father, the brotherhood is increasing in numbers, and we would like to build a monastery." Antonij was glad and said, "Blessed be God in all things! May the

---

[79] On the question of whether Antonij personally tonsured his first disciples, see M. Heppell, "The *Vita Antonii*," 55–56.
[80] See below, Discourse 8, pp. 32–33. Nestor does not give the number of monks living in the cave when Feodosij came to Kiev.
[81] I.e., the new buildings begun by Feodosij towards the end of his life and completed under his successor Stefan. See below, Discourse 8, p. 78.
[82] For a reconstruction of the chronology of Antonij's life, especially the period he spent as a recluse, see Heppell, "The *Vita Antonii*," 54–56.

prayer of the holy Theotokos and of the fathers on the Holy Mountain be with you." Having said this, he sent one of the brethren to Prince Izjaslav, saying, "O pious prince, God increases the number of brothers, and their place is small. We entreat you to give us the hill above the cave." Hearing this, Prince Izjaslav was very glad, and he sent one of his boyars to them and gave them the hill.[83] The superior and the brethren laid the foundations of a large church and monastery, surrounded it with a fence, built many cells, erected a church, and adorned it with icons. And henceforth it began to be called the Caves Monastery, because the monks first lived in a cave. And henceforth it was called the Caves Monastery, which is under the blessing of the Holy Mountain.[84]

When the monastery was completed and while Varlaam was superior, Prince Izjaslav built a monastery dedicated to St. Demetrios and brought Varlaam to be superior there, as he wished to exalt it above the Caves Monastery, relying on his wealth.[85] For many monasteries have been built by rulers and nobles using their wealth, but they are not like those which have been built by tears and fasting, prayer and vigil. Antonij had neither silver nor gold, but attained his purpose by tears and fasting, as I have said.

After Varlaam's departure to the monastery of St. Demetrios, the brethren took counsel and went to the elder Antonij and said to him, "Father, appoint a superior for us." He said to them, "Whom do you want?" They said to him, "Whomsoever God wills and the most pure Theotokos and you, honorable father." And the great Antonij said to them, "Who is there among you like the blessed Feodosij? He is obedient, meek, and humble. Let him be your superior." All the brethren rejoiced and prostrated themselves before him to the ground,

---

[83] This information is not included in Nestor's Life of Feodosij. Perhaps it was included in the "Antonij" material, with which Nestor does not appear to have been familiar.

[84] On the "doublet" formed by these last two sentences, see Appendix I, n. 686.

[85] In spite of the motives here attributed to Izjaslav Jaroslavič, it seems that the relations between the two monasteries were quite cordial, at least until the death of Feodosij in 1074. See, for example, Discourse 8, n. 198. It is possible, however, that they were not so good by the time Nikon was superior (ca. 1077–1088), since the monk Lavrentij went to the Monastery of St. Demetrios when Nikon refused to allow him to live as a recluse in the Caves Monastery. See Discourse 26, p. 146. Priselkov, *Očerki*, 191–93, without any foundation, attributes the hostile tone of this passage to Nikon, who feared that the Monastery of St. Demetrios might become a rival to the Caves Monastery as a nursery of bishops for Rus'.

and they appointed Feodosij as their superior.[86] The brethren then numbered twenty.

When Feodosij took over the monastery, he began to practice severe asceticism, fasting, and prayer with tears. He began to gather together many monks, assembling in all one hundred brothers. He began to seek a monastic rule. At that time there was an honorable monk from the Stoudios Monastery named Michael, who had come from the Greeks with Metropolitan George.[87] He began to ask him about the rule of the Stoudite fathers and copied down what he found out from him. He established in his own monastery how to sing the monastic offices; how to make prostrations; how to arrange the readings; where people should stand in church and all the rules of behavior in church; where people should sit at table; and what should be eaten on which days—all arranged according to rule. Having found this out, Feodosij established it in his monastery, and all the monasteries of Rus' received the rule from this monastery. Therefore, the Caves Monastery became honored as the first of them all and the most prestigious of all.

When Feodosij was in the monastery, observing a virtuous life and the monastic rule and receiving everyone that came to him, I, the wretched and unworthy servant Nestor[88] came to him, and he accepted me. I was then in my seventeenth year.[89] I have set down in writing the year in which the monastery was founded, and why it is called the Caves Monastery.[90] Later we shall speak again of the life of Feodosij.

---

[86] According to Nestor's Life of Feodosij, it was the monks who chose Feodosij as their superior, and Antonij accepted their decision. See below, Discourse 8, p. 43.

[87] Here again the *Account* differs from the Life of Feodosij, according to which Feodosij obtained a copy of the Stoudite Rule from a monk named Efrem, who was a former monk of the Caves Monastery but was then living in Constantinople. See below, Discourse 8, n. 152, for an explanation of this discrepancy. On George (Georgios), Metropolitan of Kiev from ca. 1065 to ca. 1076, see Poppe, "Die Metropoliten," 286.

[88] The name "Nestor" is omitted from the PVL version of the *Account* (PSRL 1:160, 2:149). On its presence here, see Appendix I, n. 690.

[89] This passage indicates that Feodosij probably followed the custom prevailing in most Byzantine monasteries, including Stoudios, of not accepting candidates below the age of 16. See P. de Meester, *De monachico statu iuxta disciplinam byzantinam* (Rome, 1942), 352–53.

[90] The author of this version of the *Account* implies that the monastery was founded in 1051, but it is quite possible that its first members assembled many years earlier. See Heppell, "The *Vita Antonii*," 50–56.

*Discourse 8. May 3. The Life of our venerable father
Feodosij, superior of the Caves Monastery, written by
Nestor, a monk of that same monastery.*

I thank Thee, Jesus Christ, my Lord and Master, that Thou hast vouchsafed me, unworthy as I am, to recount the lives of Thy holy servants. For after first writing about the life, murder, and miracles of the blessed passion-sufferers Boris and Glěb,[91] I have been moved to undertake a second narrative. The first one was beyond my powers, and I was not worthy of undertaking it, since I am crude and foolish; moreover, I had not been instructed in any kind of learning. But I remembered Thy word, O Lord: "If ye have faith as a grain of mustard seed, ye shall say unto this mountain, Go and be planted in the sea; and without doubting it should obey you."[92] I, the sinful Nestor, taking hold of these things in my mind and fortifying myself with the faith and hope that all things are possible from Thee,[93] began to write this account of the life of our venerable father Feodosij, formerly superior of the Caves Monastery of our holy Mistress, the Theotokos, the archimandrite of all Rus' and founder [of our monastic life].[94]

Brothers, as I called to mind the life of this venerable man, which has not been written down by anyone, I was daily overcome by grief, and I would pray to God that He would consider me worthy to record everything in order about the life of His servant, our father Feodosij, so that the monks who come after us, having received and read this narrative and seen the valour of this man, might praise God, glorify His servant, and be strengthened to further endeavors, especially as such a man and servant of God appeared even in this land. For it was of him that the Lord said, "Many shall come from the east and west, and shall sit down with Abraham, Isaac, and Jacob in the kingdom of heaven,"[95] and also,

---

[91] A reference to Nestor's *Lesson concerning...Boris and Glěb*. See above, Discourse 7, n. 72.
[92] A partially garbled conflation of Matt. 17:20 and Luke 17:6.
[93] See Matt. 19:26; Mark 10:27, 14:36.
[94] The words "archimandrite of all Rus' and founder [of our monastic life]" (архимандрита всея Русіи и начальника) do not occur in the oldest copy of the Life of Feodosij, that of the *Uspenskij Sbornik* (hereafter UspSb). They were presumably added by a later copyist or editor after it had become customary to bestow this title on the superiors of the Caves Monastery as a mark of special honor. The first superior to have this title was Polikarp, who died in 1182 (see Discourse 38).
[95] Matt. 8:11; cf. Luke 13:28–29.

"Many that are last shall be first."[96] For this man, though he appeared late in time, showed himself superior to the first fathers, since in his life he emulated the holy founder of the monastic life, I mean the great Antony, and closely resembled his namesake Theodosios, archimandrite of Jerusalem, and the same things came to pass in his life. Both of them passed their lives in the same fervent service of our Lady, the Theotokos, and received from the One whom she bore the same recompense, and they pray to the Lord unceasingly for us, their children. It is indeed remarkable, as is written in the books of the fathers, that "the last generation will be weak."[97] Yet in this last generation Christ revealed such a man as this as His husbandman, a shepherd for His monks, and a guide and teacher of universal truth for His holy sheep, for from his youth he was adorned by a pure life and good deeds, and especially by faith and understanding.

From now on I shall begin to tell you about the blessed Feodosij right from his youth. But listen, brothers, with close attention, since this discourse is full of profit for all who hear it. I beg you, beloved, do not despise my crudeness, for I am constrained by love of the holy man for whose sake I have tried to record all these things. Moreover, I take care that it should not be said of me, "Thou wicked and slothful servant, thou ought to have taken my money to the exchanges, and then at my coming I should have received mine own with usury."[98] So, brothers, it is not fitting to conceal God's wonderful acts, especially since the Lord said to His disciples, "What I tell you in darkness, that speak ye in light, and what ye hear in the ear, that preach ye on the housetops."[99] It is my wish to write all these things for the profit and edification of all with whom we converse, so that they may thereby glorify God and receive their recompense and reward. Now I am about to begin my discourse and embark on my story, but first I shall pray to Thee, O Lord: "O Master Lord Almighty, giver of blessings, Father of our Lord Jesus Christ, come to my aid and enlighten my heart so that it may understand Thy commandments, and open my lips so that they may proclaim Thy wonderful works

---

[96] Matt. 19:30; cf. Luke 13:30.
[97] Nestor refers here to a passage in the *Book of Holy Men*. See Introduction, pp. xx–xxi. Cf. PL 73, bk. 5, no. 4; *Cod. Slav. Vindob. 152*, item 152; *The Old Church Slavonic Translation of the* Ἀνδρῶν ἁγίων βίβλος [hereafter Ἀνδρῶν ἁγίων βίβλος], eds. D. Armstrong et al. (The Hague, 1975), 148.
[98] Matt. 25:26–27; cf. Luke 19:22–23.
[99] Matt. 10:27; cf. Luke 12:3.

and praise Thy servant, so that Thy holy name may be glorified, for Thou art the helper of all who hope in Thee, forever. Amen."

The birth of the holy Feodosij[100]

About fifty *poprišče* from Kiev, the capital city, there is a town called Vasyl'kiv.[101] Here the parents of the holy one lived in Christian faith and adorned with every kind of piety. They bore this blessed child, and on the eighth day they brought him to God's priest, as is the custom of Christians, to give the child a name. The priest looked at the child, foresaw within his heart that from his youth he would dedicate himself to God, and named him Feodosij.[102] When the child was forty days old, he was baptized. He grew up under his parents' care and God's grace was with him, for from youth the Holy Spirit dwelt in him.

Who will proclaim the mercy of God? For He did not choose a shepherd and teacher for His monks from among wise philosophers or from rulers of cities but—for this may the Lord's name be glorified—a man who, although simple and unlettered, showed himself to be wiser than the philosophers. O hidden mystery! For the bright morning star shone forth for us from a place where it was not expected, so that we beheld its radiance from all lands and ran towards it, scorning all else, and satisfied by that light alone. O divine grace! For from the very beginning He marked out and blessed this place, since He wished His spiritual sheep to graze there until He chose a shepherd.

It happened that the blessed one's parents moved to another town, called Kursk,[103] by the prince's order, or rather I should say by God's will, so that the life of this valiant child might shine forth there. For it is fitting that our morning star should come from the east and gather round itself many other stars who await the sun of righteousness and say, "Master, here am I, and the children whom I have nourished with Thy

---

[100] These headings in the *Paterik*'s version of the Life of Feodosij are absent in the copy of the UspSb, and these were probably not part of Nestor's original composition. They probably originated as marginal notes in a manuscript and were later entered into the text by a copyist.

[101] Vasyl'kiv is situated on the Stuhna River, southwest of Kiev, and was one of the key defensive points for Kievan territory. See Toločko, "Kievskaja zemlja," 31–33. It was probably founded by Volodimer, whose baptismal name was Vasilij. On *poprišče* as a unit of measure, see below, n. 184.

[102] Presumably Feodosij was the name he received when tonsured, not when baptized, as Nestor here implies.

[103] Kursk was situated on the River Sejm, a tributary of the Desna, about two hundred miles east of Černihiv.

spiritual food. Here, Lord, are my disciples. For I have brought to Thee those whom I have taught to despise all the things of this life and to love only Thee, the Lord God. Behold, Lord, this flock of Thy rational sheep, over whom Thou didst make me shepherd and whom I tended in Thy holy pasture and brought them to Thee, Lord, having kept them pure and undefiled." Then the Lord said unto him, "O good servant, you have faithfully increased the talent entrusted to you. Take therefore the crown prepared for you and enter into the joy of your Lord."[104] And to the disciples He said, "Come, good flock, rational sheep of a valiant pastor, who have hungered and toiled for my sake. Receive the kingdom prepared for you from the foundation of the world."[105] So, brothers, let us equal and imitate and follow the life of our venerable father Feodosij and his disciples, whom he sent to God before himself, so that we too may be deemed worthy to hear that voice which comes from our Almighty Master, "Come, ye blessed of my Father, receive the kingdom prepared for you from the foundation of the world."[106]

The holy Feodosij's childhood struggles

Let us now return, brothers, to the first narrative about this holy child. Growing in body and drawn in his soul to the love of God, he would daily go to God's church and listen to the divine Scriptures with the utmost diligence. Moreover, he would not approach other children when they were playing, as young people usually do, but despised their games. His clothes were patched; his parents often urged him to dress himself in fine clothes and go out to play with other children, but he would not obey them, preferring to be like one of the poor. He also begged his parents to let him study the divine books with one of the teachers. This they did, and he soon learnt all sacred Writ, so that everybody marveled at the child's wisdom and understanding and at the speed with which he learned. Who shall recount the submissiveness and obedience which he showed in his studies, not only towards his teacher, but to all who studied with him?

When the blessed Feodosij was thirteen years old, his father passed away. Henceforth he grew more zealous in his labors, so that he would go out to a village with his slaves to work with the utmost humility. But his mother restrained him from such activity and forbade him to do it,

---

[104] Cf. Matt 25:21–23.
[105] See Matt. 25:34.
[106] See Matt. 25:34.

and again begged him to dress in fine clothes and go and play with children his own age. She would say, "By going about this way, you bring disgrace on yourself and your family." But he did not heed her, so that she frequently became furious with him and beat him. For she had a strong, powerful body, like a man; anyone who heard her talking, but could not see her, would have thought she was a man.

The holy one's departure on a pilgrimage

Meanwhile this blessed youth was pondering how and by what means he might be saved. Then he heard about the holy places where our Lord walked in the flesh, and wanted to go there and revere them. He prayed to God, "My Lord Jesus Christ, hear my prayer and deem me worthy to go to Thy holy places and revere them." While he was then praying, some pilgrims came to the town. Seeing them, the blessed youth rejoiced and ran and greeted them, kissing them affectionately and asking where they were from and where they were going. They replied, "We are from the holy places and, God willing, we will go back there." The holy one begged them to take him as their traveling companion. They promised to take him and to conduct him to the holy places. When the blessed Feodosij heard their promise, he was filled with joy and went home.

When the pilgrims were about to leave they informed the youth about their departure. That night he arose, unbeknownst to anyone, and left home secretly, taking nothing with him except the clothes which he was wearing—and they were very shabby. Thus he departed in the wake of the pilgrims.

But the good God did not allow him to leave this land, since He had designated him from his mother's womb to be a shepherd of His rational sheep in this land. If the shepherd departed, the pasture which God had blessed would become desolate, thorns and briers would come upon it, and the flock would be scattered.[107] Three days later his mother learned that he had left with the pilgrims and set off after him, taking along her only [other] son, who was younger than the blessed Feodosij. They pursued him for a considerable distance, overtook them, and seized him. Out of fury and rage his mother took him by the hair, flung him on the ground, and trampled on him with her feet. The pilgrims protested greatly and she let go, but returned home, leading him tied up like some malefactor. She was so possessed by anger that she beat him until her

---

[107] Cf. Isa. 5:6, 7:23–24, 32:13; Matt. 26:31.

strength gave out. Then she took him into a room, tied him up, shut him in, and departed. The blessed youth accepted all these things with joy and prayed to God about them all.

Two days later his mother came and let him out and gave him something to eat, but as she was still gripped by anger she put irons on his feet and ordered him thus to walk about, taking care lest he run away from her again. He went about like this for many days. Then her heart softened towards him and she began to beg and urge him not to run away from her, since she loved him more than the others and accordingly could not bear to be without him. When he promised that he would not leave her, she removed the irons from his feet and told him to do whatever he wanted. The blessed Feodosij then returned to his former labors and went daily to church.

How the holy one baked sacramental loaves[108]

He saw that often there were no sacramental loaves for the liturgy, because none had been baked. He was very grieved[109] about this, and in his humility he resolved to set himself apart for this task, which he did. So he began to bake loaves and sell them. If there was anything left over cost, he gave it to the poor. With the money he received he bought more grain, ground it with his own hands, and made more loaves. Thus was it God's will, so that pure loaves be brought to His church by a pure and innocent child. This went on for two years or more.[110] All his young companions, prompted by the enemy, mocked and reproached him on account of this work, but the blessed one gladly accepted all their reproaches and maintained silence.

When the enemy—the hater of good—saw himself vanquished by the humility of this holy child, he did not give up, since he wanted to turn him away from this work. He began to incite his mother to forbid him to go on with this activity. Because she could not bear her son to be in disgrace and she began to speak to him affectionately, "I beg you, my child, give up this work, for you are bringing disgrace on your family. I cannot bear to hear you insulted by everybody because of this work. It is

---

[108] *Prosfury* were round-shaped loaves with a cross imprinted on them, specially prepared for use in the liturgy.

[109] I have used here the Arsenian reading жаляше (so too the UspSb), as it makes better sense: see Abramovyč, *Pateryk*, 25, n. 42.

[110] Both the UspSp and the Arsenian texts read "12 years" here (Abramovyč, *Pateryk*, 25, n. 48), but the Cas. II reading makes better sense. This is also the view of Golubinskij, *Istorija russkoj cerkvi*, 1, 2:572–73.

not fitting for you, a child, to do such work." The blessed Feodosij answered her meekly, "Listen, mother, I entreat you! The Lord God Jesus Christ Himself became poor and was humbled, giving us an example, so that we might humble ourselves for His sake. He was reviled and spat upon and beaten and endured all these things for the sake of our salvation. How much more fitting it is for us to endure them, so that we might receive Christ. As for this work of mine, listen: When our Lord Jesus Christ sat down for supper with His disciples, He took bread, blessed it and broke it, and gave it to His disciples, saying, 'Take and eat, this is my body, broken for you and for many for the remission of sins.'[111] If our Lord called bread His flesh, should I not all the more rejoice that our God has considered me worthy to make His flesh?" When his mother heard this, she marveled at the child's great wisdom and from then on left him alone.

The enemy, however, did not desist, but goaded her to forbid her child to show such humility. For a year later, when she again saw him baking loaves and being blackened by soot from the oven, she was greatly distressed and again began to reproach him, now tenderly, now with threats; sometimes she beat him to make him stop doing such work. The blessed youth was very unhappy about this and perplexed as to what he should do. Then he got up at night and secretly left home and went to another town not far away; he lived with the priest and continued his work as usual.

His mother looked for him in her town and was in great distress when she failed to find him. Then many days later she heard where he was living and hurried after him in a great rage. When she came to the aforementioned town she looked for him and found him in the priest's house. She took hold of him, beat him, and dragged him back to her town. After she had brought him home, she locked him up and said, "Henceforth you will not go away from me. Wherever you go, I shall come and find you and tie you up and bring you back to my town." Then the blessed Feodosij prayed to God and daily went to God's church.

The holy one's service to the governor and his humility

He was indeed lowly in heart and submissive towards everyone, so that the governor of the town, seeing that the boy was so meek and

---

[111] Matt. 26:26, 28. The entire passage recalls the consecration of the communion loaf at the liturgy.

submissive, felt a great love towards him and told him to stay by his church. He also gave him some fine clothes in which to go about. The blessed one did this for a few days, as though he was carrying a heavy burden, but then took the clothes off and gave them to the poor; he himself dressed in shabby clothes and thus went about. The governor saw him thus going about and gave him another set of clothes, better than the first, and begged him to wear it. But he took this off too and gave it away; he did this many times. When the judge[112] learned of this he began to love him even more, and marvelled at his humility.

After this the blessed Feodosij went to one of the blacksmiths and told him to make him an iron chain, which he took and girded round his loins, and he went around like this. The iron was tight and cut into his body, but he went on as though this caused him no discomfort.

When many days had passed and a feastday came, his mother began to urge him to dress in fine clothes to serve at table, since all the town's magnates would be dining at the governor's table that day and the blessed Feodosij had been ordered to stand by and serve. This was why his mother had told him to put on fine clothes, especially when she had heard that the governor had arranged for all the town's magnates to dine with him. While he was putting the fine clothes on, being an innocent-minded youth he was not on his guard with her, but she was watching him closely and saw blood on his shirt. She wanted to find out the true state of affairs and realized that the blood was caused by the chain biting into him. She was inflamed with anger against him and got up in a furious temper, tore off his shirt, beat him, and snatched the chains from his loins. The blessed youth got dressed as though he had received no harm and went to serve the diners with the utmost meekness.

The holy one departs for Kiev, leaving his mother

Some time later he heard the Lord in the Gospel saying, "Whosoever hath not forsaken his father and mother and followed after me is not worthy of me,"[113] and, "Come unto me, all ye that labor and are heavy laden and I will give you rest. Take my yoke upon you, and learn of me; for I am meek and lowly in heart: and ye shall find rest unto your souls."[114] Having heard these words, the divinely inspired Feodosij was inflamed with love for God; inspired by zeal towards God, he pondered

---

[112] Here the word is судія, apparently referring to the governor (властелинъ).
[113] Matt. 10:37–38.
[114] Matt. 11:28–29.

daily and hourly how and where he could be tonsured and hide from his mother.

By divine Providence his mother went away to a village and was to stay there many days. The blessed one rejoiced, and after praying to God, he secretly left home, with nothing but his clothes and a little bread on account of the weakness of his body. Thus he set out for the town of Kiev, since he had heard about the monasteries there.[115] As he did not know the way, he prayed to God that he might find traveling companions who would direct him on the journey he wished to make. By divine Providence some merchants on heavily loaded carts came by that way. When the blessed one learned that they were going to that town, he rejoiced in his heart and praised God Who had fulfilled his heart's desire. He kept at a distance and did not reveal himself to them; when they stopped for the night the blessed one did not go up to them but simply kept within sight of them and rested there, God being his only protection. Traveling thus for three weeks, he reached the aforementioned town. Since he wanted to become a monk, after his arrival he went round all the monasteries and begged them to accept him. But when they saw the boy's simplicity and his shabby clothes, they were unwilling to take him. This was God's will, so that he should be led to that place to which God had called him from youth.

The holy one's visit to the great Antonij, and his tonsure

Then he heard about the blessed Antonij, who was living in a cave.[116] His spirits soared, and he set out for the cave and came to the venerable Antonij. When he saw him he fell down and prostrated himself before him and begged him with tears to accept him. The great Antonij said to him, "My son, do you not see that this cave is a wretched place, narrow and confined? As you are still a child, I think, you will not be able to endure the discomfort of this place." He said this not only to test him, but he also had foreseen with prophetic vision that he would build up that spot and make a glorious monastery to assemble many

---

[115] Almost nothing is known about monastic life in Rus' before the emergence of the Caves Monastery. The earliest known foundations were the monasteries of St. George and St. Irene founded by Jaroslav Volodimerovič in 1037 (PVL 1037, PSRL 1:151, 2:139). In his *Sermon on Law and Grace* (ca. 1049) Ilarion remarks that already in Volodimer's reign "monasteries arose on the mountains," but this may only be a rhetorical flourish. See Müller, *Des Metropoliten Ilarion Lobrede*, 106.

[116] For a possible chronology of Antonij's life, see Heppell, "The *Vita Antonii*," 54–57.

monks. The divinely-inspired Feodosij answered him meekly, "You see, honored father, that Christ our God, Who cares for all His creatures, whosoever they are, has brought me to your holiness and told me to seek my salvation through you. Therefore, whatever you bid me, I shall do" The blessed Antonij said to him, "Blessed be God, my son, Who has sustained you for this undertaking. You stay in this place." Once again Feodosij fell down and prostrated himself before him. Then the elder blessed him and commanded the great Nikon to tonsure him, since he was a priest and an experienced monk.[117] He took the blessed Feodosij and tonsured him according to the custom of the holy fathers and dressed him in monastic garments in the year 1032,[118] in the reign of the pious prince Jaroslav Volodimerovič.

Our father Feodosij dedicated himself entirely to God and the venerable Antonij, and henceforth gave himself up to a life of physical austerity: he spent whole nights in vigil, praising God and casting off the heaviness of sleep, striving to subdue his flesh. He also worked with his hands, remembering daily the words of the psalm: "Look upon mine affliction and my trouble; and forgive all my sins."[119] Thus he humbled himself by self-denial in every way and tormented his body with labors and abstinence, so that the venerable Antonij and the great Nikon marveled at his meekness and submissiveness and at such virtue, steadfastness, and good cheer in a youth, and they both glorified the all-merciful God on this account.

His mother's arrival in Kiev

His mother searched long for him in her own town and in neighboring towns. When she did not find him, she wept bitterly, beating her breast as though for the dead. An order was sent throughout the whole land that if anyone had seen such a child anywhere he should come and inform his mother and receive a reward for the information. Some

---

[117] It has generally been assumed that Nikon tonsured Feodosij, and also Varlaam and Efrem, because Antonij was not a priest. The *Account*, however, states clearly that Antonij himself tonsured his first disciples (see above, pp. 20–21). Perhaps Antonij was already living as a recluse by the time Feodosij came to Kiev in the early 1050s, and Nikon was acting as head of the community. See Heppell, "The *Vita Antonii*," 55–56.
[118] This date, which is an interpolation in the Cas. I and Cas. II copies of the *Paterik* (Abramovyč, *Pateryk*, 29, n. 15), is erroneous, since it is clear from the context that Feodosij must have come to Kiev in the early 1050s. For an explanation of this insertion, see Heppell, "The *Vita Antonii*," 53, n. 56, and 54, n. 59.
[119] Ps. 24:18.

people came from Kiev and told her, "Four years ago we saw him walking about in our town, asking to be tonsured in one of the monasteries." When she heard this, the woman went there without delay, not lingering nor fearing the length of the journey. She came to the aforementioned town in search of her son, and after arriving there, she went round all the monasteries seeking him.

Finally she was told, "He is in the cave with the venerable Antonij." She went there to find him and began by summoning the elder deceitfully, saying, "Tell the venerable one that I have come a long way and ask him to come out. Say that I have come to converse with him and prostrate myself before his holiness and receive his blessing." The elder was informed about her, and he went out to her. When she saw the elder, she prostrated herself before him to the ground. The elder said a prayer and blessed her. After the prayer, they both sat down, and she began to talk to him at length. Finally she revealed the reason she had come. She said, "I entreat you, father, tell me if my son is here. I am greatly troubled about him as I do not know whether he is alive." Because of the simplicity of his mind the elder did not perceive her trick and said to her, "Your son is here. Do not grieve over him, for he is alive." Then she said to him, "May I not see him, father? I have traveled a long way and come to this town simply to see my son and then return to my town." The elder said to her, "If you want to see him, go away now and I shall go and tell him, because he does not want to see anybody. Then come back tomorrow morning and you will see him." When she heard this, she departed, expecting to see him the next day.

The venerable Antonij went into the cave and reported everything to the blessed Feodosij. When he heard this, he was very distressed that he could not hide from his mother. The next day the woman came again. The elder several times urged the blessed one to go out and see his mother, but he did not want to go. Then the elder went out and told her, "I have begged him many times to come out to you, but he is unwilling." She then began to address the elder not at all meekly, but shouted very angrily, "O the violence of this elder! He has concealed my son in the cave and does not want to show him to me. Bring out my son, elder, so that I may see him, for I cannot bear to live if I do not see him. Show me my son, lest I suffer a cruel death! For I shall kill myself before the doors of this cave if you do not show him to me!"

Then Antonij was very distressed and went into the cave and begged the blessed one to go out to her. He did not want to disobey the elder, and went out to her. When she saw her son in such a pitiable state—for his face had changed with so much labor and self-denial—she embraced him and wept bitterly for a long time. When she had comforted herself a little, she began to urge Christ's servant, "Come home, my son, and whatever is necessary for the salvation of your soul do at home as you wish. Only do not leave me. When I die, you can bury my body and then return to this cave, if you want to. For I cannot bear to live if I do not see you."

The blessed one said to her, "Mother, if you want to see me every day, come to this town and enter one of the women's monastaries and be tonsured there. Thus you could come here and see me and also save your soul. But if you do not do this, I tell you truly that from now on you will not see my face." He daily continued to exhort his mother with such and many other precepts, but she did not want to do this and would not even listen to his words. Whenever she left him, the blessed one would enter the cave and pray to God fervently for his mother's salvation and that her heart might be turned to obey Him. God heard His servant's prayer, for as the Prophet said, "The Lord is near to all that call upon Him in truth. He will perform the desire of them that fear Him: and He will hear their supplication."[120]

Now one day his mother came to him and said, "My son, I shall do everything you have told me to do. I shall not return to my town, but, God willing, I shall enter a women's monastery, be tonsured there, and abide there for the rest of my days. Your teaching has made me discern that this transient world is nothing." Hearing this, the blessed Feodosij rejoiced in his soul and went and told the great Antonij. When the venerable one heard the news, he glorified God Who had turned her heart to such penitence. The great Antonij went to her and instructed her at length for the good of her soul and told the princess[121] about her. She admitted her to the women's monastery dedicated to St. Nicholas,[122] and there she was tonsured and clad in monastic dress. After living a virtuous life for many years, she peacefully reposed in the Lord.

Such was the life of our blessed father Feodosij from his early years until he came to the cave. His mother related these things to one of the brethren named Feodor, who was cellarer in the time of our father

---

[120] Ps. 144:18–19.
[121] Perhaps Jaroslav's wife Ingigerd, daughter of King Olaf of Sweden, but she died in 1050, which is rather early for Feodosij's arrival in Kiev some four years before Varlaam and Efrem (see Heppell, "The *Vita Antonii*," p. 53, n. 56). Possibly she was one of Prince Izjaslav's sisters.
[122] Golubinskij, *Istorija russkoj cerkvi*, 1, 2:746, no. 4, says that this women's monastery was founded by Izjaslav Jaroslavič but gives no further information.

Feodosij. I heard all these things directly from him, and I have written them down for the recollection of all who read them. But let me move on to the remaining story of the youth's perfection, and God, Who sets us aright, will indicate to me the fulfillment of the tale....[123]

Our holy father Feodosij also showed himself to be victorious over evil spirits in the cave. After his mother was tonsured and he had cast off all worldly care, he strove with greater labors to acquire zeal towards God. Three lights shone forth in the cave, expelling the demonic darkness by prayer and fasting: I refer to the venerable Antonij, the blessed Feodosij, and the great Nikon. They were in the cave, praying to God, and God was with them, for it is said, "Where two or three are gathered together in my name, there am I in the midst of them."[124]

Varlaam, the son of the boyar Ioann

At this time there was a certain man named Ioann who was foremost among the prince's boyars. This man's son often came to the venerable ones and enjoyed the honeyed words which flowed from the mouths of these fathers. He loved them greatly and wanted to live with them, since he despised all the things of this life and counted glory and riches as nothing. For he had been touched by the word of the Lord: "It is easier for a camel to go through the eye of a needle, than for a rich man to enter the kingdom of heaven."[125] He told only Antonij about this idea, saying, "Father, if it is pleasing to God, I should like to be a monk and live with you." The elder said to him, "Your wish is a blessed one, and your idea is full of grace. But take care, my son, lest the riches and glory of this world turn you back. For the Lord said, 'No man, having put his hand to the plough, and looking back, is fit for the kingdom of heaven.'[126] So a monk who returns to the world in thought and concerns himself with worldly things cannot set himself on the right path to eternal life." The elder talked to the youth about many other things, and a fervent love of God was kindled in his heart. Then he departed to his home.

On the next day he dressed himself in clean and sumptuous clothing, then got on his horse and came to the elder. Around him were his servants, leading other horses in splendid trappings in front of him, and

---

[123] The text appears to be unstable at this point: Abramovyč, *Pateryk*, 215, n. 42.
[124] Matt. 18:20.
[125] Matt. 19:24; Mark 10:25; Luke 18:25.
[126] Luke 9:62.

thus in great splendor he came to the fathers' cave. They came out and prostrated themselves before him, as it is fitting before nobles, but he prostrated himself in front of them, right to the ground. Then he took off his boyar's dress and laid it before the elder and then set before him the horse with its trappings, saying, "Here, father, are all the fine allurements of this world. Do what you want with them, for I have already rejected these things and wish to be a monk and live with you in the cave. Henceforth I shall not return to my own house."

The elder said to him, "Take care, my son, to whom you make your vow and whose soldier you wish to be. For God's angels stand by unseen and receive your vows. If your father should come here to take you away, exercising his great authority, we would not be able to help you, and then you will appear before God as a liar and a traitor." The youth said to him, "I have faith in my God, father, so that even if my father should start to torture me I would not obey him and return to the world. I beg you, father, to tonsure me quickly." Then the venerable Antonij told the great Nikon to tonsure him and clothe him in monastic dress. After reciting the usual prayers, Nikon tonsured him, dressed him in the monastic habit, and gave him the name of Varlaam.

The eunuch

At that time there came a certain eunuch from the prince's household, a favorite of the prince, who looked after everything in his household. He begged the elder Antonij [to receive him], as he too wished to become a monk. After instructing him about the salvation of his soul, the elder entrusted him to the great Nikon to be tonsured. He tonsured him, dressed him in the monastic habit, and gave him the name of Efrem.[127]

It is not fitting to conceal the fact that the enemy brought trouble to the venerable ones on account of these two.[128] The enemy, the devil, the hater of good, seeing himself vanquished by the holy flock and realizing that henceforth this place would be glorified, wept at his downfall. Then he began with his evil trickery to inflame the heart of the prince against the venerable ones, so that he would at last scatter the holy flock. But he

---

[127] It is interesting that Efrem was not refused admission to the monastery, although he was a eunuch. In theory eunuchs were not accepted on Mount Athos at this time. See Meester, *De monachico statu*, 350. But it appears that this prohibition was not strictly observed in the first half of the eleventh century. See P. Meyer, *Die Haupturkunden für das Athosklöster* (Leipzig, 1894), 173, 181.

[128] I.e., Varlaam and Efrem.

was unable to do this, and was himself put to shame by their prayers, and fell into the pit that he had made.[129] For his trouble shall return on his own head, and his unrighteousness shall come down on his own crown.[130]

The misfortune visited upon the holy ones

When Prince Izjaslav found out what had happened to his boyar and his eunuch, he was very angry and gave orders that he who had dared to do such things should be brought before him. [His servants] quickly went out and at once brought the great Nikon before him. The prince looked at Nikon angrily and said, "Are you the one who tonsured the boyar and the eunuch without my permission?" Nikon answered, "By God's grace I tonsured them with the permission of the heavenly King and of Jesus Christ, Who called them to the ascetic life." The prince said, "Either you persuade them to return home or I shall send you and your companions to prison and dig up your cave." To this Nikon answered, "My lord, you do whatever is pleasing in your eyes, but it is not fitting for me to turn away a soldier from the heavenly King."

Antonij and those with him took their clothes and left their own place, intending to go to another district.[131] While the prince was still angrily reproaching Nikon, one of his servants entered and informed him that Antonij and those with him were about to leave the city for another district. Straightway the prince's wife said to him, "Listen, my lord, and do not be angry. The same thing also happened in our country: the monks fled because of some trouble, and much evil was done in the land on their account. Take care, my lord, lest this happen in your district."[132] When the prince heard this, fearing the wrath of God, he dismissed the great Nikon and told him to go back to the cave. He sent after the others with a message begging them to return. When they were told this, just three days later, they returned to their cave, like brave men from battle who had vanquished their foe, the devil, and they prayed to

---

[129] Cf. Ps. 7:15.

[130] See Ps. 7:16.

[131] On a later occasion Antonij incurred the anger of Prince Izjaslav, presumably by protesting against his treatment of Vseslav Brjačeslavič of Polack, and fled from Kiev, taking refuge with Svjatoslav Jaroslavič of Černihiv. See PVL 1074, PSRL 1:193, 2:185, and Heppell, "The *Vita Antonii*," 55, n. 70.

[132] Izjaslav's wife was the Polish princess Gertrude, the sister of Bolesław II of Poland. The episode to which she refers is described in more detail in the account of Moisej the Hungarian (Discourse 30).

God continually day and night. But even so the devil took no rest in his struggle with them.

The firmness of the blessed Varlaam

When the boyar Ioann discovered that the Christ-loving prince Izjaslav had inflicted no harm on them, he was furious with them on account of his son. Taking a large number of servants, he went to the holy flock and scattered them. Entering the cave, he took hold of his son, the blessed Varlaam, and dragged him out. He took off his holy mantle and flung it into a deep hole. So also he removed the helmet of salvation on his head and cast it aside and seized hold of him and dressed him in fresh and sumptuous clothing befitting nobles. But Varlaam flung the clothes down and would not even look at them; he did this many times. Then his father ordered that his hands be bound, that he be dressed in his previous clothes, and that he thus go through the town to his home. But Varlaam, who was truly ardent in his soul in love of God, caught sight of a little cleft filled with rubbish along the way. He quickly entered it and with God's help tore off his clothing and trampled it under his feet in the filth, at the same time also trampling down the evil designs of the cunning enemy.

When they had entered their home, his father told him to sit down with him at table. He sat down, but refused to taste any food and remained downcast, looking at the ground. After the meal his father sent him to his own quarters but first placed servants there to see that he did not go away. Then he ordered his son's wife to dress up in all her finery in order to entice the youth, and that a multitude of servants serve in his presence. But Varlaam, a true servant of Christ, went into a room and sat down in a corner. His wife came up to him, as she had been ordered, and begged him to sit down on the bed. When he saw her foolish behavior he realized that his father had arranged for her to entice him, and he began to pray continually in the secrecy of his heart to the all-merciful God Who could save him from this temptation. He remained sitting in that place for three days without getting up or tasting any food or putting his clothes on, but remained in only his shirt.

The venerable Antonij, those with him, and the blessed Feodosij were greatly distressed on his account and prayed to God for him. God heard their prayer, for it is written: ''The righteous cried, and the Lord hearkened to them, and delivered them out of all their afflictions. The Lord is near to them that are of a contrite heart; and will save the lowly in spirit."[133] When blessed God saw the boy's meekness and endurance, He moved his father's hard heart to show mercy towards his son. His servants told him, "This is now the fourth day that he has not eaten or dressed." Hearing this, his father was very sad on his account and anxious that he should not die of hunger and cold. So he summoned him, kissed him affectionately, and let him go.

Then there was such a state of affairs: a great lament as though for the dead. The male and female servants lamented for their lord because he was leaving them; his wife came, sobbing bitterly because she was losing her husband; and his father and mother lamented because he was going away from them. So they all saw him off with lamentation. Thus did Christ's warrior depart from his father's house, like a bird set free from a net or a wild goat from a snare.[134] Running quickly, he came to the cave. The fathers were filled with joy when they saw him and stood up and glorified God, for He had heard their prayer. From then on many people came to the cave to receive the blessing of the holy fathers, and by God's grace some of them became monks.

The departure of the holy Nikon

At that time the great Nikon and another monk from the Monastery of St. Menas,[135] known as the Bulgarian,[136] took counsel and went away, as they wished to reside on their own.[137] Reaching the sea, they separated, just as the apostles Paul and Barnabas did to proclaim Christ,

---

[133] Ps. 33:16–18.

[134] Nestor borrowed this simile from the Life of St. Sabbas by Cyril of Scythopolis, one of his basic literary models. For the passage, see I. Pomjalovskij, ed., *Žitie svjatogo Savy Osvjaščennogo, sostavlennoe Kirillom Skifopol'skim* (St. Petersburg, 1890), 109.

[135] Golubinskij, *Istorija russkoj cerkvi*, 1, 1:746, no. 6, says that it is not certain whether this monastery was in Kiev, although he so lists it; no other Rus' sources refer to it.

[136] The UspSb, Arsenian, and Cas. I copies give the alternate reading of болярина ("the boyar"): Abramovyč, *Pateryk*, 35, n. 44.

[137] The reasons for Nikon's departure from Kiev are not clear. Priselkov, *Očerki*, 174, has suggested that he left because of his resistance to Izjaslav over the tonsuring of Varlaam and Efrem. But since Izjaslav acquiesced and apparently bore the Caves Monastery no ill will, this is not a very convincing explanation. Possibly Nikon did not approve of the foundation of the Monastery of St. Demetrios by Izjaslav and feared that it might become a rival to the Caves Monastery (cf. the statement in the *Account*, Discourse 7, p. 22); or he may simply have wished to establish his own monastery, which is what he actually did.

as it is written in the Acts of the Apostles.[138] The Bulgarian went to Constantinople, found an island in the middle of the sea, and settled there. He lived for many years, enduring cold and hunger, and then reposed in peace. To this day that island is called Bolgarov.[139] But the great Nikon departed to the island of Tmutorokan', found an empty place near the town, and settled on it.[140] By God's grace the place flourished, and he built on it a church dedicated to the holy Theotokos. It became a glorious monastery even to this day, and it had the Caves Monastery as its model.

Some time after this the eunuch Efrem departed to Constantinople and lived in one of the monasteries there.[141] Later he was brought back to this country and became bishop of Perejaslav.[142] We have already added many stories to our main discourse, but from this point let us return to our subject.

The holy one's ordination

After the departure of these holy fathers our blessed father Feodosij was ordained priest by the order of the venerable Antonij. Every day he celebrated the divine liturgy with the utmost humility, for he was submissive by disposition, tranquil in his thoughts, innocent in mind, full of all spiritual wisdom, and possessing pure love for all the brethren. There were now fifteen brothers gathered together.

The departure of the great Antonij

As the venerable Antonij had been accustomed to live alone and could not endure all the noise and disturbance, he shut himself in a single cell of the cave, after placing the blessed Varlaam, the son of the boyar Ioann, in charge of the brotherhood in his stead.[143] From there again the

---

[138] Cf. Acts 15:39.
[139] I.e., "the Bulgar's." The other MSS read боляровъ, "the boyar's."
[140] No evidence suggests why Nikon chose to make the long journey to Tmutorokan'; possibly he had contacts with some of the leading families there.
[141] It is not known why Efrem decided to leave the Caves Monastery. He probably settled in the Stoudios Monastery, since it was he who supplied Feodosij with information about the Stoudite "rule." See below, p. 44.
[142] On the circumstances of his appointment and its "titular" character, see A. Poppe, "Russkie mitropolii konstantinopol'skoj patriarxii v XI stoletii," *Vizantijskij vremennik* 28 (1968):97–108.
[143] It was common practice in the early days of Byzantine monasticism for the leader of a small community to choose his own successor either just before his death or if he

venerable Antonij moved to another hill. Having dug out a cave, he lived in it, and never left that place;[144] his honored body lies there to this day.

The blessed Varlaam straightway built above the cave a small church dedicated to the holy Theotokos, so that the brotherhood could assemble there for divine worship. Henceforth the place was revealed to everyone, whereas formerly it had been unknown to many people.

At first they lived in the cave, and God alone knows how much discomfort and misery they experienced on account of the confined space; it cannot be related by human lips. In addition, their diet was only bread and water. On Saturdays and Sundays they ate pulses, but often no pulses were available on those days, so they boiled herbs and that was all they ate. They also worked with their hands: they either plaited sandals, or made cowls, or did other kinds of manual work. They took their products to town, sold them, and bought grain with the proceeds. They divided this, so that at night each ground up his share to make bread. Then they began to sing the morning office, and after that they did manual work. Some dug in the kitchen garden to grow herbs until it was time for the morning service. Then they all went into church together, sang the office, and celebrated the holy liturgy. Then they ate a little bread, and each one took up his work again. Thus they labored every day and dwelt in love towards God.

Our father Feodosij bore all these things in a humble and obedient frame of mind; because of his asceticism and bodily austerity he was physically gentle and submissive. He served everyone diligently, carrying water, bearing wood from the forest on his back, and keeping vigil every night in praise of God. Sometimes when the brethren were asleep, the blessed one took the grain which had been distributed, ground each person's share, and put it in his place. Sometimes when there were many gnats and flies he would go out at night onto the top of the cave, strip his body to the waist, and sit spinning wool and singing the Psalter. His whole body would become bloodied by the multitude of gnats and flies, and they ate his flesh and drank his blood. But our father Feodosij

---

wished to live as a solitary. See Meester, *De monachico statu*, 116, and the references there cited. If Antonij originally retired to a cave above the Dnieper ca. 1033, as I have suggested in "The *Vita Antonii*," 56, n. 80, Varlaam cannot have been his first successor, as Nestor implies here.

[144] For the chronology of Antonij's life as a recluse and his involvement in the life of the community during this period, see Heppell, "The *Vita Antonii*," 56–57.

remained unmoved and would not rise until it was time for the matins.[145] Then he was to be found in church before everybody, and remained undisturbed and unruffled in mind as he performed the divine service. Then he left the church last of all. Because of this they all loved him greatly, marveling at his meekness and submissiveness.

The appointment of the holy Feodosij as superior

After this the blessed Varlaam, the superior of the brethren in the cave, was transferred on the prince's order to the Monastery of the Holy Martyr Demetrios and appointed superior there.[146] Then the brethren in the cave assembled and informed the venerable Antonij that they had unanimously named the blessed father Feodosij as their superior, because he had mastered the monastic life and knew God's commandments well.[147] Although our father Feodosij accepted the position of seniority, he did not alter his humility and conduct, bearing in mind the Lord's words: "Whosoever among you will be elder, let him be the least of all and the servant of all."[148] So he humbled himself and made himself least of all and the servant of all, setting an example himself, going out to work before everybody and taking his place before them in the celebration of the holy liturgy. Henceforth the place flourished and grew through the prayers of the righteous man. For it is written: "The righteous shall flourish as a palm tree: he shall be increased as the cedar in Libanus."[149] For henceforth the brethren increased and the place flourished through their good deeds and their prayers for other pious people, so that many nobles came there for a blessing and gave them a small part of their possessions.

Our venerable father Feodosij, who was indeed an earthly angel and a heavenly man, saw that the place was uncomfortable and cramped and inadequate for them all (for the brotherhood had increased) and that the church was too small for them to assemble. But he never became

---

[145] Cf. a similar episode in E. C. Butler, trans., *The Lausiac History of Palladius* (Cambridge, Eng., 1904), 48–49, which describes how the Egyptian ascetic Macarius exposed his bare flesh to gnat bites.

[146] See above, Discourse 7, p. 22.

[147] This is the first reference to members of the community participating in choosing their superior. The *Account*, however, gives a different version of the appointment of Feodosij, stating that the monks left the decision to Antonij and that he chose Feodosij. See above, Discourse 7, p. 22.

[148] Cf. Matt. 20:26–27; Mark 10:43–44; Luke 22:26.

[149] Ps. 91:12.

gloomy or despondent because of this, and daily comforted the brethren and taught them not to be anxious about the things of the flesh, and reminded them of the words of the Lord, "Take no thought, saying, What shall we eat? What shall we drink? Wherewithal shall we be clothed? For your heavenly Father knoweth that ye have need of all these things. But seek ye first the kingdom of heaven; and all these things shall be added unto you."[150] Thus the blessed one thought, and God provided abundantly for their needs.

The building of the Caves Monastery

For then the great Feodosij found an empty place not far from the cave. Realizing that it was adequate for erecting a monastery, and enriched by God's grace, fortified by faith and hope, and filled with the Holy Spirit, he began to work to settle the brethren there. With God's help, in a short time on that place he built a church dedicated to the most glorious and holy Theotokos, the ever-virgin Mary, put a fence round it, established many cells, and then moved to that place with the brethren in the year 1062. Henceforth the place flourished by God's grace and became a famous monastery, which it is to this day. We call it the Caves Monastery, which was established by our father Feodosij.[151]

After this the blessed one sent one of the brethren to Constantinople to Efrem to have the entire rule of the Stoudios Monastery copied and brought back.[152] He at once carried out the order of the venerable father, wrote down the complete monastic rule, and sent it to him.[153] After he

---

[150] Matt. 6:31–33; Luke 12:29–31.

[151] Cf. the *Account* (above, Discourse 7, p. 22): "From that time it began to be called the Caves Monastery, which is under the blessing of the Holy Mountain." This reference to Mt. Athos may derive from the use of the "Antonij" source by one of the *Account*'s compilers.

[152] According to the *Account* (Discourse 7, p. 23), Feodosij first found out about the Stoudite Rule in Kiev from a monk named Michael, who had come from Constantinople with the metropolitan George; there is no mention of Efrem. But the two sources could be complementary. Feodosij made preliminary inquiries from Michael and then sent to Efrem for a copy of the rule.

[153] The typikon sent to Feodosij was presumably that of the monastery founded by Patriarch Alexios the Stoudite ca. 1034, whose Greek original is lost but which is preserved in a Slavic translation. See V. Grumel, *Les regestes des actes du Patriarcat de Constantinople*, vol. 1, fasc. 2 (Paris, 1936), 255–56 (no. 841). It is generally accepted that this typikon was based on the monastic life practiced in the Stoudios Monastery under its famous superior Theodore (d. 826), though this view was challenged by M. Lisicyn, *Pervonačal'nyj slavjano-russkij tipikon* (St. Petersburg, 1911), 167–71, 198, 208–9, 237–80, whose arguments are complicated and somewhat contradictory: they

had received this, our father Feodosij ordered it to be read out before the brethren, and henceforth he began to do everything in his monastery according to the rule of the holy Stoudite house, as his disciples maintain it, even to this day.

Whenever anyone who wished to be a monk came to him, he never refused anyone, rich or poor, but received them all eagerly, since he himself had been tested in this way, as has been said above, when he came from his town and wanted to become a monk, and he had gone round all the monasteries and they had not wanted to take him; for God had thus tested him. The venerable one remembered all these things and recalled the misery a man suffers if he is spurned when he wishes to be tonsured. For this reason he received with joy all who came to him. However, he did not tonsure a man immediately but would order him to go about in his own clothes, until he was accustomed to all aspects of the organization of the monastery. After that he would dress him in monastic clothing and test him further in all forms of service. Then he would tonsure him and dress him in a mantle. Only when he had been tried and tested in the life of purity did Feodosij consider him fit to receive the Great Angelic Habit, and then he placed on him the cowl.[154]

Every year during Lent our father Feodosij departed to the cave where his honored body has been buried, and there shut himself up alone until Palm Sunday. On the Friday of that week at the hour of vespers he would come to the brethren, stand at the church doors, exhort them all,

---

show that while this typikon diverges from other texts of Stoudite provenance in details, it was certainly Stoudite in spirit. The Church Slavonic version of this typikon remains unpublished, although extracts are cited by Lisicyn, as well as by Golubinskij, *Istorija russkoj cerkvi*, 1, 1:611–624. For a description of the MS in which the text is preserved, see A. Gorskij and K. I. Nevostruev, *Opisanie slavjanskix rukopisej Moskovskoj sinodal'noj biblioteki*, pts. 1 and 2 (Moscow, 1855, 1857), no. 330.

[154] Nestor appears to describe a graduated "novitiate" falling into four stages and culminating in the bestowal of the Great Habit, of which the cowl (*koukoullion*) was the symbol. He does not indicate the length of any of the stages, and it is interesting to note that Patriarch Alexios appears to have prescribed a novitiate of one year only. See Meester, *De monachico statu*, 359. But this might have been a "postulant" phase for a novice with no experience of any kind of monastic life rather than a period of formal training. Nestor's description implies that the bestowal of the Great Habit was the culmination of a monk's ascetic training, and Patriarch Alexios's typikon provided a special form of service for this. See A. A. Dimitrievskij, *Opisanie liturgičeskix rukopisej xranjaščixsja v bibliotekax Pravoslavnogo Vostoka*, pt. 1, *Typika* (Kiev 1895), 228. However from Polikarp's account of Pimin the Sufferer (below, Discourse 34, p. 200; Discourse 35, pp. 204–5), it seems that by the late eleventh century the Great Habit was conferred in the Caves Monastery only when death was imminent.

and comfort them in their fasting and asceticism, saying that he was unworthy because in a single week he could not equal their labors.

The holy one's victory over unclean spirits

In the cave he experienced much misery and visions from evil spirits, even receiving wounds from them, just as it is written about the holy great Antony.[155] But when he ventured to show himself to this man, he gave him invisible strength from heaven to vanquish them. For who will not marvel at this blessed man, who remained alone in such a dark cave and did not fear the multitude of unseen hosts of demons, but stood firm, like a strong and valiant man, praying to God and calling on our Lord Jesus Christ to help him? Thus he conquered them through Christ's power, so that henceforth they dared not come near him, though they still caused him visions from afar. For when he sat after the evening office he never lay down. If he wanted to sleep, he sat on a bench, and after a short nap would get up again, continue his nocturnal singing, and prostrate himself on his knees. When he sat down, as we said, there was a clattering sound made by the multitude of demons in the cave, as though some of them were riding on wagons and others were beating drums and yet others accompanying them on pipes, and they were shouting, so that the cave rocked from the din of the multitude of evil spirits.[156] When our father Feodosij heard all this, his spirit was not afraid, nor did he feel any terror in his heart. But fortifying himself with the sign of the cross, he got up and began to sing the Psalter, and straightway the great noise died away. Then he sat down once more, after saying a prayer, and again the voices of countless demons sounded again, as they had before. So the venerable one again got up and began to sing that Psalter, and the sound ceased again. Thus the evil spirits behaved towards him for many days and nights, not allowing him to sleep even for a short time, until he conquered them through Christ's grace and received power over them from God, so that henceforth they dared not approach the place where the blessed one was praying.

It also happened that damage was done by evil spirits in the room where the brethren made bread sometimes they scattered the flour, sometimes they upset the kvass set up to make the bread, and did much damage in other ways. Then the senior cook told the blessed Feodosij about

---

[155] See the Life of St. Antony, PG 26:85; *The Life of St. Antony by Saint Athanasius*, trans. R. T. Meyer, Ancient Christian Writers, 10 (New York, 1950), 27–29.
[156] Cf. Meyer, *Life of St. Anthony*, 28.

the damage of the evil spirits.[157] And he, trusting that he had received power over them from God, got up in the evening and went to that building, shut the doors behind him and stayed there in prayer until matins, so that from that hour no demons appeared in that place, nor did they do any damage of any kind, on account of the venerable one's prohibition and prayer.

How the holy one watched over and admonished his disciples

Now the great Feodosij had the following custom: every night he would go round all the monks' cells, as he wanted to find how each was conducting his life and being diligent towards God. When he heard someone praying, he stood up and glorified God on his account, but when he heard someone chatting, if two or three had gathered together after vespers, he knocked on the door with his hand, and after thus signifying his visit he would go away. The next morning he would summon them, but he would not accuse them directly, but would admonish them indirectly through parables, saying that he wished to find out their diligence towards God. If a brother was gentle in his heart and ardent in his love for God, he would quickly realize his fault, prostrate himself, and beg for forgiveness. But if a brother's heart was clouded by demonic darkness, he would sigh, thinking that Feodosij was talking about someone else, and would make himself out to be innocent until the blessed one accused him and dismissed him, after fortifying him with a penance.

Thus he taught them all to pray diligently to God, and not to chatter after vespers nor go from cell to cell, but to pray to God in their own cells, each according to his ability, and to work daily with their hands, having the Psalter on their lips. He spoke to them as follows, "I beg you, brothers, that we should labor in prayer and fasting and be concerned about the salvation of our souls. Let us turn away from our sins and deceitful ways—adultery, theft, slander, idle chatter, strife, drunkenness, gluttony, and hatred of brethren. Let us shun these things, brothers, and abominate them, so that thereby we do not defile our souls. But let us travel along the Lord's road leading us to paradise, and let us seek God with tears and sobs, with fasting and vigils, and in humility and obedience, so that we may receive mercy from Him. Let us also hate this world still more, always bearing in mind the word of the Lord: 'If any

---

[157] The term "senior cook" (старѣи пекущимъ) suggests organized work in the kitchen, in which all monks had to take their turn. Cf. Bishop Simon's description of the three years spent by Svjatoša working in the kitchen (below, Discourse 20, p. 131).

man will not forsake father, and mother, and wife, and children, and such for my sake and that of the Gospel, he is not worthy of me;'[158] and also: 'He that findeth his life shall lose it: and he that loseth his life for my sake shall find it.'[159] So, brothers, as we too have rejected the world and renounced those living in it, let us hate every kind of unrighteousness and do nothing that belongs to this world, and let us not return to our former sins like a dog to its vomit. 'For no man,' said the Lord, 'having put his hand to the plough, and looking back, is fit for the kingdom of heaven.'[160] How shall we escape eternal torment if we complete the span of this life in idleness and without repentance? For us, brothers, who are called monks, it is fitting to repent our sins daily, for repentance is the key to the kingdom of heaven. It is not fitting for anyone to live without it; repentance is the way leading to paradise. Let us keep firmly to this way, brothers; let us keep our footsteps fixed on it. The wily serpent does not approach this road. The stages of the journey are now beset with afflictions, but in the end they will be full of joy. So, brothers, let us move forward towards that day, so that we may receive these blessings. Let us shun all those who wish to dwell in unrighteousness and not live in repentance."[161] Thus did the holy teacher speak and instruct the brethren. They received his words like earth thirsting for water and brought to God the fruits of their labors—some a hundredfold, some sixty, and some thirty. Though on earth they appeared as men, yet in their lives they were like angels, and the monastery was like heaven, in which our father Feodosij shone forth in his good deeds more brightly than the sun, as I have told you.

How the holy one was glorified, and a divine light shone forth

This is what appeared to Sofronij, the superior of the Monastery of the holy Archangel Michael. As he was heading for his monastery one night—it was a dark night—just above the monastery of the blessed Feodosij he saw a light. He marveled and praised God, saying, "How great is Thy goodness, O Lord, that Thou has shown forth such a lamp in this holy place—this holy man, who thus shines forth and illuminates his

---

[158] Matt. 10:37; Luke 14:26.
[159] Matt. 10:39; Luke 17:33.
[160] Luke 9:62.
[161] In using sermons to train monks in the ascetical life, Feodosij was following the example of Theodore the Stoudite. See Dobroklonskij, *Prep. Feodor*, 526–34. On Feodosij's sermons, see Eremin, "Literaturnoe nasledie Feodosija Pečerskogo," 159–84.

monastery." Many others saw the same thing and often related what they had seen.

When the princes and the boyars heard about the monks' virtuous life, they would come to the great Feodosij, confess their sins to him, and depart after receiving much profit.[162] They would also come again and bring him something from their possessions to comfort the brethren and help towards building the monastery. Some of them also gave villages for the needs of the church and the brethren.

The Christ-loving prince Izjaslav, who was then occupying his father's throne, especially loved the blessed one. He often summoned Feodosij to his house, and many times went himself to see him; he would drink his fill of spiritual words and then depart. Henceforth God magnified that place and multiplied the blessed ones within it through the prayers of His servant.

Our father Feodosij had instructed the porter that he was not to open the gates to anybody after dinner time, and that no one was to enter the monastery until vespers, since the brethren rested in the middle of the day from the night prayers and the morning singing.

Prince Izjaslav's visit

One day at noon the Christ-loving prince Izjaslav came, as was his custom, with only a few servants; for when he wished to go to the blessed one, he dismissed all his boyars to their own homes and came to him with only five or six servants.[163] He came, as I have said, and dismounted from his horse, since he never entered the monastery's courtyard on horseback, and went up to the gates and told the porter to open them, as he wished to come in. The porter said to him, "Our great father has given orders that we are not to open the gates to anyone until it is time for vespers." Then the Christ-loving prince told him, so that he would know who it was, "It is I, open the gates for me alone." But the porter, not knowing that it was the prince, answered, "I told you, the superior ordered me that even if the prince should come, the gates are not to be opened. But if you will, be patient for a little while, until vespers." He answered, "I am the prince. Won't you open the gates for me?" The

---

[162] Feodosij's role as a spiritual father and counselor to members of the Kievan nobility must have contributed considerably to the spiritual and cultural influence of the monastery outside its walls.

[163] The words "five or six servants" occur only in the UspSb and Arsenian MSS: Abramovyč, *Pateryk*, 43, n. 8.

porter looked up and recognized the prince. He was filled with fear[164] but did not open the gates; he ran and told the blessed one. Meanwhile, the prince stood patiently before the gates, in this respect imitating St. Peter, the chief apostle. For when he was led out of prison by an angel and came to the house where the disciples were and knocked at the door, the maidservant got up and saw Peter standing there; for gladness she did not open the gate, but ran and told the disciples about his arrival.[165] Similarly this man from fright did not open the gates, but quickly ran and announced the arrival of the Christ-loving prince to the blessed one.

Then the blessed one came out, saw the prince, and prostrated himself before him. After this the Christ-loving prince Izjaslav said, "Father, what is your order about which this monk spoke, that even if the prince should come he is not to be admitted?" The blessed one answered, "The order, my good master, is so that the brethren should not depart from the monastery in the middle of the day, but should then rest on account of the service at night. Your zeal for our holy Lady, the Theotokos, is divinely inspired and full of blessing and profitable for your soul, and we rejoice at your arrival." They both went into the church, the blessed one said a prayer, and they sat down. And so the Christ-loving prince drank his fill of the honeyed words that came from our venerable father Feodosij and, receiving great profit from them, departed for his house, praising God. From that day he began to love Feodosij much more and considered him as one of the first holy fathers. He was very obedient to him and did everything which our great and venerable father Feodosij told him to do.

The blessed Varlaam's death

The blessed Varlaam, the son of the boyar Ioann and superior of the Monastery of St. Demetrios founded by the Christ-loving prince Izjaslav, left for the holy city of Jerusalem, and after visiting the holy places there, he returned to his monastery. Some time after this he went to Constantinople, where he visited all the monasteries and bought necessities for his own monastery and then came back to his own country. While on his way and actually already in his own country, he fell seriously ill. When he reached the town of Volodymyr, he entered a nearby monastery called

---

[164] I have followed the UspSb reading here: Abramovyč, *Pateryk*, 43, n. 22.
[165] See Acts 12:12–14.

the Holy Mountain[166] and reposed peacefully in the Lord, having come to the end of his life. He told his companions to take his body to blessed Feodosij's monastery and bury it there, and he gave orders that the things which he had bought in Constantinople—icons and other necessities—should be given to the blessed one.[167] They did as he had instructed them: they brought his body, buried it in blessed Feodosij's monastery, on the right side of the church, where his tomb is to this day, and gave everything to the venerable one, as he had ordered.

The departure of the blessed Isaia

After this the Christ-loving prince Izjaslav chose one of the brethren from blessed Feodosij's monastery called Isaia, who shone forth in the monastic life, and appointed him superior of his own Monastery of St. Demetrios. Later he was made bishop of Rostov because of his virtuous life, and there they honor him among the saints, since he received from God the gift of working miracles.[168]

The arrival of the holy Nikon

After the death of Rostislav, prince of that island[169] [Tmutorokan'], the great Nikon was asked by the people there to go to prince Svjatoslav and ask him to let his son sit on that throne.[170] When he arrived at the

---

[166] See Golubinskij, *Istorija russkoj cerkvi*, 1, 2:750. There appear to be no other references to this monastery in medieval Rus' sources.

[167] That Varlaam could dispose of his purchases for the Monastery of St. Demetrios without reference to its founder, Prince Izjaslav, indicates that he paid for them out of his own personal resources. Possibly he still retained some of his personal wealth, in spite of his dramatic gesture of renunciation when he asked to be received into the community of monks living in the cave (see above, p. 37), perhaps he accepted gifts from his family after they became reconciled to his decision to become a monk.

[168] Isaia of Rostov was present at the consecration of the Caves Monastery's church in 1089 (see above, Discourse 6, p. 16). He is also mentioned in Bishop Simon's list of monks from the Caves Monastery who became bishops (see Discourse 14, p. 118).

[169] Rostislav Volodimerovič, grandson of Jaroslav Volodimerovič (d. 1054) and a son of his eldest son Volodimer (d. 1050), fled to Tmutorokan' in 1064 and expelled the ruling prince, Glěb Svjatoslavič (PVL 1064, PSRL 1:164, 2:152). According to the PVL, he was poisoned by a Byzantine envoy because "the Greeks" feared his power and influence in the northern Black Sea area (PVL 1066, PSRL 1:166, 2:155).

[170] I.e., Glěb Svjatoslavič, whom Rostislav had expelled. In spite of the PVL's laudatory necrology for Rostislav (PVL 1066, PSRL 1:166, 2:155), it seems that the inhabitants of Tmutorokan', at least those who had any political weight, wanted to have Glěb back. It is not clear from Nestor's account where Nikon met Prince Svjatoslav, who was then ruling in Černihiv.

city, he came to blessed Feodosij's monastery. When they saw each other, they both fell down together and prostrated themselves. Then they embraced each other and wept a lot, since they had not seen each other for a long time. After this the blessed Feodosij begged him not to depart from him while they were both in the flesh. Then the great Nikon gave his promise, saying, "I shall just go, arrange things for my monastery, and then I shall at once return here."

This he did. For when he arrived at the island with Prince Glěb and the latter settled on the town's throne, Nikon did return. He came to the monastery of our great father Feodosij and gave all his possessions into the blessed one's hands and gladly subordinated himself to him. The blessed Feodosij loved him greatly and regarded him as a father. So if he went away anywhere, he entrusted him with looking after the brethren and instructing them, since he was senior to them all. Moreover, when he himself was instructing the brethren in church with spiritual discourses, he told the great Nikon to teach them by reading from books, and he likewise instructed our venerable father Stefan, who was then prior;[171] later he became superior of the monastery after blessed Feodosij's death, and finally became bishop of Volodymyr.[172] Now that I have told you about those people, I shall confine myself to my account of the blessed Feodosij and those worthy achievements which he accomplished through God's grace.

The holy one's industry and diligence

Now I shall discuss this shining light, our great and holy father Feodosij. For he was indeed a man of God, a light visible in the world shining forth to all his monks in humility of mind and obedience, and in his other labors. Every day he worked with his hands, and he often went out into the bakehouse and worked with those who were doing the baking, rejoicing in his spirit as he kneaded the dough and baked the loaves; for, as I said before, he had a strong and powerful body. He exhorted and strengthened all those who were laboring so hard and comforted them,

---

[171] In the Cas. II text Stefan is described as уставникъ; the UspSb has ексиархъ, and the Arsenian has еклиархъ: Abramovyč, *Pateryk*, 45, n. 25. Slavonic уставникъ probably corresponds to Greek ὁ κανονάρχης, the monk generally responsible for directing the church services. I am grateful to Professor Anastasios Bandy for this suggestion. Elsewhere (above, Discourse 4, p. 13) he is described as деместььвьникъ, "choir master."

[172] For Stefan's subsequent career, see below, pp. 86–87.

urging them not to slacken their zeal in any way in the work they were doing.

One day, when they wanted to celebrate the holiday of the holy Theotokos, there was no water. The aforementioned Feodor, who told me many things about this illustrious man, was then cellarer. He went and told the blessed Feodosij that there was no one carrying water. Then the blessed one quickly got up and began to carry water from the well. One of the brethren, seeing him carrying water, quickly went and fetched some of the brethren, who came eagerly and carried water, until there was more than enough.

On another occasion when no wood had been gathered for cooking, the cellarer Feodor went to the blessed Feodosij and said, "Father, would you please tell one of the brethren who is idle to go and prepare the wood that is needed?" The blessed one said, "Look, I am idle, I shall go." It was then time for dinner, and the blessed one told the brethren to go to the refectory, but he himself took an axe and began to cut wood. As the brethren were going out after their meal, they saw their venerable superior cutting wood and working hard at it, and each one took up his axe too and prepared enough wood for many days.

Such was the diligence towards God of our blessed and spiritual father Feodosij, for he possessed true humility and great meekness, in this imitating Christ, the true God, Who said, "Learn of me, for I am meek and lowly in heart."[173] Thus casting his mind back to this teaching, he humbled himself and made himself least of all, working and serving others in this way, going out to work before everyone, and taking his place in church before everybody as well.

Often when the great Nikon was sitting and binding books,[174] the blessed one would sit near him and spin the threads needed for this task; such was his humility and simplicity. No one ever saw him lying down or pouring water over his body; he washed only his hands.[175] His clothing was a hair shirt, which pricked his body; over this was another shirt, of very poor quality, which he put on so that the hair shirt which he wore would not be visible. Many thoughtless people mocked and insulted him

---

[173] Matt. 11:29.

[174] The word used here in the Cas. II text is строащу with the variant reading of дѣлающю: Abramovyč, *Pateryk*, 46, n. 35. This could mean "composing books," but the context indicates that Nikon was engaged in bookbinding.

[175] Abstention from washing was a popular form of asceticism among the Desert Fathers. See *Life of St. Antony*, 60, and the references cited in n. 171, and *Lausiac History*, 15.

because of his poor clothing, but the blessed one gladly accepted their reproaches, always bearing in mind the words of the Lord and rejoicing and taking comfort from them: "Blessed are ye when men shall revile you, and shall say all manner of evil against you falsely, for my sake. Rejoice in that day and leap for joy, for great is your reward in heaven."[176] Recalling these things, the blessed one took comfort from them and bore patiently the reproaches and insults of everybody.

The driver

One day the great Feodosij went to see the Christ-loving prince Izjaslav on some business. As he was a long way from the town, Feodosij stayed until the evening on account of his business. The Christ-loving prince ordered him to be taken to the monastery in a cart, so that he should have some rest during the night. As soon as he was on his way, the driver, seeing what sort of clothes he was wearing and reckoning that he was a pauper, said to him, "Look here, monk, you are idle every day, but I work hard and can't ride a horse. Let me rest in the cart and you mount the horse, if you can ride a horse." The blessed one got up and with the utmost humility mounted the horse while the driver lay down in the cart. Thus he continued on his way rejoicing and praising God, and when sleep threatened him he got off the horse and walked beside it until he became worn out and then he mounted the horse again. When it was dawn, some nobles who were riding to meet the prince recognized the blessed one from afar, dismounted from their horses, and prostrated themselves before him. Then he said to the servant, "My son, it is already light, mount your horse." When the servant saw how they were all prostrating themselves before him, he was terrified and mounted his horse trembling. He continued his journey thus while the venerable Feodosij sat in the cart. All the boyars prostrated themselves before him when they saw him, and the driver became even more terrified. Then when he reached the monastery all the brethren came out and prostrated themselves before him right to the ground, and the servant was absolutely terrified, thinking to himself, "Who is this man before whom everybody prostrates?" The venerable one took him by the hand, led him to the refectory, and ordered that he be allowed to eat and drink as much as he wanted; he also gave him some *kuna*[177] and then dismissed

---

[176] Matt. 5:11–12; Luke 6:22–23.
[177] The *kuna* was a monetary unit in Rus', a subdivision of the *grivna*. See Vernadsky, *Kievan Russia*, 122–23.

him. It was the servant himself who told the brethren these things; the blessed one did not reveal it to anyone.

Every day he instructed the brethren not to exalt themselves for any reason, but to be humble monks and make themselves the least of all, not to be puffed up, but to be submissive towards everybody. He would go about and speak to them with his hands folded on his breast, "Let none of you seek to excel in humility, but prostrate yourselves before each other, as is fitting for monks. Do not go from cell to cell, but each of you praise God in his own cell." Every day he instructed them continually by means of these and other sayings.

If he heard from the brethren that someone was struggling with demonic visions, he would summon him, and because he had been thoroughly tested himself, he would teach and instruct him to stand firm against the devil's wiles; not to succumb or be weakened by the misery caused by demonic visions; not to depart from that place, but to fortify himself by prayer and fasting; and continually to call upon God for victory over the evil spirit. He would say to them, "So it was with me at first. One night when I was singing the usual psalms in my cell, a black dog stood before me, so that I could not prostrate myself; it stood before me for many hours.[178] Being goaded in this way I wanted to strike him, and then he vanished from my sight. Such fear and trembling seized me that I would have run away from that place, if God had not helped me. For recovering a little from fright, I began to pray fervently to God and make frequent genuflections, and thus my terror left me, so that from that hour I have not feared them, even if they have appeared before my very eyes." He would also say many other things, strengthening them against the evil spirits, and then dismiss them, and they would rejoice and glorify God for having received such instruction from their valiant guide and teacher.

About Ilarion

One of the brethren, called Ilarion, also told me, "The evil spirits were causing me a great deal of trouble in my cell. As I was lying on my bed, a multitude of demons came and seized me by the hair, trampled on me, and dragged me down, while others scaled the walls and said, 'Drag him round here so that we can crush him against the wall.' They treated me like this every night. As I could not endure it, I went and told the

---

[178] Cf. *Life of Saint Anthony*, 27, which describes how Anthony was attacked by demons in the form of dogs.

great Feodosij about the trouble with the demons and said that I wanted to leave that place for another cell. But the blessed one entreated me, 'No, brother, do not leave that place, lest the wicked demons boast that they have vanquished you and caused you harm. After that they will do you greater harm, since they will have received power over you. Rather, pray fervently to God in your cell, and when God sees your endurance He will give you victory over them, so that they will not dare approach you.' I said to him again, 'I beseech you, father, after this I cannot abide in that cell because of the great number of demons.' Then the blessed one made the sign of the cross over me and said, 'Go to your cell. Henceforth the wily demons will not inflict any torment on you, nor will you see them again.' I believed him and prostrated myself before the holy man and went away. That night I slept soundly in my cell in complete silence. Henceforth the crafty demons dared not approach near that place, since they had been driven away by the prayers of our venerable father Feodosij.''

This same monk Ilarion also told me this. He was skilled in writing books,[179] and every day and night he used to write books in the cell of our blessed Feodosij, who would quietly sing the Psalter and with his hands spin wool or perform some other task. One evening, as each of them was doing his work, the steward entered and told the blessed one, ''Tomorrow we shall have nothing with which to buy food for the brethren and for other necessities.'' Then the blessed one said to him, ''As you see, it is evening and tomorrow is far away. So go and be patient for a little while, and pray to God that He will have mercy on us and take thought about us, if He wishes.'' After hearing this the steward departed. The blessed one got up at once and went into his inner cell, to sing in accordance with his customary rule. After his prayer he came and sat down and continued his task as before. Again the steward entered and told him the same thing. The blessed one replied to him, ''Did I not tell you to pray to God? Tomorrow you will go to the town and borrow money from the merchants to buy necessities for the brethren. Later when God is beneficent, we shall repay the debt. For He is faithful Who said, 'Take no thought for the morrow: for the morrow shall take thought for itself,'[180] and He will not cast us out from His grace.''

---

[179] Бѣяше бо книгам хитр писати: It is not clear from the context whether Ilarion was copying or composing books.
[180] Matt. 6:34.

The gold sent from God

When the steward had departed, a handsome servant in military dress entered. He prostrated himself and, without saying anything, put a gold *grivna* on the table and then silently went out. The blessed one got up and took the gold, having prayed to the Lord with tears. He summoned the porter and asked him whether anyone had come to the gates that night. He replied on oath, "The gates were shut while it was still light, and thereafter I did not open them, nor did anyone come up to them." Then the blessed one summoned the steward and gave him the gold *grivna*, saying, "Why do you say, brother Anastasij, that we have nothing with which to buy what the brethren need? Now go and buy what the brethren need, and tomorrow God will again take thought for us." The steward, discerning God's grace, fell down and prostrated himself before him, begging the venerable one's forgiveness. The blessed one admonished him, "Do not be despondent, brother, but persevere in faith and cast all your care upon God. For He takes thought for us, if He so wishes. Make a feast for the brethren today, for this is a divine visitation." God again gave without stint what was necessary for His chosen flock through the prayers of the venerable one.

Every night the blessed one remained awake, praying to God with tears about these things and frequently genuflecting to the ground, so that the church stewards often heard him when it was time for matins and they wished to receive his blessing. One of them quietly went and stood listening and heard him praying and greatly weeping and often striking his head on the ground. Then the steward withdrew a little and began to approach with even footsteps, and when Feodosij heard the footsteps he became silent, making it appear to the steward that he was asleep. And when the steward touched him and said, "Give your blessing, father," the blessed one was silent until the steward touched him three times, saying, "Give your blessing, father." Then, as though woken from sleep, he said, "May our Lord Jesus Christ bless you, my son." Then he took his place in church before everybody. People related that he so acted every night.

The priest Damian[181]

There was a certain elder in the blessed one's monastery, called Damian, a priest by rank, who in his zeal and meekness imitated the life

---

[181] For a fuller narrative about Damian, see below, Discourse 12, pp. 108–9.

of our venerable father Feodosij. Many people testify about his good life and meekness and the submissiveness which he showed towards all. Especially those who lived with him in his cell[182] saw his meekness, his nightly vigils, his diligent reading of the Scriptures, and how he frequently rose to pray; they also relate many other things about him.

Once when Damian was ill and near his end, he prayed to God with tears, "O my Lord, Jesus Christ, grant that I may be deemed worthy to partake in the glory of Thy saints and to share Thy kingdom with them. Do not separate me, I beseech Thee, Lord, from my father and teacher, the venerable Feodosij, but include me with him in the world that Thou hast prepared for Thy righteous ones." As he remained praying thus, the blessed Feodosij suddenly stood before his bed and fell on his breast and kissed him tenderly, saying, "See, my son, you prayed to the Lord about me,[183] and now He has sent me to tell you that your prayer will be granted, and that you will be numbered with His saints and be with the rulers of the kingdom of heaven. And when the Lord God commands you to depart this world and come to Him, you will not be separated from me, but we shall be together in that world." After saying this, he disappeared from his sight.

Damian understood that this had been a vision from God, since he had not seen him enter through the door or depart through it; but he had appeared on that very spot and then vanished from his sight. He quickly called for the monk who was serving him and sent for the blessed Feodosij. The latter came at once and Damian said to him with a joyous face, "Father, will it be as you promised me when you appeared just now?" The blessed one, who knew nothing about this, answered, "I cannot say, my son, since I do not know the promise of which you speak." Then Damian told him how he had prayed and how the venerable one himself had appeared to him. Hearing this, the God-inspired Feodosij smiled slightly, shed a few tears and said, "Yea, my son, it shall be as you were promised. For an angel appeared in my form. How can I, a sinner, promise that glory which has been prepared for the righteous?" Nevertheless, Damian was glad when he heard the holy one's promise.

---

[182] It was apparently an exceptional privilege for a monk of the Caves Monastery to have a private cell. The monk Svjatoša in the early twelfth century received one after a long period of service in the community (see Discourse 20, p. 131). The only other example recorded in the *Paterik* is the monk Feodor, who received a private cell in his old age (see Discourse 33, p. 181).

[183] The reading here is о нем же, lit. "about whom," but it is clear that Feodosij is talking about himself.

Then the brethren assembled and he kissed them all and commended his soul in peace into the hands of the Lord when the angels came for him. Then the blessed one ordered that the board be struck, so that the rest of the brethren should assemble, and with great solemnity they buried the honored body of His servant, where they bury all the brethren.

After this the brotherhood increased, and it was necessary for our illustrious father Feodosij to enlarge the monastery and build more cells, because of the multitude of newcomers and the monks already there. He himself worked with the brethren, building the courtyard of the monastery, but although it was surrounded by a palisade, this did not protect them.

The visit of some robbers, and a miracle which occurred

One night when it was very dark, some robbers came against us. They thought that our property was hidden in the church precincts, and so they did not go to any of the cells but made their way to the church, where they heard the sound of people singing. They reckoned that it was the brethren singing vespers and departed. After lingering a little while in a thicket in the woods, they reckoned the office would be finished, and again they came to the church. They heard the same sound and saw a marvelous light in the church, and a sweet fragrance was issuing from it, for angels were singing there. Reckoning that the brethren were singing the midnight office, they departed and waited for them to finish; then they could go and take everything that was in the church. So they came many times and heard the same angelic voices. When the hour for matins arrived, the sacristan called out as usual, "Give thy blessing, father," as he asked a blessing, and then began to strike the board for matins. Then the robbers withdrew into the woods a short distance, sat down, and said, "What are we to do? It seems as though there is a phantom in the church. When they are all assembled there, then we shall go and hide behind the doors and kill them all and take their property." Thus did the enemy goad them, as he wished by this means to uproot the holy flock from that place. But he was unable to do this and was himself vanquished by them with God's help through the prayers of our venerable father Feodosij.

Then these wicked men lingered a little while, and when the venerable flock was assembled in the church with their blessed teacher and pastor Feodosij, as they were singing the morning psalms, they rushed toward them like wild beasts. They came up, and suddenly an awesome miracle occurred: the church and those who were inside it were lifted from the earth and raised into the air, beyond the range of their arrows. The blessed one and those inside the church were unaware and heard nothing, but the robbers were terrified when they saw the miracle and returned to their homes in fear and trembling. Henceforth their hearts were softened not to do evil to anyone, and their leader, with three others, came to our blessed father Feodosij to repent for this and told him what had happened. When the blessed one heard this story, he glorified God Who had saved them from such a death, and he instructed them about the salvation of their souls and dismissed them, praising God and giving thanks for all things.

A similar miracle which occurred in the same Caves Monastery

On another occasion one of the boyars of the Christ-loving prince Izjaslav saw the same thing. He was walking at night in a field fifteen miles[184] from the monastery and saw the church in the clouds. Filled with terror, he pushed on with his servants, as he wanted to see what church it was. When he reached the blessed one's monastery, as he was looking on, the church descended and stood in its usual place. He knocked on the gate, and when the porter opened it, he went to the blessed one and told him what had happened. Henceforth he often came to see him, drinking his fill of his spiritual words, and made grants from his property towards the building of the monastery.

The boyar Kliment

Another boyar of the same Christ-loving prince Izjaslav was on campaign with the prince against the foe, and as they were preparing for battle he made a vow to himself, "If I return home safely I shall give to the holy Theotokos in the monastery of the blessed Feodosij two gold *grivna*, and I shall make a metal crown for the icon of the holy Theotokos." The battle was joined and many of both armies fell by the sword, but finally the foe was defeated and those who were still alive returned to their own homes.

The boyar, however, forgot his promise to the Theotokos. Some days later, as he was sleeping in his room at midday, a terrifying voice called him by name, "Kliment!" He started up and sat on his bed, and

---

[184] According to V. Dal', *Tolkovyj slovar' živogo velikorusskogo jazyka*, vol. 3 (St. Petersburg, 1882), 306, a *poprišče* could mean a distance covered in a day's journey, i.e., about 20 versts, or about 12 miles. In this case 15 *poprišče* would be over 180 miles, which cannot be correct in this context.

then he saw the icon of the holy Theotokos from the blessed one's monastery standing before his bed. A voice came from it, "Kliment, why have you not given me what you promised? Lo, I am now telling you to get up and fulfill your promise." Having said this, the icon disappeared from his sight. Then Zdeislav Ggeuevič—for this was his former name[185]—was in great terror, and he took what he had promised, carried it to the monastery, and gave it to the blessed Feodosij; he also made a crown for the icon of the holy Theotokos.

A few days later this same boyar decided to donate a gospel to the blessed one's monastery. He came to the great Feodosij in the monastery with the holy gospel concealed under his arm. After a prayer, they were about to sit down (he still had not revealed the holy gospel), and the blessed one said to him, "First, my brother Kliment, bring out the gospel which you have under your arm and which you promised to give to the holy Theotokos, and then let us sit down." Hearing this, he was awestruck at the foresight of the venerable one, for he had not informed anyone about it. So he brought out the gospel and gave it into the blessed one's hands and sat down. After he had enjoyed his spiritual conversation he returned to his own home. Henceforth he had a great love for the blessed Feodosij and often came to see him and derived great benefit from him.

When people came to see the blessed one, after giving them instruction on divine matters he would offer them a meal of monastic food—bread and pulse. The Christ-loving prince Izjaslav frequently used to partake of this food, and rejoicing, he would say to the blessed Feodosij, "As you know, father, my house is filled with all the good things of this world, but I have never eaten such tasty food as I now do here. Although my servants think up varied and costly dishes, they are not so tasty as these. I beseech you, father, where does your food get its fine flavour?" Then our divinely-inspired father Feodosij, wishing to strengthen his love of God, would say, "If you want to know these things, my good lord, listen to me and I shall tell you. When the brethren of this monastery are going to cook or bake bread or perform any service, they have this rule. First, one of them goes and receives a blessing from the superior; then he prostrates himself three times before the holy altar

---

[185] At this time most Christians in Rus' seem to have had a Greek, as well as a "secular" (Slavic) name, and were usually referred to by the latter. Abramovyč, *Pateryk*, 216, n. 61, says that the boyar's "secular name" does not appear in either the UspSb or Arsenian MSS. He suggests reading Sudislav instead of Zdeislav, but confesses ignorance as to the origin of Ggeuevič.

right to the ground; then he lights a candle from the holy altar and kindles the fire from it.[186] And as he pours water into the cooking pot he says to the elder, 'Father, give your blessing,' and the elder says, 'May God bless you, brother.' So all their service is performed with a blessing. Your servants, as you say, quarrel and poke fun and revile each other as they work; they are often beaten by overseers; and all their service is performed in sin.'' Hearing this, the Christ-lover said, ''Indeed, father, it is as you say.''

The holy one's inspection

Our venerable father Feodosij, who was indeed filled with the Holy Spirit, increased the talents given him by God and settled the place with a multitude of monks, and what had once been a deserted place he now made into a famous monastery. Furthermore, he did not wish to establish a stock of possessions in it, but inclined his heart to God in faith and hope and did not rely on worldly possessions. For this reason he often went round the cells of his disciples, and if he found anything, whether prepared food to eat or clothing beyond that ordained by the rule or any private possessions, he took these things and threw them into the stove, as being the portion of the enemy and an enticement to sin.[187] He would say to them, "Brothers, it is not right for us as monks who have cast off worldly things to make a collection of possessions in our cells. For how can we offer to God a pure prayer if we keep a hoard of possessions in our cells? Concerning this you have heard the Lord saying, 'Where your treasure is, there will your heart be also.'[188] While of those who accumulate possessions He says, 'Thou fool, this night thy soul shall be required of thee: then whose shall those things be, which thou hast provided?'[189] So, brothers, let us be content with the clothing set forth in the rule and with the food set out in the refectory by the cellarer, and let us have no such possessions in our cells, so that we can offer to God a pure prayer with the utmost zeal and with our whole mind.'' He taught them these things and many others and instructed them all with tears and with the

---

[186] Cf. Discourse 14, p. 113. The Stoudite typikon specifies that the kitchen fire was to be lit in this way. See Golubinskij, *Istorija russkoj cerkvi*, 1, 2:619.

[187] Feodosij was strict about the monks not having private possessions, but other passages in the *Paterik* indicate that many monks did have them, and that there were distinctions betwen rich and poor. See, e.g., Discourse 19, p. 129; Discourse 22; Discourse 28, p. 154 (although here the possessions appear to have been books); and Discourse 33, p. 4.

[188] Matt. 6:21; Luke 12:34.

[189] Luke 12:20.

utmost meekness, for he was in no way hot-tempered or irascible, nor did his eyes flash with rage, but he was quiet, gentle, and merciful towards everybody.

If any member of the holy flock weakened in his heart and left the monastery, the blessed one was very sorrowful and in great distress on his account, and he would pray to God that the sheep which had strayed from the flock might come back. He would remain thus every day, praying to God with tears for his sake, until that brother came back. Then the blessed one would receive him joyfully and instruct him not to weaken because of the enemy's wiles and not to allow them to come upon him, but to stand firm; for, he would say, a valiant soul does not yield to these miserable afflictions. After telling him this and many other things and having comforted him, he would dismiss him in peace to his cell.

The monk who frequently left the monastery

There was one brother who, being weak, often left the blessed one's monastery. When he would return, the blessed one gladly received him, saying, "God will not leave him in this state, lest he die outside the monastery. Even though he often goes away from us, he will nonetheless end his life in this monastery."[190] He prayed tearfully to God on his behalf, beseeching that he might have patience. After he had left many times, he came once to the monastery and begged the great Feodosij to admit him. Feodosij, who was indeed merciful, joyfully received him, like a sheep who had strayed, and included him in his flock. Then this monk, who had acquired a little property by working with his hands—for he was a tailor—brought this and laid it before the blessed one. The holy man said to him, "If you wish to be a perfect monk, take this, as the fruits of disobedience,[191] and throw it into the fiery stove." Being ardent in faith, he took it and threw it into the stove as the blessed one had ordered, and so it was burned. Henceforth he lived in this monastery and passed the rest of his days there, and there also, according to the blessed one's prediction, he reposed in the Lord's peace.

Such was the love and loving-kindness which the blessed one had for his disciples that not one of his flock strayed; he looked after them all together like a good shepherd, tending, instructing, comforting, and exhorting them with his sayings. He nourished their souls with the

---

[190] A recurrent theme in the *Paterik* is the special grace bestowed on those who died in the monastery; this is stressed by Bishop Simon in Discourse 14.

[191] I follow the UspSb and Arsenian readings here: Abramovyč, *Pateryk*, 56, n. 23.

imperishable food of eternal life, and gave them to drink without ceasing from a spring of water. Thus he led many to an understanding of God and set many on the path to the heavenly kingdom.

And now let us come once more to the story of our father Feodosij.

The lack of food

One day the cellarer came to the blessed one and said, "We have nothing to put before the brethren for food today, nor anything to cook." The blessed one said to him, "Be patient, and go and pray to God. Does He not take thought for us? If He does, cook some wheat and mix it with honey and put that on the table for the brethren.[192] However, let us put our trust in God, Who in the wilderness gave His rebellious people bread from heaven and quails from the rain;[193] He is able to give us food today." Hearing this, the cellarer departed.

The blessed one prayed to God continually about these things. Then the aforementioned boyar Ioann,[194] God having inspired him, filled three carts with provisions—bread, cheese, fish, pulse, millet, and honey—and sent them to the blessed one's monastery. When the blessed one saw this, he glorified God and said to the cellarer, "Do you not see, my brother Feodor, that God will not abandon us if we trust Him with all our heart? Go and make a great feast for the brethren, for this is a visitation from God." The blessed one rejoiced with the brethren at table with spiritual joy, but he himself ate dry bread and vegetables cooked without oil and drank water, for this is what he always ate.[195] He never appeared downcast or frowning at table, but illuminated by the grace of God.

The compassion of holy Feodosij

On one occasion some robbers in bonds were brought to the blessed one; they had been seized in one of the monastic villages, where they wanted to steal something. Seeing them bound up like this and in such a wretched state, the blessed one felt very sorry and was moved to tears.

---

[192] This kind of cake was served as a special treat (see below, p. 67). Something of this kind was apparently included in the Stoudite typikon, but there is no indication of the form it took. See Golubinskij, *Istorija russkoj cerkvi*, 1, 2:614.

[193] See Exod. 16:9–18.

[194] See above, p. 36. Ioann evidently bore the monastery no ill will, even though it had won the battle for his son Varlaam.

[195] This was the diet prescribed by the typikon for weekdays in Lent, apart from Wednesdays and Fridays, when no vegetables were allowed. See Golubinskij, *Istorija russkoj cerkvi*, 1, 2:616.

He ordered them to be untied and given something to eat and drink, and then he instructed them at length not to harm or do evil to anyone. He gave them what was sufficient for their needs from the monastery's possessions and then dismissed them in peace. They departed praising God and the blessed Feodosij, and henceforth their hearts were softened and they did no harm to anyone but were content with their own labors. Such was the meekness of our great father Feodosij. Indeed, if he saw a beggar or a pauper badly dressed and in a miserable state he was filled with compassion towards him and showed his pity by tears. For this reason he built a house close to his monastery, erected a church dedicated to the holy protomartyr Stephen, and ordered that the beggars, the blind, the lame, and the sick be housed there. He supplied their needs from the monastery and gave a tithe from everything that belonged to the monastery. Every Saturday he used to send a cart of loaves for those who were in prison or in bonds.[196]

The priest who asked for wine

One day a priest from the town came to the venerable Feodosij, asking for wine to celebrate the holy liturgy. The blessed one straightway summoned a church steward and told him to pour out the wine in the vessel and give it to him. But he replied, "There is not much wine, only enough for the holy liturgy for two, three, or four days." The blessed one replied to him, "Pour it all out for this man, and God will take thought for us." The steward went out and, disregarding the blessed one's order, poured only a little wine into the priest's vessel and left some for the morning church service. The priest took the small amount which the steward had given him and showed it to the blessed Feodosij. He summoned the steward once more and said, "Did I not tell you to pour it all out and not to take thought about tomorrow? For God will not leave this church without a service tomorrow, but will this very day give us wine in abundance." The steward then went and poured out all the wine for the priest and so dismissed him. As they were sitting down in the evening, after their meal, lo! three carts with barrels of wine were brought in, according to the blessed one's prediction; a certain woman who supervised everything in the household of the pious prince Vsevo-

---

[196] On the philanthropic traditions of Byzantine monasticism, see D. J. Constantelos, *Byzantine Philanthropy and Social Welfare* (New Brunswick, N. J., 1968), 88–110.

lod[197] had sent them. Seeing this, the steward glorified God and marveled at the prediction of the blessed Feodosij, since he had said that God would send them that day wine in abundance, and so it had happened.

The disobedience of the cellarer

One day, when it was the feast of the great and holy martyr Demetrios, the day on which he received a martyr's death for Christ's sake, the venerable Feodosij and the brethren went to the Monastery of St. Demetrios,[198] some people brought to him loaves of the finest quality, which he ordered the cellarer to put on the table for the rest of the brethren to eat. But the cellarer disobeyed him, saying to himself, "Tomorrow, when all the brethren arrive, I shall put out these loaves for them to eat, but now I shall put out the ordinary loaves of the monastery for the brethren." As he thought, so he acted.

The next day, as they were sitting at table and these loaves were being cut, the blessed one looked and saw what kind of loaves they were, and he summoned the cellarer and asked him where the loaves had come from. He replied, "They were brought yesterday, but I did not give them out yesterday because there were very few brethren, and I decided to put them out today for all the brethren to eat." The blessed one said to him, "It is not fitting to take thought of the coming day, but to act according to my order. Now our Lord, Who eternally takes thought for us, would have taken thought for us and given us what we needed." Then he ordered one of the brethren to collect the pieces of bread in a basket and carry them to the river and scatter them, and he imposed a penance on the cellarer because he had committed an act of disobedience. He used to act thus whenever he heard of an action being performed without a prior blessing, since he did not wish the holy flock to taste food prepared without a blessing, as it was the fruit of disobedience. Because he regarded it as the enemy's portion, sometimes he ordered it to be thrown into the fiery stove and sometimes into the rapids of the river.

---

[197] Vsevolod Jaroslavič, prince of Perejaslav (1054–78) and Kiev (1078–93). The PVL's necrology comments on his piety, saying that "he loved monks very much" and "ministered to their needs" (PVL 1093, PSRL 1:216, 2:207).

[198] Despite the *Account*'s statement that Prince Izjaslav wished to make the Monastery of St. Demetrios superior to the Caves Monastery (above, Discourse 7, p. 22), the two monasteries apparently maintained friendly relations, at least while Feodosij was superior. It is significant that Izjaslav twice chose a superior for the Monastery of St. Demetrios from the Caves Monastery, first Varlaam and then the monk Isaia, who later became bishop of Rostov.

DISCOURSE 8

The holy one's command about disobedience

A similar example of a disobedient action occurred after the death of our blessed father Feodosij. Although it is not suitable to relate such matters here, nevertheless I have recalled it and will add this account to the one just related:

It was after the expulsion of our venerable father and superior Stefan from the monastery, when the great Nikon received the office of superior.[199] The time of the great and holy fast was drawing near, and it had been arranged by our venerable father Feodosij that on the Friday of the first week of abstinence, as they were laboring like good ascetics, they should have loaves of the finest quality, some of them made with butter[200] and honey. Nikon ordered the cellarer to do this according to the custom. But the cellarer lied and said, "We have no flour for making such loaves." God, however, did not despise the labors and prayers of His venerable ones, lest the practice established by the blessed Feodosij be upset. For as they were going to their Lenten dinner after the holy liturgy, a cart containing these particular loaves was brought in from an unexpected source. Seeing this, the brethren praised God and the holy Feodosij, marveling that God always took thought for them and gave them everything they needed through the prayers of their father and teacher Feodosij.

Two days later the cellarer ordered loaves to be baked for the brethren from that flour which he had said previously he did not have. As those who were baking the bread were kneading the dough and pouring in warm water, a frog was found there—it had been cooked in that water —and so this task performed disobediently was defiled in this way. For it was God's will towards the feeding of his holy flock that they should perform this feat of asceticism in that holy week and not eat such loaves; so God through this reptile, defiled them, as being the enemy's portion, and so that this incident should be an example for the future.

Let none of you despise me because I have interrupted my narrative to record this incident, for I have recorded this in order that you should realize that it is not fitting for us to disobey our teacher and superior in any matter. Even if we conceal something from him, nothing is hidden from God, and He will speedily avenge the one whom He has appointed

---

[199] The exact date is uncertain (probably ca. 1077); Nikon remained in office until his death in 1088 (PVL 1088, PSRL 1:207, 2:199).

[200] The Cas. II text has масломь ("with butter or oil") the other MSS have макомь ("with poppy seed"): Abramovyč, *Pateryk*, 59, n. 23.

to be our elder and pastor, so that we should all obey him and do everything according to his will. Let us, however, now return to our previous narrative about the blessed Feodosij.[201]

The shortage of oil

Once, when the feast of the Dormition of the holy Theotokos was approaching, there was no oil with which to fill the lamps. The church steward had the idea of squeezing oil from flax seeds and using this to fill and light the lamps. He asked the blessed Feodosij about this, and he told him to do as he had suggested. When he was about to pour the oil into the lamps, he saw that a mouse had fallen into it and was floating dead in it. He quickly went and told the blessed one, "I covered the vessel containing the oil with the utmost care. I do not see how this creature jumped in and drowned." The blessed Feodosij decided that this was a visitation from God and reproached himself for his lack of faith. He said to him, "It would have been better for us, brother, to have placed our hope in God and trusted that He would give us what we need, and not to have acted without faith, which was not fitting. Go and pour that oil onto the ground; then let us be patient for a little while and pray to God that He will give us plenty of oil this very day." Then when it was time for vespers, a certain rich man brought in a large barrel full of oil. When the blessed one saw this, he glorified God that He had so quickly heard their prayer. When they had filled all the lamps, most of the oil was still left, and so on the next day they celebrated the solemn feast of the holy Theotokos.

The devout prince Izjaslav, who was indeed ardent in his faith towards our Lord Jesus Christ and His most holy Mother, and who afterwards laid down his life for his brother,[202] according to the Lord's commandment—he, as I have said, had an exceptional affection for our father Feodosij and often came to see him and drink his fill of his spiritual words.

---

[201] Nestor's digression on the monk's duty to obey his superior may reflect the disciplinary troubles which afflicted the monastery after Feodosij's death and probably led to the expulsion of Stefan.

[202] Izjaslav was killed on October 3, 1078, in battle against his kinsmen Oleg and Boris Svjatoslavič and Boris Vjačeslavič (PVL 1078, PSRL 1:201, 2:193).

How a cask of mead was filled according to the word of the holy one[203]

One day when the prince had come and they were sitting in the church conversing about spiritual matters, it was the time for vespers, and so the Christ-lover took his place with the blessed one and the honorable brethren at the evening office. Just then by God's will it began to rain heavily. Seeing such a downpour, the blessed one summoned the cellarer and told him to prepare food for the prince's repast. Then the keybearer came to him and said, "O lord and father, we have no mead[204] for the prince and his attendants to drink at dinner." The blessed one said, "Haven't you even a little?" He answered, "Not any, father. I turned the vessels upside down and laid them on their sides." The blessed one said again, "Go and look more carefully. Perhaps there is a little left." He replied, "Believe me, I turned the vessel in which the mead is kept upside down, and then laid it on its side." Then the blessed one, who was indeed filled with the Holy Spirit and with spiritual grace, said to him, "Go, and according to my word, in the name of our Lord Jesus Christ, you will find mead in the vessel." As he had faith in the blessed one, he left and came to the storehouse, and according to the word of our holy father Feodosij he found the cask placed upright and full of mead. Awestruck, he quickly went and told the blessed one what had happened. The blessed one said to him, "Keep silent, my son, and do not say a word about this to anyone. But go and carry as much as you need for the prince and his attendants, and give the brethren some of it to drink too, for this is a blessing from God." When the rain stopped, the prince departed for his home. The blessing was so great in that house that it sufficed them for many days.

The expulsion of demons

One day a monk came from one of the monastery's villages to our blessed father Feodosij, saying, "There are demons living in the shed where they shut up the cattle and are doing much harm there; they will

---

[203] The title of this chapter, which appears only in the Cas. II redaction (Abramovyč, *Pateryk*, 61, n. 7) appears misplaced. It belongs above, immediately before the words "The devout prince Izjaslav...."

[204] This is the only drink consumed in the Caves Monastery specifically referred to in the Life of Feodosij. The Stoudite typikon prescribed wine as the standard drink, except during Lent, but as wine was a luxury in Rus', one would not expect it to be drunk regularly in the monastery, especially in view of its precarious financial position. Mead was popular in Rus', but it is not clear whether it was the monastery's usual drink or was reserved for special occasions, such as a princely visit.

not let them be fed. The priest has often said a prayer and sprinkled the place with holy water, but even so the evil demons remain and continue to harm the cattle." Our father Feodosij fortified himself against them by prayer and fasting, according to the word of the Lord: "This kind goeth not out but by prayer and fasting."[205] Thus confident that he would expel them from that place, as he had previously done from the bakehouse, he went to the village. In the evening he entered alone into the shed where the demons had made their abode, shut the doors, and remained there praying until matins. And from that hour no demons have appeared at that place, nor have they harmed anyone in that village, since they had been expelled from it by the prayers of our venerable father Feodosij as though they had been attacked with weapons. The blessed one returned to his own monastery like a mighty warrior, having vanquished the evil demons who were making trouble in the holy one's region.

How a quantity of flour was increased as the holy one predicted

One day the senior baker came to our venerable and blessed father Feodosij and said, "We have no flour with which to bake bread for the brethren." The blessed one said to him, "Go and look round the storehouse, and perhaps you will find a little flour there. Until now God has always taken thought for us." Knowing that he had swept the granary and that in one corner alone there was a little bran, he replied, "I tell you truly, father, I myself have swept the place out and there is nothing there but a little bran in one corner." The father said to him, "Believe me, my son, that God is able to fill the place with flour from those few grains of bran. He did this for the widow in the time of Eliu, making a large quantity of flour from a few grains, so that she and her children fed themselves during a time of famine until there was an abundance among the people.[206] He is the same even now and likewise able to create much from little for us. Go and see whether God's blessing will be there." Hearing this, he departed, and when he entered the building, he saw the granary, which had previously been empty, now filled with flour by the prayers of our venerable father Feodosij, so that it was now spilling through the walls onto the ground. Awestruck at seeing this marvelous miracle, he returned to the blessed one and told him. The holy one said

---

[205] Matt. 17:21; Mark 9:29.
[206] See 3 Kings 17:8–16.

to him, "Go, my son, and do not reveal this to anyone, but bake loaves as usual for the brethren. For God has bestowed His mercy upon us by the prayers of our venerable brotherhood, granting everything we need, if we ask Him."

Such was the blessed one's diligence towards God, such was the hope of our holy father Feodosij, and such was his trust in our Lord Jesus Christ that he placed no hope in earthly things nor trusted this world in any matter, but directed his whole mind and soul towards God and placed all his trust in Him, taking no thought for the coming day and remembering daily in his heart the Lord's saying, "In nothing be anxious; behold the fowls of the air: they sow not, neither do they reap, nor gather into barns; yet the heavenly Father feedeth them. Are ye not much better than they?"[207] Every night, therefore, he would pray with tears, "Lord, Thou hast gathered us together in this place. If it pleases Thy holy grace that we should live in it, be Thou our helper and giver of all good things. For this house has been founded in the name of Thy holy Mother, and we are gathered together in it in Thy name. Do Thou, O Lord, keep and preserve us from every counsel of the all-cunning enemy and deem us worthy to receive eternal life. Place always in our hearts the fear of Thee, so that we may inherit those good things which have been prepared for the saints."

Thus he remained every day, teaching, exhorting, and comforting the brethren, urging them not to weaken but to persevere in their monastic labors; thus did he diligently tend his flock, taking care that no cunning wolf should enter in and scatter this divine flock.

The light sent from God

We shall now relate how certain things were revealed to a Christ-loving and God-fearing man in a vision about our venerable father Feodosij, his most stainless prayers, and this holy monastery, indicating through him that they should move to another place.

There is a small hill situated above the monastery, and as this man was going over it one night, he saw this miracle and was filled with terror. The night was dark but there was a marvelous light above the blessed one's monastery alone. When he looked up at it, he saw the venerable Feodosij standing in that light in the middle of the monastery before the church, holding up his hands to heaven, and praying earnestly to God. As he watched in wonder, another miracle appeared to him: a

---

[207] Matt. 6:26; cf. Luke 12:24.

great flame like an arc issued from the very top of the church, came to the other hill and stood on its end where our blessed father Feodosij had marked out the site for building a church. Later he began to build it, and a famous monastery is there to this day.[208] Thus did the flame appear to this man as an arc with one end at the top of the church and the other on the place I have mentioned until he rode behind the hill and saw it no more. He himself saw this and related it to one of the brethren of the blessed one's monastery; it is the truth.

So it is right for us to say, with the divine patriarch Jacob, "The Lord is in this place; it is a holy place, and none other than the house of God and the gates of heaven,"[209] and moreover to say that it is similar to what is described in the life of the great and holy Sabbas.[210] For as he was praying one night and coming out of his cell, there appeared a pillar of fire reaching up to heaven. When he reached that spot he found a cave there, and within a few days he established a famous monastery in it. Here too we should understand that God indicated the place, so that soon afterwards a famous monastery might appear there, which flourishes to this day through his prayers.

Such was the prayer for his flock and this place offered to God by our blessed father Feodosij, and such were his vigils and nightly abstinence, and thus did he shine forth in the monastery like a bright light, and so by his prayers the blessed and merciful God revealed another miracle about that place.

The remarkable appearance of the holy angels

Certain men living nearby subsequently related this incident to all the brethren. One night they heard the sound of countless people singing. When they heard this sound they rose from their beds, went out of their houses, stood on a high place, and looked in the direction of the

---

[208] The arc indicates the site of the new stone church of the monastery, described in Discourses 1–4. A similar portent is recorded in PVL 1110, PSRL 1:284, 2:260–61, but in this case the arc stretched from the stone refectory to Feodosij's tomb. The chronicler interpreted it as an angelic visitation, foreshadowing the successful campaign of the Rus' princes against the Cumans in 1111. The literary paradigm of this omen was probably the pillar of fire which guided the Israelites by night on their journey out of Egypt (Exod. 13:21).

[209] Gen. 28:16–17.

[210] The Life of St. Sabbas appears to have been Nestor's principal literary model, though this is the only occasion when he cites it directly. The textual resemblances between the two Lives are noted by A. A. Šaxmatov, "Neskol'ko slov o Nestorovom Žitii prep. Feodosija," IORJAS 1 (1896):46–65.

sound. A great light was shining above the blessed one's monastery and they saw a multitude of monks coming out of the old church and walking towards the place mentioned above. Those in front were carrying the icon of the holy Theotokos and all those walking behind were singing and holding lighted tapers in their hands, while before them went their venerable father and teacher Feodosij. When they reached that place, they sang and prayed and then turned around, and, as they watched them, the monks again entered the old church, still singing. Not one, not two, but many people saw this and related what they had seen. Now it must be understood that it was angels who appeared in this manner, though not a single one of the brethren understood them to be such, for this was the will of God, Who had hidden this mystery from them. When they heard about it later they glorified God, Who had worked such great miracles and sanctified that place and illuminated it through the prayers of our venerable father Feodosij. Now that we have related this incident, brothers, it is fitting to continue our eulogy of the blessed one and to proceed with the story of his meritorious deeds, and to give a true account of his zeal for our Lord Jesus Christ.

How the holy one preached the Christian faith to the Jews

The blessed one had the custom of getting up at night without anyone's knowledge and going out to the Jews to argue with them about Christ, reproaching and reviling them, and calling them rebellious and lawless, because he wanted to be killed preaching about Christ.[211]

The holy one's unflinching asceticism and fasting

When he departed to the aforementioned cave during Lent, he would often get up at night without anyone's knowledge and, with God as his only protector, depart alone to a monastic village. There he would prepare a cave in a hidden place, without anyone's knowledge, and remain until Palm Sunday. Then again at night he would come to his first cave. On the Friday before Palm Sunday he would come out to the brethren, so that they thought he had stayed there during Lent. Thus did he spend his time, giving himself no rest from vigil and prayer throughout the night, praying to God for his flock, and calling on Him to help them in all their labors. Every night he would go round the

---

[211] H. Birnbaum, "On Some Evidence of Jewish Life and Anti-Jewish Sentiments in Medieval Russia," *Viator* 4 (1973):231, accepts this passage as reliable evidence for the existence of a Jewish community in Kiev in the late eleventh century.

monastery's courtyard and say a prayer, thereby fortifying it as with a strong wall and taking care that the crafty serpent should not enter and capture any of his disciples. Thus he fortified all parts of the monastery.

On one occasion some men committing a robbery were captured by some people who were guarding their houses, and they were tied up and brought before the judge in the town. By God's will it chanced that they came past one of the monastery's villages. One of the bound malefactors indicated the village with his head and said, "One night we came to that village to commit a robbery and take everything there, but we saw a wall, so high that we could not approach the village." For thus had God invisibly protected their property through the prayers of this righteous and venerable man. So the blessed David testified, "The eyes of the Lord are over the righteous, and His ears are open to their prayer."[212] For the Master Who created us always inclines His ear to those who truly call upon Him, and having heard their prayer He saves them and does all things according to their wish and request for those who hope in Him. Thus He acted for our venerable and most blessed father Feodosij as he tended his flock with the utmost piety and singleness of heart, at the same time spending his own life in asceticism and self-denial.[213]

The holy one's courage and steadfastness.

At that time the cunning enemy somehow instigated dissensions among the three princes, brothers according to the flesh: two of the brothers made war on their elder brother, the Christ-loving prince Izjaslav, who was thus expelled from Kiev, the captial city.[214] When they had entered that city, they sent for our blessed father Feodosij and urged him to come and have dinner with them and take part in their unrighteous deliberations. But the venerable one, filled with the Holy Spirit, having realized that the expulsion of the Christ-loving prince had been unjust, told the messenger that he would not come to the table of Beelzebub and partake of food full of bloodshed and murder.[215] He said many

---

[212] Ps. 33:15.

[213] I follow the UspSb and Arsenians reading here: Abramovyč, *Pateryk*, 66, n. 10.

[214] In 1073 Izjaslav's younger brothers, Svjatoslav of Černihiv and Vsevolod of Perejaslav, joined forces against him (PVL 1073, PSRL 1:182, 2:172). The chronicler declares that Svjatoslav was the instigator because he wanted more power; Vsevolod is represented as being more reluctant.

[215] Feodosij's denunciation of Svjatoslav for usurping his senior brother's position and thus violating Jaroslav's so-called "Testament" (PVL 1054, PSRL 1:161, 2:150) is identical with the judgment expressed in the PVL's 1073 entry. A. A. Šaxmatov, *Razys-*

other things and then dismissed the messenger, saying, "Report everything to those who sent you." But when the two of them heard these things they could not be angry with him, since they saw that he was a God-fearing and righteous man. But neither did they heed him, and they pressed on with the banishment of their brother and chased him right out of the region. Then they returned and one of them settled on the throne of his father and brother, while the other returned to his own territory.[216]

Our venerable father Feodosij, being filled with the Holy Spirit, began to point out to him that he had acted unrighteously and contrary to the law in settling on this throne and in expelling his elder brother, as it were his father. He continued thus to accuse him: sometimes he wrote letters and sent them to him; sometimes when his nobles came to visit him he accused the prince of having expelled his brother unjustly and told them to tell him. Finally he wrote him a very long, reproachful letter in which he said, "The voice of your brother's blood cries out to God, like that of Abel against Cain." He adduced many other ancient persecutors, murderers, and brother-haters. Through these examples he pointed out everything pertaining to the prince, and having written this letter he sent it to him. When the prince read the letter he was furious, roared like a lion, and flung it on the ground. He vowed that henceforth the blessed one would be sentenced to imprisonment. Then the brethren were greatly distressed and begged the blessed one to stop and not to go on accusing the prince. Many boyars came and told him that the prince was angry with him and begged him not to oppose him, saying, "The prince will send you to prison." When the blessed one heard what they said about him going to prison, he rejoiced in his soul and said to them, "Indeed, brothers, I rejoice, for nothing in this life is particularly blessed for me. When did wealth or the deprivation of possessions exercise any constraint on me? When did the loss of villages make me sorrowful?

---

kanija o drevnejšix russkix letopisnyx svodax (St. Petersburg, 1908), ch. 17, suggested that both the chronicle entry and Feodosij's attitude reflected the political views of the monk Nikon, who tonsured Feodosij. A. Poppe "Le Prince et l'église en Russie de Kiev depuis la fin du Xe siècle et jusqu'au début de XIIe siècle," *Acta Poloniae Historica* 20 (1969):103, more cautiously points out that Feodosij simply followed the traditional precepts and practice of Byzantine monasticism in upholding the rights of the legitimate ruler, and stresses also that in Rus' only the Caves Monastery expressed this attitude so forcefully; there is no record of any opposition to the princes on the part of the metropolitans and the higher clergy.

[216] The word область (lit. "district") does not convey the element of political power enjoyed by a regional prince in Rus'. Svjatoslav Jaroslavič ruled in Kiev from 1073 to 1076.

We brought none of these things into this world; we were born naked, and so it is fitting that we likewise depart from it naked. Therefore I am prepared for either imprisonment or death." Henceforth he upbraided the prince for his enmity towards his brother, for he very much wanted to go to prison. The prince, however, even if he was very angry with the blessed one, dared not do him any harm, since he saw that he was a righteous and venerable man. Indeed, previously he had often envied his brother on account of him, because he had such a shining light in his territory (for a monk named Paul, the superior of a monastery in his own principality, had told the prince about him). Having been earnestly entreated by the brethren and the magnates, our blessed father realized that he would have no success with these words and left the prince alone; henceforth he did not reproach him but thought to himself that it would be better to beseech him by prayer to restore his brother to his territory.

Prince Svjatoslav's humility toward the holy ones.

A few days later, when the pious prince realized that the blessed Feodosij's anger towards him had passed, he took comfort in this discovery and felt very glad, since he had long wished to talk with him and enjoy his spiritual conversation. He sent to the blessed one to ask whether he would permit him to come to the monastery or not, and when he was told to come the prince got up joyfully and came to the blessed one's monastery with his boyars.[217]

The great Feodosij came out of church with the brethren, and when he saw the prince he prostrated himself in the customary way, as is fitting before a prince; the prince for his part kissed the blessed one. Then the pious prince said to him, "I dared not come to you, father, since I thought that you would be angry with me and not admit me to the monastery." The blessed one said, "Good lord, what has my anger availed against your power? Yet it is right for us to accuse you and to speak to you about the salvation of your soul, and it is right for you to obey." They went into the church, said a prayer, and then sat down. The blessed Feodosij began to speak to him from the Scriptures and taught him many things about loving one's brother; for he had inflicted many wrongs on his brother and because of this he did not want to make peace with him. After a long conversation the prince went home again, praising God that He had deemed him worthy to converse with such a

---

[217] Cf. the passage above, p. 49, which says that Izjaslav would dismiss his boyars when he came to visit the monastery.

man. Henceforth he came often to see him and drank his fill of that spiritual food; better than honey and the honeycomb were the blessed one's words which issued from those honeyed lips. And often the great Feodosij visited him and reminded him of the fear of God and of love towards his brother.

One day our blessed and God-bearing father Feodosij went to visit him. As he entered the room where the prince was sitting, he saw many people playing instruments in front of him: some were playing on dulcimers, others were raising their voices in tuneful notes, while yet others were playing on the organ; they were thus all making merry and playing music, as is customary before a prince. The blessed one sat down near him and looked at the ground, and after making a slight prostration he said, "Will it be like this in the world to come?"[218] The prince's heart was immediately touched by the blessed one's words, and he shed a few tears and told the musicians to stop. Henceforth whenever he ordered them to perform and heard of the arrival of the blessed Feodosij, he would tell them to keep quiet and make no sound. Often when he learned of the blessed one's arrival he would joyfully go out and meet him before the doors of his house, and then they would both go into the house together. He would say to the blessed one, since he was feeling glad, "I tell you truly, father, even if I were told that my father had risen from the dead, I should not rejoice so much as at your arrival, and I should not feel so much fear or misgiving before him as I do in the presence of your venerable soul." The blessed one said, "If you fear me, then do my bidding and restore your brother to the throne which your pious father entrusted to him." But the prince fell silent at this, since he did not know what to answer, for the enemy had so inflamed him with anger against his brother that he did not even want to hear his name mentioned. Our father Feodosij prayed to God daily and nightly for the Christ-loving prince Izjaslav, and also ordered his name to be remembered in the litany,[219] as he was the chief prince and the most senior of them all, whereas he said that the one who was sitting illegally on the throne was not to be remembered in his monastery. It was only when the

---

[218] The Church's traditional opposition to secular music, strolling players, and other similar forms of amusement, was still strong in the sixteenth century; it appears frequently in the *Stoglav*, promulgated in 1551. See E. Duchesne, *Le Stoglav* (Paris, 1920), items 19, 20 (p. 119) and 23 (p. 123).

[219] The ектенїа (ἐκτένεια) was a litany recited by a deacon during the liturgy while the celebrant prayed secretly; it consisted of nine petitions, each of them answered by the choir with a threefold kyrie.

brethren begged him to do so that he told them to remember the latter together with the former—however the Christ-loving one first, then the pious one.

The great Nikon, seeing such strife among the princes, departed with two monks to that aforementioned island, where he had founded a monastery.[220] The blessed Feodosij begged him many times that they should not be parted while they were both alive and asked Nikon not to leave him, but he did not obey him in this matter and departed to his own place, as we have said previously.

The building of the great church of the Caves Monastery

Then our father Feodosij, being full of the Holy Spirit, began to labor with divine grace to move to another place, and with the help of the Holy Spirit he began to build a large stone church dedicated to the holy Theotokos and ever-virgin Mary, since the first church was made of wood and too small to accommodate the brethren.[221] At the beginning of this undertaking a multitude of people gathered, and some pointed to one place for the foundations, and some to another. But none of these places was really suitable compared with a nearby field belonging to the prince. By Divine Providence the pious prince Svjatoslav was passing that way. Seeing the large crowd, he asked what they were doing there. On finding out he turned aside his horse and, as though directed there by God, he pointed to the place in his field and told them to build the church there. They said a prayer, and the holy place was revealed by the dew sent from heaven, then by the dryness of the ground, and by the bush being burnt by fire, as has already been related in detail in the account of the foundation of the church.[222] After the prayer the pious prince himself started the

---

[220] See above, p. 41. Priselkov, *Očerki*, 212, suggests that the reason for Nikon's second departure from the Caves Monastery might have been his disapproval of Feodosij's willingness to receive Svjatoslav in the monastery. But it could equally well have been due to a desire not to embarrass the superior, once he had yielded to the pressure of the boyars and at least some of his own monks and decided to try tactics of persuasion with Svjatoslav, since outright opposition to his expulsion of Izjaslav had had no effect.

[221] See also PVL 1073, PSRL 1:183, 2:173.

[222] See above, Discourse 2, p. 8. The passage "They said a prayer...foundation of the church" occurs only in the Cas. II text: Abramovyč, *Pateryk*, 69, n. 24. It is at variance with the rest of this part of Nestor's narrative, since he had not said anything about the way in which the site for the church was chosen and appears to have known little about its origins. The material in Discourses 2 and 3 to which the interpolated passage refers was written by Bishop Simon early in the thirteenth century and therefore could not have

digging, and the blessed Feodosij himself labored and toiled daily on the construction of the building. But he did not complete it in his lifetime; after his death, when Stefan was superior, the task was completed and the church was built with God's help and the prayers of our venerable father Feodosij. Then the brethren resettled there, though a few remained in the old place, together with a priest and a deacon, and the holy liturgy was celebrated there daily.

This is the life of our venerable and blessed father Feodosij from his youth up to this point; I have written only a few things out of many. For who can record in order all the good deeds of this blessed man? Who can worthily extol his courage? Even though I have tried to praise him adequately according to his merits, I have been unable to do so, since I am crude and ignorant; but I have spoken about the holy one to the extent that my powers permit.

Princes and nobles frequently wished to test the blessed one by getting the better of him in conversation, but they failed and recoiled as though they had hurled themselves against a rock; for he was fortified by faith and hope in our Lord Jesus Christ and had made himself an abode of the Holy Spirit.

He was a protector of widows, a helper of orphans, and a hope for the poor. Simply put, he comforted and instructed all who came to him, and gave to the poor what was required for their needs and their food. Many foolish people reproached him, but he accepted all these reproaches with joy. Even though he was often reproached and insulted by his own disciples, he continued to pray to God for them all. Many ignorant people mocked and ridiculed him because of his shabby clothes, but this did not distress him; rather he rejoiced at being reproached and insulted, and was very glad and glorified God for this. Indeed anyone who did not know him and saw him in such clothing would not think him a superior, but one of the monastery's poor servants.

The deliverance of a poor widow

One day as the blessed one was going to see the workmen where they were building the church, he was met by a poor widow who had been unjustly treated by the judges. She said to the blessed one, "Tell me, monk, is the superior in your monastery?" The blessed one said to her, "What do you want with him, since the man is a sinner?" The woman said to him, "I do not know whether he is a sinner or not. I only

---

been accessible to Nestor.

know that he has saved many from misery and trouble. That is why I have come, so that he might help me, since I have been unjustly treated by the judges." After learning about her situation, the blessed one took pity and said to her, "Go home now, woman, and when our superior comes I shall tell him about you and he will deliver you from your trouble." Hearing this, the woman went home. The blessed one went to the judge, told him what he knew about her and delivered her from his extortion,[223] so that he sent and returned everything which had been taken from her. Indeed, our blessed father Feodosij defended many people before princes and judges and delivered them, since they could not disobey him in any matter, knowing that he was a righteous and holy man. They did not honor him because of any fine apparel or sumptuous garments or many possessions, but on account of his pure life and radiant soul and the many exhortations which flowed from his lips through the Holy Spirit. For to him goatskin was like fine and costly apparel and a hair shirt like the most honorable imperial purple; it was thus that he wished to achieve greatness.[224]

How the holy Feodosij was summoned to God

Having spent his life in a manner pleasing to God and having reached the end of his days, he had foreknowledge of his departure to God and the day of his repose, for to the righteous death is rest. He then ordered the entire brotherhood to assemble, including those in the villages and those absent for any other purpose. After calling them all together, he charged the officials, stewards, and servants to continue performing whatever service had been entrusted to them with the utmost diligence in the fear of God and in humility and love. He thus instructed them with tears about the salvation of their souls and a life pleasing to God; about fasting, being diligent in attendance at church, and standing there; about love for the brethren; and about being submissive not only towards elders, but also showing love and submissiveness to those of the same age. After saying these things, he dismissed them.

Then the pious prince Svjatoslav came to visit the blessed one. He opened his guileless lips and instructed him about his religious duty and how he should preserve Orthodoxy and care for the holy churches. To this he added, "I pray to the Lord God and His ever-virgin Mother for

---

[223] The word used in the text is насилие ("violence"), but the context indicates that the injustice suffered by the woman was some kind of financial extortion.

[224] I follow the Arsenian reading here: Abramovyč, *Pateryk*, 71, n. 11.

your piety and your governance, that He may grant you a quiet and undisturbed reign. I entrust to your piety this holy Caves Monastery, the house of the holy Theotokos, which she herself wished to be founded. Let no archbishop or any cleric from St. Sophia acquire control over it. Let only your authority watch over it, and your children after you, up to the last of your family."[225]

After this the blessed one was shivering from cold and burning with a violent fever, and he could do nothing. He lay on his couch and said, "May God's will be done, and may He accomplish in me whatever is His will. Yet I pray, my Lord Jesus Christ, that Thou wilt have mercy on my soul, that the cunning enemy will not seize it, but that Thy angels may take it and bring it through the valley of the shadow to the light of Thy mercy." After this he fell silent and the brethren were filled with grief and sorrow on his account.

For three days he could neither speak nor signal with his eyes, so that many thought that he had already died; only a few of them perceived that his soul still dwelt in his body. After three days he got up, and when all the brethren had assembled, he said to them, "My fathers and brothers, the span of my life is now finished, for the Lord revealed to me when I was in the cave that I should depart from this world. You now discuss among yourselves whom you wish me to appoint as superior in my place."[226] On hearing this the brethren were overcome by great sorrow and weeping. Then they went out and discussed among themselves, and

---

[225] This entire paragraph does not appear in either the UspSb or the Arsenian texts: Abramovyč, *Pateryk*, 72, n. 3. It implies a hostile relationship between the Caves Monastery and the metropolitans of Kiev in the late eleventh century, for which there is no contemporary evidence. But the sentiment fits well with the religious climate in mid-fifteenth-century Kiev. In 1460 the metropolitan of Kiev was Gregory, the friend and protégé of Isidore, metropolitan of Kiev and all Rus' from 1436 to 1448, who had aroused strong opposition for supporting the Act of Union with the "Latins" signed at the Council of Florence in 1439. Thus the interpolated passage might well have been composed by Cassian himself. This was the opinion of A. Kubarev, "O redakcii Paterika Pečerskogo," *Čtenija*, 1858, no. 3:199, one of the earliest students of the *Paterik*; but not that of Abramovyč, *Issledovanija*, IORJAS 7, no. 1:243, who believed that the passage was inserted towards the end of the twelfth century, after the quarrel between the superior Polikarp and Metropolitan John IV.

[226] Cf. the account in Discourse 7, p. 22 where the monks, after dicussing among themselves, asked Antonij to choose a successor to Varlaam. Nestor's narrative shows that by the time a successor was required for Feodosij the feelings of the brotherhood were the determining factor.

unanimously declared that Stefan, who was then choirmaster in the church, should be superior.[227]

The holy Feodosij's passing

The next day our blessed father Feodosij again summoned all the brethren and said to them, "What have you decided among yourselves, my children, as to who would be a worthy superior?" They all said, "Stefan is worthy of becoming superior after you." The blessed one summoned him, blessed him, and named him superior in his place. He instructed the brotherhood at length to submit themselves to him and then dismissed them, after telling them the day of his death, and saying, "On Saturday, as the sun rises, my soul will be separated from my body." Then he summoned Stefan by himself and instructed him about caring for the holy flock. Stefan refused to leave him but looked after him humbly, since he was already greatly weighed down by his sickness.

When it was dawn on Saturday, the blessed one summoned all the brethren and kissed them all individually, while they wept and sobbed at the departure of such a shepherd. The blessed one said to them, "My beloved children and brothers! I have kissed you all with love, since I am departing to our Lord Jesus Christ. You have as superior the man whom you yourselves wanted.[228] Obey him, regard him as your spiritual father, fear him, and do everything according to his will. God performs all things according to His word and wisdom, and He will bless you and protect you from the intriguer, so that henceforth you may preserve your faith firm and unshaken in unity and love, remaining together until your last breath. May you have grace to labor without spot or blemish, and may you be united in body and soul in humility and submissiveness. Be perfect, even as your heavenly Father is perfect.[229] The Lord be with you. This I solemnly beseech you: bury me in the cave where I stayed during Lent, in these clothes which I am now wearing. Do not wash my body, and do not let any of the people see me. But bury my body by yourselves in the place I have mentioned." When the brethren heard

---

[227] According to PVL 1074 (PSRL 1:186–87, 2:176–77), the monks asked Feodosij himself to choose his successor, and he chose a monk named Jakov (James), but he was unacceptable to the brotherhood because he had come to the Caves Monastery from another monastery, and so the monks then asked for Stefan.

[228] I.e., Stefan, and not Jakov, whom Feodosij would have preferred.

[229] See Matt. 5:48.

these words from the lips of the holy father, tears gushed forth from their eyes as they wept.

The holy one's commission and promise to his disciples

The blessed one again comforted them, saying, "My brothers and fathers, I promise you that although I depart from you in the body, I shall always be with you in spirit. And whichever of you shall die in this monastery or in any place where he may be sent as superior, I shall answer for him before God, even though he may have committed sins; but whoever leaves this place of his own accord, I shall have nothing to do with him.[230] You will discern my position[231] at God's court thereby: when you see an increase of all good things in this monastery you will know that I am close to the heavenly Master; but when you see want and poverty, understand that I am far from God and lack the confidence to pray to Him."

After these words he dismissed all the brethren and would not let anyone stay with him. One of the brethren, who had always looked after his needs, made a small chink in the wall and looked through it. The blessed one arose, lay down on his knees, and prayed tearfully to the merciful God for the salvation of his soul, calling on all the saints to help him, especially our holy Mistress the Theotokos, and he prayed to the Lord God, our Savior Jesus Christ, for his flock and this place. After his prayer he again lay down on his bed. After lying down for a little while he looked up to heaven and with a loud voice and radiant countenance said, "Blessed is God! If He is such, then I am not afraid, but rather rejoice that I am leaving this world." As he spoke thus, it is to be understood that he had seen a vision of some kind. Then he straightened himself, stretched out his legs, placed his hands on his breast in the form of a cross, and commended his soul into God's hands, and he was united with the holy fathers in the year 1074 at sunrise on Saturday, May 3, as he had predicted.[232]

---

[230] The notion that a special grace was attached to spending one's whole life in the Caves Monastery and dying there became an important element in the monastery's tradition and appears in other parts of the *Paterik*, notably in Bishop Simon's letter to Polikarp (Discourse 14), written over a century and half after the death of Feodosij.

[231] The term дьрзновение ($\pi\alpha\rho\rho\eta\sigma\iota\alpha$), here translated first as "position at God's court" and then as "confidence," implies both the standing and the boldness to intercede before a greater authority on a lesser client's behalf.

[232] PVL 1074, PSRL 1:188, 2:178, notes more precisely that Feodosij died in the second hour of the day, on the second Saturday after Easter, May 3, in the eleventh year

Then they wept over him a great deal, took him up and carried him to the church, and sang the customary office over him. Suddenly, as though by some divine revelation, a multitude of the faithful drew near, moved by their zeal. They came and stood before the gates, waiting for the blessed one to be brought out. The pious prince Svjatoslav was staying not far from the blessed one's monastery, and he saw above the monastery a column of fire from the earth up to heaven. No one saw this except the prince, and he realized from it that the blessed one had passed away and said to those with him, "Look! I think that the blessed Feodosij has passed away today." For he had been with him earlier and had seen how very seriously ill he was. He sent to learn if he really had passed away and wept much at the news that it was so.

The burial of the holy Feodosij

The brethren closed the gates and did not admit anyone, in accordance with the blessed one's wishes. They stayed sitting over him, waiting until the people had dispersed, when they could bury the blessed one, as he had ordered. Many boyars had come and were standing before the gates. Lo, under God's providence, the sky suddenly clouded over and it began to rain, whereupon the people dispersed. At once the rain stopped and the sun shone, and they carried him to the aforementioned cave, laid him there, and sealed it up. Then they departed and remained all that day without food.

That summer, through the prayers of our blessed father Feodosij, there was an increase of all good things in the monastery, and also in the villages[233] there was an abundance of crops and livestock, more than there had ever been. Discerning this and recalling the holy father's promise, his disciples glorified God, because He had deemed their teacher and mentor worthy of such grace. It is clear even to this day that everything in his monastery has increased through his prayers: even when all the surrounding districts had been plundered by soldiers there was an increase in the blessed one's monastery through the prayers of our father Feodosij. It is indeed true, as the Lord God said, "I will honor them that honor me,"[234] and as the divine Scriptures say, "The righteous, though he dies, will live for evermore; the pains of Hell will not touch him; his reward is with the Lord and his hope is with the most

---

of the indiction.
[233] I use the UspSb and Arsenian readings here: Abramovyč, *Pateryk*, 74, n. 33.
[234] 1 Kings 2:30.

High."[235] Indeed our venerable father Feodosij, though separated from us in body, nevertheless is always with us in spirit, as he himself said. Now I shall relate to you a miracle that happened after the blessed one's death.

The holy one's miracle for a boyar

There was a certain boyar who had incurred the violent anger of the prince, so that many people told him, "The prince will send you to prison." Then he prayed earnestly to God and called on our holy father Feodosij for aid, saying "I know, father, that you are holy. Now the time has come: arise and entreat the heavenly Master to deliver me from this misfortune." One day, as he was sleeping at midday, our venerable father Feodosij appeared to him, saying, "Why are you so sad? Or do you think that I have left you? Although I am separated from you in body, yet in spirit am I with you always. Tomorrow the prince will summon you and will not be angry with you at all, but will restore you to your position." This magnate did not see him in his sleep, as it were, but as he woke up with a start he saw the blessed one behind him, going out of the door. And it turned out as the blessed one had said. Henceforth this man had a very strong affection for the monastery of the blessed Feodosij.

The holy one's miracle concerning some stolen silver

A certain man was about to set out on a journey. He had a little basket full of silver, and he brought it to the monastery of our blessed father Feodosij and entrusted it for safekeeping to a monk named Konon, whom he regarded as his friend. One of the brethren named Nikolaj saw this and, goaded by a demon, stole it and hid it. When Konon went into his cell and looked around and could not find it, he was greatly distressed and prayed tearfully to God, frequently invoking our holy father Feodosij that he might not be shamed by the man who had given him the silver for safekeeping. Then he fell asleep for a little while, and in his sleep he saw the blessed Feodosij saying to him, "The monk Nikolaj, prompted by the devil, took what you are so distressed about and hid it in the cave." And he showed him the place and said, "Go, tell nobody about this, take your property." He woke up and rejoiced. He arose quickly, lit a candle, went to the designated place, and found the silver, according

---

[235] Wisd. of Sol. 5:16.

to the words of the holy father. He took it and carried it to his cell, praising and glorifying God and His servant, the blessed Feodosij.

The sick cleric

It is told also that one of the clergy of the great cathedral church of St. Sophia was very ill with a burning fever. Coming to himself for a little while, he prayed to God and our holy father Feodosij about the weakness caused by his illness. Then when he had again fallen asleep he saw the blessed Feodosij giving him his own stick and saying, "Take this and walk with it." He took it and felt that his illness and fever had left him. He told those who were with him about the blessed one's appearance and later, when he was able, he went to the blessed one's monastery and told the brethren how God had cured him of his illness through the prayers of our holy father, since He had given such grace to His blessed servant.[236] And now let us come to the end of our story.

Stefan's period of office as superior

After the falling-asleep of our blessed father Feodosij, Stefan became superior and labored to build the church which the blessed one had begun. By the grace of Christ and the prayers of our venerable father Feodosij in a few years the church was built and the monastery completed.[237] All the brethren moved there, but a few remained in the former place, as we have already said, since it was their custom to bury the brethren who had died there. Both monasteries are close to each other, and between them is the courtyard which our venerable father Feodosij built for receiving beggars, so they all form a single group of buildings, divided by courtyards.[238] Our father Stefan also ordained that the holy liturgy should be celebrated every day in the old church for the brethren who had died. God provided all necessities and the place increased in numbers by the grace of God and through the prayers of our holy father Feodosij.

---

[236] It is interesting that both these miracles take the form of visions; as Feodosij was buried in an unknown place in the Caves (see above, p. 84), there was no tomb available to act as a locus for working miracles.
[237] See PVL 1075, PSRL 1:198, 2:189.
[238] See above, p. 65.

DISCOURSE 8

The expulsion of Stefan, later bishop of Volodymyr

The enemy, the hater of good, who wages perpetual war against God's servants and will not let them live in peace, but rises up against them with his evil designs, stirred up strife among these people. And where there is strife he always has many victories, and the warfare which has arisen continues without ceasing.[239] Satan caused such a rebellion in their midst that they joined together in a plot and ejected Stefan from his position as superior. The devil so inflamed them with anger that they even expelled him from the monastery.[240]

Many boyars were his spiritual sons and had been entrusted to him by the blessed one. They were very distressed that their spiritual father had suffered so much and been driven out of the monastery, since he had received it from our venerable father Feodosij. They gave him gifts from their property both for his physical needs and other requirements.[241] With God's help and the prayers of his venerable teacher Feodosij, Stefan founded a monastery at Klov and built a church dedicated to the holy Theotokos, named after its model in Constantinople which is called Blachernai.[242] Every year on July 2 they celebrate a solemn feast there in honor of the holy Theotokos.

Nikon's period of office as superior

After Stefan's expulsion the monks in the monastery of the venerable Feodosij unanimously appointed as their superior the great Nikon, who, after the blessed one passed away, had come to the monastery from his own place.[243] In my opinion, his appointment was in accordance with God's will, because he was senior to them all, and indeed our venerable father Feodosij was deemed worthy of being tonsured by his hand and of

---

[239] I follow the more extended UspSb and Arsenian readings here: Abramovyč, *Pateryk*, 77, n. 4.

[240] Nestor does not give any specific reasons for the rebellion against Stefan and his expulsion from the monastery. Perhaps the monks objected to the strict discipline of the Stoudite Rule, which Feodosij had maintained only by constant vigilance and the charismatic power of his personality.

[241] I use the UspSb and Arsenian readings here: Abramovyč, *Pateryk*, 77, n. 16.

[242] See above, Discourse 4, p. 13, which says that Stefan dedicated his monastery to Our Lady of Blachernai in honor of the miracle which brought the craftsmen to Kiev from Constantinople. Stefan's church is not mentioned by Janin, *La géographie ecclésiastique*, among those dedicated to Our Lady of Blachernai outside Constantinople.

[243] Nikon had left the Caves Monastery and returned to Tmutorokan' when Svjatoslav established himself in Kiev. See above, pp. 77–78.

receiving from him the Holy and Angelic Monastic Habit. Many times the enemy tried to make trouble for him also and to stir up rebellion against him, but he was unable to do so.

However, let us now end our narrative here, since we have composed a history about Feodosij derived from many different kinds of information. For as much as I heard earlier by inquiring from fathers older than myself who were there in his time—this I, the sinful Nestor, the least of all the monks in the monastery of our venerable father Feodosij, have written down. I myself was received into the monastery by the venerable superior Stefan and was tonsured and invested with the monastic habit by him, and then ordained deacon by him, though I was not worthy of this, since I am crude and ignorant, and, moreover, I have been filled with a multitude of sins from my youth. Nevertheless, I have accomplished this task through God's will and out of love toward Feodosij.

Since, brethren, I often heard about the good and pure life of our venerable and God-fearing father Feodosij, I was filled with joy and gave thanks that he had lived and labored thus in most recent times. Then I saw that nobody had written it down, and my spirit was overcome with sadness and sorrow. So, constrained by my love for our great and holy father Feodosij, I tried in the crudeness of my heart to write down a few of the many things I had heard about him, to the glory and honor of the great God and our Savior Jesus Christ, to Whom with the Father and the Holy Spirit be glory, now and forever, Amen.

Discourse 9. August 14. A discourse by Nestor, a monk of the Caves Monastery, about the translation of the relics of our most venerable father Feodosij of the Caves Monastery.[244]

People rejoice [to commemorate] the memory of holy men with eulogies, says the most wise Solomon.[245] For it is customary, during the divine celebration of a festival, to feel spiritual joy at the thought of godly men. According to the saying of the most wise Solomon, "A righteous man, even though he dies, still lives, and the souls of the righteous are in the hands of God."[246] For the Lord honors them that honor Him,[247] and it pleased Him to reveal as acceptable in His sight this blessed and valiant man, a man of exalted life, marvelous virtues, and outstanding miracles—the blessed Feodosij. And God did indeed act thus eighteen years after the death of the venerable one.

In the year 1091 a multitude of those practicing the monastic life in the most holy Caves *lavra*[248] gathered together with their teacher and superior,[249] and unanimously decided that the relics of the venerable Feodosij should be translated. It is right, therefore, to invoke you: blessed indeed are you, fathers, and goodly your counsel. O divinely appointed assembly! O mighty fasters! O most honorable host! O blessed congregation! For the psalm of David[250] has been fulfilled in

---

[244] A slightly shorter version of this discourse appears in PVL 1091, PSRL 1:209–11, 2:200–3, but with no indication of the author, whereas in the *Paterik* he refers to himself in the title and also three times in the text as "Nestor"; presumably he is identical with Nestor, the author of the Life of Feodosij. The question whether the inclusion of the name represents a genuine tradition or an erroneous interpolation is discussed by Šaxmatov, "Žitie Antonija i Pečerskaja Letopis'," 125, 127, and S. A. Buhoslavs'kyj [Bugoslavskij], "K voprosu o xaraktere i o ob"eme literaturnoj dejatel'nosti prep. Nestora," IORJAS 19, no. 1 (1914):178–81. Šaxmatov and Abramovyč take the former view, Buhoslavs'kyj the latter.

[245] Cf. Prov. 10:7.

[246] Cf. Wisd. of Sol. 3:1, 4:7.

[247] 1 Kings 2:30.

[248] Apparently the earliest use of the word *lavra* to describe the Caves Monastery. While this monastery was essentially a *lavra* in the Palestinian sense, i.e., a collection of individual monks gathered together under one leader, the word is also used honorifically to denote its special position and prestige.

[249] The superior at this time was Ioann, who is mentioned elsewhere in the *Paterik* (Discourses 6, 25, 27, 31, and 36).

[250] The word used in the text is богоотьць (θεοπάτωρ), "ancestor of God," a common reference to David. See G. W. H. Lampe, *A Patristic Greek Lexicon* (Oxford, 1961), 89.

you: "See now! what is so good, or what so pleasant, as for brethren to dwell together?"[251] Your counsel was indeed good, most illustrious fathers, and the words of your concord sound forth like trumpets.

Desiring their true pastor, they did not say, "We are deprived of our father and teacher," but they all, as with one voice, said, "Let us take up the honorable relics of our beloved father Feodosij. For it is not right that we should be deprived of our pastor, nor is it fitting that the shepherd should abandon the sheep entrusted to him by God, lest the wild beast should come and scatter Christ's flock of rational sheep. But let the shepherd come into his sheepfold and play on his spiritual pipe, so that the shepherd's reed might ward off the assault of the crafty beast." Then they called upon our Preserver and on their guardian angels and said to one another, speaking with a single voice, "It is fitting, brothers, that we should have the coffin of our father Feodosij always before our eyes, and that we should always pay him due reverence, as our true father and teacher. It is not right that our venerable father Feodosij should remain outside his monastery and church, for he founded it and gathered the monks together." Having made their decision, they at once ordered a place to be prepared for depositing the holy one's relics, and they set up a stone coffin.

The feast day of the Dormition of our most holy Lady, the Theotokos, was drawing near, and three days before this festival the superior ordered [some of the brethren] to go into the cave and mark the place where the relics of our holy father Feodosij lay. By his command I, the sinful Nestor, was deemed worthy of this task, and I was the first to see his holy relics, by the order of the superior. So I am telling you everything exactly as it happened, since I did not hear it from others, but was myself in charge of this affair. The superior came to me and said, "Let us go into the cave, my son, to our venerable father Feodosij." We came to the cave without informing anyone. The superior looked around to see where to dig, pointed to a place outside the mouth [of the cave], and then said to me, "Do not tell anybody, but take whomever you want to help you, and apart from him let none of the brethren know anything until we have carried the relics of the holy one out in front of the cave."

In the course of seven days I fixed up shovels with which to dig. It was then Tuesday, and late in the evening I took with me another

---

[251] Ps. 132:1.

monk,[252] a man of remarkable virtues; no one else knew. When we came to the cave we recited prayers and supplications, prostrated ourselves, sang the appointed psalms, and then set to work. I started digging and worked hard, and then I yielded to the other brother. We dug until midnight, but we could not find the holy one's relics. We began to feel very miserable, and our eyes began to fill with tears. I thought that perhaps the holy one did not wish to reveal himself. Then another thought came to me, that perhaps we should dig to one side. I took the spade and began to dig diligently. The monk who was with me was standing before the cave, and when he heard the church board being struck for matins, he called out to me that they had struck the board, but I had dug through to just above the relics of the holy one. And when he told me about the board being struck, I answered, "Brother, I have dug through to them!" But when I had done this a great fear overwhelmed me and I began to cry out, "Lord, have mercy upon me, for the sake of the venerable Feodosij!"

There were two monks then keeping watch in the monastery until the superior, who had concealed himself with some [of the monks], should secretly bring out the relics of the venerable one; they were keeping a careful watch in the direction of the cave. And when the church board was struck for matins they saw three columns, like arcs of fire,[253] which came to rest on the church of the most holy Theotokos, where the venerable Feodosij is buried. All the monks saw this as they were coming to matins. So did many pious people in the town, for they had been informed earlier about the translation of the relics of the holy one. They said, "Look! They are bringing the relics of the venerable Feodosij out of the cave." When it was morning and the day broke, it became known throughout the town, and a multitude of people came with candles and incense.

The estimable and renowned Stefan, who was previously mentioned in the Life of the blessed one and who succeeded him as superior but then left the monastery and founded his own monastery at Klov, later by the grace of God became bishop of Volodymyr.[254] At this time he was staying in his monastery, and at night he saw across the field a great light above the cave. Reckoning that they were bringing out the honorable relics of the holy Feodosij—for he had been informed [about this]

---

[252] The text has два мниха ("two monks"), but is clear from the context and the use of dual verbal forms in the following sentences that Nestor had only one companion.
[253] See Discourse 8, p. 71, where a similar portent indicated the site of the stone church.
[254] Cf. Discourse 8, p. 87, and also Discourse 4, n. 41.

earlier, on the previous day—he was extremely grieved that they should translate the relics without him. That very moment he mounted his horse and rode swiftly towards the cave, taking with him Kliment, whom he appointed superior in his place. On their way they saw a great light above the cave, but when they approached it they saw nothing and realized that it was an angelic light. When they came to the entrance of the cave, we were sitting by the holy one's relics. When I had dug through [to them] I sent to the superior and said, "Come, father, let us carry out the relics of the venerable one," and the superior came with two of the brethren. When I had dug deep, they prostrated themselves, and we saw his remains lying there in a manner befitting his sanctity: all his limbs were whole and uncorrupted; his hair had remained dry on his head; the countenance of the venerable one was radiant; his eyes were shut and his virtuous lips closed. We thus placed his honorable and holy relics on a bier and carried them out before the cave.

The next day, by God's will, all the bishops assembled and came to the cave: Efrem of Perejaslav,[255] Stefan of Volodymyr, Ioann of Černihiv,[256] Marin of Jur'ev[257] and Antonij Poroskij;[258] all the superiors came from all the monasteries with many of their monks, and pious people came too. They took the sacred relics of the holy Feodosij from the cave with many candles and with incense; as previously mentioned, people had come from the town to meet the holy one, holding candles in their hands. They carried him into the most holy God-founded church, and the most holy church rejoiced to receive its servant. What a sight was to be seen in the church! The daylight hidden by the light of candles; the bishops touching each other as they kissed the holy one's relics; priests prostrating themselves and kissing them affectionately; monks

---

[255] Cf. Discourse 8, p. 41.
[256] Cf. Discourse 6, p. 16, and n. 56.
[257] Marin is included in Bishop Simon's list of bishops (see Discourse 14, p. 119) but is not mentioned among those present at the consecration of the stone church in 1089.
[258] The geographic designation following Antonij's name does not correspond to any see known to exist in the eleventh century. See H. Gelzer, *Ungedruckte und ungenügend veröffentlichte Texte der Notitiae Episcopatuum* (Munster, 1901), 585; reprint, J. Darrouzès, *Notitiae Episcopatuum Ecclesiae Constantinopolitanae* (Paris, 1981), 367. He might have been Marin's predecessor as a bishop of Jur'ev, since an "Antonij, bishop of Jur'ev," is mentioned as present at the consecration of the stone church in 1089. See Discourse 6, p. 16 and ibid., n. 58. See also Abramovyč, *Pateryk*, 218, n. 81, and Golubinskij, *Istorija russkoj cerkvi*, 1, 1:689. No mention of Jur'ev is made in the account of the consecration of the church (PVL 1089, PSRL 1:208; 2:199), which includes a certain Антонїи Гурьговскыи, while the 1091 entry mentions Маринъ Гуревскыи as one of the bishops present (PSRL 2:203).

running forward and touching the holy one's garments, raising up to God spiritual songs bearing praise and thanksgiving to the holy one! Then they laid him in his own church of the Mother of God, on the right side, on Thursday, August 14, at the first hour of the day, and thus that day solemnly celebrated the festival.[259]

In the year 1108 the superior Feoktist[260] began to urge and entreat the pious prince Svjatopolk[261] that the name of the holy and venerable father Feodosij should be mentioned in the *sinodik*,[262] since this was God's will. Svjatopolk was glad and promised to do this, for he knew about his life, and Svjatopolk began to tell everybody about the life of the venerable Feodosij. The metropolitan[263] did as he requested and ordered Feodosij's name to be inscribed in the *sinodik*, and ordered all the bishops to do this too. All the bishops gladly inscribed the name of our holy and venerable father Feodosij, and he is mentioned in all the services to this day.

A prophecy of the holy one

It would not be right to pass over in silence [what I am about to say], but I shall tell you briefly how a prophecy of our holy father Feodosij was fulfilled. While the great Feodosij was still alive, serving as superior and directing the flock entrusted to him by God, he showed concern not only for his monks but also for people in the world, as regards the salvation of their souls. He showed a special concern for his spiritual sons, and comforted and instructed all those who came to him; sometimes he went to their houses and gave them his blessing.

There was a certain pious magnate, a spiritual son of the holy one, named Jan.[264] One day Feodosij came to visit Jan and his wife Maria in their house. They were both pious people, living in chastity in

---

[259] Cf. the complete account of the translation in PVL 1091, PSRL 1:209–11, 2:200–3.
[260] PVL 1108, PSRL 1:283, 2:259. Feoktist was Ioann's successor; it is not exactly known when he took office.
[261] Svjatopolk II Izjaslavič ruled in Kiev from 1093 to 1113. He is presented unfavorably in the first part of Discourse 31 (see below), but under the influence of the monk Proxor Lobednik seems to have experienced a sincere change of heart, and during the latter part of his reign he was very devoted to the Caves Monastery. See Discourse 31, pp. 173–74.
[262] The *sinodik* (synodikon) was a list of the deceased to whom special honor was to be paid. Most scholars equate Feodosij's inscription in the *sinodik* with canonization.
[263] Nikephoros, who was metropolitan in Kiev from 1104 to 1121.
[264] This may be the Jan who died at age 90 and was buried in the Caves Monastery. See PVL 1106, PSRL 1:281; 2:257.

accordance with [the injunction] of the devout Paul, keeping their marriage pure. The blessed Feodosij loved them because of this, since they lived according to God's laws and dwelt in love for each other. As soon as he came to them he taught them about giving alms to the poor, about the kingdom of heaven which the righteous would receive, while torment would be the fate of the wicked, and about the hour of death. He still spoke about this and many other sacred writings until the relevant words came to him,[265] and he spoke to them about their bodies being laid in their tomb.

The pious woman, Jan's wife, suddenly interrupted the venerable one and said, "Honored father Feodosij, who knows where my body will be laid?" The divinely-inspired Feodosij, filled with the gift of prophecy, said to her, "I tell you truly, wherever my body shall be laid, there you too will be laid to rest, after some time has passed." Eighteen years after the blessed one departed this came to pass. For the venerable Feodosij departed eighteen years before the translation of his body, and when they translated the relics of the holy one, in the same year and month Jan's wife Maria died, on August 16. The monks came and sang the customary hymns, carried her out, and buried her in the church of the holy Theotokos in the Caves Monastery, opposite the tomb of Feodosij, on the left side. The venerable one was laid there on August 14, and this woman on August 16.

Just consider this remarkable man! For this prophecy of the venerable Feodosij did indeed come to pass. He was a good shepherd who faithfully tended his rational sheep, guarding them carefully and meekly, watching over them, and praying for the flock entrusted to him, and for all Orthodox Christians, and for the land of Rus'. Since his departure from this life he prays for the faithful people and for his disciples who, as they gaze on his honorable coffin, recall his teachings and his self-denial and praise God. And I, his sinful and unworthy servant and disciple Nestor, do not know how to praise his good life and self-denial, but I will say these few words: Rejoice, father and teacher, who despised the tumult of the world and loved silence! Rejoice, you who obeyed God in the quietude of the monastic life and brought to yourself every gift of God! Rejoice, father, for you excelled in fasting and hated the lusts of the flesh, and rejected the beauty and desires of the world. Rejoice, for you followed in noble footsteps, emulating the fathers, exalting yourself in silence, adorning yourself with humility, and delighting in the words of

---

[265] дондеже к нему доиде словеси. The syntax of this passage is confusing.

books! Rejoice, for you fortified yourself with the hope of eternal blessings, which you have indeed received! Rejoice, for you mortified the desires of the flesh, unmasked iniquity, and stamped down rebellion, O venerable one! Rejoice, for you fled from the devil's wiles and snares! Rejoice, father, that you have gone to your rest with the righteous, receiving the reward of your labors! Rejoice, for you were the heir of the fathers, following their teaching, their way of life, their self-denial, their devout standing in prayer; and especially emulating the great Theodosios,[266] imitating his habits and manner of life, following his ways, passing from works to better labors and offering the customary prayers to God in a sweet-scented fragrance, bearing the thurible of prayer with its fragrant incense! Rejoice, for you conquered the desires of the flesh and the ruler of the world and prince of this age! Rejoice, for you set aright your enemy the devil and overcame his wiles, opposing his arrows and standing against him with unflinching purpose! Rejoice, for you fortified yourself with the armor of the Cross, with invincible faith, and with the help of God! Therefore, honorable shepherd of Christ's flock, O wise Feodosij, pray for us, and for me, your servant Nestor, that we may be delivered from the snares of the devil, and protect us by your prayers from our enemy and foe, through Jesus Christ our Lord, to Whom be glory, honor, and reverence together with his eternal Father and His most holy, blessed and life-giving Spirit, now and forever. Amen.

Discourse 10. The decoration of our venerable father Feodosij's coffin.[267]

After some time Georgij, the son of Simon and grandson of Afrikan,[268] wished to decorate the coffin of our venerable father Feodosij, which he did. He sent one of his boyars named Vasilij from the town of Suzdal'[269] to the Caves Monastery in the God-named city of Kiev to plate the coffin of the venerable Feodosij. Georgij gave him 500 *grivna* of silver and 50 *grivna* of gold to plate the venerable one's coffin. Having received this, Vasilij set out unwillingly on his journey, cursing his life and the day he was born, saying to himself, "What gave the

---

[266] A reference to Theodosios the Cenobiarch (d. 529), one of the founders of cenobitic monasticism in Palestine.
[267] This took place in 1129 or 1130. See PRSL 2:293.
[268] See Discourse 1, p. 1.
[269] Suzdal' was one of the regions controlled by the descendants of Vsevolod Jaroslavič (father of Volodimer Monomax), to whose household Georgij's father was originally attached.

prince[270] the idea to waste so much money? What reward will he get for decorating the tomb of a dead man? Just as this wealth was gained for nothing, so it has been thrown away for nothing. Woe is me, since I alone dare not disobey my lord! Why have I left my home? For whose sake am I making this unpleasant journey? By whom shall I be honored? I have not been sent to the prince or any other magnate. What shall I say, what words shall I utter to that stone tomb, and who will give me an answer?'' This and many other similar remarks he spoke to those who were with him.

The holy one appeared to him in a dream, saying meekly, "My son, I wanted to give you the reward of your labors, but if you do not repent you will suffer many troubles." But Vasilij did not cease grumbling, and the Lord inflicted much misfortune on him because of his sins: all his horses died; their clothes were stolen;[271] and the thieves took everything except the treasure-chest which had been sent with their baggage. Vasilij opened the treasure-chest which had been sent for decorating the holy one's coffin, took from it a fifth part of the gold and silver, and spent this on his own needs, and to buy horses; he did not realize that God was angry because of his blasphemy. When he came to Černihiv, he fell from his horse and injured himself so badly that he could not even move his arm. Those who were with him put him on a boat and took him to the outskirts of Kiev; it was then evening.

That night the holy one appeared to him saying, "Vasilij, did you not hear the Lord saying, 'Make to yourselves friends of the mammon of unrighteousness; that, when ye fail, they may receive you into everlasting habitations?'[272] My son Georgij pondered well the Lord's saying: 'He that receiveth a righteous man in the name of a righteous man shall receive a righteous man's reward.'[273] You were about to receive a crown for your labors, since no one has received such glory as you would share with him, but now you are stripped of everything. Yet do not despair of your life. There is no other way for you to be cured except by repenting this sin. Give orders that you are to be carried to the Caves Monastery, to the church of holy Theotokos, and placed on my coffin. You will

---

[270] If the boyar Vasilij is referring here to was Georgij Simonovič, he apparently had the title of prince, although he was not a member of the Rurikid dynasty. The word may have been used inaccurately; the Cas. I text has the word старѣишина (Abramovyč, *Pateryk*, 84, n. 18), which in this context could mean "master."

[271] I have used the reading from the Cas. I text here: Abramovyč, *Pateryk*, 84, n. 21.

[272] Luke 16:9.

[273] Matt. 10:41.

recover and find untouched the gold and silver which you have spent." This was revealed to Vasilij that night, but not in a dream; it was in the evening that the venerable Feodosij appeared to him.

The next day Prince Jurij Volodimerovič[274] came [to see] him with all his boyars and saw that he was seriously injured; very grieved on this account, he departed. But Vasilij had faith in his vision of the holy one and gave orders to be taken to the Caves Monastery. While he was on the river bank a stranger went to the superior and said, "Go quickly to the river bank, bring Vasilij here, and place him on the tomb of the venerable Feodosij. He will give you a treasure-chest. Charge him in front of everybody with having taken a fifth of it. If he repents, give it back to him." Having said this, he disappeared. The superior[275] looked for the man who had appeared to him, but no one had seen him enter or leave. He went to the Dneiper, took Vasilij up the hill, and placed him on the holy one's coffin. Vasilij stood up, his entire body whole and well, and gave the superior 400 *grivna* of silver and 40 *grivna* of gold. "My son, where is the remaining 100 *grivna* of silver and 10 *grivna* of gold?" said the superior. Vasilij then began to repent and said, "I took it and spent it. Give me a little time, father, and I shall return it all to you. I wanted to hide my theft and not reveal it; I thought I could conceal it from God, Who sees everything." Then he shook out the money from the vessel in which it had been sealed, counted it in front of everybody, and found it complete: 500 *grivna* of silver and 50 *grivna* of gold; and they all glorified God and the holy Feodosij. Then Vasilij began to tell them everything in due order about his vision and the holy one's deed.

The next day the prince came to the aforementioned place, bringing his physicians with him to cure Vasilij, but did not find him. When he learned that he had been taken to the Caves Monastery he thought that he had already died. He rode quickly to the monastery and found him well, as though nothing had ever ailed him. And when the prince heard from him about these wonderful miracles, he was awestruck and filled with spiritual joy, and he came and prostrated himself before the miracle-working tomb of the great Feodosij; then he departed.

When the chiliarch Georgij Simonovič heard about this, his devotion to the holy Theotokos and the holy Feodosij increased, and in

---

[274] The younger son of Volodimer Monomax and brother of the reigning Kievan prince, M'stislav Volodimerovič. He is often referred to as Jurij Dolgorukij ("Long-Arm").

[275] If the decoration of the coffin took place in 1130, the superior would have been Timofej. See PSRL 2:293.

addition to his many gifts he gave a *grivna* containing the weight of a 100 *grivna* of gold, and wrote the following letter:

"I, Georgij, the son of Simon, the servant of our most holy Lady, the Theotokos, and of the holy Feodosij, who received a blessing from his most holy hand, once suffered for three years from a disease in my eyes and could not see the rays of the sun. By his word I was healed, for I heard from his lips, 'See!' and I saw. So I write this letter to the last of my family, lest any of them be separated from the house of the most holy Lady, the Theotokos, and from the venerable Antonij and Feodosij. Even if any of them should come to the last stages of poverty and cannot make any gifts, at least let them be buried in the villages of this church, since the prayers of Antonij and Feodosij give protection everywhere. For once, when we advanced against Izjaslav M'stislavič with the Cumans,[276] we saw a high town[277] in the distance. We at once marched against it, although no one knew which town it was. The Cumans were fighting beside it, and many were wounded and fled from the town. Later we learned that it was a village belonging to the Caves Monastery of the holy Theotokos. There had never been a town there, nor did the people in the village understand what had happened. But when they came out the next morning they saw the bloodshed and marveled at what had taken place.

"So I write to you: all your names are inscribed in the prayer of the holy Feodosij, who promised my father Simon that he would pray for us, just as [he prays] for his monks.[278] My father told me to place this prayer in his hands when he was about to be laid in his tomb, since he had set his hopes on the holy one's promise. My father once appeared plainly to one of the God-bearing fathers and said, 'Tell my son Georgij that I have received all blessings through the holy one's prayers. Do you

---

[276] Abramovyč, *Pateryk*, 218, n. 87, identifies this as the campaign fought in 1149 by Jurij Volodimerovič of Suzdal', aided by Cuman auxiliaries, in which he temporarily ousted from Kiev his nephew Izjaslav M'stislavič, who had established himself there in 1146. See PSRL 1:320–22, 2:372–94. But this implies (i) that Georgij Simonovič was still able to take part in a campaign in 1149, although by that time he must have been quite old, and (ii) that he did not write the letter until twenty or more years after he commissioned the decoration of the tomb. Perhaps the letter in its extant form was written by a son or perhaps even a grandson of the Georgij Simonovič who sent the boyar Vasilij to Kiev, probably on the basis of a letter written by him shortly after 1130. In any case, the family clearly preserved a tradition of being under the special protection of Feodosij and the Caves Monastery. Cf. Pritsak, *The Origin of Rus'*, 1:420–21.

[277] The word градъ signifies a fortified enclosure, not necessarily a full-fledged town.

[278] See Discourse 1, p. 4.

too, my son, strive to follow me in good works.' And whosoever does not want the prayer and the blessing of our holy father Feodosij and inclines away from him, he loves a curse, and may it come upon him."

For this reason his great-grandsons[279] have an affection for St. Demetrios[280] and have their own place there. If any one of them should reject it, they will be under the curse of their fathers and ancestors, because of their own free will they rejected the prayers of the holy one and the blessings and promise of our venerable father Feodosij.

Discourse 11. An encomium to our venerable father Feodosij, superior of the Caves Monastery in the divinely-protected city of Kiev.

When the righteous are praised, the people will rejoice.[281] For it is a day of joy and gladness when a righteous and venerable man reaches the end of his life; when he sees rest from his labors; when he abandons sorrow and enters into joy; when he leaves behind the earth and all earthly things and goes forth into heaven; and when he leaves mankind, joins the company of angels, and is deemed worthy to behold God. It is on this day that our teacher, guide, and pastor departed to eternal life—our father Feodosij, great among the fathers, a bright light, a steadfast warrior and miracle-worker in the land of Rus'.[282] Where, indeed, is there greater joy than this, that we have been vouchsafed to behold the departure to the Lord of our father and teacher, who received a crown of incorruption and serves forever by the throne of the Lord, emboldened to pray to Him for us? For not only the son but also the servants rejoice when they see their lord serving an earthly prince after many labors and victories over the prince's enemies. So we, the sons and servants of our master, rejoice and celebrate, praising his achievements and his victory over unclean spirits; he has received great honor from the Lord

---

[279] This reference to Georgij's great-grandsons indicates that the final passage was a later addition, even if the extant form of the letter was not composed until after 1149.

[280] This reference to St. Demetrios may indicate a church in Suzdal' which had some connection with the Caves Monastery. Such a church might have been founded by the former Caves monk Efrem after he became bishop of Perejaslav, since a passage in the 1089 PVL entry describes Efrem as an energetic builder (PSRL 1:208–9, 2:200). The buildings described there, including a stone bathhouse as well as churches, are all in Perejaslav, but Efrem probably visited Suzdal', since politically it was part of the Perejaslav area. See Abramovyč, *Pateryk*, 218, n. 88.

[281] Prov. 29:2.

[282] This encomium was composed some centuries after Feodosij's death on May 3, 1074.

Almighty, and by his intercession has obtained everlasting life for many people.

Who can worthily praise and magnify this earthly angel and heavenly man? We saw the light of faith through our apostle, Prince Volodimer, sent by God, as a people sitting far off in darkness and shadow; he, having come to the knowledge of God through holy baptism, showed Him to us alone, removing the veil of darkness from our souls, so that we were illuminated by the light of the divine Trinity. And there is another way, which Christ showed to his disciples, saying: "Everyone that hath forsaken father and mother, towns and villages, shall receive a hundredfold here and in the world to come and the heavenly kingdom."[283] From whom did we learn about this way and about the light yoke of Jesus? Who showed us how to take up the Cross and follow Christ? Who but our venerable father Feodosij? There were those before him who left this world and walked along the narrow way, but it was he who gave form and structure to all the monasteries of Rus'.[284] No one before him manifested a life of perfect mortification, for he and his teacher Antonij fulfilled the word of the Lord: "Except a corn of wheat falleth into the ground and die, it abideth alone: but if it die, it bringeth forth much fruit."[285] Having died to the whole world, he lived in Christ, and brought forth much fruit, which he generated through the Spirit and nurtured with virtue and righteousness, increasing the talent given to him by God. And [now] he hears the Lord's saying, "Good and faithful servant, thou hast been faithful over a few things; I will make thee ruler over many things."[286] It was of him that Christ said, "Many that are last shall be first, and the first [shall be] last."[287] This man, though born in a recent generation, yet surpassed in steadfastness and in the love of God which shone forth in him many who had lived before him.

During his earliest years he spurned earthly things and occupied his mind with those of heaven, even as a young boy. From his mother's womb he was an unsullied vessel of the Holy Spirit. He did not love the glory of this world, but of his own free will accepted poverty and imitated his Lord in all things. He gave no thought to the good things that pass away and desired only the time when age would come and he would

---

[283] Matt. 19:29; Mark 10:30; Luke 18:30.
[284] A reference to Feodosij's introduction of the Stoudite Rule. See Discourse 8, pp. 44–45.
[285] John 12:24.
[286] Matt. 25:21; Luke 19:17.
[287] Matt. 19:30; Mark 10:31; Luke 13:30.

appear before the face of God and converse in prayer with Him alone. He received many cruel wounds from his mother; by this means our wicked enemy wished to turn the holy child away from his holy purpose, since that accursed deceiver saw that he would be vanquished by him, and therefore he visited many troubles on him. But the grace of God beheld him there where it shines forth like the sun in the vaults of heaven, illuminating the whole world with its rays. He accepted what was done to him and was not deprived of the power of vision, but as the days passed he ascended to better things, forgetting those things which are behind and reaching forth into those things which are before, according to the words of the Apostle.[288] He was tested in obedience by his mother, but all the more conducted himself according to God's commands, for he understood, through the wisdom of the Holy Spirit, that concern for worldly things is a stumbling-block to a man anxious to fulfill divine commandments. Casting all else aside, he surrendered himself to the Lord,[289] thinking that it was better to cause his mother pain for a short time, until God should grant her wisdom to separate herself from the vanities of the world, than that she should be deprived of the Lord's kingdom.

He came to the city of Kiev and sought a leader and guide who would show him the true way of God. He sought for a long time, and he found one, for the Lord does not deprive those who desire profitable things. He found a remarkable man, far advanced in wisdom and understanding and possessing the gift of prophecy, named Antonij. The blessed Feodosij came to him, young in years but old in wisdom, zealously carried out all the orders of his teacher, and held fast to his commands. He was, in the words of Job, "the eye of the blind and the foot of the lame."[290] He kept continually in his heart the Apostle's words: "Bear ye one another's burdens, and so fulfill the law of Christ."[291] This blessed man bore the burden not only of one or two, but he took upon himself the tasks of all the brethren and through his own efforts lightened the burden of them all, and many of them obtained rest through his labors. With the help of God, who gave him physical strength, he acted thus every day: he was never absent from the congregation in the church, never broke the rule of the cell, and diligently

---

[288] Phil. 3:13.
[289] I have used the Arsenian reading here: Abramovyč, *Pateryk*, 88, n. 21.
[290] Job 29:15.
[291] Gal. 6:2.

observed those things contained in the rule of the fathers,[292] which he wrote down for those who came seeking good works and blessed obedience.

Therefore the Lord exalted him: he was appointed pastor, father, and teacher over those for whom he had labored as the last and least worthy of them all, considering himself the servant of all. For when the superior Varlaam was removed by the prince and installed elsewhere, Feodosij could not disobey his teacher Antonij, though it was much against his will; he recognized that it was God's decision [that he should become a superior] and reluctantly undertook the task, addressing himself to even greater spiritual efforts. He thought to himself, "Even if I have taken much thought for bodily needs, it is still better to apply myself steadfastly to those of the spirit." The holy Feodosij would say to himself, "Pile labors upon labors, achievement upon achievement. Otherwise how will you appear to your Lord if you have not nurtured his flock well? Or how can you say, 'Behold I and the children which Thou hast given me, my God.'"[293] Therefore he remained whole nights without sleep, sometimes standing in prayer, sometimes walking round the cells and rousing the brethren to prayer. When he held a position of seniority he did not abandon his good habits: sometimes he carried water, sometimes he chopped wood, and thus by his own action set an example to the brotherhood.

When the Great Fast drew near, then Feodosij, Christ's valiant soldier, spurned all earthly things and separated himself from the community of men; he would leave the brethren, shut himself alone in a cave, and remain there throughout the forty days, conversing in prayer with God alone. Who shall relate his pains and efforts, his sobs and tears, his rigorous fasting, his struggle with evil spirits? And when the glorious day of the Resurrection of our Lord Jesus Christ approached, the venerable one would come forth like Moses from Mount Sinai, his spirit more radiant than the countenance of Moses; throughout his life he never transgressed this rule.

Then it was vouchsafed to him by a divine revelation to know the day of his departure from this world to everlasting life. When he was ordered to pass on, he did not hide from his friends and disciples that he was going to God, and promised to pray to Him for the house of the most

---

[292] уставу отечьскому, presumably referring generally to teachings found in the writings of the Desert Fathers, particularly in the *Book of Holy Men*. These did not of course constitute a formal rule.

[293] Cf. Isa. 8:18.

holy Mother of God and for the flock of his children, even until the coming of our Lord God. As he promised, so he acted. Inasmuch as he was deemed worthy to receive great gifts from God, in such measure will he bestow the Lord's grace on us at every time and season coming and visiting us, protecting and preserving us, and guarding his flock from the enemies of our souls. For who has ever sought things profitable for the salvation of his soul at the holy one's coffin and not received them? Who, having sinned, has not found hope? Who, having called upon his holy name with faith, has not found deliverance and healing for the wounds of his soul and the sickness of his body? He is our apostle and preacher, our shepherd and teacher, our ruler and guide, our strong wall and defense, our great glory and our intercessor before God.

Today, brethren, it is fitting that we should rejoice and be filled with spiritual gladness, that we should put on fine apparel and make a joyful celebration, since we have always before our eyes our venerable father Feodosij's coffin, in which on this day his holy and much-suffering body was laid and which sends forth rays of miracles to all corners of the land of Rus'. This coffin has received a treasure which cannot be stolen, a vessel of the Holy Spirit, a divine instrument—the noble body of our father and teacher. As we look at this, it is as though we gaze upon his very self. For although the holy one has been laid in his tomb, yet in spirit he is always with us and can see [us]. If we live according to his precepts and observe his commandments, he rejoices, draws near to us with loving-kindness, and guards and preserves us as his beloved children. But if we cease to work for our salvation and do not observe his injunctions, we deprive ourselves of his help. O holy father Feodosij, who have yourself made good our failings by your virtues, without your help we are unable to accomplish any good thing. But on the day of your passing we call upon you, having formed from ourselves a choir filled with love.

Rejoice, light of the Rus' land, for like the morning star which appears in the west and shines forth in the east[294] you illuminate the whole of our land! Rejoice, you who have prescribed and given us an example of the true way, our guide, director, and teacher of the monastic life! Rejoice, O leader and warrior, helper and assistant to all those who desire to be saved! Rejoice, you who increased the flock of rational sheep in the house of the Mother of God; there was none like you in our land before your time nor after it! Rejoice, you who planted Christ's

---

[294] So the text says, but it would be more logical for the morning star to appear in the east.

vineyard, so that its shoots have spread to the sea and its branches to the rivers, for no country or place is without the vines of your vineyard! Rejoice, you who received God's revelation and founded the house of the most holy Mother of God, which you built and adorned with all greatness and brought as a gift for the Theotokos! Rejoice, you who increased the talent of your Lord; having received ten talents, you furnished Him with a thousand! Rejoice, for you filled the meadows of Christ's vineyard with rational sheep in great abundance; and the sheep of other lands, having tasted the nourishment there, shut themselves up with your faithful children! Rejoice, sweet spring of water, from which the monastic hosts have drunk deep and received divine refreshment, and then traversed without difficulty the straight way and settled where the mighty waters flow forth! Rejoice, O pastor and teacher, who preserved the flock from the crafty wolf whole and undefiled and brought it to Christ, our leader and shepherd. Rejoice, O pillar of fire, brighter than that which shone in the time of Moses![295] For that pillar gave forth a physical light, whereas you spiritually illumined the new Israel, led it through the desert of the temptation of this life of vanity, struck terror into the cunning Amalek[296] with your spiritual rays, and lead [your children] into the promised lands, or rather the meadows of paradise, where your disciples sing your praise. Rejoice, earthly angel and heavenly man, servant and laborer of the most holy Mother of God! For she found no other to establish her house except you, whom she loved and promised to visit with the favor of her gifts; and so it was.

Rejoice, O father Feodosij, our glory and splendor! Your *lavra* glories in you, and its name is renowned to the ends of the earth. All lands marvel at the fathers who formerly dwelt there, that they shone forth like stars in the vault of heaven,[297] revealing themselves as men who carry out God's commands, miracle-workers, men deemed worthy to receive from God prophetic powers, and from the Holy Spirit the gift of discernment, teachers of the word of God. Emperors hastened to them, princes bowed down before them, magnates submitted to them, powerful men trembled, and people from other lands were filled with awe as they beheld these heavenly men walking about the earth, gathering together in the house of the Mother of God as though before the

---

[295] Cf. Exod. 13:21.
[296] See Exod. 17:8–14. The Israelites were attacked by Amalek and his troops on their journey out of Egypt, and as long as Moses held up his hands to heaven they were victorious.
[297] I follow the reading of all the other MSS: Abramovyč, *Pateryk*, 91, n. 16.

Lord's throne, ceaselessly singing angelic songs, and together with the angels drawing near to the Lord's altar. Some had angelic visions, others conversed with angels in mind and spirit and knew in their souls when the divine angels were about to draw near, and still others visibly drove out evil spirits, striking terror into them. Such are the shoots of your vineyard; such are the branches of your root; such are the pillars of your dwelling; such are the children you brought forth; such are the fathers of your *lavra*. It was fitting, father, that such disciples should come from such a teacher, for a stream of the Holy Spirit did indeed flow forth from your mouth, the river of which Christ Himself, the Son of God, spoke when He taught the Jews, "He that believeth on me, out of his belly shall flow rivers of living water."[298] This He said of the Spirit which those who believed in Him should receive. This same river, as it stops somewhere along its course, continually gives its children [water] to drink to the end of time. The apostles, having released this river, brought all nations to God; the martyrs, having drunk of this river, took no thought for their bodies, but surrendered them to all kinds of wounds and torments; the fathers, having drunk of this river, left towns and villages, homes and riches, and dwelt in mountains, dens, and caves in the earth; your disciples, having drunk of this river, despised earthly things and thought only of heaven, and having received those things which they desired, they moved into the divine world, the dwelling place of incorporeal choirs.

Following in their footsteps we sought refuge in the house of the Mother of God and in your hope and your defense; we placed all our trust in the most pure Virgin Theotokos and in you, most blessed father Feodosij. Even if we have not succeeded in traveling along the way of your earlier disciples, yet we remember those words spoken by thy holy lips: "Whoever ends his life in the house of the most holy Mother of God, and in my hope, even if he has not attained to great ascetic achievements, I shall complete his work and pray to God for him and his fellow laborers."[299] Hoping in this, therefore, we call upon you in prayer. You know, venerable one, even though we keep silent, that in our time we have forsaken the vanities of this world, we have raised ourselves up a little, we have accepted Christ's yoke and sought refuge in the house of our most holy Lady, the Theotokos, and in your holy habitation. Do not hand us over to the enemies of our souls, for they have armed themselves against us; each hour they hold us captive and pierce our hearts with

---

[298] John 7:38.
[299] See Discourse 8, p. 83.

divers evil designs, leading us away from the understanding of God, forcing us to love transient and corporeal things, and finally plunging us into the depths of sin. But we turn to you, our helmsman: direct us to a quiet haven, still the tempest in our minds, and pray for us to the Lord of all, that He may grant us to do as He commands, in speech and writing, in thought and deed. If we have turned aside from the way of the Lord's commandments and through our sloth failed to observe the rule which you committed to us, for the sake of our one faith in the most holy Virgin and in [our love] for you, O holy father Feodosij [we pray] that she will number us among the company of your children, who walk undefiled in paths of righteousness, and not separate us from the light of your radiant countenance when she takes us away from here.

While we are still in this life, we pray that you will visit us and preserve us from all diabolic snares and from deeds which lead us away from God, grant us by your prayer a pure and godly life, raise up our minds which through sloth have fallen down to the ground, and grant us courage, a guard within, and the remission of our former sins. Even if slackness has taken possession of our minds, yet if we remain in your *lavra*, with you as our helper, always at our side, we hope through your prayer to appear before God free and unvanquished by enemies visible and invisible. For you yourself said to your disciples when the command came from God to leave this world, "Let it be clear to you, my children, that if after my departure to God this place increases in numbers and the monks have an abundance of all things they need, you must understand from this that I can approach God boldly and that He accepts my prayer."[300] And we, venerable father, know clearly that because of your angelic life and passion-suffering asceticism you boldly approached Almighty God before your departure. How much the more, then, after your departure! You made it clear by prophecy that this house of the most holy Theotokos, your holy *lavra*, would grow and increase in greatness and glory, and you declared that you would pray continually for your holy dwelling. Indeed this true and sincere promise has been fulfilled, for since your passing no one has conquered or destroyed your house, but year after year it has flowered and come to surpass all others.

When our sins increased, when our iniquities could go no further, when our wickedness angered God—then, for our sins, God permitted our religious houses to be destroyed, our monasteries to be reduced to ruins, our towns to be captured, and our villages to be desolated by an

---

[300] See Discourse 8, p. 83.

unknown people, a people without mercy or shame,[301] a people having neither the fear of God nor possessing bowels of human compassion. We still live in bondage under them, in grievous affliction and bitter suffering.[302] Thus we prostrate ourselves before thee and pray to you:

"Lift up thy hands for us to our Lady, the Virgin and most holy Theotokos, that she may remember her ancient mercy towards this house, which was given to her as a worthy offering; that she may lighten the burden of our bitter grief and banish our crafty foes and those who blaspheme our Orthodox faith;[303] that she will make impregnable her holy church, which she willed to raise up as a dwelling-place for herself; and that she may increase the flock of thy habitation, and visit it, as in former times, guarding and strengthening it, preserving and keeping it from enemies visible and invisible, so that we may be free in soul and in body, that in this transitory life we may live in a manner pleasing to God and like the fathers of old acknowledge no ruler but the most pure Theotokos and you, venerable Feodosij."

Knowing your gentleness of heart, I have ventured to open my lips to praise you, not because I can extol you as you deserve, but because I hope, father, to obtain some benefit from you, some lessening of my sins and [my inclination] toward other unbecoming observations and exercises. For the heavenly powers have glorified you; the apostles have accepted you; the prophets have received you as one of their own; the martyrs have embraced you; the hierarchs rejoice together with you; the host of monks came to meet you; the most pure Empress herself, the Lord's Mother, has exalted you. She raised you up, making you known to all ends of the earth, you faithful servant of the Lord. How can I worthily praise you, since my lips are vile and my tongue unclean? But since I have nothing to bring you on the day of your passing [I offer] this paltry eulogy, like a small and stinking stream which has poured itself into the wideness of the sea, not to fill the sea, but to be cleansed from its foulness. Therefore, holy father, venerable Feodosij, do not be angry with me, sinner that I am, but pray for me, your servant, that our Lord

---

[301] I follow the Arsenian reading here: Abramovyč, *Pateryk*, 93, n. 21.
[302] These words apparently refer to the conquest of Rus' by the Mongols and indicate that the eulogy was composed while Kiev and the surrounding area were still under the "Tatar yoke," i.e., probably sometime during the fourteenth century, since by the end of that century Kiev was no longer under Mongol rule, but had become part of the Grand Duchy of Lithuania.
[303] This could refer to the Mongols, who had accepted Islam in the fourteenth century, or the "Latins" of nearby Poland. Even after the conversion of their ruler Jogaila (Jagiełło) to Catholicism in 1386, the Lithuanians were tolerant of Orthodoxy.

Jesus Christ may not judge me on the day of His coming, to Whom be glory with His eternal Father and the most holy, blessed, and life-giving Spirit now and forever.

> *Discourse 12. The first holy and blessed monks of the Caves Monastery, who shone forth in godly virtues in the house of the most pure Mother of God, in the holy Caves Monastery, in fasting, vigil, and the gift of prophecy.*[304]

A most remarkable miracle was in truth to be seen, brethren, in that the Lord gathered together such monks as these in the dwelling of His Mother. They shone in the land of Rus' like bright lights, some in fasting, others in vigils, yet others in making prostrations. Some fasted throughout the day or for two days; some ate bread and water; others ate cooked vegetables, and yet others ate raw food. They all dwelt together in love: the younger ones submitted to their seniors and did not venture to speak in front of them but did everything with great obedience and meekness; likewise the seniors showed love towards the younger ones, instructing them and comforting them like their beloved children. If any brother fell into some transgression, they comforted him, and out of their great love three or four would share the penance of this one man. Such was the divine love, self-denial, and meekness in that holy brotherhood. And if a brother left the monastery, all the brethren would be sad on his account and would send after him, calling him to come back to the monastery. And when that brother did return they would go to the superior and prostrate themselves on his behalf and beg the superior [to take him back]; for their part, they joyfully received the brother back into the monastery.

Such were the monks at that time, fasters, and ascetics. I will now mention some of these remarkable men. First there was a presbyter named Damian. He fasted to such an extent that until the day of his death he ate nothing but bread and water. And whenever anyone brought in a child with some illness, people would bring the child to the monastery to the venerable Feodosij, who would order Damian to say a

---

[304] This title is misleading, since the monks mentioned here were active in the monastery in the second half of the eleventh century and thus were not the earliest disciples of Antonij, the founder of the monastery. See Heppell, "The *Vita Antonii*," 56. The title is omitted in the Arsenian redaction, and considerably shorter in Cas. 1: *Pateryk*, Abramovyč, 94, n. 10.

prayer over the sick person. He at once would do so and anoint him with holy oil, and those who came to him were healed.

Once when the blessed Damian had fallen ill and was on the verge of death, lying helpless, an angel came to him in the form of Feodosij and promised him the kingdom of heaven as a reward for his labors. Afterwards the great Feodosij came to him with the brethren and sat beside him; he was still very weak. He looked to the superior and said, "Father, do not forget what you promised me tonight." The great Feodosij realized that he had seen a vision and said to him, "Brother Damian, what I promised you will come to pass." Damian then closed his eyes and gave up his soul into the hands of God. The superior and all the brethren buried his body with due solemnity.[305]

There was another brother, called Ieremej, who remembered the baptism of the land of Rus'.[306] He had received from God the gift of seeing what would come to pass. If he saw anyone lost in deep thought, he would reproach him privately and instruct him to be on his guard against the devil. If any brother was thinking of leaving the monastery, he would go to him, reprove his intentions, and comfort him. If he said anything to anyone, good or bad, the words of the elder were fulfilled.

There was another elder named Matfej, who had the gift of discernment.[307] Once when he was standing in his place in the church he raised his eyes, looked around among the brethren who were standing and singing on both sides, and he saw a demon walking around, in the form of a Pole[308] and carrying in his robe some flowers called *lepki*. He would take a flower from the fold [of his garment] and throw it at somebody. If the flower stuck to one of the brethren who was standing there, the brother would remain standing for a while, but then his will would weaken and he would make up some excuse, leave the church, go to sleep, and not return to the service. But if he threw it at another monk standing there and the flower did not stick to him, that brother would stand firm during the singing until matins were over; then each would go to his own cell.

---

[305] Cf. Discourse 8, pp. 57–58. Nestor does not mention Damian's gift of healing.
[306] I.e., the baptism of Volodimer in 988.
[307] Literally, "he was прозорливъ" (διορατικός), i.e., he had the power to "see into the mind and soul of another person," as distinct from prophecy, the gift of predicting future events.
[308] This image may reflect the unpopularity of Prince Izjaslav's reliance on Polish troops to help him regain the Kievan throne. See PVL 1069, PSRL 1:173, PSRL 2:162.

This elder had the following habit: after matins had been sung and the brethren were dispersing to their cells, this blessed elder would leave the church last of all. Once when he was on his way [to his cell] he sat down under the board[309] to rest, since his cell was a long way from the church, and he saw what looked like a large crowd coming out of the gates. He looked up and saw a demon sitting on a pig and swanking, and many others running around him. "Where are you going?" the elder said to them. "For Mixail Tobol'kovič," said the demon sitting on the pig. The elder made the sign of the cross and went to his cell. When the day dawned the elder realized the meaning of his vision and said to his disciple, "Go and ask whether Mixail is in his cell." And his disciple said, "He's not there now; he went outside the monastery's enclosure after matins." The elder related his vision to the superior and the senior brethren, and the superior summoned that brother and strengthened him.[310]

During the lifetime of the venerable Matfej, the blessed superior Feodosij passed away and Stefan became superior in his place, and Nikon after him, and this elder was still alive.[311] He saw many other visions, and departed to the Lord in peace in the holy Caves Monastery.[312]

Discourse 13. The blessed Nifont, formerly bishop of Novgorod: how he saw the holy Feodosij in a divine revelation in the Caves Monastery.

The blessed Nifont had been a monk in the Caves Monastery, emulating the holy fathers in the manner of his life, and as a reward for his many virtues he was appointed bishop of Novgorod.[313] He had great

---

[309] The клепало was the board used to sound the call to prayer.
[310] This sentence is omitted in some MSS: Abramovyč, *Pateryk*, 96, n. 61.
[311] Although it is not explicitly stated that Matfej, like Ieremej, remembered the conversion of Rus', it appears that he lived to advanced old age.
[312] A similar account of these "first monks" forms part of the PVL 1074 entry, PSRL 1:188–91, 2:179–82. There are some differences, notably a malicious anecdote about Nikon, which appears in the chronicle but not in the *Paterik*: Matfej looked up in church to where the superior usually sat and saw an ass sitting there, from which he deduced that the superior had not yet arisen (PSRL 1:191, 2:182).
[313] Nifont was not the first monk of the Caves Monastery to be bishop of Novgorod. He had at least one predecessor, Nikita the Solitary, who became bishop of Novgorod in the late eleventh or early twelfth century. See Discourse 25, p. 146. Bishop Simon also mentions a bishop of Novgorod named German. See Discourse 14, pp. 118–19. As Nifont died in 1156, he cannot have been the immediate successor of Nikita.

faith in and love for the most holy Theotokos and for Antonij and Feodosij, the venerable fathers of the Caves Monastery. As soon as he heard that the metropolitan Constantine was coming to Rus', sent by the ecumenical patriarch, he was filled with spiritual joy. He thought to himself that he could accomplish two things simultaneously: he could stay in the house of the most pure [Theotokos] and venerate the venerable ones, and receive a blessing from the metropolitan. He therefore came to Kiev in the year 1156. While he was staying there, awaiting the metropolitan's arrival—for he had been told that the metropolitan was coming from Constantinople—Metropolitan Klim accepted the metropolitan's throne without the blessing of the patriarch of Constantinople.[314] Klim urged the blessed bishop Nifont to celebrate the liturgy with him, but Nifont said, "Because you have not received a blessing from the holy ecumenical patriarch of Constantinople I do not wish to serve with you nor recall your name in the holy liturgy. But I will recall the name of the holy patriarch of Constantinople." Klim was very insistent and set against him Prince Izjaslav[315] and his own supporters, but was unable to do him any harm. The patriarch of Constantinople heard about Nifont and sent him a letter,[316] blessing him for his depth of understanding and his steadfastness, and adding his name to those of saints of former times who had stood firm for Orthodoxy. Nifont read the patriarch's letter, and his attitude became even more firm and resolute. He was on affectionate terms with Prince Svjatoslav Ol'govič, for Svjatoslav had previously resided in Novgorod.[317]

While the blessed bishop Nifont was staying in the holy Caves Monastery, filled with great faith in the venerable ones, as has been mentioned, after a short time he fell ill, and related a remarkable vision. "Three days before my illness," he said, "as I was coming from matins

---

[314] For a discussion of the circumstances of Klim's appointment and the subsequent division of opinion among the Rus' bishops, see Obolensky, "Byzantium, Kiev and Moscow," 64–67.

[315] Izjaslav M'stislavič of Kiev. See Discourse 10, n. 276. Although Izjaslav was driven out of Kiev by Jurij of Suzdal' in 1149 and again in 1151, he was able to recover his position on both occasions.

[316] See Grumel, *Regestes*, 1, fasc. 3, no. 1027, pp. 98–99. For the text of the letter (the Greek original has been lost), see Makarij, *Istorija russkoj cerkvi*, 3rd ed., vol. 3 (St. Petersburg, 1888), Appendix 1, 297. For an English translation, see below, Appendix II.

[317] Svjatoslav Ol'govič belonged to the Černihiv branch of the Rurikid dynasty, descended from Prince Svjatoslav Jaroslavič. According to Baumgarten, *Généalogies*, Table IV, no. 15, Svjatoslav's second wife was Catherine, daughter of the *posadnik* (chief magistrate) of Novgorod, whom he married in 1136.

I rested for a little while and immediately fell into a light sleep. And behold! I found myself in Svjatoša's place[318] in the church of the Caves Monastery, earnestly and tearfully praying to the most holy Theotokos that I might see the holy venerable father Feodosij. Many of the brethren were assembling in the church, and one of them came up to me and said to me, 'Do you want to see our holy father Feodosij?' I answered, 'Yes, very much. If you can, show him to me.' He took me and led me to the altar and there showed me the holy father Feodosij. I saw the venerable one, ran up to him joyfully, fell down at his feet, and prostrated myself before him to the ground. He lifted me up, blessed me, embraced me, kissed me affectionately, and said, 'Welcome, my brother and son Nifont. From now on we shall never be parted.' The venerable one held a scroll in his hand. I asked him to give it to me, and I unrolled and read it. At the beginning were written the following words: 'Behold I and the children which God has given to me.'[319] After this I awoke, and now I know that this illness is a visitation from God.''

Nifont was ill for thirteen days, and reposed in peace on April 8, in Holy Week.[320] He was buried with due solemnity in Feodosij's cave, and [so] came to his beloved, as the venerable Feodosij had promised him. They stand together before the Mother of Christ, delighting in the indescribable beauties of heaven and praying for us their children. Such were the remarkable men in the holy Caves Monastery; many of them shared in the work of the apostles and occupied their thrones, as the content of this epistle reveals clearly to us.

---

[318] For a detailed account of the monk Svjatoša, see Discourse 20.
[319] Isa. 8:18.
[320] A parallel account of Bishop Nifont's visit to Kiev just before his death appears in *Hyp.* 1156, PSRL 2:483–84, but here the vision of Feodosij is placed before the account of Nifont's opposition to Klim's appointment as metropolitan. The *Laurentian Chronicle* contains only a brief notice of his death (PSRL 1:347).

*Discourse 14. An epistle from the humble
bishop Simon of Vladimir and Suzdal' to Polikarp,
a monk of the Caves Monastery.*[321]

Brother, sit down in silence,[322] collect your thoughts, and say to yourself, "You wretched monk! Did you not leave the world and parents according to the flesh for the Lord's sake?" If, even here, when you have come to seek your salvation, you neglect spiritual things, why have you been invested in a monastic name? Your black garments will not save you from torment.

You know that you are accounted as blessed by princes and boyars and by all others. They say, "He is indeed blessed, since he has hated this world and its glory, and moreover takes no thought for worldly things, but desires those of heaven." But you are not living as a monk should, and I am thoroughly ashamed of you! If those who here call us blessed precede us into the kingdom of heaven and dwell in peace [there], shall we not cry out in grievous torment? And who will have mercy on you, who brought about your own downfall? Rise up, brother, think seriously about your soul, and serve the Lord with fear, and with all humility and wisdom. Do not be meek today, then angry and bad tempered tomorrow, keeping silence for a while, and then grumbling at the superior and those who serve him.

Do not tell lies and absent yourself from the congregation in church for bodily reasons. For just as the rain matures seeds, so does the church draw the soul to good works. For whatever you do in your cell, it is of no value—whether you read the Psalter, or sing twelve psalms, this cannot be compared to a single "Lord, have mercy" said in the congregation.[323] And understand this, brother: when Peter, the head of the apostles, who was himself the church of the living God,[324] was seized by Herod and thrown into prison, did not the prayers of the church deliver him out of Herod's hands?[325] And David prayed, "One thing have I asked of the Lord, this will I earnestly seek: that I should dwell in the house of the Lord all the days of my life, and that I should behold the fair

---

[321] Abramovyč, *Issledovanie*, IORJAS 7, no. 3 (1902):67–69, has pointed out the ways in which this letter shows the influence of the *Paraenesis* of Ephraim the Syrian.

[322] The word used here is безмолвіи (ἡσυχία). This means not only abstention from speaking, but also a state of inner stillness and "recollection," leaving the mind open to divine influence; it is sometimes translated as "holy quiet."

[323] Cf. Ἀνδρῶν ἁγίων βίβλος, 243, lns. 16–18.

[324] Cf. 2 Cor. 6:16.

[325] See Acts 12:1–7.

beauty of the Lord and visit His holy church."[326] The Lord Himself said, "My house shall be called the house of prayer,"[327] and "Where two or three are gathered together in my name, there am I in the midst of them."[328] And when there is such a large company gathered together, more than one hundred brethren, so much the more have faith that our God is present.

Their dinner is kindled from that divine fire[329] of which I would rather have a single crumb than all that is set before me for my dinner. The Lord is my witness that I have partaken of no other food except morsels of bread and the pulses cooked for the holy brotherhood. But today, brother, you do not praise those dining at the table, and in the morning you grumble at the cook and the brother who is serving, and in this way you make trouble for the elder. You will find yourself eating dung, as is written in the Book of the Fathers.[330] The elder saw those who grumbled at their food eating dung and those who praised it eating honey, just as the same elder had predicted about their different kinds of food.[331] Whatever you eat or drink, you should praise the Lord. If you complain about your food you will destroy yourself. As the Apostle said, "Whether ye eat or drink, do all for the glory of God."[332]

Brother, bear insults patiently, for he who endures to the end will be saved, and saved without difficulty. If it happens that you are insulted, and someone comes and tells you that you have been wrongly accused, say to the person who tells you, "Even if he insulted me, he is still my brother, and I deserve it. He did not do this of himself, but our enemy the devil goaded him to do it, to create enmity between us.[333] May the Lord wreak vengeance on the deceitful one, and forgive my brother." You say that someone insulted you to your face in front of

---

[326] Ps. 26:4.
[327] Matt 21:13; Mark 11:17; Luke 19:46.
[328] Matt. 18:20.
[329] Simon is here referring to the practice of kindling the fire in the kitchen from (presumably) a candle on the holy table. Cf. Discourse 8, p. 61.
[330] Simon is probably referring here to the *Book of Holy Men*, i.e., the Church Slavonic translation of the Ἀνδρῶν ἁγίων βίβλος. Cf. Nestor's reference to the "Books of the Fathers" in Discourse 8, p. 25 and n. 97.
[331] Cf. Ἀνδρῶν ἁγίων βίβλος, 295, and *Vitae Patrum*, PL 73:1000.
[332] 1 Cor. 10:31.
[333] Cf. St. John Climacus, *The Ladder of Divine Ascent*, trans. C Luibheid and N. Russell (New York, 1982), 83. Here and elsewhere Simon's thought shows the influence of the *Ladder*, a work with which he was clearly acquainted. It was available in a Church Slavonic translation at the time when Simon was writing. See D. Bogdanovič, *Jovan Lestvičnik u vizantijskoj i staroj srpskoj književnosti* (Belgrade, 1968), 205.

everybody. Do not grieve about this, or be quickly moved to anger, but fall down and prostrate yourself to the ground before that brother, and say, "Forgive me, brother!" Put right the transgression in yourself, and then you will overcome all the power of the enemy.[334] If you answer back when you are insulted, you do yourself double injury. Are you greater than King David? When Semei insulted him to his face, one of the king's servants, who could not endure to see his king insulted, said, "I shall go and cut off his head. Why should a dead dog curse my lord the king?" And what did David say to him? "O son of Saruia, let him curse David, so that the Lord may look upon my affliction and return me good for his cursing."[335] Consider, my son, one greater than these: how our Lord humbled Himself and became obedient to His Father unto death.[336] When reviled, He threatened not,[337] when He was told, "Thou hast a devil," and when He was beaten and struck on the face and spat upon, He was not angry, but prayed for those who crucifed Him.[338] And so He taught us: "Pray for your enemies, do good to them that hate you. Bless them that curse you."[339] As for what you did in negligence, enough of that! For that reason it is fitting that you weep, since you abandoned the sacred noble Caves Monastery of the holy Antonij and Feodosij and of the holy monastic fathers who were with them, and went to be superior of the Monastery of the Holy Cosmas and Damian, the silverless ones.[340] But now you have acted well and abandoned that pointless enterprise and have not yielded to your enemy's intrigues, for the enemy wished and intended to ruin you. Do you not know that a tree which is not frequently watered and even transplanted quickly withers?[341] Out of disobedience you separated yourself from your father and your brothers and abandoned your own place; such a man will quickly perish. For a sheep staying in the flock remains unharmed, but quickly perishes when separated and is devoured by a wolf.

---

[334] Cf. Ἀνδρῶν ἁγίων βίβλος, 271, lns. 16–19.
[335] 2 Kings 16:5–12.
[336] See Phil. 2:8.
[337] See 1 Pet. 2:23.
[338] See Luke 23:34.
[339] Luke 6:27–28.
[340] безмѣздника, the Church Slavonic rendering of ἀνάργυροι "without money, taking no payment," an adjective commonly applied to healing saints, especially Cosmas and Damian. See Lampe, *A Patristic Greek Lexicon*, 118, and Sreznevskij, *Materialy*, 1:60. For this monastery, see Golubinskij, *Istorija russkoj cerkvi*, 1, 2:747. This mention in Simon's letter appears to be the sole reference to the monastery.
[341] Cf. Ἀνδρῶν ἁγίων βίβλος, 196, lns. 5–9.

You should have considered earlier why you wanted to leave the holy and noble Caves Monastery, the place of salvation, which is wonderful for anyone who would be saved. I believe, brother, that this was God's work, since He could not endure your pride: He cast you down, as formerly He cast down Satan and his rebellious hosts, because you were unwilling to serve that holy man, your lord, our brother Archimandrite Akindin.[342] For the Caves Monastery is a sea which does not keep anything foul within it, but casts it out.[343]

As for what you wrote to me about the insults you suffered—woe unto you! You have destroyed your own soul! Let me ask you: how do you wish to be saved? Even if you fast and practice temperance in all things, become like a beggar and remain without sleep, but cannot endure an insult, you will not be saved. But now the superior and all the brethren rejoice on your account, and we too at what we have heard about you; we have taken comfort from the fact that you were lost and are now found.

Then you again yielded to your own will and not to the superior's, because you wanted to go to be superior of the Monastery of St. Demetrios,[344] and had the prince and I not prevented you, you would have done this. Understand, brother, that your seniority in rank is displeasing to God, and therefore the Lord has given you a weakness in your eyes. But you did not in any way restrain yourself when it was fitting to say, "It is good for me that Thou hast afflicted me; that I might learn Thine ordinances."[345] I have seen you as an ambitious man, one who seeks glory from men and not from God. Do you not believe, accursed one, what is written: "No man taketh this honor unto himself, but he that is called of God."[346] If you do not believe the Apostle, you will not believe in Christ either.

---

[342] Little is known about Akindin. He may have succeeded the priest Vasilij, who was elected in 1182 (see Discourse 38) and was still in the monastery in 1187 (PSRL 2:707).

[343] Abramovyč, *Pateryk*, 220, n. 104, compares this passage with one in the *Ladder* of St. John Climacus. The only relevant comparison here would seem to be with a passage in Step 4 (on Obedience): "The sea has to be stirred up, provoked and made angry so as to jettison onto dry land the hay, the corruption carried into it by the rivers of passion." See *The Ladder of Divine Ascent*, 108.

[344] The monastery founded by Prince Izjaslav Jaroslavič. See above, Discourse 7, p. 22, Discourse 8, pp. 43, 66.

[345] Ps. 118:71.

[346] Heb. 5:4.

Why do you seek rank from men and not from God?[347] For you are unwilling to submit yourself to the things that are of God and are thinking about high positions. Formerly such men were cast out of heaven. "Am I not worthy to be trusted with a position of responsibility," you say, "or am I inferior to the steward or the brother who assists him?" Not having achieved your desire, you have become restless: you often want to wander from cell to cell and to set one brother arguing with another, saying unprofitable things. Or you think to yourself and say, "This man is a superior and this one is a steward," when all that matters is to please God. There is no salvation anywhere else, but why cannot people understand this?[348] This is the devil's work, and for you these things are nothing but vanity. If you do achieve some success and stand on the topmost rung, do not forget humility and wisdom, so that when you come down from the heights, you will find the path of humility and not fall into various kinds of troubles.

Princess Verxoslava, Rostislav's wife,[349] writes to me that she would like you appointed bishop either in Novgorod in place of Antonij, or in Smolensk in place of Lazar, or in Jur'ev in place of Aleksej, "even if I have to spend a thousand pieces of silver on behalf of you and Polikarp," she says. I said to her, "My daughter Anastasia,[350] what you want to do is not pleasing to God. If he had remained in the monastery and not left it, keeping his conscience pure, obeying the superior and the brethren, and practicing temperance in all things, then not only would he have been clothed in priestly garments, but would have been worthy of the higher [heavenly] kingdom."

Did you covet a bishophric, brother? The thing you desire is good, but listen to what the apostle Paul says to Timothy,[351] and after reading this you will understand whether you have amended your life in a manner befitting a bishop. If you had been worthy of that rank, I would have not let you leave me,[352] but with my own hands I would have

---

[347] Cf. Ἀνδρῶν ἁγίων βίβλος, 135, lns. 19–21.
[348] The wording and syntax of this passage are unclear.
[349] See Baumgarten, *Généalogies*, Table X, no. 7. She was a daughter of Vsevelod "Great Nest" of Suzdal', and in 1181 married Rostislav Rurikovič of Ovruč.
[350] Anastasia was the princess's "Christian" name. It was a common practice, at least in princely and boyar families, to give children two names, a Slavic ("secular") and a Christian name, usually of Greek origin. See Discourse 8, p. 61, n. 185.
[351] See 1 Tim. 3:1–7.
[352] In his account of Alimpij the Icon-painter Polikarp says he had seen the church in Rostov to which Volodimer Monomax had taken an icon painted by Alimpij. See Discourse 34, p. 197. Presumably this was when he had been visiting Bishop Simon.

ordained you as my fellow-bishop in both sees, Vladimir and Suzdal', as Prince Georgij[353] wished. But knowing your spiritual poverty, I forbade this. And if you disobey me, if you submit yourself to the office of bishop or superior, it will be a curse for you and not a blessing, and moreover you will not enter that holy place where you were tonsured.[354] Like a worthless vessel you will be cast away, and afterwards you will weep much, but to no purpose. For perfection does not lie in being honored by all men, brother, but in amending your life and keeping yourself pure.

Brother, many bishops have been appointed from the Caves Monastery dedicated to the most holy Mother of God, just as the apostles were sent throughout the whole world by Christ our God Himself, and they illuminated the whole land of Rus' through holy baptism, like bright lights. First Leontij, bishop of Rostov, a great prelate whom God glorified with incorruption. He was the first to occupy that see, and suffered many torments at the hands of unbelievers; he was the third citizen of the land of Rus', together with the two Varangians,[355] to be crowned by Christ, for whose sake he suffered.[356] You yourself have read in the Life of the holy Antonij about Metropolitan Ilarion, who was tonsured by him and later considered worthy of the priesthood. After that there were Nikolaj and Efrem at Perejaslav[357] Isaia in Rostov,[358] German in

---

[353] Georgij Vsevolodovič of Suzdal', a son of Vsevolod "Great Nest," succeeded his father as prince of Vladimir. He was killed in 1238 in the battle against the Mongols on the River Sit'. See Baumgarten, *Généalogies*, Table X, no. 6.

[354] Here again Simon seems to be strongly influenced by John Climacus, in this case by what he says about the need for a monk to obey his spiritual father completely. Cf. *The Ladder of the Divine Ascent*, 92–93.

[355] See PVL 983, PSRL 1:82, 2:69–70.

[356] For further information about Leontij, the circumstances of his martyrdom, and an analysis of the content of different redactions of his Life which have survived, see N. N. Voronin, "Žitie Leontija Rostovskogo i vizantijsko-russkie otnošenija vtoroj poloviny XII veka," *Vizantijskij vremennik*, 23 (1963):23–46. See also E. S. Hurwitz, *Prince Andrej Bogoljubskij: the Man and the Myth* (Florence, 1980), which includes the reproduction (in Appendix IV, pp. 94–95) of the short version of the Life published in *Pamjatniki drevnerusskoj pis'mennosti, Pravoslavnyj Sobesednik*, 1858, pt. 2, 300–11, and an English translation of this text (pp. 79–81).

[357] For Efrem, see Discourse 8, p. 41, and Discourse 9, p. 91. There are no other references to Nikolaj in the *Paterik*.

[358] See Discourse 8, p. 51; Discourse 6, p. 16; Discourse 25, p. 144.

Novgorod, Stefan in Volodymyr,[359] Nifont in Novgorod,[360] Marin in Jur'ev,[361] Mina in Polack, Nikolaj in Tmutorokan', Feoktist in Černihiv,[362] Lavrentij in Turov, Luka in Bilhorod[363] and Efrem in Suzdal'. If you want to know them all, read the old Rostov chronicle.[364] There are more than thirty altogether, and then with those who came later, up to myself, sinner that I am, nearly fifty, I think.[365]

Consider, brother, how great is the glory and honor of this monastery! You should be ashamed of yourself, and repent, and prefer this tranquil and untroubled life to which the Lord has called you. I would gladly leave my bishophric and work for the superior in the holy Caves Monastery. I say this, brother, not to exalt myself, but to inform you. You know what authority I have as a bishop. Who does not know me, the sinful bishop Simon, [lord] of this cathedral church, the ornament of Vladimir, and the other church of Suzdal' which I founded myself?[366] How many towns and villages they possess! And they collect tithes throughout this whole region; and I, unworthy as I am, am lord of all this. I would have left all this, but you know what important spiritual matters hold me back. I pray to the Lord that He will give me time to amend my life—and the Lord knows our secrets. I speak truly to you when I say that I would [swiftly] regard all this glory and honor as dirt!

---

[359] See Discourse 9, p. 91; Discourse 4, p. 13.

[360] See Discourse 13, p. 110.

[361] See Discourse 9, p. 91.

[362] See Discourse 25, p. 145.

[363] See Discourse 6, p. 16.

[364] This "old Rostov chronicle" has not survived as an independent text. A chronicle usually designated by this name is included in the *Archive Collection = Sbornik Moskovskogo glavnogo arxiva Ministerstva inostrannyx del*, no. 20/25, f. 1v–620r, but the title is not accurate, since the context indicates that it belongs to a group of "national-Russian" chronicles of Muscovite provenance, supplemented by local annals. See A. A. Šaxmatov, *O tak nazyvaemoj Rostovskoj Letopisi* (Moscow, 1904), 9. It is possible, however, that the annals were kept at the episcopal court in Rostov. According to A. A. Šaxmatov, *Obozrenie russkix letopisnyx svodov XIV–XVI vv.* (Leningrad, 1938), some source of this kind was used by the compiler of the *Ermolin Chronicle* in the fifteenth century.

[365] Here Simon stresses the importance of the Caves Monastery as a training ground for native bishops, which greatly enhanced the prestige of the monastery as an "all-Rus'" institution. This is reflected in the title of L. K. Goetz's book, *Das Kiever Höhlenkloster als Kulturzentrum des vormongolischen Russlands* (Passau, 1904).

[366] The "ornament of Vladimir" must have been the cathedral of the Dormition, restored by Vsevolod III. See G. H. Hamilton, *The Art and Architecture of Russia* (London, 1954), 34. The church in Suzdal' was probably the one restored by Georgij Vsevolodovič (ibid., 38), apparently at Bishop Simon's instigation.

If I could be swept up with the dung in the Caves Monastery and be trampled by men, or if I could be one of the poor before the gates of that sacred *lavra*, and become a beggar,[367] it would be better for me than this transitory glory. One day in the house of the Mother of God is more than a thousand years; and I would have chosen to stay there rather than live in these "tents of the sinners."[368]

I ask you in truth, my brother Polikarp, where have you heard of more wonderful miracles than those which occurred in the holy Caves Monastery. Who is more blessed than these fathers, who shine forth like rays of the sun to the ends of the world? In this present narrative I shall give you a true account of them, in addition to what I have already told you. And now, brother, I shall tell you why I have such fervent faith in the holy Antonij and Feodosij.

> *Discourse 15. A narrative written by Simon, bishop of Vladimir and Suzdal', about the holy monks of the Caves Monastery, and about why we should feel fervent love for the venerable fathers Antonij and Feodosij of the Caves Monastery.*[369]

I heard the most remarkable incident from the blessed elders, and they say they heard it from eyewitnesses to the miracle, which occurred when Pimin was superior of the holy Caves Monastery.[370]

There was a man perfect in every virtue called Onisifor, a presbyter by rank, to whom God had granted the gift of discernment, so that he could see every man's transgressions.[371] Other accounts of his virtuous actions are related, but I shall recount only this one. This blessed Onisifor had a spiritual son, a monk and friend whom he loved. This monk did not sincerely emulate the life of the holy man. He appeared to fast and falsely made himself out to be chaste, but in secret he ate and drank

---

[367] The typika of most Byzantine monasteries stipulated that food should be distributed each day at the main gate. See Constantelos, *Byzantine Philanthropy*, 90.

[368] Cf. Ps. 83:10.

[369] This rather clumsy title has several variants in different MSS: Abramovyč, *Pateryk*, 104, n. 1.

[370] There is no clear evidence of the dates of Pimin's period of office. Since this incident occurred some years before Simon himself entered the monastery in the late twelfth century, but within the living memory of more senior monks, Pimin might have been the predecessor of Archimandrite Polikarp, who died in 1182. See Discourse 38.

[371] Cf. Ἀνδρῶν ἁγίων βίβλος, 97, lns. 5–14, which describes how a certain bishop could tell from his communicants' faces which of them were sinners.

and lived a filthy life; thus he spent his life. This was hidden from his spiritual father, and none of the brethren could understand it. Then one day the monk died suddenly, although he was in good health. No one could approach his body because of the stench that came from it, and they were all gripped by fear. They dragged him out by force, but they could not sing [the funeral service] over him because of the stench; so they laid him down and sang the customary office standing some distance away. Then some people, holding their nostrils, carried him away and laid him inside the cave; he stank so horribly that they fled from the cave without a word. Often a sound of bitter weeping could be heard, as though he were being tormented.

The holy Antonij appeared to Onisifor the presbyter and said severely, "Why have you done this? You have laid here such a filthy, unclean, impious, and sinful man as has never been buried here. He has defiled this holy place." Arising[372] from this vision and falling on his face, he prayed to God, "Oh Lord, why didst Thou hide the deeds of this man from me?" An angel approached him and said, "This is a sign for all who sin without repentance, that having seen it, they may repent." After saying this the angel vanished.

Then the presbyter went and told the superior Pimin all these things. The next night he had the same vision. He was told, "Cast him out quickly for the dogs to eat! He does not deserve to stay here." Once more the presbyter had recourse to prayer, and a voice said to him, "If you wish, help him!" He conferred with the superior [and they decided] that they would compel some people to drag him out and throw him into the water, since no one would voluntarily approach the hill where the cave was.

The holy Antonij appeared to him again, saying, "I have had pity on the soul of this brother, since I cannot break the promise I made to you that every person buried here will be forgiven, even though he is a sinner.[373] The fathers who are here with me in the cave are not inferior to those who formerly pleased God according to the Law. I have prayed to the Lord my God and to His most pure Mother that not a single member of this monastery may be judged worthy of torment. And the Lord spoke to me, so that I heard His voice, [saying], 'I am He that said to Abraham:

---

[372] I have used the Arsenian reading въставъ here: Abramovyč, *Pateryk*, 105, n. 1.

[373] Only here in the *Paterik* is the promise of salvation to those who die in the Caves Monastery attributed to Antonij; it is usually associated with Feodosij (see Discourse 8, p. 82) and may have been "transferred" here.

For the sake of twenty righteous men I shall not destroy this city.'[374] How much the more, then, for your sake and those who are with you I will have mercy on a sinner and save him. If he succeeds in dying here, he shall rest in peace." Hearing these words from the holy one, Onisifor related everything he had seen and heard to the superior and all the brethren, from among whom I found one who told me this story [as he had heard it] from these first monks.

The superior Pimin was greatly perplexed on account of this terrible affair and prayed to God with tears for the salvation of the souls of the brethren. And a revelation came to him from God, speaking as follows, "Although many sinners have been buried here, they have all been forgiven for the sake of the holy ones in the cave who pleased me, and I have had mercy on the soul of this accursed man for the sake of my servants Antonij and Feodosij and through the prayers of the holy monks who are with them in the cave. And let this be a sign of the change to you: the stench has been transformed into a fragrant odor." Hearing this, the superior was filled with joy. He summoned all the brethren, related the vision to them, and went with them to the cave to see what had happened. They all smelled the fragrant odor from his body; there was no more stench, nor any sound of sobbing. They all delighted in the fragrant odor and glorified God and His holy servants Antonij and Feodosij because of the salvation of the brethren.

For this reason I, the sinful bishop Simon, weep in grief and misery, [praying] only that I may be buried in that sacred earth and receive some slight absolution for my many sins through the prayers of the holy fathers, through Jesus Christ our Lord, to Whom be glory now [and forever. Amen].

---

[374] Gen. 18:31.

Discourse 16. Blessed Evstratij the Faster.[375]

A certain man came from Kiev to the cave to become a monk,[376] having distributed all his property to the poor, leaving a little for his relatives to distribute after his death. This monk Evstratij was a faster and obedient to everybody. This same blessed man, together with many other Christians, was taken prisoner and sold to a Jew. He instructed and and entreated his fellow captives, "Brothers, since many of you have been baptized and come to believe in God, let us not abjure our vow made in holy baptism. For Christ has redeemed us from the curse [of the Law],[377] and begotten us by water and the Spirit, and made us sons and heirs. Whether we die, we die unto the Lord; whether we live [we live unto the Lord].[378] If we die for Christ, by our death we buy life, and He will give us eternal life."

This Evstratij was captured by the godless Hagarenes[379] and sold to a Jew. After a few days the captives began to die of hunger and to grow weak from thirst: some after four days, some after seven days, the strong ones after ten days—they all died of hunger and thirst. There were fifty of them, thirty workers from the monastery and twenty from Kiev. After fourteen days only this monk remained alive, since he had fasted since childhood. The Jew, seeing that this monk was the cause of his losing the gold which he had given for the captives,[380] crucified him.

When the day of Christ's Resurrection drew near, he mocked the holy Evstratij—what they did to our Lord Jesus Christ, and how He was mocked, is written in the Gospel—and so also this blessed man was nailed to a cross. On the cross he gave thanks to God, and remained

---

[375] Discourses 16 and 17 each have as their theme the fate of prisoners captured during raids by the Cumans. The PVL first mentions such raids in 1068 and frequently thereafter (e.g., in 1092, 1093, and 1096). A successful counterattack by a coalition of Rus' princes in 1111 provided some respite from the Cumans, but by the mid-twelfth century they once again became a threat and were a major factor in the political decline of southern Rus'.

[376] The Caves Monastery was outside the walls of Kiev proper.

[377] See Gal. 3:13.

[378] See Rom. 14:8. The bracketed part of this verse is omitted in the text, which here contains the words бытію долъжнаа послужим, which suggest a different train of thought and are difficult to construe here. Probably Bishop Simon was writing from memory, and we have here a "half-remembered" sentence.

[379] Evstratij was probably, though not certainly, captured in the Cuman raid of 1096 on the Caves Monastery. See PVL 1096, PSRL 1:232, 2:222–23.

[380] These words imply that Evstratij had urged the captives to refuse to eat food prepared by the Jews and thus indirectly caused their death by starvation.

alive for fifteen days. The Jews said to him, "Now, you fool, eat your fill of the food prescribed by the Law, so that you may live, for Moses received the Law from God and gave it to us, and it is said in these books, 'Cursed is everyone that hangeth on a tree.' "[381] The monk said, "God vouchsafed to me great grace to suffer today, and He said to me, as He said to the thief, 'Today shalt thou be with me in paradise.'[382] For He Himself cast out the curse of the Law and brought in grace. Of him Moses said, 'Thy life shall be in suspense before thine eyes,'[383] and David said, 'They pierced my hands and my feet,'[384] and 'They parted my garments among themselves and cast lots upon my raiment.'[385] And of this day he said, 'This is the day which the Lord has made: let us exult and rejoice in it.'[386] Today you and the Jews with you will weep and lament, for God will call you to account because of my blood and that of all the Christians, for the Lord hates your Sabbaths, and changed your festivals to days of mourning, because the instigator of your iniquity has been killed."[387] Hearing these words, as the crucified man taunted him, the Jew took a spear and pierced him, so that the blessed Evstratij commended his spirit to the Lord.[388]

And the soul of the venerable one was seen [being] borne on a chariot of fire, and the horses were made of fire, and a voice was heard, saying in Greek, "This good man has been named as a citizen of the heavenly city, and for this reason he will be called *Protostrator* in your calendar."[389]

---

[381] Deut. 21:23; Gal. 3:13.
[382] Luke 23:43.
[383] Deut. 28:66.
[384] Ps. 21:16.
[385] Ps. 21:18.
[386] Ps. 117:24.
[387] The syntax of this sentence is obscure. Evstratij's prophecy that the person responsible for his death will himself be killed does in fact come to pass toward the end of the discourse.
[388] If Evstratij was captured in 1096, he must have died that same year. But Šaxmatov, *Razyskanija*, 276, n. 1, has suggested that he died in either 1087, 1092, or 1098, since Discourse 16 suggests that he died on Easter Day, which only in those years fell on March 28, Evstratij's feast day.
[389] This "translation" resembles that of Elijah (4 Kings 2:11), with the important difference that Evstratij was not bodily "translated," as was Elijah. The voice speaking in Greek has long puzzled scholars. Both Golubinskij, *Istorija russkoj cerkvi*, 1, 1:765, n. 1, and Priselkov, *Očerki*, 242–43, think that the words: "and for this reason he will be called *Protostrator* in your calendar" were added by Bishop Simon. In this case, however, one would expect the words "*our* calendar" and not "*your* calendar." Golubinskij considered *Protostrator* a corruption of the Greek πρωτοστάτης (literally "he who stands

Immediately, that very day, a message came from the emperor against the Jews: all the Jews were to be expelled, their property confiscated, and their elders killed.[390]

That happened in this way. There was a certain Jew, a rich and very brave man, who had been baptized. Because of this the emperor received him and a few days later appointed him eparch. But when he had obtained this position, he secretly rejected Christ and His faith, and encouraged the Jews throughout the Greek Empire to buy Christians to work for them. But this wicked eparch was exposed and killed, as the blessed Evstratij had said, and the Jews who were spending the winter in Cherson had their property confiscated, and the one who had acted against the blessed Evstratij was hung. "His trouble shall return on his own head, and his unrighteousness shall come down on his crown."[391] The holy one's body was cast into the sea, where it performs many miracles. The faithful searched for his holy relics, but they could not find them; for this holy man did not want glory from man, but from God. The accursed Jews, having seen an awe-inspiring miracle, were baptized.

Discourse 17. The meek and long-suffering monk Nikon.

Another monk, named Nikon, was held captive in fetters. A certain man came from Kiev to ransom him, but this did not please him, since he came from one of the city's important families. This Christ-lover returned home after ransoming many captives. When Nikon's relatives heard of this, they came to ransom him, bringing a great deal of money.

---

first"). In fact, the word πρωτοστράτωρ was current in eleventh-century Byzantium; originally it had meant the chief of the stable attendants, but was now applied nonfunctionally to persons of high rank or holding important office. See R. Guilland, "Études de titulature et de prosopographie byzantine. Le Protostrator," *Revue des études byzantines* 7, no. 2 (1950):156. It therefore seems reasonable to assume that the whole passage was spoken by the "heavenly voice," and that it derived from a tradition, oral or written, emanating from Cherson, where Evstratij was crucified, and where Greek was the official language, so that πρωτοστράτωρ would have been known and used. This "legend," together with other facts about Evstratij's death and its aftermath, could have reached Kiev through merchants from Cherson or by way of escaped captives such as Nikon the Dry, whose experiences are described in Discourse 17.

[390] No Byzantine sources record any such action against the Jews in Cherson, but this does not mean that it did not take place. Trading in captives was officially forbidden under Byzantine law, but a local incident might not be considered worth recording by historians whose main interest was centered on Constantinople. See I. Malyševskij, "Evrei v južnoj Rusi i v Kieve v X–XII vekax," *Trudy Kievskoj duxovnoj akademii*, 1878, no. 9:488.

[391] Ps. 7:16.

The monk said to them, "Don't waste your wealth uselessly. If the Lord had wished me to be free, He would not have delivered me into the hands of these impious men—the most cunning in the whole world. He said, 'I am He that delivered my priests into captivity.' If we have received good things from the hand of the Lord, shall we not endure evil things?"[392] The relatives reproached him and departed, taking their riches with them.

The Cumans, seeing themselves deprived of what they wanted, began to torture the monk relentlessly. For three years he was daily beaten and bound, cast into the fire, fettered hand and foot, and almost killed by hunger and thirst through exposure in the burning sun. Sometimes he did not taste any food for a whole day, and sometimes none for two or three days. And he gave thanks to God for all these things, and prayed ceaselessly. In the winter he was cast out into the cold and snow.

The accursed Cumans did all this to him in order to obtain a large ransom for him. But he would tell them, "Christ will deliver me from your hands without any payment. For I have already learned this, since my brother whom you sold to the Jews to be crucified has appeared to me. They will be condemned together with those who said, 'Away with him, away with him, crucify him. His blood be on us, and on our children!'[393] You, accursed ones, will forever be tortured with Judas, as impious traitors and lawbreakers. For the holy Gerasim[394] told me, 'Within days you will be in the monastery through the prayers of the holy Antonij and Feodosij and the holy monks with them.'" Hearing this and reckoning that he wished to escape, the Cumans cut his shinbones, so that he could not run away, and placed him under a strong guard. Two days later, while they were all sitting near him with weapons ready, he suddenly vanished at the sixth hour, and they heard a voice saying, "Praise the Lord from the heavens." Thus was he brought invisibly to the church of the holy Theotokos in the Caves Monastery at the time when they were beginning to sing the *kinanik*.[395]

All the brethren ran together towards him and asked him how he had gotten there. At first he wished to conceal this remarkable miracle. But when they saw the heavy irons he was wearing, his unhealed

---

[392] See Job 2:10.
[393] A conflation of John 19:15 and Matt. 27:25.
[394] Gerasim is not otherwise identified. Possibly he was identical with Evstratij the Faster. See Šaxmatov, *Razyskanija*, 276, n. 1.
[395] кинаникъ: The "communion verses" recited by the priest at the liturgy when he is about to communicate.

wounds, his whole body suppurating from the wounds, his fetters, and the blood still dripping from the cuts on his shins, they would not believe it. Finally he revealed the truth to them and would not allow the irons to be removed from his hands and feet. The superior[396] said, "Brother, if the Lord had wished you to be held thus in bonds, He would not have brought you away from that place; so now submit to our will." They removed the irons from him and used them to make what they needed for the altar.

Many days later the Cuman who had guarded this blessed man came to Kiev to arrange a peace and entered the Caves Monastery. When he saw the elder he told the superior and the brethren all about him; after that he did not return home, but was baptized with his family and became a monk. They ended their lives there in penitence, working for their captive, and were buried in the narthex of the church.

Many other of the blessed Nikon's virtuous deeds are related. There is no time now to write about them, but I shall tell you this one. When this blessed man was in captivity, the captives one time fell ill from hunger and hardship. The blessed one ordered them not to eat anything prepared by the pagans. He himself healed them through his prayers, although he was in fetters, and caused them to escape without being noticed. Again, when that Cuman we have mentioned was about to die, he ordered his wives and children to stretch the monk over him. The blessed one prayed and healed him; he foresaw that he would ultimately repent, and saved himself from a cruel death. This Nikon is called "The Dry" in our calendar: his body had shrivelled up from loss of blood and suppurating wounds.

To Polikarp

Brother, how can I tell you about the holy men who were formerly in the noble and blessed Caves Monastery, through whose virtuous lives pagans were baptized and became monks? On account of the blessed Gerasim, the martyr for Christ previously mentioned, Jews were baptized, while because of the passion-sufferer Nikon, Cumans became monks. You have also heard many other things from me, the sinful bishop Simon, the least worthy of the bishops, who is not worthy to sit at the feet of those holy monks. In my opinion, no one in the world, nor

---

[396] As the events described in Discourses 16 and 17 occurred in the last decade of the eleventh century, the superior would have been Nikon's successor Ioann, who held office from 1088 to 1108.

this writer himself is capable of describing their miracles. For to them the Lord said, "Let your light so shine before men, that they may see your good works, and glorify our Father, which is in heaven."[397] But what is this betrayal of our vow, this change in the manner of our life that has caused us to fall from such heights into the depths of worldliness? For we have leaders and teachers who are the equals of incorporeal beings, our first mediators and intercessors before the Creator; they are like angels, and crowned with martyrs' crowns.

Discourse 18. The holy martyr Kukša and Pimin the Faster.

How can I willingly pass over the blessed martyr Kukša, a monk of this same Caves Monastery? Everyone knows[398] how he expelled evil demons, baptized the Vjatičians,[399] brought down rain from heaven, caused a lake to dry up, and performed numerous miracles.[400] After many torments he was beheaded, together with his disciples. Pimin, the blessed faster, died on the same day. He had received foreknowledge of his departure to the Lord two years earlier; he prophesied many other things and healed the sick. [One day] he called out loudly in the middle of the church, "Our brother Kukša was killed at daybreak!" Having said this, he passed away at the very same hour and on the same day[401] as those holy ones.[402]

Note to Polikarp

I omit many things that could be said about these holy ones. If the discourse you have heard from my own lips is not sufficient, then my written words will not lead you to belief; if you do not believe them, you will not have faith, even if somebody rose from the dead.

---

[397] Matt. 5:16.
[398] Abramovyč, *Pateryk*, 222, n. 129, suggests that this brief account of Kukša was based on oral traditions still current in the monastery when Simon was writing.
[399] The Vjatičians, a group of Slavic tribes mentioned several times in the PVL, originally lived some distance northeast of Kiev; they were not brought under the rule of the princes of Kiev until they were subdued by Prince Svjatoslav I in 966 (PSRL 1:65, 2:53). Later they rebelled, but were again conquered, this time by Volodimer (PVL 982, PSRL 1:82, 2:69).
[400] For Kukša's missionary work, see Golubinskij, *Istorija russkoj cerkvi*, 1, 1:208–9.
[401] The words "on the same day" occur only in the Arsenian text: Abramovyč, *Pateryk*, 111, n. 10.
[402] I.e., the monks killed at the same time as Kukša.

Discourse 19. Holy Afanasij the Solitary, who died, revived two days later and remained alive for twelve years.[403]

There was in that same holy monastery a brother named Afanasij, who lived a life that was holy and well pleasing to God and then died after a long illness. Two brothers sponged down his dead body, wrapped him in a shroud as befits a dead man, and departed. By chance some people came along, saw that he was dead, and also departed. The dead man remained unburied for a whole day; he was very poor and possessed nothing of this world, and because of this he was neglected. For everybody hastens to serve the rich, both during their life and at the point of death, in order to inherit something. Then at night someone appeared to the superior and said, "This man of God has been left unburied for two days, but you make merry." Having learned about this, the superior came to the dead man with all the brethren the next day, and they found him sitting up and weeping. They were filled with terror when they saw that he had returned to life, and questioned him, "How did you return to life, and what did you see?" He made no reply, except to say, "Save yourselves!" They kept entreating him, so as to hear from him something useful. But he said to them, "If I speak to you, you will not believe me." The brethren told him on oath, "We will keep to everything you tell us." He said to them, "Obey the superior in all things, repent hourly, and pray to the Lord Jesus Christ, to His most pure Mother, and to the venerable Antonij and Feodosij that you may end your lives here and be deemed worthy of being buried in the cave with the holy fathers. For these things are better than all the virtues. Even if one succeeds in achieving these in due order, do not be puffed up. Now do not ask me any more questions, but forgive me, I beseech you." Then he went into the cave, shut the door behind him, and remained there, without speaking a word to anyone for twelve years. When he was about to pass away, he summoned all the brethren and told them the same things about obedience and repentance as he had on the first occasion, and said, "Blessed is he who is deemed worthy of being buried here." Having said this, he reposed peacefully in the Lord.

There was a certain brother who had suffered for many years from a kidney disease. He was brought to the cave and Afanasij was placed

---

[403] For similar incidents, see Ἀνδρῶν ἁγίων βίβλος, 113, lns. 2–10, and *The Ladder of Divine Ascent*, 134. The parallel in this latter work is very close, except that the dead man, Hesychius the Horebite, was "absent from the body" for only one hour.

over him. After embracing the blessed one's body he was healed from that hour, and for the rest of his life he had no more pain in his kidneys nor anywhere else. The man who was cured was called Vavila, and he related to the brethren: "I was lying down and crying out from pain, and this blessed man suddenly entered and said to me, 'Come, I will heal you.' As I was about to ask him when and how he had come there, he suddenly vanished." Henceforth they all realized that he had pleased the Lord, for he had never gone out [of the cave] or seen the sun for twelve years, nor had he stopped weeping day and night. He ate only a little bread and drank a little water, and that only once a day. This I heard from that Vavila who was healed by him.

If anyone finds what I have written hard to believe, let him read the Lives of our holy fathers Antonij and Feodosij, the founders of monasticism in Rus', and so let him believe. If it does not seem so, they are not guilty, for it is fitting that the parable told by the Lord should be fulfilled: "A sower went forth to sow his seed, and some fell along the path, and some among the thorns."[404] As for those who are choked by life's anxieties, of them the prophet said, "The heart of this people has become gross, and their ears are dull of hearing,"[405] and "O Lord, who has believed our report?"[406]

To Polikarp

My son and brother, do not follow after these. For it is not for their sake that I write this [epistle] to you, but in order to win you over. I give this advice to you: strengthen yourself with piety in the holy Caves Monastery; do not desire power, or the office of superior or bishop; it will be sufficient for your salvation that you ended your life there. You yourself know that I could relate whole books of similar narratives which would profit you and me. In fact, I am telling only a few of the many things performed and heard about in this divine and holy Caves Monastery.

---

[404] Matt. 13:3–4, 7; Mark 4:3–4; Luke 8:5, 7.
[405] Cf. Isa. 6:10.
[406] Isa. 53:1.

Discourse 20. The venerable Svjatoša, prince of Černihiv.

The blessed and pious prince Svjatoša, who was David's son and Svjatoslav's grandson[407] and whose name was Nikola,[408] decided that the delusions of this vain world and everything in it flow on and pass away, whereas the blessings of the world to come are eternal and without limits and the heavenly kingdom, which God has prepared for those who love Him, is everlasting. So he abandoned his princely authority—his honor and glory and power—and considering these things to have no value, he came to the Caves Monastery and became a monk on February 17, 1106.[409] All the monks there know about his virtuous life and his obedience. He spent three years in the kitchen working for the brethren, and with his own hands he chopped the wood needed to prepare the cooked pulses and often carried wood from the river bank on his own shoulders; his brothers Izjaslav and Volodimer[410] had difficulty in stopping him from doing such work. Since his obedience was sincere, he begged that he might work in the kitchen for the brethren yet another year. Thus he was tested and made perfect in every respect.[411] After this he was placed at the monastery's gate, where he remained for three years without going anywhere, except to church. Then he was ordered to serve in the refectory. And so, by the wish of the superior and all the brethren he was ordered to have a cell for himself,[412] which he built (to this day it is known as "Svjatoša's"), and also a garden, which he planted with his own hands. They say about him that throughout all the years of his monastic life no one ever saw him idle; his hands were always busy with some handiwork, and what he made with his hands sufficed for his own

---

[407] Svjatoslav Jaroslavič was prince in Černihiv (ca. 1054–1073) and Kiev (1073–1076). His son David ruled briefly in Smolensk (1095–1096) and thereafter in Černihiv until his death in 1123.

[408] Nikola was either his baptismal or monastic name, but Rus' sources usually refer to him as Svjatoša, a diminutive of the secular name Svjatoslav.

[409] See PVL 1106, PRSL 1:281, 2:258. In 1097 Svjatoša had taken part in the campaign against David Igorevič, who had captured and blinded his cousin Vasil'ko (PSRL 1:272, 2:247).

[410] Izjaslav Davidovič ultimately ruled in Kiev three times (1155, 1157–58, 1161). Volodimer Davidovič died in 1154 as prince of Černihiv.

[411] This seems to correspond to the "novitiate" described in Nestor's Life of Feodosij. See Discourse 8, p. 45.

[412] This was presumably a reward for his long period of obedience and service, as well as a recognition of his spiritual maturity. Premature retirement to solitude, without the superior's permission, was discouraged; the potentially dangerous consequences are graphically illustrated in Discourses 25 and 36.

clothing. He had on his lips the Jesus Prayer continually: "Lord Jesus Christ, Son of God, have mercy upon me."[413] He had never tasted any food except what was provided by the monastery, and although he had considerable possessions, he gave everything away to provide for the needs of strangers and beggars and for maintaining the church buildings. Many of his books are still there.

While he was still ruling, the blessed prince Svjatoša had a highly skilled physician, a Syrian by birth named Peter, who came with him to the monastery.[414] When Peter saw Svjatoša's voluntary poverty and the way he worked in the kitchen and sat at the gate, he left him and went to live in Kiev, where he treated many people. He often came to the blessed one, and when he saw him in a very bad state and fasting immoderately, he admonished him, "Prince, you should consider your health, lest you destroy your body with so much labor and abstinence, because there are times when you are very weak and lack the strength to bear the yoke laid upon you, which you have chosen for God's sake. For God does not wish a man to fast and labor beyond his strength, but desires only a pure and contrite heart. You are not accustomed to these privations which you are inflicting on yourself by working like a slave who has no choice. Your pious brothers Izjaslav and Volodimer have been severely reproached on account of your poverty, and because you have come from such honor and glory to a state of extreme deprivation and are killing your body and destroying your health with unsuitable food. I am astonished at the moisture in your stomach, which used to be weighed down with tasty food and yet now takes raw vegetables and dry bread without complaint. Take care that your ill health does not some day spread to every part of you and that, if your strength fails, you soon lose your life. I shall not be able to help you, and you will leave your brothers weeping and inconsolable. Even the boyars who once served you and thought that they would become great and famous because of you are now deprived of your affection; they built large houses and reside in

---

[413] The passage about the Jesus Prayer does not occur in the oldest Arsenian redaction: Abramovyč, *Pateryk*, 114, n. 10. These words, therefore, cannot be taken as evidence that Svjatoša used the Jesus Prayer, but they are important as an indication of its use in the mid-fifteenth century, when the Second Cassian redaction of the *Paterik* was compiled.

[414] Syria was a well-established center of medical knowledge at this time. See S. H. Nasr, *Islamic Science. An Illustrated Study* (Westerham, Kent, 1976), 179–81, and also L. A. Oganess'an, *Istorija mediciny v Armenii*, vol. 5, pt. 2 (Erevan, 1946), 229–32, whose list of physicians practicing medicine in Armenia in the eleventh and twelfth centuries includes some Syrians.

them in a state of great distress. You have nowhere to lay your head, but you sit on this rubbish heap, and people think you have gone out of your mind. What prince has ever done this? Did your blessed father David or your grandfather Svjatoslav? Or who among the boyars has ever done this or wished to follow this path, apart from Varlaam who was formerly superior here? If you disobey me, you will receive judgment before judgment is due!" Peter often said such things to him, sometimes while sitting with him in the kitchen and sometimes by the gate, having been instructed to do this by Svjatoša's brothers.

The blessed one replied, "I have often reflected on this subject, brother Peter, and I have decided not to spare my flesh, so as not to wage war against myself once more, and so that my body, crushed by the weight of toil, may find peace. For it is said, brother Peter, 'strength is made perfect in weakness.'[415] The sufferings of this present time are not to be compared with the future glory that will be revealed in us. I thank the Lord that He has freed me from worldly work and made me a servant of His servants—these blessed monks. As for my two brothers, let them look to themselves; everybody is responsible for his own time, and my princely authority is sufficient for them. I have left all these things for Christ's sake—wife, children, home, power, kinsmen, friends, servants, and estates, and because of this I hope to inherit eternal life; indeed, to gain this I made myself a beggar for God's sake. Whenever you treat patients, do you not order them to avoid food? For me, to die for Christ is gain; and as for sitting on this rubbish heap, I am sharing the throne with Job.[416] Even if no prince has done this before me, let me be the one to go ahead and show them the way. Whoever would attempt to do likewise, let him follow this way and me. In the future look to yourself and to those who have instructed you."

When the blessed one fell ill, the physician would see him and prepare herbal remedies for every possible disease, whether it was a burning fever or cholera, but before he could arrive the prince would recover without taking any medicine. This often happened. Once Peter himself fell ill and Svjatoša sent him a message, saying, "If you don't drink any more medicinal herbs, you will soon be well, but if you disobey me, you will suffer a great deal." But Peter, wishing to display his skill and get rid of his disease, drank the herbal mixture and almost died. Through the holy one's prayers, he recovered. Then he fell ill again, and the holy one sent him the message, "You will recover within three days,

---

[415] 2 Cor. 12:9.
[416] See Job 2:8.

provided you do not take any medicine." The Syrian obeyed him, and within three days he was well, as the blessed one had said.

Then the blessed one summoned him and said to him, "Be tonsured, for in three months I will depart from this world." He meant that he would die, but the Syrian did not understand what was going to happen to him. Peter fell at his feet and said to him with tears, "Woe is me, my lord, my benefactor, my very life! Who will look after me in a foreign land? Who will feed the many children of those in need? Who will protect the wronged and have mercy on the poor? Did I not tell you, prince, that you would leave your brothers weeping and inconsolable? Did I not tell you that I would be healed through God's word and power, and by your prayers? Where are you going now, good shepherd? Tell me, your servant, about this deadly wound, so that if I cannot heal it, my head may be given for your head, and my soul for your soul. Do not depart silently from me, but tell me, my lord, where this knowledge comes from, so that I may give my life for you. If the Lord has informed you, entreat him that I may die for you. If you leave me, where shall I sit and lament my loss—on this footstool or at this gate, where you usually are? What shall I inherit from your property? You yourself are naked, but when you depart this life you will be buried in these patched garments. Give me your prayer, as in olden times Elijah gave Elisha his cloak,[417] so that I might part the depths[418] and pass over into the realms of paradise, the marvelous abode of the house of God. Wild beasts know how to herd together after sunset and lie down in their dens: a bird finds a shelter, and the turtledove a nest for its young. But you have been here six years[419] in the monastery, and I have not found out where your place is."

The blessed one said to him, "It is good to put one's trust in the Lord and not to rely on man. The Lord knows how to feed all His creatures and can protect and save the unfortunate. As for my two brothers, let them not weep for me, but for themselves and their children. I have no need of medicine during my life, for a dead man cannot see life, nor can physicians raise from the dead." They went out together to the cave, and Svjatoša dug a grave for himself and said to the Syrian, "Which of us desires this grave more?" The Syrian said, "You know if

---

[417] See 4 Kings 2:13–14.
[418] Elisha struck the water of the Jordan with Elijah's cloak; the waters then parted and he was able to pass over.
[419] The Arsenian text says five years: Abramovyč, *Pateryk*, 116, n. 41.

anyone wants it, but please stay alive and bury me here." The blessed one said, "It shall be as you wish."

So Peter was tonsured and wept without ceasing day and night for three months. The blessed one comforted him, saying, "Brother Peter, do you want me to take you with me?" He said with weeping, "I want you to let me go first, so that I may die for you, and you pray for me." The blessed one said to him, "Have courage and prepare yourself. You will depart this life in three days." Then Peter partook of the sacred, life-giving, and deathless mysteries, lay down on his bed, prepared himself for death, stretched out his legs, and commended his spirit into the hands of the Lord.

The blessed prince Svjatoša remained alive for a further thirty years, never leaving the monastery until he passed on to eternal life. On the day of his passing practically the whole town gathered together. When his brother heard about this, he sent to the superior and asked if he might have, as a token of blessing, the cross which his brother used to wear on his paramandyas,[420] also his pillow, and the prayer stool on which he used to prostrate himself. The superior gave him these things, saying, "Be it unto you according to your faith." The prince accepted these things and held them in honor and gave the superior three *grivna* of gold, so that he did not take these tokens of his brother without payment.

Once this same Izjaslav fell ill and everybody despaired of his recovery, since they saw that he was at the point of death; his wife, children, and all his boyars were sitting at his bedside. He raised himself, requested water from the well of the Caves Monastery, and then fell silent. They sent for some water and wiped the tomb of Feodosij, and the superior gave them a hair shirt from the prince's brother Svjatoša to put on him. Before the man bringing these things entered [the room], the prince called out, "Go quickly outside the town to meet the venerable Feodosij and Nikola!" When the messenger entered with the water and the hair shirt the prince exclaimed, "Nikola! Nikola! Svjatoša!" They gave him some water to drink and dressed him in the hair shirt, and he recovered immediately. They all praised God and His servants. Whenever the prince fell ill, he would put on this hair shirt, and would recover.

Izjaslav wanted to march against his brother, but was restrained by the bishops then in office. Whenever he went on a campaign, he wore the hair shirt, and so remained unhurt. But once he had committed a sin

---

[420] On the парамандии (παραμανδύας), see N. F. Robinson, *Monasticism in the Orthodox Churches* (London, 1916), 49–50.

and did not dare to put it on, and so he was killed in battle;[421] he had previously given instructions that he was to be buried in it.

Many virtuous deeds performed by this man are related, and there are monks who know about the blessed prince Svjatoša to this day.

To Polikarp

Again I address a sermon to you. Have you ever done anything like this? Have you abandoned great riches? You never had any! Have you renounced your glory? You did not attain to this [yourself]; you came to glory and all good things from poverty.[422] Consider this prince! No other prince in Rus' has done what he did, for none of them has entered monastic life voluntarily; this man was indeed superior to all Rus' princes. How can the insults you have suffered be compared to his hair shirt? You were called to nakedness, and you deck yourself with fine clothes! You will be stripped bare because of them, and you will be condemned for failing to wear the bridal robe of humility. What does the blessed John write in the *Ladder*? "A Jew longs for food, so that he might celebrate according to the Law."[423] You are like them, concerned as you are with food and drink, and thereby making yourself renowned. Listen to the blessed Evagrios: "A monk, if he sins, has no festival on earth."[424] Do not feed your body, lest it become your adversary, and do not go to extremes in seeking high office; when you fail to achieve this, you bring reproach upon yourself. Take the holy fathers as your model, so that you may not be deprived of divine glory. If you cannot succeed in being crowned with the perfect, at least try to win praise with those who have pleased [God]. Yesterday you entered the monastic life, and

---

[421] See *Hyp.* 1162, PSRL 2:518. Izjaslav Davidovič, Svjatoša's brother, was killed in an interprincely quarrel on March 6, 1162, and buried in the Church of SS. Boris and Glěb in Černihiv.

[422] A clear indication of Polikarp's humble origins, which are hinted at in Discourse 14.

[423] Simon appears to be referring here to a passage in Step 14 of the *Ladder* (on Gluttony): "The Jew celebrates on Sabbaths and feast days." See *The Ladder of Divine Ascent*, 165.

[424] Abramovyč, *Issledovanie*, IORJAS 7, no. 3 (1902):73, n. 99, refers to a sermon entitled *O umilenii duši* (On the Emotion of the Soul) but admits that he has been unable to find the Greek original. It does not correspond to any of the Evagrian writings in PG 40, nor is it certain that the author actually was Evagrios of Pontus. The full Church Slavonic text of the sermon is found in the *Prolog* under October 27, and in the Great Menologion compiled in the sixteenth century by Metropolitan Makarij. See *Pamjatniki slavjano-russkoj pis'mennosti* (St. Petersburg, 1880), 1963–66.

already you are making your vows.[425] Before you have grown accustomed to the monastery you want to be a bishop and show yourself as a firm legislator; before becoming submissive yourself you want to subdue everybody else. You want to be wise in lofty matters, giving orders with the proud and contradicting others. I have heard these things from your own lips—how you think of earthly things and not those of heaven, of the things of the body rather than of the spirit, of bodily passions and not of self-control, of riches and not of poverty. You have abandoned the light and given yourself over to darkness; you have rejected life and prepared for yourself eternal torment. Having armed yourself against the enemy, you have turned those weapons against your own heart. Rise up, brother, and consider the danger to your life! Do not let your mind and your thoughts stray from that holy place!

And now, brother, I shall tell you about the monk Erazm—a story which deserves your close attention.

Discourse 21. *The monk Erazm, who spent his property on holy icons and found salvation through them.*

There was a monk in the Caves Monastery named Erazm, who was very rich. He spent all he had on the needs of the church and decorated with metal many icons which hang above the altar to this day. He became extremely poor and was neglected. He fell into despair because he had not received any recompense from the money he had spent on the church, and he had nothing with which to give alms. The devil put these ideas into his heart, and he began to be idle and to neglect everything and pass his days without any fixed plan. He fell seriously ill and remained speechless and blind for eight days, with only a little breath in his chest. On the eighth day all the brethren came to him, and when they saw his frightful breathing they marveled, saying, "Alas! Alas for the soul of this brother! For he has lived a life of idleness and sin, and now he sees something and is agitated, unable to depart from this life." Then Erazm got up, as though he had never been ill, sat down, and said to them, "My brothers and fathers, listen to me! This is truly how it is: you all know that I am a sinner and that up to this day I have not repented. Today the saints Antonij and Feodosij appeared to me, saying, 'We have prayed to God, and the Lord has given you time for repentance.' I saw both the holy Theotokos holding her Son Christ our God in her arms and all the

---

[425] Such vows were normally made at the end of a lengthy trial period. See Discourse 8, p. 45, n. 154.

saints with her. She said to me, 'Erazm, because you decorated my church and exalted it with icons, I shall glorify you in the kingdom of my Son, for you have the poor always with you. But rise up, repent, and receive the Great Angelic Habit.[426] In three days I shall take you, thus purified, to myself, for you have loved the beauty of my house.'"

After saying this to the brethren, he began to confess unhesitatingly before them all whatever sins he had committed. Rejoicing in the Lord, he was tonsured into the Habit, and three days later departed to the Lord in the fullness of faith. This I heard from the holy and blessed elders who actually saw what happened with their own eyes.

To Polikarp

Knowing this, brother, do not think, "I have spent my substance in vain." For before God everything is reckoned up to the uttermost farthing. Hope that you receive grace from God in return for your labors. You have completed two doors for the great and holy church of the holy Theotokos in the Caves Monasery, and she will open the doors of mercy to you. For the priests continually sing of such things in the church: "Sanctify, O Lord, those that love the beauty of Thy house, and glorify them with Thy holy strength."[427] Remember the patrician who ordered a cross to be made of pure gold, and the young man who, striving to emulate him, added his small amount of gold and inherited all his property.[428] If you spend what you have to glorify God and His holy Mother, you will not lose your reward. But say with David, "I praise Thee more and more,"[429] so that God may say to you, "I will honor them that honor me."[430] For you yourself said to me, "Woe is me! I am spending everything I have on the needs of the church. Let it not be spent in vain and destroyed by war or thieves or fire." I praised your good intentions. For the scripture says, "Vow, and pay your vows,"[431] and "It is better that thou shouldest not vow, than that thou shouldest

---

[426] The highest degree of monastic profession in the Eastern Church.
[427] This prayer comes at the conclusion of the Liturgy. See Abramovyč, *Pateryk*, 222, n. 136.
[428] Abramovyč, *Pateryk*, 222, n. 137, refers this incident to the *Sinajskij Paterik*, the Church Slavonic version of the *Pratum Spirituale* of John Moschos, but it does not appear in the text of the *Pratum Spirituale* in PG 87.
[429] Ps. 70:14.
[430] 1 Kings 2:30.
[431] Ps. 75:11.

vow and not pay."[432] If it should happen that such things are stolen by thieves or destroyed by war, do not blaspheme or be upset, but praise God for it, saying with Job, "The Lord gave, the Lord has taken away."[433]

And in addition I shall relate to you the story about the monk Arefa.

Discourse 22. The monk Arefa, the theft of whose property was regarded as charity, and so he was saved.

There was a monk in the Caves Monastery named Arefa, by birth a native of Polack. He had a great deal of wealth in his cell[434] and never gave either a single farthing or any bread to the poor. He was so stingy and hardhearted that he himself was dying of hunger. One night some thieves came and stole all his property. Arefa was so miserable on account of his stolen gold that he wanted to kill himself. He made life very difficult for innocent people and tormented many unjustly. We all begged him to stop asking questions, but he took no notice at all. The blessed elders comforted him, saying, "Brother, cast thy care up to the Lord, and He shall sustain thee,"[435] but he answered them with harsh and offensive words.

A few days later he fell seriously ill and was already at the point of death, but still he did not stop his grumbling and reproaches. But the Lord, Who wishes to save all men, showed him a vision[436] of advancing angels and a host of demons. He began to call out, "Lord, have mercy! Lord, I have sinned, it is Thine! I am not complaining!" After he recovered from his illness, he told us about his vision:

"When the angels came, demons entered too and began to dispute about my stolen property, saying, 'Since he complains and does not praise [God], he is ours and has been handed over to us.' The angels said to me, 'Accursed man! If you had given thanks to God for this, it would have been counted to your credit, as it was with Job. For if anyone gives alms, this is a great thing in the sight of God, but you must do it of your own free will. But if he thanks God for what has been taken away from him by force, this is better than charity. For if the devil has plunged a

---

[432] Eccles. 5:4.
[433] Job 1:21.
[434] This was strictly forbidden by the Stoudite Rule, and Feodosij was very vigilant in seeing that monks did not accumulate private possessions in their cells.
[435] Ps. 54:22.
[436] The word видѣник (vision) occurs in the Arsenian text and other MSS: Abramovyč, *Pateryk*, 121, n. 16.

man into complaining, and the man surrenders everything to God, this is more than charity; it is giving thanks as well.' After the angels said this to me, I cried out, 'It is Thine! Lord, have mercy! Lord, forgive me! Lord, I have sinned! It is all Thine, Lord! Lord, I shall not complain!' Straightway the demons disappeared and the angels rejoiced, and recorded the lost silver as almsgiving."

Hearing this, we glorified God, Who had made these things known to us. The blessed elders discussed the matter and said, "It is indeed right and proper to give thanks to God for all things." We saw Arefa daily praising and glorifying God, and we marveled at the change in his mind and character. Whereas previously no one could stop his complaining, now he was always crying out the words of Job: "The Lord gave, and the Lord has taken away: as it seemed good to the Lord so has it come to pass; blessed be the name of the Lord."[437] If he had not seen the vision of the angels and heard those words, he would never have stopped grumbling; and we used to believe that this was his true nature. If this were a small matter, the elder in the *Paterikon* would not have prayed to God that thieves might come and take everything he had; his prayer was heard, and he handed everything he possessed over to them.[438]

To Polikarp

I have now instructed you, brother, with all kinds of precepts. Pray to the Lord God that you may end your life here in repentance and in obedience to your superior, Akindin. These three things surpass all other virtues, as Afanasij the Solitary bore witness. Now I will tell you yet another remarkable miracle, which I myself witnessed. It happened as follows in the same holy Caves Monastery.

Discourse 23. The priest Tit and the deacon Evagrij, two brothers who were on very bad terms with each other.

There were two spiritual brothers, the deacon Evagrij and the priest Tit. They loved each other deeply and sincerely, so that everybody marveled at their harmony and boundless mutual affection. But the devil, that hater of good who is always roaring like a lion seeking someone to devour, made enmity between them and instilled such hatred that

---

[437] Job 1:21.
[438] Abramovyč, *Pateryk*, 222, n. 138, refers this incident to the *Sinajskij Paterik*. Cf. PG 87:3103–6 (no. 212).

they would not look at each other. The brethren often begged them to be reconciled, but they would not listen. When Evagrij was standing in the church and Tit came in with the censer, Evagrij would avoid the incense; and if he did not do so, Tit would go past without censing him. They remained for a long time in the darkness of sin, since when Tit was celebrating Evagrij refused to accept absolution and received communion in anger. It was the enemy that put them up to this.

One day Tit fell seriously ill, and as he lay in despair he began to weep for his loss and sent to the deacon in a spirit of contrition, saying, "Forgive me, brother, for God's sake, for being angry with you!" But Evagrij cursed him with violent words. The elders, seeing that Tit was dying, forcibly dragged Evagrij in to forgive his brother. When the sick man saw him he rose up a little and fell down at his feet, saying with tears, "Forgive me, father, and give your blessing." But the cruel and hardhearted Evagrij refused and said in front of all of us, "I will never be reconciled with him, neither in this world nor in the next!" He tore himself away from the elders' arms and immediately fell down. When we tried to get him to his feet, we found that he was dead. We were unable to stretch out his arms or close his lips as though he had been dead for a long time. Meanwhile the sick one got up quickly, as though he had never been ill. We were filled with terror at the sudden death of the one and the rapid recovery of the other.

After much weeping we buried Evagrij with his lips and eyes open and his arms outstretched. We asked Tit what had happened, and he told us, "I saw some angels moving away from me and weeping over my soul, while demons rejoiced at my anger. Then I began to beg my brother to forgive me. When they brought him to me, I saw a pitiless angel holding a fiery lance. When Evagrij refused to forgive me, the angel struck him and he fell down dead, but the angel gave me his hand and lifted me up."

When we heard this, we were filled with the fear of God Who said, "Forgive, and you shall be forgiven."[439] For the Lord said, "Whoever is angry with his brother without a cause shall be in danger of the judgment."[440] And Ephraim says, "If any man should die in a state of enmity, he will be judged without mercy."[441] If this man does not

---

[439] Matt. 6:14; Luke 6:37.
[440] Matt. 5:22.
[441] Abramovyč, *Pateryk*, 222, n. 139, refers this quotation to the *Paraenesis* of Ephraim the Syrian. So far I have not been able to locate it; it does not appear in the *Paraenesis II ad poenitentiam*, published in *Ecclesiae Anglicanae. Vindex Catholicus*, ed. W. W. Har-

receive absolution through the holy Antonij and Feodosij, woe unto him, vanquished as he is by such a passion.

To Polikarp

Be warned by this story and take care, brother, not to give any room to the demon of anger, for whoever is subject to him becomes his slave. Rather you should fall down and prostrate yourself before your enemy, lest you be delivered over to the pitiless angel. May the Lord preserve you from any feeling of anger, for He said, "Let not the sun go down upon your wrath."[442] To Him be glory with the Father and the Holy Spirit now and forever.

Discourse 24. A second epistle, to Archimandrite Akindin of the Caves Monastery about the holy and blessed monks of that monastery, written by Polikarp, a monk of the Caves Monastery.[443]

With the Lord assisting me and confirming my words [I address myself] to your piety, my father and lord Akindin, most honorable archimandrite of all Rus'.[444] Incline your gracious ears, so that I may pour into them the lives, deeds, and portents of those marvelous and blessed men who formerly lived in this Caves Monastery about which I heard from Simon, bishop of Vladimir and Suzdal', your brother, who was once a monk in this Caves Monastery. He told me, sinner that I am, about the holy and great Antonij, the founder of monastic life in Rus', about the holy Feodosij, and about the lives and achievements of the holy and venerable fathers after their time who ended their lives in the house of the most pure Mother of God. May your wise understanding pay heed to my immature and imperfect thoughts.

You asked me once to tell you about the deeds of these monks. Knowing how crude and lacking in refinement I am, and aware that I am always terrified when I tell any tale in your presence, how could I recount clearly the marvelous signs and wonders performed by them? I told you a little about these remarkable miracles, but I forgot most of

---

vey, vol. 2 (Cambridge, 1842), 318–34.
[442] Eph. 4:26.
[443] For a suggested reconstruction of the original content of this epistle, see Appendix III.
[444] For the introduction of this honorific title for the superior of the Caves Monastery, see above, Discourse 8, p. 24, n. 94, and also Discourse 38.

them from fright, since I felt ashamed in the presence of your piety, and I told my tale stupidly. So I have felt constrained to send you a written account of our holy and blessed brotherhood, so that the monks who come after us may know of the grace of God which formerly dwelt in this holy place, and may glorify our heavenly Father Who revealed such shining lights in the land of Rus', in the holy Caves Monastery.

Discourse 25. Nikita the Solitary, who later became bishop of Novgorod.

While the venerable Nikon was superior,[445] there was [in the monastery] a brother named Nikita. He wished to be honored by men and conceived a great deed, but not for God's sake: he began to ask the superior to allow him to withdraw into solitude. The superior forbade him to do so, saying, "My son, it is not profitable for you to sit idle, since you are young. It is better for you to stay among the brethren and work for them. You will not risk losing your reward. You yourself have seen how our brother the holy Isaakij the Cave-dweller was seduced by demons.[446] Had he not been saved by God's grace, through the prayers of the venerable fathers Antonij and Feodosij, who to this day work many miracles, he would have been lost." Nikita said, "I will certainly not be seduced by such a trick. I will ask the Lord God to grant me the gift of working miracles." Nikon answered, "What you are asking is beyond your powers. Take care, brother, lest you exalt yourself and then have a fall. Our humility orders you to serve the holy brotherhood, for whose sake you will be crowned as a reward for your obedience." Nikita remained unmoved by the superior's words and did exactly what he wanted: he shut the door behind him and remained [in the cave] without going out.

Before many days had passed he was seduced by the devil. While he was singing, he heard a voice praying with him and smelled an indescribably fragrant odor. He was deceived by this and said to himself, "If this were not an angel, he would not be praying with me, nor would there be this fragrant odor of the Holy Spirit." He began to pray diligently, "Show Thyself plainly to me, O Lord, that I may see Thee." Then a voice said to him, "I shall not reveal myself to you because you are young and lest you be puffed up and then fall." The solitary said with tears, "I shall in no way be deceived, O Lord, since I have been

---
[445] I.e., between 1078 and 1088.
[446] See below, Discourse 36.

instructed by my superior to pay no attention to the wiles of the devil; but I shall do everything that Thou dost command." Then the serpent, that slayer of souls, assumed power over him and said, "It is impossible for a man to behold me while he is still in the flesh. I shall send my angel to stay with you. Act according to his will." Straightway a demon stood before him in the guise of an angel.[447] The monk fell down and venerated him as an angel. The demon said to him, "Do not pray, but read your books. Through them you will find yourself conversing with God, and you will be able to give useful advice to people who come to visit you.[448] I shall pray continually to my creator for your salvation."

Having been seduced, the monk did not pray, but applied himself diligently to reading and studying. He would see the demon continuously praying for him, and he rejoiced that an angel was praying for him. He conversed for the good of their souls with those who came to visit him, and began to prophesy. This brought him great fame, so that everyone marveled at the way in which his prophesies were fulfilled. One day Nikita sent a message to Prince Izjaslav,[449] saying, "Today Glěb Svjatoslavič has been killed at Zavoloč'e.[450] Quickly send your son Svjatopolk to rule in Novgorod." And it happened exactly as he said; a few days later Glěb's death became known. From then on the Solitary became famous as a prophet, and princes and boyars paid close attention to him. In fact a demon does not know what will come to pass but, acting on his own, instructs evil men either to kill or to steal and makes those things known;[451] the monk would prophesy these things, which did indeed come to pass.

No one could dispute with him about the books of the Old Testament, since he knew them all by heart: Genesis, Exodus, Leviticus, Numbers, Judges, Kings, and all the Prophets in order; and he knew all

---

[447] Cf. the experience of Isaakij, recorded below in Discourse 36.
[448] It was a well-established custom in medieval monasticism for solitaries to be visited by people seeking practical advice and spiritual guidance. See Heppell, "The *Vita Antonii*," 55.
[449] Izjaslav Jaroslavič, three times prince of Kiev (1054–68, 1069–73, 1078).
[450] Glěb Svjatoslavič, prince of Tmutorokan', was killed in battle against his uncle Izjaslav Jaroslavič on May 30, 1078. See PVL 1078, PSRL 1:199, 2:190.
[451] I have used the Arsenian reading here: Abramovyč, *Pateryk*, 126, nn. 14–15.
[452] These were probably other books in the Old Testament, and probably some in the Apocrypha. This passage provides interesting evidence of what parts of the Old Testament were known and read in Rus' in the eleventh century; there was no complete text of the Bible until the time of the Gennadij Bible in 1499.

the Jewish books as well.[452] But as for the Gospel and the Apostle,[453] the holy books given to us by grace to confirm us [in the faith] and set our lives in the right path, he did not wish to see, hear, or read them, nor would he allow anyone else to talk to him about them. From this it became clear to everybody that he had been seduced by the enemy.

The venerable fathers—the superior Nikon, Ioann who succeeded him as superior, Pimin the Faster,[454] Isaia who became bishop of Rostov,[455] Matfej the Percipient,[456] holy Isaakij the Cave-dweller,[457] Agapit the Physician,[458] Grigorij the Miracle-worker,[459] Nikola who became bishop of Tmutorokan',[460] Nestor who wrote the chronicle,[461] Grigorij the creator of the canons,[462] Feoktist who became the bishop of Černihiv,[463] and Onisifor the Percipient[464]— could not accept this. These God-bearers came to the man who had been tempted, prayed to God, and expelled the demon from him; after this Nikita did not see him. They led him outside and questioned him about the Old Testament, as they wished to hear something [about this] from him. He swore that he had never read these books. This man, who had known the Jewish books by heart, now did not know a single word, to put it simply. The blessed fathers could scarcely teach him letters.

---

[453] I.e., the Pauline Epistles.
[454] If this "Pimin the Faster" is the same as the one in Discourse 18, then Kukša must have been killed towards the end of the eleventh century. It is also possible that this Pimin is identical with the Pimin of Discourse 35.
[455] Cf. Discourse 8, p. 51, Discourse 6, p. 16, Discourse 14, p. 118.
[456] See Discourse 12, p. 109.
[457] See Discourse 36.
[458] See Discourse 27.
[459] See Discourse 28.
[460] See Discourse 14, p. 119.
[461] The connection of Nestor with the PVL is one of the most disputed questions associated with the chronicle. See A. G. Kuz'min, Načal'nye ètapy drevnerusskogo letopisanija (Moscow, 1977), 133–54.
[462] Nothing more is known of this Grigorij. He presumably was engaged in adapting the Byzantine chant to the Rus' version of Church Slavonic (or vice versa). In this connection it is interesting to note a brief item sub anno 1073 in the *Novgorod Fourth Chronicle* (PSRL 4:117) about the arrival of three singers from Greece with their families.
[463] See Discourse 14, p. 119.
[464] At first sight this monk would seem to be identical with the monk Onisifor of Discourse 15, who also had the gift of discernment. But as the incident described there relates to the mid-twelfth century, there must be some other explanation. Possibly Polikarp did not remember accurately at this point and confused Onisifor with Matfej, whom he had already mentioned.

From then on he devoted himself to self-denial and obedience and to living a pure and humble life, so that he excelled everybody in virtue; later he was made bishop of Novgorod on account of his many virtuous deeds.[465] He performed many miracles: once during a drought he prayed to God and brought down rain from heaven and extinguished a fire in the town. Now this holy and blessed Nikita is honored with the saints.

Discourse 26. Lavrentij the Solitary.

Some time later another brother named Lavrentij wished to retire into solitude, but the holy fathers absolutely forbade him to do so. Lavrentij went to the Monastery of St. Demetrios, founded by Prince Izjaslav, and lived as a recluse there.[466] Because of his austere life, the Lord granted him the gift of healing.

A certain man was brought to him from Kiev, who was possessed by a demon which the solitary was unable to cast out. It was a ferocious demon, like wood, which ten men could scarcely carry, and yet this monk single-handedly took hold of him and bound him. He remained there unhealed a long time, and the solitary ordered him to be taken to the Caves Monastery. Then the demoniac began to cry out, "To whom are you sending me? I dare not approach the cave because of the holy ones buried there. There are only thirty in the monastery whom I fear. I'll fight with the others." Those who were dragging him along knew that he had never been in the Caves Monastery and knew no one there. They asked him, "Who are those whom you fear?" The demoniac gave the names of all of them. "These thirty," he said, "will drive me out by a single word." There were then 180 monks in all. They said to the demoniac, "We are going to shut you in the cave." The demoniac said, "What is the use of me fighting with dead men? For they can now approach God more boldly on behalf of their monks and pray for those who come to them. But if you want to see me fight, take me to the monastery." Then he began to speak in Hebrew and Latin and also in Greek, in short in languages which he had never heard, so that those taking him were terrified by his change of languages and diversity of tongues.

Before he arrived at the monastery he recovered and began to think clearly. The superior and the brethren came to [see] him, but after his

---

[465] Nikita was bishop of Novgorod from 1096 to 1108. See Golubinskij, *Istorija russkoj cerkvi*, 1, 1:672.

[466] See above, Discourse 7, p. 22, n. 85, and Discourse 8, p. 66.

recovery he did not know a single one of the thirty people whom he had mentioned while possessed.[467] Those who had brought him asked, "Who cured you?" He looked at the miracle-working icon of the Theotokos and said, "Thirty holy fathers (whom he mentioned by name) came with her to meet me, and I was healed." He knew all their names, but not a single one of these elders personally. So together they all rendered glory to God, His most holy Mother, and His blessed servants.

I have written this down for you, my lord Akindin, in order not to conceal in darkness or hide from view the wonderful miracles, signs, and virtuous deeds of our blessed and venerable fathers, and in order that others may learn about the holy life of our brotherhood—how on one occasion there were as many as thirty monks with the power to cast out demons by a single word: demoniacs dared not approach the cave, because the holy fathers Antonij and Feodosij and the other holy monks whose names are written in the Book of Life were buried there. Blessed is he who has been considered worthy of being buried with them, and blessed and saved is he who has been considered worthy of having his name inscribed along with theirs. May the Lord in His mercy consider me also worthy of being with them in the Day of Judgment, thanks to your prayers. Amen.

Discourse 27. The holy and blessed Agapit the Physician, who took no fee.

There was a certain man from Kiev named Agapit, who was tonsured in the time of our blessed father Antonij;[468] having seen Antonij's good deeds for himself, he followed his angelic way of life. Just as that great man concealed his sanctity and healed the sick by giving them some of his own food—it seemed to them that he was giving them medicinal herbs, and then they recovered through his prayers—so the blessed Agapit helped sick people, emulating the holy elder. When any of the brethren fell ill, he would leave his cell, go to the sick brother, and serve

---

[467] Polikarp describes all the typical symptoms of demonic possession: abnormal physical strength, fear of specific spiritual forces, knowledge beyond the victim's normal experience, and complete oblivion after recovery. See T. K. Oestereich, *Possession, Demoniacal and Other, among Primitive Races, in Antiquity, the Middle Ages and Modern Times*, trans. I. D. Ibberson (London, 1930), 17 ff.

[468] If Agapit was one of Antonij's earliest disciples and came to him before he withdrew into solitude ca. 1033, he would have been very old by the time the incidents related in this discourse took place, since they can be assigned to the last two decades of the eleventh century. See below, n. 475.

him (for there was nothing worth stealing in his cell).[469] He would lift him up, carry him away with his own hands, and give him some of his own food (cooked greens), and so the sick man would recover through his prayers. If his sickness lingered—since it pleased God to increase the prayers and faith of His servant in this way—the blessed Agapit would pray to God for him without ceasing, until God restored the patient to health through his prayers. For this reason he was called "the Physician," because the Lord had given him the gift of healing. People said about him in the town that there was a man in the monastery who was a physician; many sick people came to him and were healed.

There lived at the same time as this blessed one a certain man, an Armenian by birth and belief, who was very skilled in medicine, better than any of his predecessors.[470] As soon as he looked at a sick man, he knew when he would die and would tell him the day and hour of his death; in no way would he change his declaration or treat the sick man. One of these patients, who had a high position in the household of Prince Vsevolod,[471] was brought to the Caves Monastery; he had been driven to despair by the Armenian, who had predicted that he would die in eight days. The blessed Agapit gave the man the greens which he was eating himself and cured him.

His fame spread throughout the land. The Armenian, however, was wounded by the arrow of jealousy and began to revile the blessed one. He sent to the monastery a man condemned to death: he ordered him to be given some deadly herbs, so that after eating them he would fall down dead in front of Agapit. But when the blessed one saw that the man was dying he gave him some food from the monastery and healed him by his prayers; thus he delivered from death one who had been under a death

---

[469] This implies that there were other monks who did have property worth stealing; clearly they were accumulating private possessions, in spite of Feodosij's vigorous efforts to prevent this. See above, Discourse 8, pp. 62, 63.

[470] Таковъ не бѣ преже его. This suggests that there had previously been other Armenian physicians in Kiev, but there are no specific references to others in any sources. Ya. Dachkévytch, "Les Arméniens à Kiev (jusqu'à 1240). Deuxième partie," *Revue des études arméniennes* 9 (1975–76):323, cites this passage as "le plus grand témoignage écrit sur les Arméniens à Kiev" relating to the late eleventh century, but later (p. 328) says, "En effet la Vie d'Agapit constitue la première mention écrite sur les Arméniens à Kiev." Oganess'an, *Istorija mediciny v Armenii*, 229–32, lists thirty-one physicians, some of them Arabs or Syrians, known to have practiced and/or written about medicine in Armenia in the late eleventh century. He includes the one mentioned here but does not cite any others working in Kiev.

[471] Vsevolod, the fifth son of Jaroslav the Wise, was the last to rule Kiev (1078–1093).

sentence. Henceforth the heterodox[472] Armenian prepared for war against Agapit and incited his fellow believers against him, telling them to give him poisonous herbs to drink, since he wished to cause his death in this way. But the blessed one drank them without harm or suffering any unpleasantness. For the Lord knows how to deliver pious men from death, having said, "If they drink any deadly thing, it shall not hurt them; they shall lay hands on the sick, and they shall recover."[473]

At this time Prince Volodimer Vsevolodovič Monomax[474] fell ill. The Armenian attended him and treated him diligently, but without success, and the illness grew worse. When he was at the point of death he sent to Ioann, the superior of the Caves Monastery, and begged him to compel Agapit to come to him, since he was then prince of Černihiv.[475] The blessed one answered, "If I go to the prince, then I must go to everybody. For the sake of glory from men I shall not betray the vow which I made before God to stay in the monastery until my last breath. If you send me away, I shall go to another county and come back when this affair has passed." He had in fact never left the monastery. When the prince's envoy saw that he would not come, he begged the monk at least to give him some herbs. At the superior's insistence he gave him some herbs from his own food to give to the sick man. When the prince tasted these herbs, he immediately recovered.

Volodimer arrived in Kiev and came to the Caves Monastery, as he wished to pay honor to the monk and see who it was who had given him the herbs and with God's help restored him to health.[476] For he had never seen him, and thought to make him a gift from his property. But Agapit,

---

[472] As non-Chalcedonians and monophysites, the Armenians were regarded as heretics. The *Nikonian Chronicle*, PSRL 9:147–49, includes under the year 1114 an account of a disputation between some Armenians and a certain bishop Ilarion, bishop of the Bulgarian town of Merlin, in which they are accused of being monophysites and also reproached for using undiluted wine in the liturgy and for fasting in honor of a dog belonging to a heresiarch named Sergej; the dog was killed by a wolf.

[473] Mark 16:18.

[474] Vsevolod Jaroslavič's eldest son, prince of Perejaslav (1094–1113) and Kiev (1113–1125).

[475] Volodimer Monomax was prince in Černihiv from 1078 until after his father's death in 1093, when under pressure he ceded the city to his cousin Oleg Svjatoslavič, whose father had previously held it (PVL 1094, PSRL 1:226, 2:217). The reference to Ioann, who succeeded Nikon as superior in 1088, narrows the date of this episode to between 1088 and 1094.

[476] There is also a reference to Volodimer experiencing a miraculous cure in the Caves Monastery in Discourse 4 (see above, p. 13). This apparently happened when he was much younger, while his father Vsevolod was still prince in Perejaslav.

who had no wish for praise, hid himself, and the prince gave the gold he had brought to the superior. After this Volodimer sent one of his boyars to the blessed Agapit with many gifts. The boyar found him in his cell, brought [out] his gifts, and put them down in front of him. Agapit answered, "My son, I have never taken anything from anybody. Shall I now lose my reward for the sake of gold which I never requested from anybody?" The boyar answered, "Father, he who sent me knows that you did not require this. But for my sake comfort your son whom you have restored to health in God's name. Take this and give it to the poor." The elder answered, "I shall gladly take it for your sake, because there are things that I need. Say to him who sent you, 'Everything you possess belongs to others. You cannot take anything with you when you depart this life. Distribute everything you have now to those in need, since that is why the Lord delivered you from death. I could have done nothing for you. Do not disobey me, lest you suffer again.'" Agapit took the gold, carried it outside his cell, threw it away, and hid himself. The boyar went out and saw that the gold and the gifts had been thrown away. He took them all and gave them to the superior Ioann, and told the prince everything about the elder. Everybody realized that he was a servant of God. The prince did not dare disobey the elder, and he distributed all his possessions to the poor, according to the blessed one's words.

After this the monk Agapit fell ill, and the aforementioned Armenian came to visit him and began to argue with him about medical skills, asking him which herbs would cure such a disease. "Those through which the Lord will give health," answered the blessed one. The Armenian realized that the monk was quite ignorant and said to his companions, "This man knows nothing!" And taking him by the hand he said, "He will die within three days. This is the truth, and my words shall not prove false. If this does not happen, I shall become a monk." The blessed one said to him angrily, "Are these your methods of healing? You tell me that I will die and that you cannot help me? If you have the skill, then give me my life. If this is beyond you, then why do you blame me, sentencing me to death within three days? The Lord has informed me that I shall die in three months." The Armenian said to him, "But you are aware that you cannot live more than two days. You are very ill and unable to move by yourself."

At that moment a sick man from Kiev was brought in. Agapit arose as though he were not ill, took some herbs which he had been eating himself, showed them to the physician and said, "Here are my herbs. Look and you see what they are." When the physician saw them he said to the monk, "These are not our herbs. I think that they come from Alexandria." The blessed one laughed at his ignorance, gave the herbs to the sick man, and restored him to health. He said to the physician, "Eat, my son, and do not complain,[477] since we are so poor and have nothing to give you to eat." The Armenian said to him, "Just now, father, we have been fasting for four days of this month."[478] The blessed one asked him, "Who are you, and what is your faith?" The physician said to him, "Have you not heard that I am an Armenian?" The blessed one said to him, "How dare you come and defile my cell and hold my sinful hand! Get away from me, you impious heterodox!"[479] The Armenian went away, covered with confusion.

The blessed Agapit remained alive for three months and then departed to the Lord after a short illness. After his death the Armenian came to the monastery and said to the superior, "I will become a monk and abandon my Armenian faith and truly believe in the Lord Jesus Christ. For the blessed Agapit appeared to me, saying, 'You promised to take the monastic habit. If you betray this vow, you will lose both your life and your soul.' And so I believe this. But if this blessed man had wanted to live a long time, God would not have taken him away from this world. Even if the Lord did take him, He gave him eternal life. I reckon that he left us of his own free will, because he desired the heavenly kingdom, but that he is still able to live with us. I thought that he would not live for three days, and for this reason he assigned himself three months. If I had said three months, he would have stayed alive for three years. Even if he has died, he has taken up his abode in this house, abiding in eternal life, and is alive there." Then the Armenian was

---

[477] I have use the variant reading жали се here: Abramovyč, *Pateryk*, 132, n. 3.
[478] Days of fasting observed by the Armenians are discussed by T. E. Dowling, *The Armenian Church* (London, 1910), 96; A. A. King, *The Rites of Eastern Christendom*, vol. 2 (Rome, 1948), 578; and R. Janin, *Églises orientales et rites orientaux* (Paris, 1955), 331–32. In addition to all Wednesdays, Fridays, and the whole of Lent (except Sundays), they included a period of fasting every month, usually before a major festival.
[479] Dachkévytch, "Les Arméniens," 329, thinks that this description of Agapit's hostile reaction represents the climate of opinion in the early thirteenth century, when Polikarp was writing, rather than that of the late eleventh century, when the encounter between the monk and the Armenian physician is supposed to have taken place. He points out that the Armenian's religious allegiance evidently did not prevent him from being accepted as a personal physician by highly placed persons in Kiev.

tonsured in the Caves Monastery and ended his life there in the fullness of faith.[480]

Such deeds and even greater ones were performed by these holy monks, recalling whose virtuous life I marvel that the great achievements of our holy fathers Antonij and Feodosij have been passed over in silence. If so great a light should be extinguished through our neglect,[481] how can rays shine forth from it—I mean these venerable fathers, our brethren? But as the Lord said, "No prophet is accepted in his own country."[482] If, most honored archimandrite, my lord Akindin, I have recorded for you the miracles of some of these aforementioned holy and venerable fathers, the ascetic achievements of some, the resolute self-denial of others, the obedience of others, and the gift of prophecy of yet others—all these things were made known to me by faith, all their signs and miracles, by your fellow monk and my master, Bishop Simon. Other people consider the things I have related to be distasteful, because of the greatness of the deeds described, but the fault lies in their lack of faith—they know me as the sinful Polikarp. But if your venerableness should order me to record those things which my mind can grasp and my memory recall, even if they are not necessary for you, let us leave them for the benefit of those who come after us, just as the blessed Nestor wrote about the blessed fathers Damian, Ieremej, Matfej, and Isaakij in the chronicle.[483] All their lives are related in the Life of the holy Antonij, though only briefly. But as for the aforementioned monks, I speak plainly, not obscurely as in former times. For if I keep silent, they will be completely forgotten, and not even their names will be remembered, as was the case up to this day. Now in the fifteenth year of your service as superior I speak of things never mentioned for 160 years.[484] Now,

---

[480] The following paragraph is Polikarp's own conclusion. For further discussion, see Appendix III.

[481] Does this obscurely refer to the Life of Antonij, which included accounts of other earlier monks of the monastery whose lives were in danger of being forgotten? See the Introduction, p. xl.

[482] Luke 4:24. Cf. also Matt. 13:57; Mark 6:4.

[483] See PVL 1074, PSRL 1:189–91, 2:180–82. A. A. Šaxmatov, "Kievo-Pečerskij Paterik i Pečerskaja Letopis'," IORJAS 2 (1897), thinks that Polikarp is referring to a lost chronicle of the Caves Monastery. But Polikarp more likely was thinking of the PVL and not of some inextant predecessor.

[484] Unfortunately, the dates of Akindin's period of office are not known, so this information does not enable us to fix the time when Polikarp was writing. See the Introduction, p. xxviii–xxx.

thanks to your love, those things which had been concealed are now being heard, and the memory of those who love God will be honored and praised forever, for those who please Him will receive a crown from Him.

It is a great thing for me to be adorned by such things, and I think that I shall conceal the shame of my deeds in this way: I shall simply call to mind the things I have heard, write them down, and think that it was I who sought out the marvelous deeds of these men. As the Lord says, "Joy shall be in heaven over one sinner that repenteth."[485] How much more will the angels rejoice over so many righteous men, for they now live in heaven and their glory is sufficient for their heirs. For while here they did not care about the flesh, but, as incorporeal beings, they despised earthly things and considered everything in this life to be as dung, so that they might attain only Christ. For they loved Him alone, bound themselves fast to His love, and commended their wills entirely to Him, so that they might receive deification from Him. He gave them on earth the gift of working miracles as a reward for their labors, and in the life to come He will glorify them with indescribable glory. For on earth nothing is given to men without the Holy Spirit, nothing that is not given from above. Therefore I, the sinful Polikarp, have recorded these things, doing this work in obedience to your will, my lord Akindin.

But tell me, and I shall relate to you one more small incident, about our blessed and venerable father Grigorij the Miracle-worker.

Discourse 28. Holy Grigorij the Miracle-worker.

The blessed Grigorij came to our holy father Feodosij in the Caves Monastery, and was instructed by him in the monastic life: voluntary poverty, humility, obedience, and other virtues. He was especially diligent in prayer, and because of this he received power over demons.[486] Even when they were a long way away they would cry out, "Grigorij, you are driving us out by your prayers!" It was this blessed man's custom to recite prayers of exorcism[487] after every office. The ancient enemy could not endure being driven out by him, and as he could not harm him in any other way, he instructed some wicked men to rob him. Actually he possessed nothing but books.

---

[485] Luke 15:7.
[486] See above, Discourse 25, p. 145, where Grigorij is mentioned by name, and Discourse 26.
[487] запрещалныя молитвы: literally "prohibiting prayers," designed to expel demons.

One night thieves came and kept watch on the elder, so that when he went out for matins they could go and take everything he had. But Grigorij was aware of their arrival, for every night he stayed awake, singing and praying ceaselessly in the middle of his cell, and he also prayed for these men who had come to rob him: "Lord, grant that Thy servants may fall asleep, since they labor in vain, giving pleasure only to the enemy." And they slept for five days and five nights, until the blessed one summoned the brothers and woke the thieves up, saying, "Until now you have kept watch over me in vain, since you wanted to rob me. Now go home." They got up but could not move as they were weak from hunger. The blessed one gave them something to eat and sent them away.

When the town governor learned this, he ordered the thieves to be tortured.[488] Grigorij was distressed that the thieves had been handed over [to torture] because of him. He went and gave some books to the governor and he released the thieves. He sold the rest of his books and distributed the money to the poor, saying, "Let no one fall into misfortune who would want to steal them."[489] For the Lord said, "Lay not up for yourselves treasures upon earth, where thieves break through and steal. But lay up for yourselves treasures in heaven, where rust doth not corrupt and thieves do not steal. For where your treasure is, there will your hearts also be."[490] The thieves, repenting on account of the miracle which had befallen them, did not return to their previous activity, but came to the Caves Monastery and went to work for the brethren.

This blessed man had a garden where he planted vegetables and fruit trees. And thieves came there too. When they had taken up their loads, intending to leave, they were unable to do so.[491] For two days they stood motionless, weighed down by their burdens, and they began to cry out, "Lord Grigorij, let us go! We have already repented our sins and we will do such things no more!" When the monks heard them, they

---

[488] There is no evidence in medieval Rus' sources of torture being a regular part of judicial procedure, as it was later in Muscovy. See D. H. Kaiser, *The Growth of Law in Medieval Russia* (Princeton, 1980), 146–47.

[489] Cf. Ἀνδρῶν ἁγίων βίβλος, 226, lns. 13–16: Abba Arsenios gave a thief a golden coin so that he would not be tempted to steal.

[490] Matt 6:19–21. Cf. Luke 12:33–34.

[491] I. Dujčev, "Épizod iz Kievo-Pečerskogo Paterika," TODRL 24 (1969):89–93, points out that the prototype of this story of a malefactor being struck motionless is the story of King Jeroboam I of Israel (3 Kings 13:1–6) and that it has many parallels in later literature. He concludes that this episode in Discourse 28 therefore "has no historical value."

came to take them but could not lead them away from that place. And they questioned them, "When did you come here?" The thieves answered, "We have been standing here for two days and two nights." The monks said, "But we always come and go and we have not seen you here." The thieves said, "If we had seen you here, we would have begged you with tears to let us go. Lo, we were incapacitated and we began to cry out. Now entreat the elder to release us."

Grigorij came and said to them, "Since you have been idle all your lives, stealing the fruits of others' labors and unwilling to work yourselves, now you must stand here in idleness for the rest of your days." They entreated the elder with tears and said that they would not again commit such misdeeds. The elder took pity on them and said, "If you are willing to work and feed others by your own labors, I will let you go." The thieves vowed, "We will obey you absolutely." Grigorij said, "Blessed be God! Henceforth you will work for the holy brotherhood and bring them what they need from the fruits of your labor." And so he let them go. The thieves ended their lives in the Caves Monastery and looked after the garden; their descendants, I believe, are here to this day.

One day three men arrived, wishing to test this blessed man. Two of them entreated the holy man, saying falsely, "Our friend has been condemned to death. We implore you to try and save him. Give him something with which to ransom himself from death." Grigorij burst into weeping from grief, since he foresaw that the end of this man's life was at hand. He said, "Woe unto this man! For the day of his destruction has drawn near." But they said, "Father, if you give something, he will not die." They said this because they wanted to get something from him and divide it up. Grigorij said, "I will give you something, but he will die." He asked them to what kind of death he had been sentenced. They said, "He will be hung on a tree." The blessed one said, "They sentenced him correctly. He will be hung in the morning." Then he descended into the cellar where he used to pray (so that his mind would not hear any earthly things, nor his eyes look upon any vanities) and brought up the rest of his books. He gave these to them, saying, "If these are not suitable, bring them back to me." They took the books and started to laugh, saying, "We will sell them and divide up the money." Then they saw the fruit trees and said to each other, "Let us come here tonight and take away his fruit."

When night fell the three men came and shut the monk in the cellar where he was praying. Then one of them—the one they had said would be hanged on a tree—climbed up and began to pick the apples and got himself entangled on a branch, which broke. The other two ran away in terror, but the first man, flying in mid air, caught his clothes on another branch, and as there was no one to help him he was choked by his necklace. Grigorij, who was locked in the cellar, could not come to join the brethren in church, and when they all came out of the church and saw the man hanging dead, they were terrified. They looked for Grigorij and found him locked up in the cellar. When they came out, the blessed one told them to take the dead man down and said to the man's friends, "See how your plan has been fulfilled! For God is not mocked.[492] If you had not shut me up, I could have come and taken him down from the tree, and he would not have died. Since the enemy has taught you falsely to guard vanities through deceit, you have abandoned feelings of compassion." When the two revilers heard that what he had spoken about had come to pass, they fell down at his feet and begged for forgiveness. Grigorij sentenced them to work in the Caves Monastery, so that from then on they should eat bread for which they had worked and be content to feed others from their own labors. And thus they ended their lives, working together with their children in the Caves Monastery for the servants of the holy Theotokos and the disciples of our holy father Feodosij.

It is fitting to relate how this blessed one suffered a violent death. Once in the monastery a vessel was defiled because an animal fell into it, and because of this the venerable Grigorij went down to the Dnieper for water. At that very moment Prince Rostislav Vsevolodovič approached, intending to go to the Caves Monastery for a prayer and a blessing, as he was going on a campaign against the Cumans with his brother Volodimer.[493] When his servants saw the elder they began revile him and to taunt him with shameful words. The monk, who realized that they were all close to death, said, "My sons, at the very time when you should have compassion and should be seeking many prayers from everybody, you are doing something evil which is displeasing to God. You should rather be lamenting your destruction and repenting your transgressions, so that you might at least obtain remission on Judgment Day. For judgment has already caught up with you: you will all die in the water together with your prince." The prince, who did not fear God and did not take the venerable one's words to heart but thought he was talking nonsense in making this prophecy about him, said, "Are you telling me that I shall

---

[492] Gal. 6:7.

[493] Immediately after the death of Vsevolod Jaroslavič in 1093, the Cumans attacked Kiev, and Svjatopolk Izjaslavič, Vsevolod's successor as prince of Kiev, asked his cousins Volodimer Monomax and Rostislav Vsevolodovič to help him to mount a counterattack. See PVL 1093, PSRL 1:219–20, 2:210–11.

die in the water, when I know how to get across it?" Then the prince got very angry, and ordered [his servants] to tie up the monk's hands and feet, hang a stone round his neck, and throw him into the water. And so he was drowned.

The brethren looked for him for two days but could not find him. On the third day they went to his cell, intending to take the rest of his things, and there he was, dead, tied up in his cell with a stone round his neck. His clothes were still wet, and his countenance was radiant, as though he were alive. They could not find out who had brought him, and his cell was shut. But glory be to the Lord, Who works marvelous miracles for His servants! The brethren carried out his body and with due honor buried it in the cave, where it remained whole and free from corruption for many years.

Rostislav did not seek forgiveness for his sin and did not come to the monastery because he was so angry. He did not desire a blessing and withdrew himself from it; he loved a curse, and it came upon him. But Volodimer did come to the monastery for a prayer. When they were at Trypillja[494] the armies met, and our princes fled from the face of their enemies. Thanks to the prayers and blessing of the holy men, Volodimer crossed the river, but Rostislav was drowned with all his soldiers, just as the blessed Grigorij has said.[495] It is said, "For with what judgment ye judge, ye shall be judged: and with what measure ye mete, it shall be measured to you."[496] Mark well, those of you that give offense—a dangerous thing—the parable told by the Lord in the holy Gospel about the merciless judge and the importunate widow.[497] She often came to see Him, and made a nuisance of herself, saying, "Avenge me of mine enemy." I tell you that the Lord will speedily avenge His servants, for He says, "Vengeance is mine; I will repay."[498] The Lord says, "Despise not one of these little ones: the angels do always behold the face of my Father which is in heaven."[499] For the Lord is righteous, and loves righteousness; His face beholds uprightness.[500] Whatsoever a man

---

[494] A town south of Kiev at the confluence of the Stuhna and the Dnieper.
[495] The Rus' princes were unable to withstand the onslaught of the Cuman archers and were forced to flee. They dived into the Stuhna. Volodimer got across safely, but Rostislav was drowned, in spite of Volodimer's efforts to save him.
[496] Matt. 7:2.
[497] See Luke 18:1–6.
[498] Rom. 12:19.
[499] Matt. 18:10.
[500] See Ps. 10:8.

soweth, that shall he also reap.⁵⁰¹ Such is the vengeance on the proud, to whom the Lord is opposed, but He giveth grace unto the humble.⁵⁰² To Him be glory with the Father and the Holy Spirit, now and forever. Amen.

Discourse 29. The much-suffering Ioann the Solitary.[503]

The offspring born on earth of the first man are similar in form and appearance, and subject to the same passions,[504] since having beheld the beauty of the fruit, he did not restrain himself; he disobeyed God and received a life of bondage to the passions. When man was created, as a divine being, he had no blemishes, for the Lord our God took dust from the earth, and with His own pure and undefiled hands created man good and virtuous. But he, like mud, loved earthly things and slithered down the slope leading to a life of pleasure; and pleasures became firmly attached to him. From then on the human race was mastered by passion and inclined towards other pleasures; we are in a constant state of war. I am alone vanquished by them; I work for them, and am troubled by the thoughts of my soul.[505] Being so painfully affected by them, I have a strong and persistent desire to commit sins. I have no equal in all the world as regards the great number of my sins, in which I remain up to this present hour. But only this one man alone, who from among all men discovered the truth, set himself apart to do God's will; he kept His commandments without spot or blemish, and preserved his body and his soul free from every kind of physical or spiritual defilement. I am referring[506] to the venerable Ioann, who shut himself up alone in a confined space in the cave and remained there for thirty years in a life of great austerity.

---

[501] See Gal. 6:7.

[502] See Prov. 3:34.

[503] This discourse mostly consists of a lengthy testimony related by Ioann the Solitary in the first person. But there are also other first-person passages in this discourse, and it is sometimes difficult to tell exactly who is speaking; Polikarp is clearly less skillful in presenting this type of material than he is in writing narratives.

[504] The text has страсти, which I have translated as "passions."

[505] This first-person speaker is the writer of the introductory section of this discourse, up to the words "set himself apart," which does not appear in either the Arsenian or the Theodosian MSS. The Arsenian text begins "Blessed indeed is this man who set himself apart...": Abramovyč, *Pateryk*, 138, n. 22. The introduction seems to have been included by a later editor or copyist who wished to add his own personal testimony to that of Ioann the Solitary.

[506] The first-person speaker here is Polikarp, the narrator.

He tormented his body by much fasting and wore heavy irons on all parts of it.

He was often visited by one of the brethren, who was troubled by his inclination towards the lusts of the flesh (this was the devil's work), and he used to beg the blessed Ioann to pray to God for him that the Lord would give him relief from his passions and subdue his physical desires. He often came and talked about this. The blessed Ioann would say to him, "Brother, be a man, and be strong; bear the Lord patiently, and strive to follow in His way. He will not let you fall into the hands [of the devil] and will not deliver you[507] into the snare of their teeth." The brother replied to the Solitary, "Believe me, father, if you do not grant me relief, I will not rest but move about from place to place." The blessed Ioann said to him, "Why do you want to deliver yourself up to be devoured by the enemy? You are like a man standing near a precipice: when his enemy comes he suddenly flings him into the abyss; such a man falls with great violence and cannot rise up. But if you stay here, in this holy and blessed monastery, you are like a man standing far from the precipice: although his enemy tries hard to drag him towards it, he cannot do so, until the Lord through your patience leads you out of the pit of your passions and away from the filthy mire and sets your feet on stone.[508]

"But listen to me, my son, and I shall tell you what I have experienced since my youth.[509] I suffered much, tormented by unchaste thoughts, and I did not know what to do for my salvation. I would remain without food for two or three days—I spent three years in this way—and often I tasted nothing for a whole week. I spent nights without sleep, and nearly killed myself with intense thirst. I wore heavy iron fetters and remained in this wretched state for three years; but even so I found no rest. Then I went to the cave where our holy father Antonij lies and addressed myself to prayer; I remained praying by his grave day and night. And I heard him saying to me, 'Ioann, Ioann, you must shut yourself up here. Through the darkness and silence you will find respite from your struggle, and the Lord will help you through the prayers of His venerable ones.' From that hour, brother, I settled here, in this confined and miserable place. I have been here for nearly thirty years, and in few

---

[507] I follow the variant reading тя here: Abramovyč, *Pateryk*, 139, n. 32. The text has нас ("us").
[508] Cf. Ἀνδρῶν ἁγίων βίβλος, 99, lns. 15–24.
[509] The first-person speaker is now Ioann the Solitary himself, who continues in the first person until almost the end of the discourse.

years have I found rest. All my life I have suffered and struggled with thoughts of the flesh; I have had a terrible experience, leading such a life, eating only enough to stay alive.[510] Then, not knowing what to do and unable to endure the warfare of the flesh, I thought I would live naked and put heavy irons on my body, which I have had on me to this day; I am wasting away from the cold and irons.

"I did something else too, which I found useful: I dug a pit[511] up to my shoulders, and when Lent approached I went into the pit and covered myself with dust, so that only my head and arms were free. I remained thus, grievously oppressed, for the whole of the fast, unable to move a single limb. But this did not stop the struggle raging in my flesh and the fire burning in my body. Our enemy the devil, moreover, tried to fill me with terror, since he wanted to drive me away from that place, but I became aware of his evil design. My legs, which were in the pit, began to burn from the bottom, so that my veins contracted and my bones rattled. The flames reached my belly and my limbs caught fire, but I forgot the intense pain and rejoiced in my soul that I was being kept pure from defilement: I preferred to burn fiercely in the fire for the Lord's sake rather than leave the pit. I saw a frightful and exceedingly cruel serpent about to devour me completely and breathing fire and sparks that burned me. The devil did this to me for many days in his desire to drive me away.

"The night of Christ's Resurrection drew near. Suddenly that cruel serpent fell upon me and took my head and arms into its mouth; the hair on my head and the hair of my beard was singed, as you see now. I was already in its throat, and from the depths of my heart I called out, *Prayer*: 'O Lord my God, my Salvation! Why hast Thou hast forsaken me![512] Have mercy on me, O Lord, for Thou alone lovest mankind! O God, Who alone art without sin, save me, sinner that I am! Deliver me from the defilement of my transgressions, that I may not be held fast forever in the devil's snares! Deliver me from the jaws of this enemy, for he goes about like a roaring lion, seeking to devour me! Raise up Thy power and come and save me! Let Thy lightning flash forth and drive this serpent away, so that he may vanish from Thy countenance!'

"When I had finished my prayer, at once there was a flash of lightning, and the fierce serpent disappeared from my sight; and from

---

[510] This is a free translation; the wording is very obscure at this point.
[511] I follow the Arsenian reading, which omits досяжущу in Cas. 2: Abramovyč, *Pateryk*, 140, n. 47.
[512] Matt 27:46; Mark 15:34.

then until today I have never seen it again. A divine light shone forth, like the sun, and I heard a voice saying to me, 'Ioann, Ioann, help has come to you. Take thought for yourself, lest you experience something worse and suffer some evil in the life to come.' I prostrated myself and said, 'Lord, why hast Thou left me to be so cruelly tormented?' He answered me, saying, 'I have visited [afflictions] on you according to the strength of your endurance, so that you might be tried in the fire like gold. For God does not allow a man to suffer attacks beyond his strength, when he can no longer fight; but, like an [earthly] master, He entrusts great and difficult tasks to His strong and powerful servants, while for the weak He devises light and lesser duties. Understand this: during this conflict with passion, which is the reason for your prayer, say a prayer for yourself to the dead man who lies opposite you, and ask him to give you some respite in your struggle against unchastity; for he is greater than Joseph[513] and can help those who are suffering and in a state of misery from such passion.' As I did not know the man's name, I began to call out, 'Lord, have mercy upon me!' Later I found out that he was Moisej, a Hungarian by birth.[514] And there came upon me the indescribable light in which I now dwell. I have no need of candles day or night. But all the worthy people who come to visit me are satiated by this light and they see clearly its great comfort; it clearly lights up the night, for the sake of the hope of the other world.[515] We have killed our reason through our love of the flesh, and Christ, who acts righteously, visits suffering on us, who have never borne fruit. But brother, I will say this to you: let us pray together to the venerable Moisej, and he will help you."

He took a single bone from the holy one's relics, gave it to him, and said, "Place it against your body." At once his suffering ceased, his limbs became as dead, and henceforth he had no further trouble. Together they gave thanks to God Who had glorified His saints; as they pleased Him in this life, so after death He enriched them with gifts of

---

[513] A reference to Joseph's resistance to the blandishments of Potiphar's wife (Gen. 39:7–12).

[514] See below, Discourse 30.

[515] This is an important passage, since it indicates that Ioann had some form of mystical experience which is not described or even hinted at anywhere else in the *Paterik*. The language here has close affinities with that used by Symeon the New Theologian (949–1022) to describe his experience of "light-mysticism." See I. Hausherr, ed., "Un grand mystique byzantine. Vie de Syméon le Nouveau Theologian par Nicetas Stethatos," *Orientalia Christiana* 12 (1928):8–10, and George A. Maloney, *The Mystic of Fire and Light* (Denville, N. J., 1975), 83–104, with lengthy citations from Symeon's writings.

healing, adorned them with incorruptible crowns, and deemed them worthy of His kingdom. To Him be glory with the Father and the Holy Spirit, now and forever.

Discourse 30. The venerable Moisej the Hungarian.

It is known of the blessed Moisej the Hungarian that he was loved by the holy Boris.[516] He was a Hungarian by birth, the brother of Georgij on whom Boris placed a golden necklace and who was killed on the Al'ta together with the holy Boris and whose head was cut off for the sake of the golden necklace.[517] Moisej was alone saved from a cruel death and escaped the bitter slaughter. He went to Jaroslav's sister Peredslava and stayed there.[518] In those days it was impossible to cross to anywhere, and this man, valiant in spirit, prayed to God until our pious prince Jaroslav, who could not restrain the warm feeling in his soul which he felt towards his two brothers,[519] marched against the lawless one and defeated the proud, godless, and accursed Svjatopolk.[520] He fled to the Poles, came back with Bolesław, drove Jaroslav out, and settled in Kiev himself.[521] Bolesław returned to Poland, taking with him both of Jaroslav's sisters, and also his boyars.[522] Among them was this blessed Moisej, who was chained hand and foot with heavy fetters; he was closely guarded, because he was strong in body and handsome in appearance.

There was a certain noble woman, young, beautiful, and possessing great wealth and power. When she saw Moisej she was struck by the beauty of the vision she had seen, and her heart was pierced with desire for this venerable man. She began to speak seductive words to him, saying, "You are a sensible man; there is no point in you experiencing such

---

[516] Boris and his younger brother Glěb were sons of Volodimer I by his Bulgar wife. When Volodimer died on July 15, 1015, his eldest son Svjatopolk became prince in Kiev. The PVL 1015 entry, PSRL 1:132–37, 2:118–21, says that Svjatopolk sent men to kill Boris of Rostov, who was then returning from a campaign against the Pečenegs with Volodimer's retinue, and Glěb of Murom (on July 24 and September 5, respectively, according to the hagiographic tradition).

[517] See PVL 1015, PSRL 1:134, 2:120. Georgij was run through as he tried to shield Boris with his body.

[518] Peredslava, Volodimer's daughter by Rogněda and therefore Jaroslav's full sister, was then in Kiev.

[519] I.e., Boris and Glěb.

[520] PVL 1015, 1016, PSRL 1:141–42, 2:128–129.

[521] PVL 1018, PSRL 1:142–43, 2:130.

[522] PVL 1018, PSRL 1:144, 2:131.

torments. You could set yourself free from this suffering and bondage." Moisej said to her, "If that be God's will." The woman said to him, "If you will submit to me, I shall set you free and make you great throughout the Polish land. You will be master of me and all my dominions." But the blessed one, aware of her lascivious desires, said to her, "What man who has taken a woman and become subject to her has ever amended his life? When Adam, the first man created, submitted to a woman he was driven out of paradise. Samson, who excelled all men in strength and was victorious over warriors, was finally betrayed to a foreign people by a woman. Solomon, who attained the most profound wisdom, worshipped idols when he yielded to a woman. Herod, after winning many victories, finally became enslaved and beheaded John the Baptist.[523] So why should I, who am now free, make myself a slave to a woman whom I have never known from the time of my birth?"

She said to him, "But I shall ransom you, and make you famous, and set you up as lord of my household. I want to have you as my husband. Just do as I wish: comfort the longing of my soul and let me have my fill of your beauty. Your desire is sufficient, for I cannot bear that your fairness should perish without reason. Let the burning in my heart cease, and let me have rest from my thoughts and respite from my passion, and you will enjoy my beauty and be lord of all I possess, the heir to my dominion, and the senior to all my boyars." But the blessed Moisej said to her, "You know very well that I shall not do as you wish. I want neither your power nor your wealth. Purity of soul and, even more, purity of body are better than all that. May it not happen that I destroy the efforts of the five years which the Lord has permitted me to suffer in these fetters. Since I do not deserve to suffer such torments, I hope that I shall be delivered from eternal torment because of them."

Then the woman, seeing that she would be deprived of his beauty and with the devil suggesting another course, thought, "If I ransom him, he will be completely subject to me, and not of his own free will." So she sent a message to the man holding him, told him to take as much [money] as he wanted, and hand Moisej over to her. This man, seeing an opportunity of acquiring wealth, took from her one thousand silver *grivna*[524] and handed Moisej over to her. She then dragged him off forcibly and shamelessly to unseemly activity. After she had gotten him in

---

[523] Abramovyč, *Pateryk*, 223, n. 155, suggests that these examples may have been taken from an anthology of the deeds of evil women found in the Bible.
[524] "Silver *grivna*" occurs only in the Theodosian MS: Abramovyč, *Pateryk*, 143, n. 48.

her power she ordered him to attach himself to her. Having released him from his fetters, she clothed him in costly garments and fed him with tasty food. Compelled by her love, she embraced him and forced him to satisfy her desire.

The venerable one, seeing the woman's folly, was even more diligent in prayer and fasting, preferring for God's sake dry bread and water drunk in purity to costly food and wine drunk in iniquity. Not only did he pull off his one shirt, like Joseph,[525] but he also removed all his clothes and fled from sin, considering the life of this world to be of no value. This so angered the woman that she tried to starve him to death. But God does not abandon His servants who put their trust in Him. He moved the heart of one of the woman's servants to compassion, and he gave him some food secretly.

Other people sought to change his mind, saying, "Brother Moisej, what prevents you from getting married? You are still young, and she is a widow who lived with her husband for only one year. She is beautiful, more than other women, and possesses immeasurable wealth and great power in Poland. If she had felt inclined to marry a prince, he would not have shunned her. Yet you, a captive dependent on her will, do not wish her to be lord? If you say, 'I cannot disobey Christ's commands,' does not Christ say in the Gospel, 'For this cause shall a man leave father and mother, and shall cleave to his wife: and the twain shall be one flesh? Wherefore they are no more twain, but one flesh?'[526] And the Apostle says, 'It is better to marry than to burn,'[527] and he orders widows to enter into a second marriage.[528] You do not follow the monastic way of life; you are free. So why do you submit yourself to wicked and miserable torments? Why are you suffering like this? If you should die in this wretched state, what glory will you have? Who from the first men until now except monks has shunned women? Did Abraham or Isaac or Jacob? Joseph won the battle for a short time, and then he was defeated by a woman.[529] If you lose your life now, you will have been defeated by a woman. Who will not laugh at your folly? It is better for you to

---

[525] See Gen. 39:12–13: Joseph ran away from Potiphar's wife, leaving his cloak in her hands. But Joseph left his cloak unwillingly, whereas Polikarp implies that Moisej refused to wear the "costly garments" provided by his temptress and removed them as a protest.
[526] Matt. 19:5–6; Mark 10:7–8.
[527] 1 Cor. 7:9.
[528] See 1 Tim. 5:14.
[529] See Gen. 41:45: Pharaoh gave Joseph "Asenath, the daughter of Potiphera, priest of On," as his wife after making him the ruler of Egypt.

submit to this woman and be free and be the master of all."

He said to them, "My brothers and good friends, you mean well. But I believe that the argument you set before me is more insidious[530] than the whispering of the serpent in the Garden of Eden. You are trying to make me submit to this woman, but I in no way can take your advice. Even if I should die in these fetters and cruel torments, I am completely confident that I will receive God's mercy. Even if all those righteous men were saved, though they had wives, I alone am a sinner, since I cannot be saved with a wife. But if Joseph had yielded to Potiphar's wife, he would not afterwards have become a ruler. God saw his patience and gave him a kingdom, and so he was honored among his people as a chaste man, although he begot children. But I do not wish to receive the kingdom of Egypt, or be master of lands, or be a great man in Poland, or appear honored throughout the land of Rus'—I have despised all these things for the sake of a higher kingdom. If I escape with my life from the hands of this woman, I shall become a monk. For what did Christ say in the Gospel? 'Every one that hath forsaken his father, or mother, or wife, or children, or home, he is my disciple.'[531] Should I not obey Christ rather than you? And the Apostle says, 'He that is married careth how he may please his wife, but he that is unmarried careth how he may please God.'[532] Now I ask you: whom is it better to serve, Christ or a wife? It is written: 'Servants, be obedient to them that are your masters for good and not for evil.'[533] Let it be clear to you, who hold me in your power, that I shall never be beguiled by a woman's beauty nor separated from the love of Christ."

When the woman heard about this, she adopted a cunning plan in her heart. She sat him on a horse, with many servants, and ordered them to take him through the villages and cities that were subject to her, saying to him, "All these things are yours, if they please you. Do what you like with all of them." To the people she said, "This is your lord, and my husband; let all who meet him prostrate themselves before him." For there were many who served her, both men and women. The blessed one laughed at her folly and said to her, "You are taking this trouble in vain. You cannot entice me with the corruptible things of this world nor rob me of my spiritual riches. Understand this, and do not trouble yourself in vain." The woman said to him, "Do you not know that you have

---

530 I have used the Arsenian reading here: Abramovyč, *Pateryk*, 144, n. 58.
531 Matt. 19:29; Mark 10:29; Luke 18:29.
532 1 Cor. 7:32–33.
533 Eph. 6:5.

been sold to me? Who will take you out of my hands? I shall never let you go alive; I shall deliver you to death after many tortures." He answered fearlessly, "I am not afraid of what you said. But he who handed me over to you has a greater sin. For my part, I shall henceforth be a monk, if that is God's will."

At that very time a certain monk from the Holy Mountain, a priest by rank, came to the blessed one, under God's direction, and invested him with the Angelic Habit. Having instructed him at length about purity and about not showing his back to the enemy and how to deliver himself from this lecherous woman, he departed from him. A search was made for this man, but he could not be found.[534]

Then the woman, despairing of her hopes, began to inflict severe wounds on Moisej: she ordered him to be stretched out and beaten with a rod until the ground was covered with blood. Those beating him said to him, "Submit to your mistress, and do as she wishes. If you disobey we shall break your body to pieces. Do not think that you will escape these tortures, but you will give up your soul in agony after prolonged torture. Have mercy on yourself, get rid of these poor clothes, and dress yourself in costly garments. Avoid the torments that are waiting for you before we touch your flesh."[535] Moisej answered, "Do as you have been told, brothers, and do not delay. It is impossible for me to renounce my monastic state and my love of God. No torture of any kind, neither fire nor sword nor wounds, can separate me from God or from this Great Angelic Habit. This shameless and deluded woman has demonstrated her shamelessness. Not only has she shown no fear of God, but she even shows contempt for human shame by wantonly forcing me to wickedness and adultery. I shall neither submit to her nor do this accursed woman's bidding."

The woman was much concerned about how to avenge her disgrace, and she sent to Prince Bolesław, saying, "You know that my husband was killed while campaigning with you, and that you have granted my wish that I may take whomever I want as my husband. I have fallen

---

[534] There is no corroborative evidence of this timely arrival of a priest-monk from Mount Athos (the Holy Mountain). It is possible that he was invented by Polikarp and that Moisej was not actually tonsured until he escaped to Kiev and joined Antonij, then living in a cave in a hill above the Dnieper. See Heppell, "The *Vita Antonii*," 51. Two scholars, however, are prepared to accept this story as authentic: V. Mošin, "Russkie na Afone i russko-vizantijskie otnošenija v XI–XII vv.," *Byzantinoslavica* 9 (1947):61, and F. Dvornik, *The Making of Central and Eastern Europe* (London, 1949), 252–53.

[535] The words "before we touch your flesh" (донелѣже не коснемься плоти твоей) are omitted in the Arsenian text: Abramovyč, *Pateryk*, 146, n. 33.

in love with one of your captives, a handsome young man. I ransomed him, took him into my house, and gave him a large amount of gold—all the gold and silver and authority in my house I have given him. But he sets absolutely no value on these things. I have often tormented him with wounds and hunger, but this was not enough for him. He was kept in fetters by his captor for five years. During the sixth year he has been with me and has suffered much at my hands because of his disobedience, which he brought on himself through his own stubborness. Now he has been tonsured by some monk. Whatever you order to be done with him, I shall do it.''

Bolesław ordered her to come to him and to bring Moisej with her. The woman came to Bolesław and brought Moisej with her. When Bolesław saw the venerable one, he tried hard to make him take the woman, but he could not persuade him. He said to Moisej, ''Is there anyone so lacking in sense as you? You are depriving yourself of so many benefits and so much honor, and have submitted yourself to these cruel tortures. You must know that from now on you are faced with a choice between life and death: either you must do as your mistress wishes, be honored by us, and have great power, or, if you disobey, you will be put to death after many tortures.'' He said to the woman, ''None of the prisoners ransomed by you is to be set free. But do as you wish, like a mistress to a slave, so that the others will not dare to disobey their masters.'' Moisej answered, ''What does the Lord say? 'What is man profited, if he shall gain the whole world? Or what shall a man give in exchange for his soul?'[536] Why do you promise me glory and honor, which you yourself will soon lose, when you will come to your grave with no possessions at all? And this wicked woman will meet with a cruel death.'' This prophecy of the venerable man was indeed fulfilled.

The woman, having gained greater power over him, shamelessly dragged him off to sin. On one occasion she forced him to lie with her on her bed, kissing him and embracing him, but she was unable by this means to entice him and make him do what she wanted. The blessed one said to her, ''Your efforts are in vain. Do not think that I am useless or unable to do this thing. For the love of God I shun you as an unclean woman.'' Hearing this, the woman ordered him to be beaten with a hundred strokes every day. Finally, she ordered his private parts to be cut off, saying, ''I shall not spare his beauty, so that no one else may enjoy it.'' Moisej lay like a dead man from loss of blood, scarcely able to

---

[536] Matt. 16:26; Mark 8:36–37; Luke 9:25.

breathe. Bolesław was filled with shame because of the woman's high position and her former love, and he gave in to her whim by instigating a great persecution of the monks and drove all of them out of his dominions.

God speedily avenged his servants. One night Bolesław died suddenly, and a serious rebellion broke out throughout the Polish land. The people rose up and killed their bishops and boyars, as we are told in the chronicle.[537] This woman was also killed at that time. The venerable Moisej recovered from his wounds and came to the holy Theotokos in the Caves Monastery, a valiant victor for Christ, bearing a martyr's wounds and a confessor's crown. The Lord granted him power over the passions. A certain brother who had been attacked by thoughts of unchastity came and begged the venerable one to help him. He said, "Whatever you advise I shall do until my dying day." The blessed one said to him, "Never speak to any woman throughout your life." He eagerly promised to do this. The holy one had a stick in his hand, for he could not walk because of his wounds, and he struck the monk with it on the breast. Immediately his private parts lost all feeling, and henceforth he had no more trouble.

These facts about Moisej are written in the Life of our holy father Antonij, since this blessed man had come during the holy Antonij's lifetime. He died in the Lord in the fullness of faith after spending ten years in the monastery; he had suffered in bonds as a captive for five years, and then a sixth year for his chastity.[538] I can remember how the monks were driven out of Poland because he was tonsured and gave himself to God

---

[537] See PVL 1030, PSRL 1:149; 2:137. Bolesław actually died in 1025, and the disturbances in Poland took place ca. 1034. See Cross and Sherbowitz-Wetzor, *The Russian Primary Chronicle*, 257, n. 158.

[538] This chronological information is important for establishing the time when Antonij's first disciples gathered together and so initiated the community which was to develop into the Caves Monastery. If Moisej was carried off to Poland in 1018 (perhaps 1019) and remained there six years altogether, he must have come to Kiev around 1025. This would coincide with the death of Bolesław in 1025 but not with the disturbances in Poland in 1034. However, Šaxmatov, "Žitie Antonija i Pečerskaja Letopis'," 133, n. 1, says that the words "a sixth year" should be amended to "six years," the reading of the Arsenian MS, and argues that Moisej came to Kiev ca. 1030. Yet the reading "six years" is not found in any variants given by Abramovyč. Thus, it seems reasonable to assume that Moisej came to Kiev ca. 1025, probably after the death of Bolesław and the woman who was holding him captive. This is a modification of the theory I expounded in "The *Vita Antonii*," 52–53, that Moisej came to Kiev ca. 1031.

whom we loved.[539] This is written in the Life of our holy father Feodosij: when our holy father Antonij was expelled by Prince Izjaslav on account of Varlaam and Efrem, his princess, who was Polish, restrained him, saying, "Do not do it or even think of it. For once it happened in our country that the monks were driven out beyond the boundaries of our land for some reason, and this brought great misfortune to the Poles."[540] This happened because of Moisej, as I have written above.[541]

I have now reached the end of this topic. I have written about Moisej the Hungarian and Ioann the Solitary and described how the Lord acted through them to His glory. Having glorified them because of their endurance, He enriched them with the gift of working miracles. To Him be glory now [and forever, world without end. Amen].

Discourse 31. The monk Proxor, who by his prayers made bread from pigweed and salt from ashes.

As it pleases God, Who loves mankind, to take thought for the human race, His creatures, at all times and in all seasons, by giving us useful experiences in expectation of our repentance, He sends down upon us sometimes famines, sometimes wars to upset existing rulers. By this means our Lord restores human negligence to the path of virtue and to the remembrance of unseemly acts; for those who commit evil and unseemly deeds will be handed over to wicked and heartless rulers because of our sins. But the rulers will not escape judgment either, since he who does not show mercy will be judged without mercy. So it was when Svjatopolk was prince in Kiev.[542] Svjatopolk committed many acts of violence against people: he destroyed the houses of powerful individuals down to the foundations for no reason, and he took away many people's goods. Because of this the Lord allowed the pagans to have dominion over him, and there were many attacks by the Cumans. In

---

[539] This first-person passage must have come from Polikarp's source, the Life of Antonij; he could not have remembered events from the early eleventh century.
[540] See Discourse 8, p. 38.
[541] This is Polikarp's own comment. There is no firm evidence that the expulsion of the monks from Poland was connected with Moisej.
[542] Svjatopolk II Izjaslavič, prince of Kiev from 1093 to 1113.

addition, there was in those days civil strife, severe famine, and acute shortages of everything in the land of Rus'.[543]

Now at that time a certain man came from Smolensk to the superior Ioann,[544] as he wished to become a monk; he was tonsured and given the name of Proxor. After he became a monk he devoted himself to a life of obedience and abstinence without limit, even depriving himself of bread. He used to gather pigweed, grind it with his own hands, and make himself bread; this was his food. He used to prepare this for a year, and in the next year prepare the same thing, and so was content to do without bread all his life. The Lord saw his endurance and great self-denial and added a sweet taste to the bitter flavor, so that after his sorrow he experienced joy, as it is said, "Weeping shall tarry for the evening, but joy shall be in the morning."[545] Because of this he was called "Lobednik,"[546] since he never tasted bread, except sacramental wafers, nor any kind of vegetables, nor any drink, but only water and pigweed, as was said above. He was never downcast, but always served the Lord with gladness. And he was never afraid when an invasion came, since he lived like one of the birds. He did not acquire estates or barns in which he gathered his goods.[547] He did not say like the rich man, "Soul, thou hast much goods laid up for many years; eat, drink, and be merry."[548] For he had nothing but pigweed, and he prepared this only for the coming year. He used to say to himself, "This night the angels shall require thy soul of thee: then whose shall the pigweed be, which thou hast provided?"[549] This man fulfilled in deed the word of the Lord: "Behold the fowls of the air: for they sow not, neither do they reap, nor gather into barns; yet your heavenly Father feedeth them."[550] Imitating them, the venerable Proxor went lightheartedly on his way along the path where there was pigweed. From there he put it on his shoulders, as though on wings, brought it to the monastery and prepared it for his food. His nourishment required neither plowed nor sown land.

---

[543] See PVL 1093–1096, PSRL 1:218–234; 2:209–224, which gave detailed accounts of the Cuman raids.
[544] Ioann held office from 1088 to 1108.
[545] Ps. 29:5.
[546] A name derived from лобеда, the Rus' word for pigweed.
[547] See Ἀνδρῶν ἁγίων βίβλος, 305, lns. 4–7, for a similar description of Abba Serapion.
[548] Luke 12:19.
[549] Based on Luke 12:20.
[550] Matt. 6:26.

When a great famine came and death from hunger descended on all the people, the blessed one kept to his task of gathering pigweed. A certain man saw him doing this and began to gather it too for himself and his household, so that they would be sustained during the famine. The pigweed on which the blessed one fed even increased at this time, and he gave himself extra work in those days, collecting plants, as I have said before, grinding them with his own hands, making bread, and distributing it to those who had nothing and had grown weak from hunger. Many people came to him during the famine, and he distributed bread to them all, and to all of them it appeared sweet, as though it contained honey. So no one wanted bread unless they received food made from a wild plant by the hands of this blessed man. To whomever he gave it with a blessing, it would be a sweet, pure, and light-colored loaf of bread; but if anyone took it secretly the bread turned out to be like wormwood.

One of the brethren secretly stole some of the bread and began to eat it without Proxor's permission, but he could not eat it because in his hands it was like wormwood and seemed to be extremely bitter. This happened several times. This brother felt so ashamed that he could not tell the blessed one about his transgression. Starving and unable to endure this natural need and seeing death before his eyes, he came to the superior Ioann, told him what had happened, and asked forgiveness for his sin. The superior could not believe what he had said, and ordered another brother to do the same thing, that is, to take some bread secretly, so that they could see whether this was really true. And when this loaf was brought it was found to be just like the brother who had stolen the loaf had said; indeed no one could eat it because of its bitterness. While the loaf was still in his hands, the superior sent and requested that they obtain a loaf from Proxor's hands and, as they were going out, to steal another loaf. When these loaves were brought back, the stolen one changed in their presence and became bitter, like dust, just like the first one, but the one which they had received from Proxor's hands was like honey and light in color. As a result of this miracle, Proxor's fame spread everywhere; he gave food to a large number of hungry people, and was of service to many.

When Svjatopolk, together with Volodar' and Vasil'ko,[551] whom Svjatopolk had blinded at the instigation of David Igorevič, began his

---

[551] Volodar' and Vasil'ko were great-grandsons of Jaroslav the Wise. Vasil'ko was prince of Terebovlja in western Rus', while his brother Volodar' ruled Peremyšl' (Przemyśl) on the San in the same area. These territories were guaranteed by the inter-princely agreement concluded at Ljubeč in 1097. See PVL 1097, PSRL 1:257, 2:231.

campaign against David because of the blinding of Vasil'ko,[552] merchants were not allowed to come from Halyč,[553] nor any ships from Peremyšl', and there was no salt throughout the land of Rus'. There was much confusion, disorder, and lawless plundering, just as the prophet said, "[Will not all the workers of iniquity know,] who eat up my people as they would eat bread? They have not called upon the Lord."[554] It was obvious then that the people were in great distress, weakened by hunger and war, and they had neither wheat nor salt with which to get through the time of scarcity.

Then the blessed Proxor, who had his own cell, gathered a large quantity of ashes from all the cells without anyone's knowledge and distributed them to people who came to him; to all it became pure salt through his prayers. However much he distributed, it increased in proportion. He would not take anything [for it] but gave it to everybody free, as much as each person wanted. Not only was it sufficient for the monastery, but laymen came to him and would take an abundant supply to satisfy the needs of their homes. It was a sight: the marketplace was empty, but the monastery was full of people coming to get salt! This roused the envy of those who sold salt, since they were unable to get what they wanted. They had thought that they would become very wealthy from the sale of salt in those days, and they were very upset about it. For previously they had been selling salt at a high price, two measures for a *kuna*, but now they were selling it at ten measures for a *kuna*, but no one would take it. So all the salt merchants rose up, went to Svjatopolk, and denounced the monk, saying, "The monk Proxor in the Caves Monastery has robbed us of much wealth. He gives salt to everyone who comes to him. No one can stop him, and we are being reduced to poverty." The prince, who wanted to please them, thought of two things to himself: he could put a stop to the unrest among them and at the same time gain wealth for himself. With this plan in mind, after consulting with his advisers, he announced a very high price for salt; his idea was that he would take it from the monk and sell it. Then he promised

---

[552] Vasil'ko was kidnapped and blinded at the urging of David Igorevič of Volodymyr, who wanted to add Terebovlja to his own larger area. This incident, which is related in PVL 1097, PSRL 1:260-73, 2:234-48, was a breach of the Ljubeč agreement. The blinding of political opponents was common in the Byzantine Empire and occasionally practiced in contemporary Poland, but not in Rus'. Finally Svjatopolk II, as prince of Kiev, was persuaded to march against David Igorevič to punish him for his crime, even though Svjatopolk himself was partly culpable.
[553] Halyč, an important source of salt, was in the territory of David Igorevič.
[554] Ps. 13:4.

the conspirators,[555] saying, "I will rob the monk for your sake," but he kept to himself his plan for gaining wealth. He wanted to afford them some small satisfaction by this means, though really he was doing them considerable harm, for enmity does not know how to perform a useful action.[556]

The prince then sent [some men] to remove all the monk's salt. When the salt was brought, the prince came, as he wanted to see it, and with him came the conspirators who had denounced the blessed one, and they all saw that what lay in front of their eyes was ashes. They marvelled greatly and asked each other what this could be; they could not understand it. As Svjatopolk wanted to find out what was at the bottom of it all, he ordered [the ashes] to be kept for three days, so that they could find out the truth; he told someone to taste them, and in his mouth they proved to be ashes. Many people came, as usual, wanting to get salt from the blessed one. When they found that the elder had been robbed, they returned empty-handed, cursing the man who had done it. The blessed one said to them, "When the ashes are scattered [on the ground], go and take them." The prince kept them for three days and then ordered them to be thrown away at night. When the ashes were thrown away they were at once transformed into salt,[557] and when the citizens learned about this they came and seized the salt. Because of this remarkable miracle the man who had committed the original act of violence was filled with terror: he could not conceal the affair because it happened in front of all the citizens. He began to make inquiries about this matter. Then they told the prince about another affair—how the blessed one had fed many people with pigweed, and in their mouths it had become bread with a sweet taste, but some people had taken a loaf without his blessing, and in their mouths it was like dust and as bitter as wormwood.

Hearing this, the prince was ashamed of what he had done, and he went to the superior Ioann in the monastery and repented before him. Previously he had been on bad terms with him, because the superior had

---

[555] The word крамольникомъ indicates that Svjatopolk had entered into a plot with the salt merchants, and possibly with some members of his retinue, to rob Proxor, although, as subsequently becomes clear in this narrative, he intended to double-cross them.

[556] I have followed the Arsenian reading here, which omits the word предпочитати included in the Cas. II text, where it distorts the structure of the sentence: Abramovyč, *Pateryk*, 153, n. 9.

[557] There may be a factual foundation to Proxor's miraculous production of salt, since pigweed only grows in salty soil and absorbs the salt into its tissues. Hence Proxor could obtain salt by burning his customary food. See A. H. Krappe, "L'arroche biblique et le *Paterik*," *Revue des études slaves* 13 (1933):244–45.

accused him of having an insatiable desire for wealth and of committing acts of violence. So Svjatopolk had seized him and imprisoned him in Turov,[558] [and he would have remained there] if Volodimer Monomax had not risen up against Svjatopolk. Svjatopolk feared that he might start an insurrection, so he quickly restored the superior to the Caves Monastery with due honor. Because of this miracle Svjatopolk began to feel a great love for the holy Theotokos and the holy fathers Antonij and Feodosij, and henceforth he greatly honored and esteemed the monk Proxor, knowing that he was indeed a servant of God. He gave his word to God that henceforward he would not commit any acts of violence against anybody. The prince further confirmed this promise to him, saying, "If by God's will I depart from this life before you, lay me in my grave with your own hands, so that your innocence may appear on me. If you pass away before me and go to the relentless Judge, then I shall carry you to the cave on my own shoulders, so that the Lord will thereby grant me forgiveness for the many sins I have committed against you." Having said this, he departed from him.

The blessed Proxor lived for many years in the fullness of faith, leading a pure and blameless life, well-pleasing to God. After this the holy one fell ill, and the prince was then on a campaign. Then the holy one sent him a message, saying, "The hour of my departure from this body has approached. If you wish, come and receive my forgiveness and carry out your promise, so that you may receive remission of your sins from God, and lay me in my grave with your own hands. I await your arrival. If you delay and I depart [from this world], the battle will not go so well for you as it will if you come to me." Hearing this, Svjatopolk dismissed his soldiers that very hour and hurried to the blessed one. The venerable one instructed the prince at length about compassion, the coming judgment, eternal life, and endless torments. He gave him his blessing, kissed all those with the prince, lifted up his hands, and gave up his soul. The prince took hold of the elder's body, carried him into the cave, and with his own hands laid him in his grave.

After the blessed one's burial he went to war and won many victories over the godless Hagarenes; he took all their land and led them [captive] to his own land.[559] This victory in the land of Rus' was granted

---

[558] Svjatopolk had moved from Novgorod to Turov in 1088, after the assassination of his brother Jaropolk Izjaslavič in 1086, to whom Vsevolod Jaroslavič of Kiev had assigned it in 1078.

[559] For these victorious campaigns against the Cumans, see PVL 1103, PSRL 1:277–79, 2:230–31.

by God according to the prophecy of the venerable one. Henceforth, when Svjatopolk went on a campaign or hunting expedition, he would come to the monastery with a thank-offering and worship before [the icon of] the Theotokos and at the tomb of Feodosij. He would go out into the cave to the holy Antonij and the blessed Proxor, prostrate himself before all the venerable fathers, and go on his way. So his reign, watched over by God, was in good order. For he himself had witnessed and openly confessed the miracles and remarkable signs of the renowned Proxor and the other venerable ones. May we all obtain grace with them through Christ Jesus our Lord, to Whom be glory with the Father and the Holy Spirit now and forever.

Discourse 32. Venerable Marko the Cave-dweller, whose orders the dead obeyed.

We sinners emulate the holy men of old by means of the written word, which explains what they were seeking with great effort and labor in the deserts, on the hills, and in the bowels of the earth. In some cases the writers themselves saw what they recorded; in others they heard about the lives, miracles, and God-pleasing deeds of venerable men; in yet others they heard of the lives and miracles and activities of those who lived before them, as we find in the *Paterik* of the Caves Monastery, in which they collected material and spoke about them.[560] As we read about them, we derive much pleasure from these spiritual anecdotes. I, unworthy as I am, have not attained understanding of the truth, and I have seen nothing of such men. But following what I have heard, that is, what I have been told by the venerable Bishop Simon, I have written these things down for your fatherhood.[561] Nor have I ever traveled round the holy places nor seen Jerusalem or the mountains of Sinai, which would have enabled me to add to my tale some of those things with which people with literary skill are wont to embellish their works. So let there be no glory for me, but only for this Caves Monastery and the holy monks who formerly lived there, and for their lives and miracles, which I recall with joy, since I, sinner that I am, desire the prayers of these holy

---

[560] Polikarp apparently refers to some written source containing material about the early monks of the monastery. As he also refers on other occasions to "the chronicle" (the PVL) and the "Life of Antonij," this source is presumably something different, though without further information it is impossible to identify it.

[561] къ твоєму отечеству: The Greek ἡ πατρότης σου, was an honorific address for bishops and superiors. See Lampe, *A Patristic Greek Lexicon*, 1053.

fathers. From this point I shall make a start on my tale about the venerable Marko the Cave-dweller.

The holy Marko spent his life in the cave, and during his lifetime our holy father Feodosij was carried out of the cave into the great and holy church.[562] The venerable Marko dug many [burial] places in the cave with his own hands, carrying out the earth on his shoulders every day and night, laboring hard in God's work. He dug many graves for the brethren and took nothing for the service, but if anyone did give him something he would take it and distribute it to the poor.[563]

One day, as he was digging away as usual and working very hard, he felt a sudden weakness and left the place he was digging narrow and not of the usual width. It happened that one of the brethren fell ill and departed to God that day, and there was no other grave available except this cramped one. The dead man was brought into the cave and placed in the grave with some difficulty, because of its tight fit. The brethren grumbled at Marko, since they could not prepare the dead man for burial or anoint him with oil because the place was so narrow. The cave-dweller, prostrating himself before them, said, "Forgive me, fathers! I did not finish my job because I suddenly felt weak." They reproached him all the more and made insulting remarks. Marko said to the dead man, "Since this place is tight, brother, sprinkle yourself with holy water, and take the oil and pour it over yourself." The dead man stretched out his hand, raised himself up a little, took the oil, anointed himself with the sign of the cross on his breast and face, and returned the vessel. Then in front of them all he prepared himself for burial, lay down, and fell asleep. When they saw this miracle they were all seized by fear and trembling at what happened.

Another brother died after a long illness. One of his friends wiped him with a sponge and went into the cave, as he wanted to see the place where his beloved friend would be buried, and so he asked the blessed one. The venerable Marko replied, "Brother, go and tell the dead brother, 'Wait until the morning, so that I will be able to dig a place for you. Then you will depart in peace to the future life.'" The brother who had come said to him, "Father Marko, I have wiped his body with a sponge; he is dead. To whom are you telling me to speak?" Marko repeated, "You can see that his place is unfinished. I am telling you to

---

[562] Feodosij's relics were translated in 1091. See Discourse 9, pp. 89–93.
[563] This indicates that, contrary to the Stoudite Rule and in spite of the efforts of Feodosij, by the late eleventh century the monks of the Caves Monastery did pay for and accept money for services.

go and say to the dead man, 'Brother, the sinful Marko says you are to stay [alive] for one more day, until he prepares a place for your burial and sends for you; in the morning you can depart to the Lord we desire.'"

The brother who had come [to the cave] obeyed the venerable one and returned to the monastery. He found all the brethren singing the customary hymn over the deceased brother. He stood at his side and said, "Marko tells you that no place is ready for you, brother, so wait until tomorrow morning." They were all amazed at his words. When the brother had spoken them before everybody, the dead brother suddenly opened his eyes, and his soul returned to his body. He remained alive throughout the day and entire night with his eyes open, not uttering a word to anyone. The next morning the brother who had previously gone [to Marko] went to the cave to find out whether the place was ready. The blessed one said to him, "Go and tell the dead man, 'Marko says that you are to leave this transitory life and come to the life eternal, since a place has been prepared for your body. Give up your spirit to God. Your body will be buried here in the cave with the holy fathers.'" The brother went and told all this to the monk who had come back to life, and he at once closed his eyes and gave up his soul in front of everyone who had come to visit him. Then he was buried with due honor in the aforementioned place in the cave. They all marveled at this miracle, that a dead man had returned to life at the word of the blessed Marko, and then died again at his command.

There were two brothers in this great Caves Monastery who had been united by sincere love from their youth, and who had one mind and one will towards God. They begged the blessed Marko to dig one grave for the two of them, so that they might both[564] be buried there when the Lord commanded it. A long time after this Feofil, the senior, went away somewhere on business. The younger one fell ill and departed to the future life, and was buried in the place that had been prepared. Some days later Feofil came back and learned about his brother. He was deeply grieved and, taking some people with him, he went to the cave, wishing to see the dead man and the location and place where he was buried. Seeing that he had been laid in the higher place,[565] he was displeased and complained at length to Marko, saying, "Why have you put him [there]? I am senior to him, but you have put him in my place."

---

[564] I follow the Arsenian reading оба (both), in preference to the Cas. II абїе: Abramovyč, *Pateryk*, 157, n. 65.
[565] This indicates that Marko had dug the grave in the form of two bunks.

The cave-dweller, who was a humble man, prostrated himself and said, "Forgive me, brother, I have sinned against you." Having said this, he said to the dead man, "Get up, brother, and give your place to the brother who has not yet died. You lie in the lower place." Suddenly, at the venerable one's words, the dead man got up and lay down in the lower place before everyone present. It was very obvious that this was a terrible and awe-inspiring miracle. Then the brother who had complained and grumbled at the blessed one fell at Marko's feet and on account of his brother's burial said to him, "Father Marko, I have sinned in moving my brother from his place. I beg you, tell him to lie in his own place again." The blessed one said to him, "The Lord has removed the enmity between us. He did this because of your grumbling, so that you would not hate me forever and have evil thoughts about me. But even a body without a soul shows such love towards you that it has yielded to your seniority, even after death. I had not wanted you to go away from here, so that you would inherit your place of seniority and be buried here this very hour. But you are not ready to depart this life, so go and take thought for your soul. After a few days you will be brought back here. As for raising the dead, that is God's work, and I am but a sinful man. But this dead man, who feared your insults and my subjection by you, could not bear this and has left you half the place prepared communally for you both. God can move him, but I cannot say to a dead man, 'Rise up, and lie down again in the higher place.' You lift him up and see whether he will obey you, as he did just now."[566]

Hearing this, Feofil was terribly cast down by Marko's terrible words. He thought he would drop dead immediately and did not know whether he would reach the monastery. When he came to his cell, he was seized by inconsolable weeping. He gave away all his possessions, right down to his shirt, leaving himself only one garment and his mantle, and waited for the hour of his death. No one could make him stop his bitter weeping or even make him take some tasty food. When daybreak was drawing near he would say, "I do not know whether I will live till evening." When night came he would say, still weeping, "What shall I do if I do not live till morning?[567] For many people have gotten up [in the morning] and not lasted until the evening, or have lain down on their beds and not gotten up from them. So what will happen to me, who has received an intimation from the venerable one that my end will come

---

[566] There are numerous examples of "speaking corpses" in early monastic literature, which may well have influenced Polikarp's presentation of this story.

[567] Cf. Ἀνδρῶν ἁγίων βίβλος, 106, lns. 15–18.

soon?" And he prayed to God with tears to give him time for repentance. He spent every day in this way—fasting, praying, and weeping hourly, expecting the day and hour of his death and separation from his body; he wasted his flesh so much that all his limbs withered. Many people tried to comfort him, but this only drove him to greater sobbing. Through his copious weeping he lost his eyesight, and thus he spent all of the days of his life in great abstinence, pleasing God by his good life.[568]

The venerable Marko, having learned the hour of his departure to the Lord, summoned Feofil and told him, "Forgive me, Brother Feofil, because I made you unhappy for many years. Now I am leaving this world. Pray for me! If I receive boldness to speak before God, I shall not forget you. May God grant that we may soon see each other and find ourselves in the same place as the fathers Antonij and Feodosij." Feofil answered with weeping, "Father Marko, why are you leaving me? Either take me with you, or grant me the restoration of my sight." Marko said to him, "Do not be sad, brother. For God's sake your physical eyes have lost their sight, but with your spiritual vision you have acquired the power to discern Him. I am the cause of your blindness, brother. I told you that you would die, as I wanted to do something that would benefit your soul and bring your exalted ideas about yourself to a state of humility, for a broken and humbled heart God will not despise."[569] Feofil said to him, "You saw, father, how I fell down before you because of my sins. I should have died in the cave, when you raised up the dead man, but the Lord granted me my life, thanks to your holy prayers, in expectation of my repentance. Now I request of you: let me depart with you to the Lord, or restore my sight." Marko said, "There is no need for you to see this transitory world. Request of the Lord that you may see His glory there [in the next world]. Do not wish for your death, for it will come to you, even if you do not desire it. Let this be a sign of your departure: three days before your passing, you will be able

---

[568] This account of Feofil's prolonged penitential weeping indicates how highly the gift of tears, as a sign of contrition, was valued in the Caves Monastery. Possibly Feofil (or Polikarp) was influenced by the Egyptian monk Arsenios the Great, who collected his tears in a basket (see *Vitae Patrum*, III, 1, PL 73:860). I. Hausherr, *Penthos*, Orientalia Christiana Analecta, 132 (Rome, 1944):42, in his study of compunction, cites Arsenios as the greatest exponent of contrition in the records of early Christian monasticism. For an interesting study of the spiritual significance of tears, drawing widely on the early monastic literature, especially Syriac, see Maggie Ross, "Tears and Fire: Recovering a Neglected Tradition," *Sobornost* 9, no. 1 (1987):14–23.
[569] Ps. 50:17.

to see, and then you will depart to the Lord and there behold endless light and indescribable glory." After saying this, the blessed Marko passed away in the Lord and was buried in the cave, where he had dug himself a place.

Feofil redoubled his sobbing. He was sorrowful in his heart because of his loss of eyesight, and he shed a fountain of tears, which increased even more. He had a bowl, and when he was occupied in prayer the tears would come, and he would put the bowl down and weep over it. For many years he filled it with tears, since every day he was expecting the venerable one's prophecy to be fulfilled. When he realized that his end and [departure] to God [was near] he prayed fervently to God that his tears might be acceptable before Him. Lifting up his hands, he began to pray saying, *Prayer*: "O Lord Master Jesus Christ, Who loves mankind, my most holy king, Who does not desire the death of sinners, but awaits their turning from their sins, Thou knowest our weakness. O good comforter, health to the sick, salvation to sinners, strength to the weak, rising up to those who have fallen! I pray, O Lord, show forth Thy grace upon me at this hour, unworthy as I am, and pour upon me the inexhaustible fount of Thy mercy, that I may not be tried by the ordeals of the princes of the air and vanquished by them. [I ask this] through the prayers of Thy servants, our great fathers Antonij and Feodosij, and all the saints who pleased Thee throughout the ages. Amen."

Immediately a handsome man stood in front of him and said, "Your prayer is good, but why do you boast about the loss of your tears?" Taking up a bowl much larger than Feofil's and filled with fragrant perfume, like sweet-smelling myrrh, he said, "Look, this comes from the tears you shed from your heart in prayer to God, which you wiped away with your hand or a towel or your clothing, or which fell from your eyes onto the ground. I have collected them all in this bowl and concealed them by the order of our Creator. Now I have been sent to bring you joyful news: you will depart to Him with gladness, for He said, 'Blessed are they that mourn, for they shall be comforted.'"[570] After saying this he disappeared.

The blessed Feofil summoned the superior[571] and told him about the angel's appearance and speech, and he showed him the two bowls, one filled with tears and the other filled with fragrant perfume; he ordered this to be poured over his body. In three days he himself departed to the Lord and was buried in the cave near Marko the Cave-

---

[570] Matt. 5:4.
[571] Ioann, who held office from 1088 to 1108.

dweller, as was fitting. He was annointed with the perfume from the angel's bowl, so that the entire cave was filled with the fragrant odor, and the bowl of tears was poured over him. For he that sows in tears shall reap in joy. They went on and wept and they cast their seed.[572] They shall be comforted in Christ, to Whom be glory with the Father and the Holy Spirit, now [and for ever and ever. Amen].

Discourse 33. The holy venerable fathers, Feodor and Vasilij.

As it is said, "Indifference to possessions is the mother of all blessings, just as avarice is the mother and root of all evil."[573] As Climacus says, "A man who loves to collect possessions will toil to his death for the sake of a needle."[574] But he who does not love possessions has come to love the Lord and has kept His commandment; such a man cannot keep possessions, but despises them in a manner pleasing to God by distributing them to all those in need. As the Lord said in the Gospel, "Whoever he be that forsaketh not all that he hath, he cannot be my disciple."[575]

Feodor followed these sayings. Having abandoned his worldly possessions and distributed his wealth to the poor, he became a monk and strove to live a virtuous life. By the superior's order he became the inhabitant of a cell called "the Varangian cave,"[576] in which he lived a life of self-denial for many years. But the enemy caused him much vexation and sadness on account of the property he had distributed to the poor. He used to think about the long years [ahead] and the weakness of the flesh, and that he would be dissatisfied with the monastic food.[577] The enemy brought him to a time of testing, and he did not ponder things in his mind nor remember the words of the Lord: "Take no thought for the morrow [saying], what shall we eat? or, what shall we drink? or, wherewithal shall we be clothed? Behold the fowls of the air: they sow not, neither do they reap; yet your heavenly father feedeth them."[578] The enemy often made him confused, wishing to drive him to despair on

---

[572] Ps. 125:5–6.
[573] Cf. 1 Tim. 6:10.
[574] See *The Ladder of Divine Ascent*, 190. This section of the *Ladder* also contains the quotation from 1 Tim. 6:10.
[575] Luke 14:33.
[576] On the Varangian Cave, see below, nn. 582 and 594.
[577] See Ἀνδρῶν ἁγίων βίβλος, 179, lns. 10–18: a monk regrets having given money away and is tempted to acquire new wealth, but the story ends differently.
[578] Matt. 6:34, 31, 26.

account of his poverty and the money he had spent and given to the poor. As he thought about these things over many days, the enemy made him feel very gloomy because of his poverty, and he openly confessed his misery to his friends.

A monk named Vasilij, one of the most spiritually advanced in the monastery, said, "Brother Feodor, I beg you: do not lose your reward. If you want possessions, I will give you everything I have. But you must say before God, 'Let everything which I gave away be for Thee.' Then you will no longer be sad,[579] since you will have acquired your possessions. But take care. Will the Lord bear with you?" Hearing these words, Feodor became filled with a great fear of divine wrath, for he had heard from Vasilij what happened in Constantinople, where a man had fallen down and died in the middle of church because of his remorse about gold which he had given away to charity; he was thus deprived of both, and lost both the gold and his life.[580] Having grasped the point of this, Feodor wept for his transgressions and blessed the brother who had led him away from this malady. The Lord says of such men, "Whoever will bring forth the precious from the worthless, he shall be as my mouth."[581] Henceforth a great love developed between Feodor and Vasilij.

Feodor made good progress in keeping the Lord's commandments and performing deeds pleasing to Him. This sorely wounded the devil, who was unable to lure him with [the promise] of property and wealth, and once again the adversary armed himself against Feodor and set before Him another snare to destroy him. Vasilij was sent away on business by the superior, and the enemy found this a suitable time for his evil purpose. He changed his appearance to resemble Vasilij and came to see the cave-dweller. At first he addressed him in profitable words, "How are you now, Feodor? Has your war with the demons stopped, or do they still trouble you with [thoughts of] love of possessions and remind you of the property which you gave away?" Feodor did not realize that this was a demon but thought that it was his brother who was saying these things to him. So the blessed one answered, "Thanks to your prayers,

---

[579] I accept the Arsenian будеши rather than the Cas. II буди: Abramovyč, *Pateryk*, 162, n. 29.

[580] I have yet to locate the origin of this story. Abramovyč, *Pateryk*, 224, n. 168, refers to the *Prolog* entry under January 19, published in *Pamjatniki drevnerusskoj cerkovnoučitel'noj literatury*, vol. 4, ed. A. I. Ponomarev (St. Petersburg, 1897), but I have been unable to find this volume; the British Library has only Part 1 of this work.

[581] Jer. 15:19.

father, I am making good progress. You have given me strength, and I will not heed demonic suggestions. Now I shall gladly do anything you command. I will not disobey you, since I have found your instruction most useful for my soul." Then the demon, the false brother, took courage, since the monk had not mentioned the Lord God, and said to him, "I shall give you another piece of advice through which you will find peace [of mind] and receive restitution for what you gave away. *I have heard from certain people that there is a Varangian treasure hoard in this cave, a large quantity of gold and silver hidden in the ground from times long ago. To this day no one has taken it out, and if you ask God,*[582] He will give you a large quantity of gold and silver. But do not let anyone come in here to see you, and do not go out of the cave yourself."

The cave-dweller promised to do this, and the demon then departed. Thus invisibly did the evil spirit bring Feodor thoughts about the treasure hoard and move him to prayer. He entreated God for the gold [and promised] that if he received it he would give it away as alms. In a dream he saw the demon radiant and splendidly attired, like an angel, showing him the treasure hoard in the cave; Feodor saw this many times. After several days he came to the place shown to him, began to dig, and found the treasure hoard—large quantities of gold and silver and expensive vessels.

At this point the demon again came in the form of his brother and said to the cave-dweller, "Where is the treasure you have been given? The man who appeared to you told me that you would be given a large quantity of gold and silver in answer to your prayer." But Feodor did not want to show him the treasure. Then the demon appeared to the cave-dweller and spoke to him, secretly insinuating into his thoughts the idea that he should take the gold and depart for another country. He said, "Brother Feodor, did I not tell you that you would soon receive restitution? For [the Lord] said, 'Everyone that hath forsaken house, or estates, or possessions for my sake, shall receive an hundredfold, and shall inherit everlasting life.'[583] Lo, you now have wealth in your hands; do what you like with it!" The cave-dweller said, "I asked God for this reason: if He should give it to me, I would distribute it all as alms; that is why He gave it to me." His opponent said, "Brother Feodor, take

---

[582] The italicized passage appears only in the "O" manuscript, based on the hypothetical primitive redaction of the *Paterik*: Abramovyč, *Pateryk*, 163, n. 17. I include it because it helps the flow of the story.
[583] Matt. 19:29. Cf. Mark 10:29–30; Luke 18:29–30.

care lest the enemy vex you again because of what you have given away, as he did before. This [treasure] was given to you in place of the money you gave away to the poor. I command you to take it and go to another country. There you will acquire estates to satisfy your needs, and there too you will be able to find salvation and escape from the snares of the demons, and after your death you will bestow this wealth on whomever you wish and will be remembered because of it.'' Then Feodor said to him, ''Shall I not be ashamed of myself? I have forsaken the world and everything in it and promised God that I would end my life in this cave. Am I now to be a fugitive and live in the world? If it pleases you, let me live in the monastery, and I shall do everything you say.'' The demon, the false brother, said, ''But you cannot hide this treasure; it will all be discovered and taken away. Take my advice and do as I tell you. If this was not pleasing to God, He would not have given it to you, or told me about it.'' Then the cave-dweller believed him, as though he were his brother, and prepared to leave the cave. Preparing carts and boxes, he packed the treasure into them, so that he might go wherever the demon ordered, and so that he might harm him by his cunning trick—that is to separate him from God and the holy place, the house of the most pure Theotokos and our venerable fathers Antonij and Feodosij.

God, however, does not wish that a single person from this holy place should perish, and He saved this man through the prayers of His saints. At that time Vasilij, who had earlier delivered the cave-dweller from evil thoughts, returned from the journey on which he had been sent by the superior. He came to the cave, as he wished to see his brother who was living there, and said to him, ''Brother Feodor, how do you stand with God now?'' Feodor was surprised at his question and by the fact that he spoke as though they had not seen each other for a long time. He said to him, ''Yesterday, and the days before that, you were always with me, telling me what to do. See, I am going where you told me.'' Vasilij said, ''Tell me, Feodor, what is this you are saying—'yesterday and the previous days you were always with me, telling me what to do?' Is this some demonic vision? Do not hide it from me, for God's sake!'' Feodor said to him angrily, ''Why are you testing me and why are you confusing my soul, sometimes talking to me in one way and sometimes in another? Which words am I to believe?'' Then he drove him away, after speaking cruel words to him. Vasilij accepted them all and went to the monastery.

The demon again came to Feodor in Vasilij's form and said, ''Brother, your accursed mind has destroyed you! I have not remembered the hurtful things you said to me last night;[584] but tonight go away and take what you have found [with you]." Having uttered these words, the demon departed. When daybreak drew near Vasilij came to him again, bringing some of the elders, and said to the cave-dweller, "I have brought these people to bear witness that it has been three months since we saw each other. This is my third day in the monastery, but you talk about 'yesterday and the previous days.' This is some demon's activity. When he comes to you, do not let him converse with you until he has said a prayer. Then you will realize that he is a demon." Then he recited a prayer of exorcism, calling the saints to his aid, and after thus strengthening the cave-dweller he departed for his own cell.

The demon no longer dared show himself to the cave-dweller, and Feodor understood the devil's trickery. Henceforth he made everyone who had come to him first say a prayer before he would converse with them, so henceforth he fortified himself against his enemies and understood their cunning. The Lord delivered him from those beasts that lurk in the mind, so that he was not their slave, as happens to many who live in the desert or in caves or in enclosures apart from their fellow men. A man must protect himself very well if he is not to perish at the hands of demons. They wanted to destroy this man, but the Lord delivered him.

Feodor dug a deep pit and put the treasure he had found there. Then he covered it up, and from that day until now no one knows where it has been hidden. In order not to be idle and provide an opportunity for laziness, he devoted himself to manual work, and so became fearless and then boldly confronted the demons. He set up some millstones in the cave and began to work for the holy brotherhood. He would take wheat from the corn bins and grind it with his own hands. At night he would not sleep, but work strenuously at his task and pray. In the morning he would put the flour into the bin and again take out some wheat. He did this for many years, working for the holy brotherhood and lightening the labor of the servants. He was not ashamed of such work and prayed to God ceaselessly that He would take from him the memory of avarice. And the Lord cured him of this malady, so that he no longer thought about the wealth which consists of gold and silver, but considered this as dirt.

A long time passed, during which he labored very hard at his work in wretched conditions. The cellarer saw how hard he worked. Once when the grain was brought in from the estates, he sent five cartloads to

---

[584] I have used the Arsenian reading сеи нощи: Abramovyč, *Pateryk*, 165, n. 10.

him in the cave, so that he need not always come out to take it and thus get tired. Feodor, after piling up the grain in bowls, began to grind it, singing the Psalter, which he knew by heart. Suddenly, as he was working, he lay down as he wanted to rest a little. All at once there was a peal of thunder, and the mills began to grind. Realizing that this was demonic activity, the blessed one got up and began to pray fervently to God, saying in a loud voice, "The Lord forbids you to do this, you all-cunning devil!" But the demon did not stop grinding the mills. Feodor once again said, "In the name of the Father, the Son, and the Holy Spirit, Who cast you out of heaven and allowed Their servants to trample you underfoot, you are commanded by me, sinner that I am, not to stop working until you have ground all the grain, so that you will also work for the holy brotherhood" Having said this, he stood in prayer. The demon did not dare disobey, and by daylight he had ground five cartloads of flour. Feodor told the cellarer to send for the flour. The cellarer marveled at this marvelous miracle: five cartloads ground in a single night! He brought the five cartloads of flour from the cave, and so five other cartloads were added to their store. This remarkable miracle took place at that time, and we still hear of it now. For the saying in the Gospel was fulfilled: "Even the devils are subject unto you through my name. I have given you power to tread on serpents and scorpions, over all the power of the enemy."[585] The demons wanted to frighten the blessed one still more, but he so bound them together in work that they cried out to him, "We will no longer come!"

Feodor and Vasilij established a God-pleasing compact that they would never conceal their thoughts from each other, but would resolve and settle [their problems] according to God's guidance. Vasilij came into the cave, but Feodor, on account of old age, came out of it and built himself a cell in the old courtyard.[586] It was then that the monastery burned down.[587] Some timber had been brought to the river bank to build the church and all the cells, and carters had been hired to take it up the hill. But Feodor, who did not wish to be a burden to others, began to carry the timber himself. But whatever Feodor carried up to build his cell was thrown down the hill by the demons to annoy him; they wanted thereby to drive the blessed one away. Feodor said, "In the name of our

---

[585] Luke 10:19.
[586] This was probably in the "old monastery." See Discourse 8, p. 86.
[587] Part of the church and some other parts of the monastery were destroyed by fire in a Cuman attack on Kiev in July, 1096. See PVL 1096, PSRL 1:232–33, 2:223.

Lord God, Who commanded you to enter into the swine,[588] He orders you through me, His servant, to carry up the hill each piece of timber on the river bank, so that those doing God's work will not have to perform this task, but with it will build a house of prayer for our most holy Lady, the Theotokos, and prepare cells for themselves. Stop bothering them and realize that the Lord dwells in this place!" That night the demons never stopped carrying logs from the Dnieper up the hill, until not a single piece of wood remained below. With this [timber] they erected the church and the cells, including roofs and the floors, and it was sufficient for the needs of the whole monastery.

In the morning the carters got up and went to the river bank, intending to take the timber [up the hill], but they found not a single piece on the bank; it was all on the hill, and not stacked in one place, but in different places, according to its purpose—material for the roof and the floor was stacked separately from the timber for the cells, which had been awkward to carry because of the long distance—but the whole lot was on the hill. This was amazing to those who saw and heard about it, since what had been done was beyond human power. To many people of other faiths it seemed incredible, because of the magnitude of the miracle, but those who had seen it glorified God, Who performs extraordinary miracles for the sake of His servants. For as the Lord said, "Rejoice not that the spirits are subject unto you; but rather rejoice, because your names are written in heaven."[589] The Lord indeed did this to His glory, through the prayers of our holy fathers Antonij and Feodosij.

The demons could not bear the humiliation: sometimes honored, venerated, and reckoned as gods by unbelievers, they were now despised, dishonored, and brought to nought by Christ's servants, working like bought slaves, carrying timber up the hill, chased away by men, fearing the threats of the venerable ones, since all their tricks had been shown up by Feodor and Vasilij. So the demon saw himself despised by men and cried out, "You cruel and wicked foes! I will not stop or rest, and I will fight you to the death!" The devil did not know that our Mediator [was preparing] two mighty crowns for them: He stirred up wicked men against them, and they stretched their bows, their cruel instruments, and their weapons shall enter their hearts[590] —as we shall narrate later.

The hired men and the carters raised a rebellion against the blessed one and asked for their pay, saying, "We do not know by what trick you

---

[588] See Matt. 8:28–34; Mark 5:1–20; Luke 8:26–39.
[589] Luke 10:20.
[590] Cf. Ps. 36:14–15.

ordered the timber to be carried up the hill." An unjust judge took the fee from them and told them to claim it from the venerable one, saying, "Let the demons who work for you help you to pay!" He failed to remember the divine judgment: that he who judges unjustly will himself be judged.

Again the devil raised a storm against the venerable ones. He found one of the prince's counsellors, a wicked and cruel man, completely evil in character and deeds. The demon came to this boyar in the form of Vasilij, since Vasilij was known to him, and said, "Feodor, who was in the cave before me, found a treasure hoard containing a large quantity of gold and silver and expensive vessels. He wanted to flee to another land with all these things, but I restrained him. Now he is acting like an idiot,[591] ordering demons to grind [corn] and carry timber up the hill from the river bank. He behaves thus and keeps the treasure hoard until such time as he can hide from me and depart with it wherever he wants. And you will find nothing."

Hearing this from the demon and thinking that he was Vasilij, the boyar took him to Prince M'stislav Svjatopolčič.[592] The demon related these facts—and more—to the prince and said, "You can quickly have this man [here] and take the treasure. If he does not give it to you, then threaten him with wounds and torture. If he still won't give it to you, hand him over to severe tortures. If even then he still won't give it to you, summon me and I will accuse him before you all and show you the place where the treasure is hidden." After delivering this evil message the demon disappeared from their sight.

Early [the next morning] the prince himself went out with a multitude of soldiers, as though going on a hunt or against a powerful warrior, and seized the blessed Feodor and led him to his house. First he questioned him gently, saying, "Father, tell me, did you find a treasure hoard? I shall share it with you, and you will be a father to me and to my father. (Svjatopolk was then in Turov.)[593] Feodor said, "Yes, I did find it, and it is now hidden in the cave." The prince said, "Father, was there much gold and silver and vessels? Who hid it?" Feodor said, "We are told in the Life of Antonij that it is a Varangian hoard, since the vessels are the kind used by the Latins, and that is why the Varangian cave is

---

[591] The word уродьствовати normally (and here) means to behave in a foolish or mischievous manner that invites taunts and insults, but for a fuller discussion of уродьство as a form of asceticism ("folly for Christ's sake"), see Appendix IV.
[592] The eldest son of Svjatopolk II Izjaslavič.
[593] See above, Discoure 31, n. 558.

so-called until today.⁵⁹⁴ There is an uncountable amount of gold and silver." The prince said, "Why don't you give it to me, your son? Take as much as you want for yourself." Feodor said, "I don't need any of it, or are you ordering me to take something that will bring me no benefit? For I don't need these things, since I have been set free from this [temptation]. I don't remember [where it is]. I would have told you, since you are a slave to this [temptation], while I have been released from it." Then the prince said angrily to his servants, "I command you to put fetters on the hands and feet of this monk, who does not want my kindness. Give him neither bread nor water for three days."

Feodor was again questioned, "Reveal the treasure!" But he said, "I do not know where I hid it." The prince ordered him to be cruelly tortured, so that his shirt was soaked with blood. Then he ordered him to be hung up in thick smoke, with his hands behind his back, and a fire kindled round him. The many people marveled at this man's endurance, since he remained in the flames as though he were standing in dew, and the fire did not touch his shirt. One of the bystanders said that Feodor had performed a miracle. The prince was filled with terror, and he said to the elder, "Why are you destroying yourself? Why will you not give me the treasure, which I ought to have?" Feodor said, "I am telling you the truth: through the prayers of my brother Vasilij I was saved [from sin] at the time when I found it, and now the Lord has removed from me the memory of avarice, and I do not know where I hid it."

The prince quickly sent to the cave for the holy Vasilij. He did not want to come, but was brought out of the cave by force. The prince said to him, "I have done everything you told me to do to this wicked man. I will regard you as a father." Vasilij said "What did I tell you to do?" The prince said, "You informed me about the treasure hoard. He would not tell me, so I tortured him." Vasilij answered, "I recognize the tricks of the wicked demon. He has deceived you and spoken falsely against me and this venerable man. You have never seen me, because I have not left my cave for fifteen years." Then all the bystanders said, "You talked to the prince in front of us!" Vasilij said, "The demon has deceived you all. I have not seen the prince or you."

The prince became very angry and ordered him to be beaten mercilessly. Unable to bear the accusation, and boisterous from wine and in a furious temper, he drew out an arrow and wounded Vasilij. When he

---

⁵⁹⁴ On "the Varangian Cave," see the references cited by Abramovyč, *Pateryk*, 225, n. 174. Stender-Petersen, *Varangica*, 145–46, thinks that there is no reason to doubt the existence of the hoard, although it has never been found.

shot him, Vasilij withdrew the arrow from his stomach and threw it at the prince, saying, "With this arrow you yourself will be wounded!" And his prophecy was fulfilled. The prince ordered them to be locked up separately, so that he could torture them cruelly the next morning; but that night they passed away in the Lord. Learning this, the brethren came and took their tortured bodies and buried them with due honor in the Varangian cave, in which they had spiritually struggled, and they were buried there in their bloody garments and shirts. Their bodies are whole to this day, for how can that before which the fire was shamed partake of corruption?

A few days later M'stislav himself was shot by an arrow on the ramparts of Volodymyr, as Vasilij had prophesied, while fighting against David Igorevič.[595] Then he recognized his own arrow, with which he had shot Vasilij, and said, "I die today because of the venerable Vasilij and Feodor, so that the Lord's saying may be fulfilled: 'All they that take up the sword shall perish with the sword.'"[596] Because he had killed unlawfully, he was killed unlawfully.[597] But Feodor and Vasilij[598] received a martyr's crown in Jesus Christ our Lord, to Whom be glory with the Father and the Holy Spirit now and forever.

Discourse 34. The venerable Spiridon, the baker of sacramental bread, and Alimpij the Icon-painter.[599]

Every simple soul is holy; there is no guile in him, nor any deceit in his heart. Such a man is sincere towards God and men and incapable of sin toward God; indeed he has no desire [to sin], since he is a divine vessel and a dwelling place for the Holy Spirit, Who illuminates his body, mind, and soul. As the Lord said, "My Father and I will come and

---

[595] This occurred in 1099 during the civil war following Vasil'ko's blinding in 1097. See Discourse 31, n. 552.

[596] Matt. 26:52.

[597] The circumstances of M'stislav's death are described in PVL 1099, PSRL 1:271–72, 2:246–47. His body was concealed by his retinue for three days. It seems that there was something unusual about it, perhaps a suspicion of treachery, which would account for Polikarp saying that he died "unlawfully."

[598] I have used the variant "O" reading here, which gives the two monks' names: Abramovyč, *Pateryk*, 171, n. 7.

[599] This discourse does not appear in the Arsenian redaction. See Introduction, p. xxx. In the opinion of Šaxmatov, "Žitie Antonija i Pečerskaja Letopis'," 123, n. 1, it did not form part of the original core of Polikarp's narratives.

make our abode with him,"⁶⁰⁰ and, "I will dwell in them, and walk in them: and I will be their God and they shall be my people."⁶⁰¹ And the Apostle says, "Brethren, you are the temple of the living God, and the Holy Spirit dwelleth in you."⁶⁰² On earth such men lived like angels, and in heaven they rejoice with them forever; as they were inseparable from them in this life, so they rejoice with them after death. We shall speak about this at the end of the discourse.

The venerable Spiridon was lacking in letters but not intelligence, since he came to the monastic life not from a town, but from a village. He laid hold of the fear of God in his heart and began to study books; he learned the whole of the Psalter by heart. By the order of the superior Pimin the Faster⁶⁰³ he baked sacramental bread with another brother, named Nikodim, similar to him in mind and character. They served well in the bakehouse for many years, performing this service honorably⁶⁰⁴ and without a single fault. From the time when he entered the bakehouse the blessed Spiridon made no change in his ascetic discipline and spiritual struggles but carried out his work with the utmost piety and in the fear of God, bringing to God a pure sacrifice from his labors. The fruits of his lips were brought to Almighty God as a living sacrifice of words for all things and all men, since he sang the Psalter ceaselessly and completed it every day. Whether he was chopping wood or mixing dough, [the Psalter] was ceaselessly on his lips.

Once when he was performing his customary work with the utmost piety this blessed man happened to light the stove, as he always did, to bake the sacramental bread, and the roof of the bakehouse caught fire from the flames. He took his mantle and closed the opening of the stove. Tying together the sleeves of his tunic, he took it and ran to the well, poured water into it, and quickly ran back, while calling to the brethren to come and put out the fire in the stove. The brethren came running up and saw a remarkable thing: the water from his tunic was not exhausted, and they quenched the fury of the fire with it.

---

⁶⁰⁰ John 14:23.
⁶⁰¹ 2 Cor. 6:16.
⁶⁰² 1 Cor. 3:16.
⁶⁰³ Probably the same as the superior Pimin in Discourse 15, who held office some time in the mid-twelfth century. See Discourse 15, n. 370. It is unlikely that he is identical with the Pimin the Faster mentioned in Discourse 18, who may possibly be the same as the Pimin in Discourse 35. See Discourse 35, n. 638.
⁶⁰⁴ I have used here the reading честно found in all MSS except Cas. 2: Abramovyč, *Pateryk*, 171, n. 24.

It would require great diligence to remember, praise, and call blessed all those who ended their lives in the Lord here in the blessed Caves Monastery, saying, like David, "Rejoice in the Lord ye righteous: praise becomes the upright. Sing to Him heartily with a loud noise on a psaltery of ten strings."[605] They did not pray to the Lord and do what was pleasing in His sight at the eleventh hour, but devoted themselves to God from their youth, and after many years they departed to the Lord in their old age without having altered their rule of life for a single day or hour. For they were planted in the house of the Mother of God, and they bloomed in the courts of our God and still bring forth increase in their ripe old age, even as this blessed one.

The venerable Alimpij was commended [to the monastery] by his parents to learn icon painting. Now in the days of the pious prince Vsevolod Jaroslavič and the venerable superior Nikon, some Greek painters, according to the will of God and His most pure Mother, were brought by force from Constantinople to decorate the church of the Caves Monastery, as we are told in Simon's epistle.[606] On that occasion God performed an awesome miracle in His church. The craftsmen were setting pieces of mosaic in the altar,[607] and the image of our most pure Lady, the Theotokos and ever-virgin Mary, was taking shape. They were all inside the altar, putting the mosaic in position, and Alimpij was helping and learning the craft. And they all beheld an amazing and awesome miracle: as they were looking at the image of our Lady, the Theotokos and ever-virgin Mary, it suddenly became brighter than the sun. They were unable to look at it and fell down in terror. Then they raised themselves up a little, anxious to see the miracle that had occurred. A white dove flew out of the lips of the most pure Mother of God,[608] flew up to the image of the Savior, and hid there. They all looked to see whether it had flown out of the church, and as they were watching, the dove flew out of the Savior's mouth and flew all round the church. It flew towards each of the saints,[609] sometimes alighting on their hands and sometimes on their heads. Then it flew down and came to rest behind the wonder-

---

[605] Ps. 32:1–3.
[606] See Discourse 4.
[607] I.e., the part of the church behind the iconostasis and the Royal Doors, corresponding to the chancel in a western church. The Orthodox term for the western altar is "holy table."
[608] For a similar but not identical story, see Ἀνδρῶν ἁγίων βίβλος, 171, lns. 11–14.
[609] I.e., the images of the saints depicted on the church walls. Cf. Discourse 3, p. 9.

working *naměstnaja ikona* of the Theotokos.⁶¹⁰ The people standing below wanted to catch the dove, and they set up a ladder but could not find it behind the icon or behind the veil.⁶¹¹ They looked everywhere but could not find where the dove had hidden. As they stood gazing at the icon, right in front of them the dove once more flew out of the lips of the Theotokos and went up towards the image of the Savior.⁶¹² They shouted to those who were standing up above, "Hold it!" They stretched out their hands to catch it, but the dove flew away again in the Savior's lips and then came out. And once more a light brighter than the sun shone upon them, blinding their vision. They fell down and prostrated themselves before the Lord.⁶¹³

The blessed Alimpij was with them, and he saw the action of the Holy Spirit abiding in the holy and noble church of the Caves Monastery. When they finished painting it, the blessed Alimpij was tonsured under the superior Nikon. He became well-versed in the craft of icon painting and was highly skilled in it. He wanted to learn this skill not in order to acquire wealth, but for God's sake. For he painted icons for the superior and all the brethren, working hard enough to supply the needs of them all but taking nothing for his work. If at any time he had no work for himself, the venerable one would take the gold and silver needed for the icons, make icons for those to whom he was indebted, and give them an icon in exchange for the debt. He often asked his friends to bring him any votive icons they might have seen in a church. These he would renovate⁶¹⁴ and return to their places. He did all this in order not to be idle, since the holy fathers had commanded the monks to work with their

---

⁶¹⁰ за иконою чюдною богородичиною намѣстною. It is difficult to find a suitable translation for намѣстная икона. It usually depicted the saint or a feast to which the church was dedicated and was usually placed to the south of the Royal Doors, in the *mestnij rjad*, or "local tier," together with images of Christ, the Theotokos, and local saints. I am grateful to Natalia Teteriatnikov of Dumbarton Oaks for this information.

⁶¹¹ Probably referring to the veil (завѣса, Greek καταπέτασμα) which separated the altar from the nave.

⁶¹² This would be the image of Christ Pantocrator, which traditionally occupied the dome of a Byzantine church.

⁶¹³ Puc'ko, "Kievskij xudožnik," 71, notes that the various places indicated in the dove's flight correspond to the traditional decorative scheme in an eleventh-century Byzantine church.

⁶¹⁴ Puc'ko, "Kievskij xudožnik," 76–77, points out that one would hardly expect there to be much need to renovate icons in late eleventh-century Rus', barely a hundred years after the conversion. He suggests that Polikarp is here "looking at things with the eyes of a man living in the early thirteenth century."

hands[615] and considered this important in the sight of God. As the Apostle Paul said, "My hands have ministered unto me, unto them that were with me;"[616] "nor did I eat any man's bread for nought."[617] So the blessed Alimpij divided the proceeds of his handiwork into three parts: one part for the holy icons, a second part for the poor, and a third part for the needs of his own body. He did this throughout his life and never gave himself a day's rest, while at night he occupied himself in prayer and singing. Then when day approached, he would take up his work again. No one ever saw him idle, but he never absented himself from the congregation in church because of his work. The superior made him a priest because of his pure life and his many good deeds, and as a priest he continued to live a good and God-pleasing life.

A wealthy man from Kiev contracted leprosy. For a long time he was treated by magicians and physicians, and he sought help from men of other faiths, but without success; in fact he found that his condition was getting worse. One of his friends persuaded him to go to the Caves Monastery and ask some of the fathers to pray for him. He was taken to the monastery, and the superior ordered him to be given some water to drink, through a sponge, from the well of the holy Feodosij. They wiped his head and face, and immediately he was so covered with pus because of his lack of faith that they all fled from him because of the stench.

He returned to his own house, weeping and lamenting. For many days he did not go out on account of the stench, and said to his friends, "Shame has covered my face; I became strange to my brethren and a stranger to my mother's children,[618] because I did not come in faith to the holy Antonij and Feodosij." Every day he expected that he would die.

One day, late at night, he came to himself, reflected on his transgressions, went to the venerable Alimpij, and repented to him. The blessed one said to him, "You have done well, my son, to confess your sins to God in my unworthy presence. For the prophet David said, 'I will confess my iniquity to the Lord against myself; and Thou forgivest the ungodliness of my heart.'"[619] Having instructed him at length about the salvation of his soul, he took up his palette, adorned his face with the

---

[615] This refers to the Desert Fathers about whom the Rus' monks had read in translated *paterika*. Manual work was also required by the Stoudite Rule. See Discourse 8, p. 42.
[616] Acts 20:34.
[617] 2 Thess. 3:8.
[618] Ps. 68:7–8.
[619] Ps. 31:5.

colors with which he painted icons, anointed his suppurating wounds, and restored him to his former handsome appearance. He led him to the divine church of the Caves Monastery, administered the holy Mysteries to him, and told him to wash with the water used by the priests to wash. His sores at once fell away from him, and he was cured.

I have noticed the wisdom of this blessed man, for he took Christ as his model. Just as our Lord, Who cured a leper and told him to show himself to the priests and bring a gift in return for his cleansing,[620] so too this holy man shunned any greatness for himself. And just as Christ cured the blind man and told him to go and bathe in the pool at Siloam,[621] so too this blessed man first adorned with his colors the face that was giving off a foul smell for lack of faith, thus conferring honor on these divine instruments,[622] so that they might share with him in the miracle. As he washed him with water, he cleansed not only the leprous sores of his body but also those from his soul.

As a thank-offering for his cleansing, the great-grandson of the healed man decorated with gold the chest that hangs above the holy table, and everybody marveled at the speedy recovery. The venerable Alimpij said to them, "Brothers, pay heed to Him Who said, 'No servant can serve two masters.'[623] At first this man served the enemy through the sin of sorcery, but ultimately he came to God. For earlier he had despaired of his salvation, and his leprosy had grown worse because of his lack of faith. 'Ask,' said the Lord, 'and do not only ask, but ask with faith, and you will receive.'[624] When he repented to God and appointed me his witness, He Who is quick to show mercy had pity on him.'' After his recovery the man went back to his home, glorifying God and the most pure Mother who bore Him, and our venerable fathers Antonij and Feodosij and the blessed Alimpij. For he was indeed to us a new Elisha, [like the one] who cured Naaman the Syrian of leprosy.[625]

Another Christ-loving man, from the same city of Kiev, built himself a church and wished to have some large icons painted to decorate it:

---

[620] See Matt. 8:2–4; Mark 1:40–44; Luke 5:12–14.
[621] See John 9:1–7.
[622] The text has служители, lit. "servants," but the context indicates that Polikarp is referring to Alimpij's colors.
[623] Luke 16:13. Cf. Matt. 6:24.
[624] A paraphrase of Matt. 7:7; Luke 11:9.
[625] The parallel is quite close, since at first Naaman did not have faith in Elisha's power to heal him and ignored his order to go and wash seven times in the River Jordan. See 4 Kings 5:10–14.

five Deisis panels[626] and two *naměstnaja* icons. This Christ-lover gave some silver to two monks from the Caves Monastery, so that they would make an agreement with Alimpij that he could receive as much as he wanted to paint the icon. But the monks said nothing to Alimpij and took from the man as much as they wanted. Then the Christ-lover sent to the monks to ask whether the icons were finished. They said that more gold was needed, and again they took gold from the Christ-lover and spent it. They had another conversation with this man and spoke against the holy one, saying that he was asking for as much again as he had already received. The Christ-lover gave it gladly. A little later the monks again said, "Alimpij wants as much again." The Christ-lover said, "Even if he asks up to ten times as much, I will give it. All I want is his blessing and prayer and the work of his hands." Alimpij knew nothing of what these monks were doing.

The man sent [to the monastery], as he wanted to see whether the icons were finished. The two monks told him, "Alimpij has taken the gold and the silver and got interest on it,[627] but he does not want to paint the icons." The Christ-lover came to the monastery with a large retinue and went to see the superior Nikon,[628] intending to stir up trouble for the venerable Alimpij. The superior summoned Alimpij and said to him, "Brother, what wrong have you done to our son?[629] He has several times given you what you asked for, at your request, and sometimes you paint without payment." The blessed one said, "Honored father, your holiness knows that I have never been lazy in my work. Now I do not know what you are talking about." The superior said, "You have had three payments for the seven icons." To prove this, he ordered Alimpij's icon panels to be brought in, and he summoned the monk who had taken the payment, so that the monk could be confronted with him. The messengers saw that the icons were skillfully painted and brought them before the superior. Seeing them, everybody marveled and they were all awestruck. Trembling, they fell down on the ground and prostrated themselves before the image, not made with hands, of our Lord Jesus Christ and His most pure Mother and His saints. The fame [of this

---

[626] A Deisis icon depicts Christ flanked by the Theotokos and John the Baptist.

[627] There are references to lending money on interest in the *Rus'kaja Pravda*. See *Medieval Russian Laws*, trans. G. Vernadsky (New York, 1947), 43, Articles 50–52.

[628] Puc'ko, "Kievskij xudožnik," 78, argues that it is unlikely that this occurred under Nikon, since he probably had died shortly after Alimpij was tonsured and before he had become a well-known icon-painter.

[629] This suggests that the superior (Nikon's successor Ioann?) was the spiritual father of the unnamed "Christ-lover."

miracle] spread throughout the city of Kiev.⁶³⁰ The two monks came and spoke out against the blessed one (they knew nothing about this) and began to argue with Alimpij, saying, "You took three payments for the icons, but did not paint them." Everybody present answered them, "Lo, the icons have now been painted by God!" When they saw this, they were filled with terror at the miracle. These monks, who had robbed the monastery, were thus shown up, deprived of their possessions, and expelled from the Caves Monastery.

This, however, did not put a stop to their malice. They made accusations against the blessed one, saying to everybody, "We painted the icons, but their owner will not give us the payment due. He deprived us of the fee and concocted this story that the icons were painted by God and not by us." And so they persuaded the people who were running to see the icons, and they prohibited them from venerating them, and for this reason people believed these monks who were telling lies about the blessed Alimpij.⁶³¹

But God glorifies His saints, as the Lord said in the Gospel, "A city that is set on a hill cannot be hid. Neither do men light a candle, and put it under a bushel, but on a candlestick; and it giveth light unto all who come."⁶³² And so the venerable Alimpij's virtuous life was not hidden: the miracle of the icons came to the ears of Prince Volodimer.⁶³³ It happened in this way. By God's will, the whole of Podil was consumed in a fire,⁶³⁴ including the church in which these icons had been set up. After the fire all seven icons were found undamaged, though the church was entirely destroyed. When the prince heard about this, he went to see the miracle that had taken place there with those icons which had been painted at God's command in a single night. He praised the Creator of all things, Who performs glorious miracles through the prayers of His servants Antonij and Feodosij. Volodimer took one of the icons, of the holy Theotokos, and sent it to the town of Rostov to be placed in a church he

---

⁶³⁰ The story of the icon "not made with hands" (нерукотворенная, Greek ἀχειροποίητος) may well have been grafted onto the original story in order to enhance Alimpij's sanctity.

⁶³¹ Puc'ko, "Kievskij xudožnik," 78, suggests that Alimpij had rivals in the monastery, but there is no concrete evidence of this.

⁶³² Matt. 5:14–15.

⁶³³ I.e., Volodimer Monomax.

⁶³⁴ Polikarp is almost certainly referring here to the fire of June, 1124, described in both the *Laurentian* (PSRL 1:293) and *Hypatian* (PSRL 2:288) chronicles. The *Laurentian* chronicle says that almost 600 churches were burnt.

had founded there;[635] it is there to this day, as I have seen for myself. While I was in Rostov the church collapsed, but the icon was undamaged and was carried into a wooden church. This too burned down, but the icon remained undamaged and showed no trace of fire.[636]

Let us come to another story about the blessed Alimpij. Another Christ-lover commissioned the blessed one to paint a *naměstnaja ikona*. A few days later the blessed Alimpij fell ill, but the icon was unpainted. The God-lover kept pressing the blessed one, who said to him, "My son, do not come and bother me. But cast all your care about this icon on the Lord. He will act according to His will, and your icon will be in place in time for the festival." The man was glad that the icon would be finished before the festival, having believed in the words of the blessed one, and went home rejoicing. The God-lover came again on the eve [of the feast] of the Dormition, wishing to take his icon, and he saw that the icon was still unfinished, and that the blessed Alimpij was very ill. He upbraided him, saying, "Why didn't you tell me about your infirmity? I would have had someone else paint the icon, so that the festival could be properly celebrated with due honor. Now you have kept back the icon and disgraced me!" The blessed one replied to him meekly, "My son, when have I ever been lazy? Is God unable to paint an icon of His mother at a single word? I am about to depart from this world, as the Lord has revealed to me, and after my death God will comfort you in every way." The man departed for home, feeling very dejected.

After he left a handsome youth entered, took up Alimpij's palette, and began to paint the icon. Alimpij thought that the icon's owner was angry with him and had sent along another icon painter, because at first he seemed like a man, but the speed of his work showed that he was an incorporeal being. Sometimes he put gold on the icon, sometimes he spread his colors on the stone, and in three hours the icon was finished. He said, "Tell me, monk, is anything missing? Have I made any mistakes?" The venerable one said, "You have done very well. God is helping you to paint this icon very skillfully, and He has done it through you." When evening came he suddenly disappeared with the icon.

---

[635] See Discourse 4, p. 13.
[636] Polikarp is presumably referring here to his visit to Bishop Simon mentioned in Discourse 14, during which he probably visited several churches. According to Puc'ko, "Kievskij xudožnik," 80–82, however, he cannot have actually seen the church in Rostov founded by Volodimer Monomax, since it burned in 1160; he must have confused it with another church.

The icon's owner could not sleep all night from misery, because the icon would not be ready for the festival; he called himself a sinner, unworthy of such grace. He got up and went to the church to weep for his sins. He opened the doors of the church and saw the icon shining in its place and he fell down in fear, thinking that he had seen an apparition. When he had recovered a little from his fright, he realized that it was the icon, and he was awestruck as he recalled the venerable one's words. He ran and woke up the members of his household. They ran joyfully to the church with candles and censers, and they saw the icon shining more brightly than the sun. They fell down to the ground, prostrated themselves before the icon, and kissed it joyfully.

The God-lover came to the superior and related the miracle that had occurred. Together they all went to the venerable Alimpij, and they saw that he was departing from this world. The superior inquired of him, "Father, how was this icon painted, and by whom?" He told them everything he had seen. He said, "It was an angel who painted it. He stands before me, about to take me." Having said this, he gave up his spirit. They prepared him for burial, carried him into the church, and sang the customary office over him. They placed him in the cave, together with the venerable fathers [in Christ Jesus our Lord, to Whom be glory with the Father and the Holy...].[637]

---

[637] The Cas. II MS contains the incomplete doxology placed here in square brackets. It is not found in any other MSS used by Abramovyč, *Pateryk*, 179, n. 7.

Discourse 35. The venerable and long-suffering father Pimin[638] and those who wish to be tonsured before their death.[639]

Having begun our discourse about Pimin, we shall go on to describe his severe suffering and illness, which he bore bravely, even giving thanks for it. This blessed Pimin was born ill, and grew up ill. Because of his sickness he was free from every kind of impurity from his mother's womb and was a stranger to sin. He often asked his parents to allow him to be tonsured, but they, like lovers of children, hoped to have him as their heir and forbade him. When he was incapacitated, he was brought to the Caves Monastery to be cured by the prayers of the holy men there or to receive from their hands the holy Angelic Habit. His parents, who loved their child dearly, never left him, and begged everybody to pray for their son and cure him of his illness. The venerable fathers tried very hard but could do nothing to help him, since Pimin's prayer prevailed over all others and he was not praying for recovery but for his illness to get worse, so that he would not be snatched away from the monastery by his parents once he was well. While his father and

---

[638] Abramovyč, *Pateryk*, 225, n. 180, points out that conflicting views have been expressed about the possible identity of this Pimin and the Pimin the Faster of Discourse 18. It is true that both monks are credited with gifts of prophecy and healing, and both had foreknowledge of the time of their death; this was in fact quite a common phenomenon in the case of holy men. However, it is more reasonable to assume that the two monks were separate individuals. There is no example in the *Paterik* of a monk having two epithets; if Pimin the Faster had been the subject of Discourse 35, he would surely have been described as such in the title. Moreover, chronological evidence, though not conclusive, suggests that the two Pimins lived at different times. The death of "Pimin the Long-suffering" occurred in 1110 (see below, n. 650). Discourse 18 cannot be precisely dated, but its context can be provisionally assigned to the mid-twelfth century. See above, Discourse 18, n. 398.

[639] It is clear from this discourse, and from other references in the *Paterik*, that in the Caves Monastery, at least by the late eleventh century, the Great Habit was normally conferred only when death was imminent or thought to be. This was contrary to the views of Theodore the Stoudite, PG 99:941, 1820, who thought that there could only be one tonsure, i.e., into the Great Habit, just as there could only be one baptism. But this practice was later modified, and the typikon of Patriarch Alexios, which regulated the life of the Caves Monastery, included a special service for monks considered worthy of the Great Habit to receive it on the third day of Easter week. See Dimitrievskij, *Opisanie*, 1:xxiii. Feodosij appears to have considered the bestowal of the Great Habit as the normal culmination of a monk's ascetic training, though not the only form of tonsure. See Discourse 8, p. 45. The evidence of Discourse 35 suggests a further change, in the direction of postponement until the end of a monk's life.

mother were sitting beside him and not allowing him to be tonsured, this blessed youth was greatly troubled and began to pray earnestly to God that his wish be granted.

One night, when they all were asleep outside, some men looking like handsome eunuchs came with candles to where Pimin was lying on his bed; they were carrying a Gospel, a tunic, a mantle, a cowl, and everything needed for tonsuring.[640] They said to him, "Do you want us to tonsure you?" He gladly promised [to obey them], saying, "The Lord has sent you, my lords. Fulfill the desire of my heart." They at once began to put questions to him, "Why have you come, brother, falling down before this holy table and before this holy assembly? Do you desire to be deserving of the Great Angelic Habit?"[641] They asked him all the other questions in order, just as it is written, then tonsured him into the Great Habit after dressing him in a mantle and a cowl and singing the obligatory office. Having bestowed on him the Great Angelic Habit, they kissed him and gave him the name of Pimin. Lighting a candle, they said that it would burn for forty days and forty nights without going out.[642] Having done all these things, they went into the church, taking his hair in a towel, and put it on the tomb of holy Feodosij.

The brothers in their cells heard the sound of singing and woke up their neighbors, thinking that the superior and some other monks were tonsuring him, or that he had already died. Together all went to the cell where the sick youth lay and found everybody asleep—his father, mother, and the servants. They went in with them to the blessed one, and they were all struck by a fragrant odor, and they saw Pimin happy and joyous, dressed in the monastic habit. They asked him who had tonsured him, [saying,] "We heard the sound of singing. Your parents who were here beside you heard nothing of this." The sick one said to them, "I think that the superior and [some of] the brethren came in here and tonsured me and gave me the name of Pimin."[643] It was that office which

---

[640] See Discourse 8, p. 45.

[641] These are the first questions put to the candidate during both the Order of the Little Habit (μανδύας, мантия) and the Order of the Great Angelic Habit, which includes the Inner Rason (ζωστικὸν ῥάσον, подрясникъ), Outer Rason (ἐξώρασον/παλλίον, ряса/палия), and Cowl (κουκκούλιον, коуколъ).

[642] Cf. Ἀνδρῶν ἁγίων βίβλος, 178–79.

[643] This is what probably happened. There is nothing in the story incompatible with the fact that Pimin was secretly tonsured by the superior and the senior members of the community, who later pretended to have no knowledge of what happened, though they never explicitly denied it; they could also have sworn the sextons to secrecy, which would explain the locked church. The deception would be justified by the desire to carry out

you heard, and they said that the candle would burn for forty days and forty nights, and they took my hair and went into the church."

Hearing this from him, they went to the church and found it locked. Rousing the sextons, they asked them if anyone had entered the church after the evening office. The sextons replied that no one had entered the church, and that the steward had the keys. Taking the keys, they went into the church and saw Pimin's hair wrapped in a towel on Feodosij's tomb. They informed the superior and looked for those who had tonsured him, but could not find them. So it became clear to them that this was God's plan. Having carefully considered this miraculous event,[644] to see whether the tonsuring could be regarded as canonical, [they decided that it was], because there was clear evidence: the locked church, the hair found on the holy Feodosij's tomb, the candle large enough to burn for one day but which burned continually for forty days and forty nights without going out. So they did not tonsure him again.

They said, "The gift bestowed on you by God is sufficient for you, Brother Pimin, as well as the name you have received." They asked him, "Who were they who tonsured you?" They showed him the books containing the rite of tonsuring and asked if anything written there had been incorrectly performed. Pimin said, "Why are you testing me, father? You came yourself with all the brethren and did to me what is written in those books, and said to me, 'It is fitting that you are suffering from illness. When the time of your departure [from this world] comes, you will recover and carry your bed in your hands.' Please, noble father, pray that the Lord will grant me patience." The blessed Pimin continued to suffer from the same illness for many years, so that those who looked after him were filled with revulsion and often left him without food and drink for two or three days at a time. He bore all these things with joy, and gave thanks to God for everything.

Another sick man was brought to the Caves Monastery and tonsured. The monks appointed to take care of the sick carried him in to Pimin, so they could look after them both together. But they neglected their service and forgot about their two patients, who grew weak from lack of water. Then Pimin said to the [other] sick man, "Brother, since those who look after us are disgusted because of our foul smell, could you continue to perform this service if the Lord restored you to health?" The man promised the blessed one that he would zealously look after the

---

Pimin's earnest wish and at the same time avoid angering his parents, who seem to have been wealthy people.
[644] I have used the Arsenian reading here: Abramovyč, *Pateryk*, 181, n. 12.

sick as long as he lived. Pimin said to him, "The Lord will take away your illness. When you are well, keep your promise and look after me and those like me. The Lord will inflict severe illness on those who perform this service reluctantly, so that they may attain salvation by being punished in this way." The sick man at once got up and began to look after Pimin, and those who had been reluctant to look after the sick were all struck down by illness, as the blessed one had predicted.

The brother who had recovered from his illness did sometimes have feelings of disgust and kept away from Pimin, leaving him hungry and thirsty because of the smell coming from his belly. He slept in a separate building, and suddenly a fever engulfed him. As he was unable to get up for three days, his thirst became unendurable, and he began to cry out, "Have mercy upon me, for the Lord's sake, for I am dying of thirst!" The monks in another cell heard this and came to him. They saw that he was seriously ill, and they informed Pimin, "The brother who looks after you is dying." The blessed one said, "Whatever a man soweth, that shall he also reap.[645] He brought this on himself: he left me hungry and thirsty, breaking his promise to God and ignoring my need. But since we are taught not to return evil for evil, go and tell him, 'Pimin calls you. Get up and come here.'"

When he was told this, the sick man recovered and immediately came to the blessed one on his own. The venerable one reproached him, saying, "How little faith you have! Now you are well; do not sin any more. Do you not know that a sick man and the one attending him receive the same reward? But the patience of the needy ones shall not perish forever. Here you have but a little misery and grief and sickness, and gladness and joy there, where there is neither illness nor sorrow nor sighing, but life eternal. For this reason, brother, do I endure these troubles. God, Who cured you of your illness through me, can also raise me from this bed and cure my weakness. But I do not want this. As the Lord said, 'He that shall endure unto the end, the same shall be saved.'[646] Already in this life I suffer oppression so that my flesh may be free from corruption and its stench may become an indescribably fragrant odor. Is it very good, brother, to stand in church, in that beautiful, pure, and holy place, sending up with the unseen angelic hosts hymns most pleasing and acceptable to God. For the church is called an earthly heaven, and those who stand in it think that they stand in heaven. What is this dark and foul-smelling room, brother? It is not a judgment before [the final]

---

[645] Gal. 6:7.
[646] Matt. 10:22, 24:13; Mark 13:13. Cf. Luke 21:19.

judgment, and a torment before the endless torment? It is enough for a sick man to say, 'I waited patiently for the Lord, and He attended to me.'[647] For the sake of such people the Apostle said to those sick in body, 'If ye endure chastening, God dealeth with you as with his sons. But if ye be without chastisement, ye are bastards, and not sons.'[648] For about such the Lord said, 'In your patience possess ye your souls.' "[649]

The venerable Pimin continued to lie in such suffering for twenty years. When he passed away, three columns [of fire] appeared above the refectory and stretched from there to the top of the church.[650] Only the Lord, Who showed forth this sign, knows whether it was for the blessed one or for some other manifestation. On the very day on which he was about to pass away the venerable Pimin, having recovered, went round all the cells, prostrated himself to the ground before all the brethren, asked their forgiveness, and announced his departure from this life. He said to the [sick] brothers, "My friends and brothers, get up and accompany me!" At his words their illness vanished, and they recovered and walked with him.

He himself went into the church, partook of Christ's life-giving Mysteries, then took up his bed and carried it to the cave, in which he had never been and which he had never seen from the time of his birth. Having entered it, he prostrated himself before the holy Antonij and indicated the place where he would be buried. He said, "This summer you buried two brothers here, one of them without the Great Habit, but you will find him wearing it. He frequently wanted to be tonsured in the Great Habit but was neglected by the brethren because he was poor, which was regarded as a sin; but his deeds were indeed worthy of the Habit, and so the Lord gave it to him. For unto everyone that hath shall be given: but from him that hath not shall be taken away even that which he hath; everyone that hath shall have abundance.[651] The other brother, whom you buried in the Habit, has had it taken away, because while he was alive he did not want it, but as he was dying, he said, 'If you see me about to depart this life, then tonsure me.' For this reason grace was taken from him, for he did not understand the words: 'The dead shall not praise Thee, O Lord, but we, the living, will bless the

---

[647] Ps. 39:1.
[648] Heb. 12:7–8.
[649] Luke 21:19.
[650] See PVL 1110, PSRL 1:284, 2:260–61, which mentions only one fiery arc.
[651] See Matt. 25:29; Luke 19:26. Also Matt. 13:12; Mark 4:25; Luke 8:18.

Lord.'⁶⁵² For it is said, 'Who will give Thee thanks in Hades?'⁶⁵³ Tonsuring into the Great Habit brings no benefit to such people, if a man's good deeds do not save him from torment. A third monk was buried here many years ago. His Habit has not perished, but has been preserved to show him up and to bring him to judgment, since according to his deeds he was not worthy to receive it. He spent his life in idleness and sin, ignorant of Him Who said, 'Unto whom much is given, of him shall be much required.'⁶⁵⁴ If the prayers of Antonij and Feodosij do not precede him, such a man is liable to judgment." Having uttered this, he said to the brethren, "Lo, they who tonsured me have come to take me!" Having said this, he lay down and reposed in the Lord. With great honor they buried him in the cave.

When they excavated the aforementioned place, they found it was as the blessed one had said. There were three monks inside: one had decomposed completely, and only his cowl remained whole; of the two recently deceased monks, the Habit had been removed from the one who had been buried in it, while the other, who had not received the tonsure, was wearing the Habit. They marveled greatly at God's inscrutable judgment, saying, "Thou, O Lord, hast given to each according to his deeds."

From this, brothers, I think we are to understand that if a man tonsured during illness faithfully asks God for life, so that he may work for Him in the monastic discipline, the Lord, the Master of life and death, if He takes him [to Himself] at the eleventh hour, will make him equal to the righteous who have already arrived.⁶⁵⁵ But if a man says, "If you see me at the point of death, tonsure me," both his faith and his tonsure are useless.

Discourse 36. Venerable Isaakij the Cave-dweller.⁶⁵⁶

Just as gold is tried in fire, so men are tested in the crucible of humility. For if the tempter was not ashamed to approach our Lord in

---

⁶⁵² Ps. 113:17–18.
⁶⁵³ Ps. 6:5.
⁶⁵⁴ Luke 12:48.
⁶⁵⁵ See Matt. 20:1–16.
⁶⁵⁶ Substantially the same account of Isaakij the Cave-dweller, but without the short introductory paragraph as found here, appears in PVL 1074 (PSRL 1:191–98, 2:182–89), where it follows the stories of the monks Damian, Ieremej, and Matfej which comprise Discourse 12 of the *Paterik*. Nothing indicates why the account of Isaakij has been separated from that of the other monks.

the wilderness, how much the more does he wish to bring temptations to men? So it was with this blessed man.

Our venerable father Isaakij, while living a secular life, was a wealthy merchant, a native of Toropec. Thinking to become a monk, he distributed his property to those in need and to monasteries, and came to the great Antonij in the cave and begged him to make him a monk. Antonij accepted him, dressed him in the monastic habit, and gave him the name of Isaakij (his secular name was Čern'). Isaakij adopted a very strict way of life. He put on a hair shirt, told someone to buy him a goat and to skin it, and put the skin on his hair shirt, so that the raw hide dried on him. He shut himself up in a gallery of the cave, in a small cell four cubits wide, and there he prayed to God with tears. His food was a single piece of sacramental bread every day, and he drank a moderate amount of water. The great Antonij would bring this to him and give it to him through a small window, just big enough for him to put his hand in it; thus he received his food. He lived in this way for seven years, never going out into the daylight nor lying down on his back, but sleeping a little in a sitting position.

One day, as evening was drawing near, he began to prostrate himself and sing the psalms, according to his custom. He did this right up till midnight, and when he grew tired he sat on his chair. While he was sitting, he put out his candle, as was his habit. Suddenly a light shone in the cave, like sunlight, bright enough to blind a man. Two very handsome youths came up to him, with faces shining like the sun, and said to him, "Isaakij, we are angels, and there is someone coming who is Christ, with His angels." Isaakij got up and saw a host of demons, whose faces were brighter than the sun. One of them was shining in their midst more than the others, with rays issuing from his face. They told him, "Isaakij, this is Christ! Fall down and prostrate yourself before Him."

Isaakij did not understand that this was demonic activity, nor did he remember to cross himself. He came out of his cell and prostrated himself before the demons' handiwork as though before Christ. The demons shouted and said, "Isaakij, you are ours!" They led him into his cell and made him sit down, and they sat round him. The cell became full of demons, and the gallery of the caves too. One of the demons, the one they called Christ, said, "Take pipes and lutes and drums and strike them, and Isaakij will dance for us!" They struck their pipes and lutes and drums and began to play. Having exhausted him, they left him almost dead, and having mocked him, they went away.[657]

---

[657] For possible prototypes of the demonic behavior as described here, see N. Challis

In the morning, at daybreak, the time drew near for him to eat some bread, and as usual Antonij came to the window and said to him, "Give me a blessing, Father Isaakij!" But he heard nothing. Antonij spoke several times, but there was no reply, and he said to himself, "Can he have passed away?" He sent to the monastery for Feodosij and the brethren. The brethren came and dug out an opening where the entrance was stopped up, and took hold of him. Thinking he was dead, they carried him out and put him down in front of the cave. They saw that he was alive, and Feodosij said that this was the demons' work. They laid him on a bed, and the holy Antonij looked after him.

At that time it happened that Izjaslav returned from Poland and was angry with Antonij because of prince Vseslav.[658] Svjatoslav of Černihiv sent for the holy Antonij by night.[659] Antonij came to Černihiv,[660] and as he liked the place called Boldiny Hills, he dug a cave and settled there. The Monastery of the Theotokos on Boldiny Hills is there to this day near Černihiv.

Learning that Antonij had gone to Černihiv, Feodosij went out with the brethren, took Isaakij, carried him to his own cell, and looked after him there. For Isaakij was weakened in mind and body and could not turn over on his side, stand up, or sit down; he just lay there on one side, and often worms collected under his thighs from his excrement and urine. Feodosij washed and tended him with his own hands; he lay there for two years while the holy one cared for him. It is a remarkable miracle that for two years he did not taste bread or water, or any kind of fruit or vegetables, nor did he speak, but lay deaf and dumb for two years. Feodosij prayed to God on his behalf, and prayed over him day and night, until in the third year he began to speak, asking to be stood up, and began to walk, like a child. He would not bother to go to church, and one could hardly drag him there by force, but after a while he began to go to church. After that he began to go to the refectory. They sat him down apart from the brethren and put some bread in front of him, but he

---

and H. W. Dewey, "Divine Folly in Old Kievan Literature: the Tale of Isaac the Cave-dweller," *Slavic and East European Journal* 22 (1978):257–58.

[658] In 1067 Vseslav of Polack tried to seize Novgorod but was thwarted by Izjaslav and his brothers Svjatoslav of Černihiv and Vsevolod of Perejaslav. Izjaslav broke his promise of safe passage, kidnapped Vseslav, and imprisoned him in Kiev. Antonij protested against Izjaslav's action and thus incurred his anger. In 1068 there was a revolt in Kiev against Izjaslav, who fled to Poland, but reestablished himself in 1069.

[659] See PVL 1074, PSRL 1:193, 2:185.

[660] One of the occasions when Antonij emerged from his seclusion. See Heppell, "The *Vita Antonii*," 55.

did not want to take it, so they put it in his hand. Feodosij said, "Put the bread in front of him, but do not put it in his hand. Let him eat it himself." For a whole week he did not eat, but after some time he looked around and put the bread in his mouth and thus learned how to eat. In this way the great Feodosij delivered him from the devil's snares and trickery.

Isaakij once more adopted a very strict way of life. Feodosij died, and Stefan succeeded him.[661] Isaakij said, "Devil, you have already deceived me once, when I was sitting in a solitary place. Henceforth I shall not shut myself up in the cave, but by God's grace I shall vanquish you in the monastery." He again put on a hair shirt, with a tight tunic over it, and he began to act like an idiot.[662] He began to help the cooks and work for the brethren. At matins he would enter church before everyone else and stand firm and motionless. When winter drew near and the frost was sharp, he would stand in sandals that were dropping to pieces, so that his feet often froze to the stone, but he would not move them until matins were over. After matins he would go to the kitchen, get the fire ready, and prepare food and water. Then the rest of the cooks would come from among the brethren.

One cook, also called Isaakij, laughed at him and said, "Isaakij, there sits a black crow! Go and catch it!" Isaakij prostrated himself to the ground, went out, caught the crow, and brought it back in front of all the cooks. They were terrified by what had happened, and told the superior and fhe brethren; henceforth the brethren began to honor him. As he did not wish to be praised by men, he began to act like an idiot and make mischief, sometimes to the superior, sometimes to the brethren, and sometimes to laymen. Some even beat him. He began to behave like an idiot outside the monastery. He took up residence once again in the cave where he had been before—Antonij had already passed away—and began to collect around him young men from the world and to clothe them in monastic dress. He was often beaten for this by the superior Nikon, and sometimes by the boys' parents. But the blessed one bore all this patiently—blows, nakedness, and cold, day and night.

One night he lit a fire in a stove in the cave. The stove was full of holes, and when the fire started to burn, flames began to come through the cracks. He had nothing with which to cover the holes so he put his bare feet against the flames until the fire burned out. Then he got down,

---

[661] See Discourse 8, p. 86.

[662] уродство творити. See Discourse 33, p. 188. For an interpretation of Isaakij's behavior, see Appendix IV.

quite unharmed. There are many stories told about him, and one other incident which I saw for myself.

Thus he gained victory over the demons and thought nothing of their terrors and fancies, as though they were no more than flies. For he said to them, "Although you deceived me at first, because I did not know about your tricks and your cunning, now I have the Lord Jesus Christ my God [to help me], and I place my hope in the prayers of my father Feodosij. I shall overcome you!" But the demons often harassed him and said, "You are ours, Isaakij, because you prostrated yourself before our elder." He would say, "Your elder is the Anti-Christ, and you are demons," and would make the sign of the cross over his face, and the demons disappeared. Sometimes they would come to him again, frightening him in a dream as a crowd of people with mattocks and spades, saying, "We are going to dig up this cave and bury this man here!" Others would say, "Come out, Isaakij! They want to bury you!" But he would say to them, "If you were men you would come by day, but you are [creatures of] the dark and come out in the dark." When he made the sign of the cross they disappeared. Sometimes they frightened him in the form of a bear, some other fierce beast, or a lion; sometimes they crawled like snakes, or frogs, or mice, or reptiles of all kinds, but they could do nothing to him. They said, "You have beaten us, Isaakij!" He replied, "When you deceived me in the form of Jesus Christ and the angels, you were unworthy of that rank. But now you appear in your true colors—as beasts and cattle and snakes and every kind of reptile. That is what you are!" Henceforth, as he himself said, he had no more trouble with them, although they had fought with him for three years. Then he began to live even more austerely, fasting and keeping vigils. While he was living thus, the end of his life approached. He fell ill in the cave and was taken to the monastery. He was ill for seven days and then departed to the Lord in the fullness of faith, without ever deviating from the path. The superior Ioann and all the brethren laid out his body and gave him an honorable burial in the cave with the holy fathers.

Such were the monks in Feodosij's monastery, who even after their death, shine like bright lights and pray to God for the brethren here in the monastery, for all those working in the house of the Mother of God, for laymen, and for those who come and make gifts from their possessions to the monastery, in which, to this day [the monks] live a virtuous life together in hymns and prayers and obedience, to the glory of Almighty God and His most pure Mother, preserved by the prayers of the holy fathers Antonij and Feodosij. May the Lord grant that we may be delivered by their prayers from the snares of the devil, who [continually] tries to trap us, and that we may find ourselves in the company of the fathers Antonij and Feodosij. Brothers, let us call upon these blessed fathers and miracle-workers, our helpers and mediators, to intercede with the Lord God, that we might be not be separated from these venerable monks, nor be snatched away from this blessed and holy place, nor be deprived of the house of the immaculate and most pure Virgin, as she herself promised. Let us continue our efforts and spend the rest of our days repenting in a manner pleasing to God. May we all receive mercy and eternal life in Christ Jesus our Lord, to Whom be glory and the kingdom with the Father and the holy and life-giving Spirit.[663]

---

[663] The conclusion here from "May the Lord grant...." is absent in the PVL's corresponding passage.

Discourse 37. The pious prince Izjaslav's inquiry about the Latins.[664]

One day the pious great prince Izjaslav, son of Jaroslav and grandson of Volodimer, came to our holy father Feodosij, the superior of the Caves Monastery, and said to him, "Father, tell me about the faith of the Varangians." Our venerable father Feodosij said, "Listen, pious prince, to what your highness has asked of our humility. Their faith is evil and their law impure. They have adopted the faith of Sabellius[665] and many other heretical beliefs, and have defiled the entire land. You must guard

---

[664] The authorship and date of this discourse are disputed. From the opening sentence it would appear to be the work of Feodosij (d. 1074) and to accord with the relationship between him and Izjaslav I as depicted in the latter part of Nestor's Life. In addition, circumstances in Izjaslav's life connect him with the "Latins": his wife Gertrude was a Polish princess who, apparently, remained a devout Catholic. See V. Meysztowicz, "L'union de Kiev avec Rome sous Grégoire VII," *Studi Gregoriani* 5 (1956):99–103, and V. L. Janin, "Russkaja knjaginja Olisava-Gertruda i ee syn Jaropolk," *Numismatika i èpigrafika* 4 (1963):149–50. Moreover, his son Jaropolk (later prince in Volodymyr) temporarily submitted to Pope Gregory VII in 1075, when his father was in exile after Svjatoslav seized Kiev in 1073. See Meysztowicz, "L'union," 96–99, and Janin, "Russkaja knjaginja," 155–56. Feodosij's authorship is accepted by Janin, 160–61, tentatively by Meysztowicz, 103, who, however, clearly has reservations, and by I. P. Eremin, "Iz istorii drevenrusskoj publicistiki XI veka: poslanie Feodosija Pečerskogo k knjazju Izjaslavu o Latinjanax," *TODRL* 2 (1935):28–34, who has made a detailed study of Feodosij's extant writings. However, this view has been challenged, convincingly in my opinion, by K. Viskovatyj, "K voprosu ob avtore i vremeni napisanja 'Slova k Izjaslavu o Latinax,'" *Slavia* 16 (1938–1939):535–67, who points out (i) that the name of Izjaslav Jaroslavič appears only in later MSS; (ii) that Feodosij could not have had access to translations of the Byzantine polemical literature on which the content of the letter is based; and (iii) that the tone of the letter is inconsistent with Feodosij's character and religious views as portrayed by Nestor; (and, one might add, with the general climate of opinion in Kiev in the second half of the eleventh century). Viskovatyj thinks that the tract was composed in the mid-twelfth century by a superior of the Caves Monastery known as Feodosij the Greek, who is mentioned in *Hyp.* 1148 (PSRL 2:366), and that it was addressed to Izjaslav M'stislavič, prince of Kiev from 1146 to 1154. He thinks the attribution to the earlier Feodosij occurred much later, perhaps in order to enhance the letter's prestige as a polemical work. Podskalsky, *Christentum*, 179–80, cautions that certain aspects of the problem of authorship require further clarification.

[665] Sabellianism (from Sabellius, who lived early in the third century) is described as "a trinitarian heresy...theologically defined by the terms of monarchianism or modalism...emphasizing the unity of the Divine Being so as to deny that the Son has a subsistence (or personality) distinct from that of the Father." See P. Lebeau, "Sabellianism," *New Catholic Encyclopedia*, 12:783. Perhaps this was regarded as being implicit in the *filioque* controversy, one of the main theological differences between the "Greeks" and "Latins."

against them, pious autocrat. Their heresies are as follows: first, they do not kiss the icons; second, they do not kiss the relics of saints; third, they draw a cross on the ground, kiss it, then get up and trample on it; fourth, they eat meat during Lent; fifth, they celebrate [the Eucharist] with unleavened bread;[666] and sixth, their priests baptize with one immersion, whereas we do so with three, and we anoint the newly baptized person with oil and perfume, while they sprinkle the mouth with salt. They do not christen with the names of saints, but with those of the parents. Therefore, it is good to shun the Latins' faith, and not to observe their customs, nor receive communion with them, nor listen to anything they say, since their beliefs are wrong and their life unclean. They eat with dogs and cats and drink their own urine—this is vile and wicked—and they eat tortoise, wild horses, asses, animals that have been strangled, and the flesh of bears and beavers. On the Tuesday of the first week in Lent they allow meat to be eaten; their monks eat lard and fast on Sundays.

"Christians[667] should not give their daughters to them in marriage, nor receive them into their own homes, nor swear any oath of brotherhood with them, nor have them as godparents, nor exchange kisses with them, nor eat with them, nor drink from any single vessel. If one of them should ask you for anything, give him something to eat for God's sake, but in his own dish; if he has no dish, give him something in your dish, then wash it and say a prayer. They do not ask for forgiveness of their sins from God, but from their priests, according to the gifts [which they give]. Their priests do not marry legal wives, but commit fornication with their servants. They celebrate the Liturgy, but think that they commit no sin in doing so. Their bishops keep concubines, go to war, and wear rings on their fingers. They bury their dead with their feet to the west, their heads to the east, their arms alongside their bodies, and their eyes, ears, and nose sealed with wax. They take their nieces in marriage. They celebrate with a dead substance, thinking that the Lord is dead, while we celebrate the Liturgy with a living body[668] and see the Lord

---

[666] The use by the Latins of "azymes," or unleavened bread, in the Eucharist was another important source of disagreement between Greeks and Latins, and figured considerably in the polemical literature that appeared before and after the schism of 1054.

[667] Cf. Discourse 1, p. 5, where "Christian" is applied only to the Orthodox. See also Discourse 1, n. 17.

[668] This refers to the fact that the "Greeks" used leavened bread in the Eucharist; the leaven, as a living substance, was considered to symbolize the risen Christ, alive after death, whereas this element was absent in the unleavened bread, or "dead substance" used by the "Latins."

Himself sitting on the right hand of the Father, Who will come again to judge the living and the dead. They [use] dead Latin substances and perform a Liturgy in which there is no life, while we, who bring to the living God a pure and undefiled sacrifice, will attain eternal life. Thus it is written, 'He shall reward every man according to his words.'[669]

"It is not good to take their loaves, since there are many evil and unrighteous things in them. Their faith is perverted and leads to destruction; they do things that even the Jews do not do. Many of them have followed the heresy of Sabellius. They are the most pagan and evil nation, because it is impossible to protect oneself against them, but one can against the pagans. The Latins have the Gospel, the Apostle,[670] and the holy icons. They go to church, but their faith and their law are unclean. They have dishonored the whole land with the multitude of their heresies, because there are Varangians throughout the land. Orthodox Christians who live among them in the same place suffer much oppression at their hands. Whoever preserves himself from them and keeps his faith pure will stand rejoicing at the right hand of God, but whoever willfully draws close to them will stand weeping bitterly with them on the left. For there is no eternal life for those living in the faith of the Latins or the Saracens, nor will they share the lot of the saints in the world to come. It is not fitting to praise their faith; anyone who does brings reproach upon himself. Or if he begins to praise continually the faiths of others and to deny Orthodox Christianity, he will appear as a man of double faith,[671] close to heresy. You must guard against such actions, my son, and have nothing to do with them. Rather flee from them, continually praise your own faith, and, as far as you can, exercise yourself in it with good deeds.

"Be merciful, Christ-lover, not only to the members of your own household, but also to strangers. If you see anyone naked, clothe him; if he is hungry or weighed down by poverty, be merciful to him. Even if he is a heretic of some other faith and a Latin, show mercy to all men and deliver them from misfortune. You will not lose your reward from the Lord, for God nourishes all men, pagans as well as Christians. Pagans and the heterodox are under God's care, but the recompense of the blessed will be different in the next world. We who live in the true faith are watched over by God here and will be saved in the life to come by our Lord Jesus Christ. If someone who professes this holy faith dies for

---

[669] Matt. 16:27. Cf. 1 Pet. 1:17; Rev. 20:13, 22:12.
[670] A liturgical lectionary containing the Pauline Epistles.
[671] двоивѣрець, from двоевѣрїе (lit. "double faith").

God's sake, he will not with confidence lose the true faith, but will die for Christ. For it is said that the saints died for their faith, so that they might live in Christ.

"If, my son, you find the heterodox disputing with true Christians and trying to entice them away from the Orthodox faith, since you truly know this Orthodoxy, do not hide within yourself, but help the Orthodox against those whose faith is evil. If you help them, you will deliver your sheep from the lion's mouth, like a good shepherd. But if you keep silent, it is as though they were snatched away from Christ and handed over to Satan, and you must answer for it on the Day of Judgment. If anyone should say to you, 'God has given this faith and that one,' then say to him, 'Who are you, you heretic? Do you think that God has two faiths? Have you not heard, accursed and perverted as you are by an evil faith, that which is written: "Thus saith the Lord, one Lord, one faith, one baptism."[672] The Lord also said, "It becometh us to fulfill all righteousness."[673] Having completed all these things, He sent His disciples to preach to the ends of the earth, and then ascended into heaven.'

"Thus you, one of evil faith, after holding to the Orthodox faith for so many years, have turned away to an evil faith and to Satan's teaching. Have you not heard [the words of] the Apostle Paul, saying, 'There are some that trouble you and would pervert the gospel of Christ, but though an angel from heaven preach any other gospel unto you than that which we have preached unto you, let him be accursed.'[674] You have renounced the preaching of the apostles and the edification of the holy fathers, and you have accepted a faith based on error and a perverted dogma leading to perdition. Therefore, you have been torn away from us and set apart, so that it is not fitting that we should share in the holy Mysteries, nor receive communion together, nor admit you to our Divine Liturgy, because there are many heresies among you."[675]

---

[672] Eph. 4:5.
[673] Matt. 3:15.
[674] Gal. 1:7–8.
[675] This last paragraph appears to be addressed to someone who had apostasized from Orthodoxy, which was not true of either Izjaslav Jaroslavič or Izjaslav M'stislavič. Possibly it is an excerpt from some other anti-Latin tract which has not survived as a separate text.

Discourse 38. The death of venerable father Polikarp, archimandrite of the Caves Monastery, and the priest Vasilij.[676]

Our blessed and venerable father Polikarp, archimandrite of the Caves Monastery, passed away on July 24, 1182, on the feast of the holy martyrs Boris and Glĕb.[677] His body was prepared for burial, and he was buried with due honor and the funeral hymns were sung, as he himself had ordered. After his death there was a great tumult in the monastery: the elders were unable to elect a superior, and there was much distress and sadness among the brethren. Indeed, it was not fitting that such a great flock should be without a shepherd, even for a single hour. On Tuesday the brethren struck the board, and they all went into the church and began to make supplications to the holy Theotokos. Lo, something remarkable happened: as though with a single voice, many said, "Let us send to Šč'kovica[678] for the priest Vasilij, so that he can become our superior and direct the monastic flock of Feodosij in the Caves Monastery." So they all went there, prostrated themselves before the priest Vasilij, and said, "All of us monks and brothers prostrate ourselves before you; we want to have you as our father and superior." The priest Vasilij, greatly upset, prostrated himself before them and said, "My fathers and brothers! I have only cherished the monastic state in my heart. Why do you think of such an unworthy person as myself for the office of superior?" They argued with him for a long time, and [finally] he promised to accept.

---

[676] Polikarp was the first superior of the Caves Monastery to be given the title of archimandrite; thereafter it was always used by superiors as a title of honor. The circumstances in which it was conferred on Polikarp were unusual, since he received the title after a dispute with the metropolitan, during which he was even suspended from his office for a time. See *Laur.* 1168, PSRL 1:254. The issue appears to have been whether the monks should observe the rules of fasting and abstinence on Wednesdays and Fridays in Lent if these days coincided with the feasts of the Lord. Polikarp apparently favored relaxing the rules in this case. It is not easy to deduce the attitude in Constantinople from the rather ambiguous wording in the Rus' chronicles. See *Hyp.* 1162, PSRL 2:520; *Laur.* 1164, 1:352. But Polikarp's practice was clearly not approved by the metropolitan; possibly some other issues were involved, touching the prerogatives and privileges of the parties concerned more closely than the abstinence controversy. In any case, it all ended well for Polikarp, since by 1174 we find him functioning normally once more, with his prestige enhanced by the title of archimandrite. See *Hyp.* 1174, PSRL 2:568.

[677] See Discourse 7, n. 72.

[678] Presumably a village or small town near Kiev, since the monks were able to walk there.

On Friday they came and went with him to the monastery. Metropolitan Nikephoros,[679] Bishop Lavrentij of Turov, Bishop Nikola of Polack, and all the superiors came to tonsure him. Metropolitan Nikephoros tonsured him with his own hands, and so he became the superior and shepherd of the monks of Feodosij's monastery in [the name of] Jesus Christ our Lord, to Whom be glory and the kingdom with the Father and most holy, blessed, and life-giving Spirit now and forever. Amen.

In the year 1463 the following sign appeared in the Caves Monastery under Prince Semen Aleksandrovič and his brother Prince Mixail,[680] when Archimandrite Nikola was superior of the Caves Monastery, and a certain Dionisij, known as Ščepa, was then in charge of the cave. On Easter Sunday he came to the cave to cense the bodies of the deceased, and when he came to the place called Obščina he censed them and said, "Christ is risen, fathers and brothers! Today is a great festival!" And like a peal of thunder they answered, "Indeed, He is risen!"

This book, called a *Paterik*, was copied by the grace of God and His most holy Mother, and with the help of our holy fathers Antonij and Feodosij of the Caves Monastery, in the house of the most pure Theotokos, the *lavra* of our venerable fathers Antonij and Feodosij, in the Caves Monastery, in the God-guarded city of Kiev, in the reign of King Zygmunt August,[681] when the noble prince Feodor Glěbovič Pronskij was *voevoda* of Kiev, Makarij was metropolitan of Halyč and All Rus',[682] and Ilarion was the most honorable archimandrite of the Caves Monastery, at the suggestion and command of the elder Aleksej of Volyn', a monk of the Caves Monastery. It was completed on March 2, 1554, in the twelfth indiction, by the deacon Nesterec, a man of many sins and least among men. As to what I have covered here, holy fathers, whoever may talk about it, for the sake of the Almighty God and His most pure Mother may he not censure, but correct me according to his own fine understanding. Do not reproach my lack of intelligence, for I

---

[679] On Metropolitan Nikephoros II (bef. 1183–after 1201), see Poppe, "Die Metropoliten," 294–95.

[680] On Semen (Simeon) and Mixail Aleksandrovič (Olel'kovič), see G. Vernadsky, *Russia at the Dawn of the Modern Age* (New Haven, 1959), 46–49.

[681] Zygmunt August, the last representative of the Jagellonian dynasty, was king of Poland and grand duke of Lithuania from 1548 to 1572.

[682] Makarij was metropolitan from 1542 to 1564.

am a sinner and not very wise. Whoever judges me will himself be judged by Almighty God and His holy Mother and the venerable Antonij and Feodosij of the Caves Monastery. Sinner that I am, I will suffer eternal torment for my evil deeds together with other sinful souls, unless I am freely pardoned by our merciful Almighty God, our Lord Jesus Christ. But for God's sake correct what is wrong, and do not censure me, sinner as I am. This has been written by the deacon Nesterec, son of Lukjan, from Sokal'.

APPENDIX I

The Sources of *Discourse 7*

Much has been written about the composition of Discourse 7, which contains the *Account of why the Caves Monastery is so called by Nestor, a Monk of the Caves Monastery*, notably by the Russian textologist A. A. Šaxmatov.[683] The central problem in using the *Account* to reconstruct the monastery's early history stems from the fact that it is based on two main sources, namely, Nestor's Life of Feodosij and the lost "Life of Antonij." In order to illustrate this, the translation of the *Account* is reproduced below, with passages derived from the "Antonij" material italicized and places where "patching" seems to have occurred also indicated.

* * *

In the reign of the pious great prince Volodimer Svjatoslavič, the sole ruler of the land of Rus', it pleased God to reveal for the land of Rus' a beacon and preceptor for those practicing the monastic life; our present account concerns him.

There was a certain pious man from the town of Ljubeč in whom the fear of God dwelt from his youth and who wished to be clothed in the monastic habit. Now the Lord, Who loves mankind, inspired him to go to the land of the Greeks and be tonsured there. He at once set out on his journey, and after traveling in the steps of our Lord, Who labored for our salvation, he arrived at Constantinople. Then he came to the Holy Mountain and went round the holy monasteries on Athos, and he saw the monasteries on the Holy Mountain and the manner of life of the fathers, higher than human nature; for while still in the flesh they imitated the life of the angels. An even stronger love for Christ burned in him, and he wished to emulate the life of those fathers. He came to one of the monasteries there and begged the superior to place on him the Angelic Habit of the monastic rank. The superior, forseeing the virtues which would develop in him, acquiesced, and after teaching and instructing him about the monastic life, he tonsured him and gave him the name of Antonij. Antonij pleased God in all things, laboring for others in meekness and humility so that all rejoiced in him. The superior said to him, "Antonij, go back to Rus', so that you may strengthen others there by your success, and may the blessing of the Holy Mountain be with you."

---

[683] See the Introduction, pp. xl–xli.

Antonij came to the town of Kiev and considered where he should live. He went round the monasteries, but felt no desire to spend his life in any of them, for this was not God's will. He began to go everywhere round the woods and hills, and he came to Berestovo and found a cave which the Varangians had dug. In this he settled and remained there, living in great austerity.

Some time after this the great prince Volodimer died, and the godless, accursed Svjatopolk settled in Kiev. He began to kill off his brothers and murdered the holy Boris and Glěb. *Antonij, seeing what bloodshed the accursed Svjatopolk was causing, fled again to the Holy Mountain. When the pious prince Jaroslav defeated Svjatopolk and settled in Kiev, [he came back].*

The God-loving prince Jaroslav liked Berestovo and its Church of the Holy Apostles and had many priests under his care. In it there was a priest named Ilarion, a devout man, knowledgeable about the Scriptures, and an ascetic. He used to go from Berestovo to a hill above the Dnieper, where the old Caves Monastery now is, and pray, for there was a thick wood there. Here he dug a small cave, fourteen feet deep, and he used to come there from Berestovo and sing the Psalter and pray to God in secret. After some time it pleased God to inspire the pious great prince Jaroslav to assemble the bishops in the year 1051, and he appointed [Ilarion] metropolitan in St. Sophia, and he abandoned his cave.

Antonij was then in the monastery on the Holy Mountain where he had been tonsured. The superior received a message from God, saying, "Send Antonij back to Rus', as I need him." The superior summoned Antonij and said to him," Antonij, go back to Rus', for God wishes it, and may the blessing of the Holy Mountain be with you, for many shall become monks through you." He blessed him and dismissed him, saying, "Go in peace."

Antonij arrived in Kiev and came to the hill where Ilarion had dug his little cave, and as he liked the place he settled in it. He began to pray to God with tears, saying, "O Lord, strengthen me in this place, and may the blessing of the Holy Mountain and of my father who tonsured me rest upon it." And he began to live there, praying to God. His food was dry bread, and he drank water in moderation. He dug the cave, giving himself no rest day or night and continuing in labors, vigils, and prayers. After some time people learned of him and would come to him, bringing whatever he needed. He became famous, like the great Antony, and those who came to him asked him for his blessing.

After some time the great Prince Jaroslav died, and his son Izjaslav assumed power and settled in Kiev. *Antonij was then renowned throughout the land of Rus'. When prince Izjaslav learned of his life, he came to him with his retinue and asked for his blessing and prayers.*[684] The great Antonij became known and honored by everyone.[685] *Some God-loving people began to come to him to be tonsured, and he received and tonsured them. A brotherhood gathered around him, twelve in number. Feodosij also came to him and was tonsured. They dug a large cave and a church and cells, which exist even to this day in the cave under the old monastery.*

When the brothers had assembled [one day], Antonij said to them, "See, brethren, God has gathered us together, and I have tonsured you by the blessing of the Holy Mountain with which the superior on the Holy Mountain tonsured me. May there rest upon you first the blessing of God and the holy Theotokos, and second that of the Holy Mountain." And he said to them, "You live with each other, and I shall appoint you a superior. But I myself will go to yonder hill and settle there alone." As I said before, he was accustomed to live in solitude. *He appointed them a superior named Varlaam and went himself to the hill, dug a cave, which is under the new monastery, and ended his life in it, having lived virtuously for forty years* without going out of the cave in which his noble relics lie, performing miracles to this day.

The superior and the brethren continued to live in the cave. The brotherhood increased in numbers and could not be accommodated in the cave, and they decided to build a monastery outside the cave. The superior and the brethren came to the holy Antonij and said to him, "Father, the brotherhood has increased in numbers and cannot be accomodated in the cave. May God and the most pure Theotokos and your prayer ordain that we place a little church outside the cave." The venerable one so ordered them, and they prostrated themselves to the ground and departed. They placed above the cave a small church dedicated to the Dormition of the holy Theotokos.

Through the prayers of the most pure Theotokos and the venerable Antonij God began to increase the number of the monks, and the

---

[684] Cf. Discourse 1, p. 2. Since Nestor does not mention any visits to Antonij by Prince Izjaslav, it seems reasonable to assume that this information came from the "Antonij" material.

[685] The doublet "*Antonij was then renowned throughout the land of Rus'*" and "*the great Antonij became known and honored by everyone*" suggests that the intervening sentence was not in the original version of the *Account*, but was inserted at some point.

brethren discussed with the superior about building a monastery. Again they went to Antonij and said to him, "Father, the brotherhood is increasing in numbers, and we would like to build a monastery." Antonij was glad and said, "Blessed be God in all things! May the prayer of the holy Theotokos and of the fathers on the Holy Mountain be with you." Having said this, *he sent one of the brethren to Prince Izjaslav, saying, "O pious prince, God increases the number of brothers, and their place is small. We entreat you to give us the hill above the cave." Hearing this, Prince Izjaslav was very glad, and he sent one of his boyars to them and gave them the hill. The superior and the brethren laid the foundations of a large church and monastery, surrounded it with a fence, built many cells, erected a church, and adorned it with icons. And henceforth it began to be called the Caves Monastery, because the monks first lived in a cave. And henceforth it was called the Caves Monastery, which is under the blessing of the Holy Mountain.*[686]

When the monastery was completed and while Varlaam was superior, Prince Izjaslav built a monastery dedicated to St. Demetrios and brought Varlaam to be superior there, as he wished to exalt it above the Caves Monastery, relying on his wealth. *For many monasteries have been built by rulers and nobles using their wealth, but they are not like those which have been built by tears and fasting, prayer and vigil. Antonij had neither silver nor gold, but attained his purpose by tears and fasting, as I have said.*

After Varlaam's departure to the Monastery of St. Demetrios, the brethren took counsel and went to the elder Antonij and said to him, "Father, appoint a superior for us." *He said to them, "Whom do you want?" They said to him, "Whomsoever God wills and the most pure Theotokos and you, honorable father." And the great Antonij said to them, "Who is there among you like the blessed Feodosij?" He is obedient, meek, and humble. Let him be your superior."*[687]

All the brethren rejoiced and prostrated themselves before him to

---

[686] These last two sentences seem to be a "doublet," possibly deriving from different versions of the *Account*. The second one, stressing the connection with Mount Athos, was probably taken from the "Antonij" material, since it was through Antonij that the Caves Monstery was linked with Athos. Contrast Nestor's statement: "We call it the Caves Monastery, which was established by our father Feodosij." (Discourse 8, p. 44).

[687] According to Nestor's Life of Feodosij, the brethren chose Feodosij as their superior and then informed Antonij of their decision (Discourse 8, p. 43); hence this version, in which Antonij made the choice, probably derives from the "Antonij" material.

the ground, and they appointed Feodosij as their superior. *The brethren then numbered twenty.*[688]

When Feodosij took over the monastery, he began to practice severe asceticism, fasting, and prayer with tears. He began to gather together many monks, assembling in all one hundred brothers. He began to seek a monastic rule. At that time there was an honorable monk from the Stoudios Monastery named Michael, who had come from the Greeks with Metropolitan George.[689] He began to ask him about the rule of the Stoudite fathers and copied down what he found out from him. He established in his own monastery how to sing the monastic offices; how to make prostrations; how to arrange the readings; where people should stand in church and all the rules of behavior in church; where people should sit at table; and what should be eaten on which days—all arranged according to rule. Having found this out, Feodosij established it in his own monastery, and all the monasteries of Rus' received the rule from this monastery. Therefore, the Caves Monastery became honored as the first of them all and the most prestigious of all.

When Feodosij was in the monastery, observing a virtuous life and the monastic rule and receiving everyone that came to him, I, the wretched and unworthy servant Nestor[690] came to him, and he accepted me. I was then in my seventeenth year. I have set down in writing the year in which the monastery was founded, and why it is called the Caves Monastery. Later we shall speak again of the life of Feodosij.

---

[688] Cf. Discourse 8, p. 43. Nestor does not say how big the community was when Feodosij became superior; this number can therefore be provisionally assigned to the "Life of Antonij."

[689] Šaxmatov, "Žitie Antonija i Pečerskaja Letopis'," 136–38, ascribes this reference to the monk Michael to the "Life of Antonij"; however, it might equally have come from annals kept at the metropolitan's court in Kiev.

[690] Šaxmatov, in two of his earlier articles, "Neskol'ko slov o Nestorovom Žitii Feodosija," 47, and "Žitie Antonija i Pečerskaja Letopis'," 141, suggested that the name "Nestor" originally appeared in a short version of the *Account* written by the author of the Life of Feodosij. Later, *Razyskanija*, 451, he changed his mind and said that it was inserted by the compiler of the *Načal'nyj svod* (the "primary compilation" ca. 1093) of the PVL. While either of these explanations is possible, it could also have been inserted by the editor Cassian, because of the similarity between the content of part of the *Account* and the Life of Feodosij. But the author of this version cannot be identical with the Nestor who wrote the Life of Feodosij, since he did not come to the monastery until after Feodosij's death, when Stefan was superior. See Discourse 8, p. 87.

APPENDIX II

Letter of Patriarch Nicholas Mouzalon of Constantinople to Nifont, Bishop of Novgorod[691]

In the name of the Holy Spirit [we address] the son and the fellow worker of our humility, the virtuous shepherd of Christ's flock of rational sheep, Nifont, lord bishop of Great Novgorod. Rejoice in the Lord!

We have heard, my lord, about your righteous suffering, which you are enduring for God's sake because of your opposition to Metropolitan Klim, who by his own arbitrary will has assumed the office of metropolitan of Kiev without our blessing. But you, honored father, refuse to allow him such extreme boldness in respect of the priestly office and will not concelebrate with him or mention his name in the divine service. You have endured many evil insults and suffered many reproaches from him, O holy man of God. For the sake of God's righteousness, O sufferer, continue to persevere and do not succumb to this evil serpent Klim and his wicked counsellors. And you, brother, will be numbered by God among the saints of old who suffered steadfastly for the Orthodox faith, and so that you will show yourself as an example of perseverance to those who later became ecclesiastics in the land of Rus'.

Peace be unto you, father, and, sufferers of Christ, May the blessing of our humility be upon you forever. Amen.

---

[691] Text in Makarij, *Istorija russkoj cerkvi*, 3rd ed., vol. 3 (St. Petersburg, 1888), Appendix 1, 297. Patriarch Nicholas IV Mouzalon (ca. 1070–1152) occupied the see of Constantinople from 1147 to 1151.

APPENDIX III

Suggested reconstruction of Polikarp's dedicatory letter

One of the unsolved problems of the *Paterik*'s composition is the original arrangement of Polikarp's narratives, which do not appear to have survived in the form in which they were first written. One of the most striking anomalies in the Cas. II text is the long conclusion to his account of Agapit the Physician (Discourse 27), which does not fit in logically with the content of the narrative. It is possible that this passage may have been part of Polikarp's dedicatory letter to Archimandrite Akindin (Discourse 24).

In the Cas. II redaction, the last sentence of this discourse reads: Понудихся писаніем извѣстити тобѣ, еже о святѣи блаженнѣи братіи нашеи, да и сущіи по насъ ҷерноризци увѣдять благодать божію, бывшую въ святѣмъ сем мѣсти и прославять отца небеснаго, показавшаго таковыа свѣтилникы в Рускои земли, в Печерьском святѣм манастыри ("So I have felt constrained to send you a written account of our holy and blessed brotherhood, so that the monks who come after us may know the grace of God which formerly dwelt in this holy place and may glorify our heavenly Father Who revealed such shining lights in the land of Rus', in the holy Caves Monastery").[692] The beginning of the relevant passage of Discourse 27 reads: Таковаа и больша сихъ съдѣашася от тѣх святых ҷерноризець, их же въспомянувъ добродѣтелное житіе, дивлюся, како премолъҷана быша великаа исправлѣніа святых отець наших Антоніа и Ѳеодосіа ("Such deeds and even greater ones were performed by these holy monks, recalling whose virtuous life I marvel that the great achievements of our holy fathers Antonij and Feodosij have been passed over in silence").[693] This latter passage, together with the rest of the conclusion of Discourse 27, could easily follow the former passage, both logically and syntactically. The dedicatory letter would then read as follows:

"With the Lord assisting me and confirming my words [I address myself] to your piety, my father and lord Akindin, most honorable archimandrite of all Rus'. Incline your gracious ears, so that I may pour into them the lives, deeds, and portents of those marvelous and blessed men who formerly lived in this Caves Monastery about which I heard

---

[692] Abramovyč, *Pateryk*, 124, lns. 21–25.
[693] Abramovyč, *Pateryk*, 132, lns. 23–26.

from Simon, bishop of Vladimir and Suzdal', your brother, who was once a monk in this Caves Monastery. He told me, sinner that I am, about the holy and great Antonij, the founder of monastic life in Rus', about the holy Feodosij, and about the lives and achievements of the holy and venerable fathers after their time who ended their lives in the house of the most pure Mother of God. May your wise understanding pay heed to my immature and imperfect thoughts.

"You asked me once to tell you about the deeds of these monks. Knowing how crude and lacking in refinement I am, and aware that I am always terrified when I relate any story in your presence, how could I recount clearly the marvelous signs and wonders performed by them? I told you a little about these remarkable miracles, but I forgot most of them from fright, since I felt ashamed in the presence of your piety, and I told my tale stupidly. So I have felt constrained to send you a written account of our holy and blessed brotherhood, so that the monks who come after us may know the grace of God which formerly dwelt in this holy place, and may glorify our heavenly Father Who revealed such shining lights in the land of Rus', in the holy Caves Monastery.

"Such deeds and even greater ones were performed by these holy monks, recalling whose virtuous life, I marvel that the great achievements of our holy fathers Antonij and Feodosij have been passed over in silence. If so great a light should be extinguished through our neglect, how can rays shine forth from it—I mean these venerable fathers, our brethren? But as the Lord said, 'No prophet is accepted in his own country.'[694] If, most honored archimandrite, my lord Akindin, I have recorded for you the miracles of some of these aforementioned holy and venerable fathers, the ascetic achievements of some, the resolute self-denial of others, the obedience of others, and the gift of prophecy of yet others—all these things were made known to me by faith, all their signs and miracles, by your fellow monk and my master, Bishop Simon. Other people consider the things I have related to be distasteful, because of the greatness of the deeds described, but fault lies in their lack of faith—they know me as the sinful Polikarp. But if your venerableness should order me to record those things which my mind can grasp and my memory recall, even if they are not necessary for you, let us leave them for the benefit of those who come after us, just as the blessed Nestor wrote about the blessed fathers Damian, Ieremej, Matfej, and Isaakij in the chronicle. All their lives are related in the Life of the holy Antonij, though only

---

[694] Luke 4:24. cf. also Matt. 13:57; Mark 6:4.

briefly. But as for the aforementioned monks, I speak plainly, not obscurely as in former times. For if I keep silent, they will be completely forgotten, and not even their names will be remembered, as was the case up to this day. Now in the fifteenth year of your service as superior I speak of things never mentioned for 160 years. Now, thanks to your love, those things which had been concealed are now being heard, and the memory of those who love God will be honored and praised forever, for those who please Him will receive a crown from Him.

"It is a great thing for me to be adorned by such things, and I think that I shall conceal the shame of my deeds in this way: I shall simply call to mind the things I have heard, write them down, and think that it was I who sought out the marvelous deeds of these men. As the Lord says, 'Joy shall be in heaven over one sinner that repenteth.'[695] How much more will the angels rejoice over so many righteous men, for they now live in heaven and their glory is sufficient for their heirs. For while here they did not care about the flesh, but, as incorporeal beings, they despised earthly things and considered everything in this life to be as dung, so that they might attain only Christ. For they loved Him alone, bound themselves fast to His love, and commended their wills entirely to Him, so that they might receive deification from Him. He gave them on earth the gift of working miracles as a reward for their labors, and in the life to come He will glorify them with indescribable glory. For on earth nothing is given to men without the Holy Spirit, nothing that is not given from above. Therefore I, the sinful Polikarp, have recorded these things, doing this work in obedience to your will, my Lord Akindin."[696]

The *Arsenian* redaction lacks all the passages in which Simon and Polikarp talk about themselves and the circumstances of their work, including Polikarp's dedicatory letter and the long conclusion to his narrative about Agapit the Physician.[697] But since they are extant in later manuscripts, there must have existed copies of the *Paterik* in which they were included. If some of these included Polikarp's dedicatory letter in the form reconstructed here, the separation of the two parts must have

---

[695] Luke 15:7.
[696] The final words of Discourse 27, "But tell me, and I shall relate to you one more small incident, about our blessed and venerable father Grigorij the Miracle-worker," would follow quite logically after the words immediately preceding the long conclusion: "Then the Armenian was tonsured in the Caves Monastery, and ended his life there in the fullness of faith."
[697] See Introduction, pp. xxix–xxx.

occurred when the personal items were replaced; there is no indication in any of the manuscripts used by Abramovyč as to why and how this happened.

APPENDIX IV

Isaakij the Cave-dweller
and the "Jurodstvo" Tradition

The account of Isaakij the Cave-dweller has aroused the interest of many students of Byzantine and East Slavic monasticism because of its connection with *jurodstvo,* or folly for Christ's sake, which became a widely practiced and highly venerated form of asceticism in Muscovy and Imperial Russia.[698] Like many distinctive elements in the East Slavic religious tradition, *jurodstvo* originated in Byzantium. There are signs of it in the earliest days of Christian monasticism in Egypt,[699] but the first detailed and well-documented portrayal of a "holy fool" is the Life of a sixth-century monk, Symeon of Emesa, by Leontios, bishop of Neapolis in Cyprus, written early in the seventh century.[700] In a recent analysis of this text, Bishop Kallistos Ware listed the specific characteristics of folly for Christ's sake as exemplified in the life of Symeon. First, an attitude of mockery towards the world: "The fool bears witness to the basic discrepancy between human and divine wisdom. Mocking all forms of conventional morality based on rules, he affirms the cardinal worth of the person."[701] Secondly, in his desire to attain and preserve the virtue of humility, he deliberately behaves in such a way as to invite taunts and insults, and to become himself an object of mockery; at the same time he thus becomes more closely identified with the outcasts and rejects of

---

[698] See E. Behr-Sigel, "Les fous pour Christ et la sainteté laïque dans l'ancienne Russie," *Irénikon* 15 (1938):554–65; I. Kologrivov, "Les 'fous pour Christ' dans l'hagiographie russe," *Revue d'ascétique et mystique* 25 (1949):426–37; I. V. Budovnic, "Jurodivye drevnej Rusi," *Voprosy istorii religii i ateizma* 12 (1964):170–95; E. M. Thompson, "The Archetype of the Holy Fool in Russian Literature," *Canadian Slavonic Papers* 15 (1973):245–73; N. Challis and H. W. Dewey, "Divine Folly in Old Kievan Literature: The Tale of Isaac the Cave-Dweller," *Slavic and East European Journal* 22 (1978):255–64; L. Rydén, "The Holy Fool," in *The Byzantine Saint,* Studies Supplementary to *Sobornost* 5 (London, 1981), 106–13; Bishop Kallistos [T. Ware], "The Fool in Christ as Prophet and Apostle," *Sobornost,* n.s. 6, no. 2 (1984):6–28.

[699] See Ἀνδρῶν ἁγίων βίβλος, 206, lns. 6–8; Ware, "The Fool in Christ," 10.

[700] *Das Leben des Heiligen Narren Symeon von Leontios von Neapolis,* ed. L. Rydén (Uppsala, 1963); A. J. Festugiére and L. Rydén, *Vie de Syméon le Fou et Vie de Jean de Chypre* (Paris, 1974). See also V. Rocheau, "St. Siméon Salos, ermite palestinien et protoype des 'Fous pour le Christ,'" *Proche-orient chrétien* 28 (1978):209–19.

[701] Ware, "The Fool in Christ," 20.

society, and with the humiliated, kenotic Christ.[702] Thirdly, the fool has a prophetic function, and a sense of mission to denounce where necessary the great and powerful people in his society. "By virtue of his utter poverty, his voluntary rejection of all outward status or security, the fool is free to speak when others, afraid of the consequences, choose to keep silent...."[703] This freedom to speak plainly is often used to make savage fun of all kinds of pomposity and self-importance.

It is at once apparent that Isaakij the Cave-dweller does not fit into this pattern, or only to a limited extent. Most of Discourse 36 is taken up with a detailed account of how Isaakij succumbed to the attacks of demons while he was living as a solitary in the cave. This left him completely shattered, mentally and physically, but he was gradually nursed back to a state of tolerable bodily and mental health by the devoted care of Antonij and Feodosij; during this time he lived with the rest of the community. As one recent study notes, "Although the story is ostensibly about Isaac, its real hero is Theodosius."[704] In fact, the dominant theme of Discourse 36 is Isaakij's slow, difficult journey form spiritual arrogance to a state of true humility,[705] of which his *jurodstvo* is simply an episode.

It is interesting to consider, however, how this episode fits into the whole story of Isaakij. It occurs immediately after one of the monks working in the kitchen tells Isaakij to go and catch a black crow. "Isaakij prostrated himself to the ground, went out, caught the crow, and brought it back in front of all the cooks." Clearly this was not the reaction which the monks working in the kitchen had expected. The story continues: "They were terrified by what had happened, and told the superior and the brethren; henceforth the brethren began to honor him." What evidently impressed them was Isaakij's immediate obedience in obeying this foolish order; obedience was a monastic virtue often in short supply in the Caves Monastery. However, Isaakij was by then well advanced on the path to humility, so "as he did not wish to be praised by men, he began to act like an idiot and to make mischief, sometimes to the superior, sometimes to the brethren, and sometimes to laymen."

---

[702] Ibid.
[703] Ibid., 21–24. In an earlier reference to the holy fool's prophetic role (p. 8), Ware notes that this was commented on by Giles Fletcher, a perceptive observer of Muscovite society in the late sixteenth century.
[704] Challis and Dewey, "Divine Folly," 262.
[705] Ibid., 261.

Thus we see that Isaakij's behavior in the latter part of his life does illustrate the second of the basic characteristics of *jurodstvo* mentioned above, but it shows no signs of the first and third, the mocking and prophetic elements. Moreover, both Symeon of Emesa and the later East Slavic *jurodivye* were pilgrims and wanderers, *stranniki* as well as holy fools, whereas Isaakij never left the Caves Monastery; indeed it was thanks to its protective care that he was able to recover from the effects of demonic attacks and continue his spiritual progress. Thus he cannot be considered a "classic" *jurodivyj*, or holy fool, in either the East Slavic or the Russian tradition,[706] but he did grasp and put into practice one important aspect of this form of asceticism, and he was the first Rus' to do so. Hence his claim to be considered the first holy fool of Rus' has some validity.

---

[706] See Behr-Sigel, "Les fous pour Christ," 557, who points out that Isaakij's *jurodstvo* is only temporary; Kologrivov, "Les 'fous pour Christ,'" 429; Challis and Dewey, "Divine Folly," 259–60, who emphasize the fact that *jurodstvo* was not the most important element in Isaakij's spiritual progress; and Ware, "The Fool in Christ," 10, who notes that for at least part of the time Isaakij's madness was "genuine rather than feigned."

BIBLIOGRAPHY

Abramovyč, Dmytro [Abramovič, Dmitrij]. *Issledovanie o Kievo-Pečerskom Paterike kak istoriko-literaturnom pamjatnike* (=*Izvestija Otdelenija russkogo jazyka i slovesnosti IAN* 6 [1901], nos. 3:207–35, 4:37–102; 7 [1902], nos. 1:233–79, 2:204–31, 3:34–76, 4:43–65).

———. *Opisanie rukopisej S. Peterburgskoj Duxovnoj Akademii, Sofijskaja Biblioteka.* Pt. 2, Čet'i Mineĭ, Prologi, Pateriki. St. Petersburg, 1907.

———. *Žitija svjatyx mučenikov Borisa i Gleba i služby im.* Petrograd, 1916. Reprint, ed. L. Müller. Slavische Propyläen, 14. Munich, 1967.

———, ed. *Kyjevo-Pečers'kyj Pateryk.* Kiev, 1930. Reprint, ed. D. Čyževs'kyj. Slavische Propyläen, 2. Munich, 1964.

Adrianova-Peretc, Varvara. "Zadači izučenija agiografičeskogo stilja drevnej Rusi." *Trudy Otdela drevnerusskoj literatury* 20 (1964):41–71.

Allatius, Leo. *De Libris et Rebus Ecclesiasticis Graecorum Dissertationes et Observationes Variae.* Paris, 1645.

Amann, A. M. *Kirchenpolitische Wandlungen im Ostbaltikum bis zum Tode Alexander Newskis. Studien zum Werden der Russischen Orthodoxie.* Orientalia Christiana Analecta, 105. Rome, 1936.

Apophthegmata Patrum. PG 65:71–440. Trans. Benedicta Ward, *The Sayings of the Desert Fathers. The Alphabetical Collection.* Library of Christian Classics, 12. London and Oxford, 1975.

Assemanus, Josephus Aloysius. *Sancti Patris Nostri Ephraem Syri opera omnia quae extant Graece, Syriace, Latine in sex tomos distributa.* Vols. 2, 3. Rome, 1732, 1743.

Athanasios, St. *Vita S. Antonii.* PG 26:835–976. Trans. R. T. Meyer, *The Life of St. Anthony.* Ancient Christian Writers, 10. New York, 1950.

Barsukov, Nikolaj. *Istočniki russkoj agiografii.* St. Petersburg, 1882.

Basil of Caesarea, St. *Regulae fusius et brevius tractatae.* PG 31:889–1035. Trans. W. K. L. Clarke, *The Ascetic Works of St. Basil.* London, 1925.

Baumgarten, Nicolas de. *Généalogies et mariages occidentaux des Rurikides russes du Xe siècle au XIIIe siècle.* Rome, 1927 (=*Orientalia Christiana* 9:1–96).

———. *Généalogies des branches régnantes de Rurikides russes du XIIIe au XVIe siècle*. Rome, 1934 (=*Orientalia Christiana* 35: 1–152).

Behr-Sigel, Elisabeth. "Les fous pour le Christ et la sainteté laïque dans l'ancienne Russie." *Irénikon* 15 (1938): 554–65.

———. *Priére et sainteté dans l'Église russe*. Russie et Chrétienté, 5. Paris, 1950. Rev. ed., Bégrolles-en-Mauges, 1982.

Beneševič, Vladimir. *Sbornik pamjatnikov po istorii cerkovnogo prava, preimuščestvenno russkogo, končaja vremenem Petra Velikogo*. Pt. 1. Petrograd, 1914.

The Book of Holy Men (Ἀνδρῶν ἁγίων βίβλος). PL 73: 852–1022. Trans. W. O. Chadwick, "The Sayings of the Fathers." In *Western Asceticism*. London, 1958, 37–189.

Boon, Dom A., ed. *Pachomiana Latina*. Bibliothèque de la Revue d'histoire ecclésiastique, 7. Louvain, 1932.

Bosley, Richard D. "A History of the Veneration of SS. Theodosij and Antonij of the Kievan Caves Monastery from the Eleventh to the Fifteenth Century." Ph. D. dissertation, Yale University, 1980.

Bubner, Friedrich. *Das Kiever Paterikon: eine Untersuchung zu seiner Struktur und den literarischen Quellen*. Augsburg, 1969.

Budge, E. A. Wallis, trans. *Stories of the Holy Fathers, Being Histories of the Anchorites, Recluses, Monks, Cenobites, and Ascetic Fathers of the Deserts of Egypt*. London, 1934.

———, trans. *The Wit and Wisdom of the Christian Fathers of Egypt*. London, 1935.

Budovnic, I. U. "Jurodivye drevnej Rusi." *Voprosy istorii religii i ateizma* 12 (1964): 170–95.

Buhoslavs'kyj, Serhij [Bugoslavskij, Sergej]. "K voprosu o xaraktere i ob"eme literaturnoj dejatel'nosti prep. Nestora." *Izvestija Otdelenija russkogo jazyka i slovesnosti IAN* 19 (1914), nos. 1: 131–86, 3: 153–91.

Čagovec, Vsevolod. "Žizn' i sočinenija prepodobnogo Feodosija." *Universitetskie izvestija* (Kiev) 41, nos. 6–7 (1901).

Cassian, John. *Collationes XXIV*. PL 99. See also E. Pichery, ed. Sources Chrétiennes, 105–7. Paris, 1964–1965 (with French translation).

———. *De Institutis Cenobiorum Libri XII*. Ed. J. C. Guy. Sources Chrétiennes, 109. Paris, 1965 (with French translation).

Challis, Natalie, and Dewey, Horace W. "Divine Folly in Old Kievan Literature: the Tale of Isaac the Cave-Dweller." *Slavic and East European Journal* 22 (1978): 255–64.

Chitty, Derwas J. *The Desert a City. An Introduction to the Study of Egyptian and Palestinian Monasticism under the Christian Empire.* Oxford, 1966.

Cod. Slav. Vindob. 152, ff. 1r–93r. (An Old Church Slavonic version of the Ἀνδρῶν ἁγίων βίβλος).

Combefis, François. *Bibliothecae Graecorum Patrum Auctarium Novissimum.* Paris, 1672.

Conev, Beno. *Opis na rŭkopisite i staropečanite knigi na Narodnata Biblioteka v Sofia.* 2 vols. Sofia, 1910–1923.

―――. *Slavjanski rŭkopisi i staropečanite knigi na Narodnata Biblioteka v Plovdiv.* Sofia, 1920.

―――. *Slavjanski rŭkopisi v Berlinskata dŭržavna Biblioteka.* Sofia, 1927 (=*Sbornik na Bŭlgarskata Akademia na Naukite* 31).

―――. "Slavjanski rŭkopisi v Viena." *Godišnik na Sofijskija Universitet* 1, *Istoriko-filologičeski fakultet* 25, no. 9 (1928–1929): 1–27.

Constantelos, Demetrios J. *Byzantine Philanthropy and Social Welfare.* New Brunswick, N. J., 1968.

Cross, Samuel H. *Medieval Russian Churches.* Ed. K. J. Conant. Cambridge, Mass., 1949.

―――, and Sherbowitz-Wetzor, Olgerd P., trans. *The Russian Primary Chronicle. Laurentian Text.* Medieval Academy of America, 60. Cambridge, Mass., 1953.

Čyževs'kyj [Čiževskij], Dmytro. "On the Question of Genres in Old Russian Literature." *Harvard Slavic Studies* 2 (1954): 105–15.

―――. *History of Russian Literature from the Eleventh Century to the End of the Baroque.* The Hague, 1960.

Dawes, Elizabeth A. S., and Baynes, Norman H., trans. *Three Byzantine Saints.* Oxford, 1948.

Dawkins, Richard M. *The Monks of Athos.* London, 1936.

Delehaye, Hippolyte. *Les légendes hagiographiques.* 3rd ed. Subsidia Hagiographica, 18. Paris, 1927.

Dimitrievskij, A. A. "Kinoval'nyje Pravila prep. Savvy Osvjaščennogo." *Trudy Kievskoj duxovnoj akademii* 1 (1890): 170–92.

―――. *Opisanie liturgičeskix rukopisej xranjaščixsja v bibliotekax Pravoslavnogo Vostoka.* 2 vols. Kiev, 1895–1901.

Dobroklonskij, A. P. *Prep. Feodor, ispovednik i igumen Studijskij.* Pt. 1, *Ego epoxa, žizn' i dejatel'nost'.* Odessa, 1913.

Drevnij Paterik izložennyj po glavam. Perevod s grečeskogo, Afonskogo Russkogo Pantelejmonova monastyrja. 2nd ed. Moscow, 1891.

Dubrovina, V. F. "K izučeniju slov grečeskogo proisxoždenija v sočinenijax drevnerusskix avtorov." In *Pamjatniki russkogo jazyka. Voprosy, issledovanija i izdanija*. Moscow, 1974, 62–104.
Dujčev, Ivan I. "Épizod iz Kievo-Pečerskogo Paterika." *Trudy Otdela drevnerusskoj literatury* 24 (1969): 88–92.
Dvornik, Francis. *Les Slaves, Byzance et Rome au IX siècle*. Paris, 1926.
———. *The Making of Central and Eastern Europe*. London, 1949.
———. *Byzantine Missions among the Slavs*. New Brunswick, N. J., 1970.
Eremin, Igor'. "Iz istorii drevnerusskoj publicistiki XI veka: poslanie Feodosija Pečerskogo k knjazju Izjaslavu o Latinjanax." *Trudy Otdela drevnerusskoj literatury* 2 (1935): 21–38.
———. "K istorii drevnerusskoj perevodnoj povesti." *Trudy Otdela drevnerusskoj literatury* 3 (1936): 37–57.
———. "Literaturnoe nasledie Feodosija Pečerskogo." *Trudy Otdela drevnerusskoj literatury* 5 (1947): 159–84.
———. "K xarakteristike Nestora kak pisatelja." *Trudy Otdela drevnerusskoj literatury* 17 (1961): 54–64.
———. *Literatura drevnej Rusi: ètjudy i xarakteristiki*. Moscow-Leningrad, 1966.
Fedotov, Georgij. *Svjatye drevnej Rusi X–XVII st*. Paris, 1931.
———. *The Russian Religious Mind. Kievan Christianity*. Cambridge, Mass., 1946.
Festugière, André-Jean, ed. *Les Moines de Palestine*. Paris, 1962–1963.
Forbes, Neville, and Mitchell, R., trans. *The Chronicle of Novgorod, 1016–1471*. London, 1914.
Goetz, Leopold K. *Das Kiever Höhlenkloster als Kulturzentrum des vormongolischen Russlands*. Passau, 1904.
———. *Kirchenrechtliche und kulturgeschichtliche Denkmäler Altrusslands*. Stuttgart, 1905.
———. *Staat und Kirche in Altrussland. Kiever Period, 988–1240*. Berlin, 1908.
Golubinskij, Evgenij. *Istorija russkoj cerkvi*. 2nd ed. 2 vols. Moscow, 1901–1904.
———. *Istorija kanonizacii svjatyx v russkoj cerkvi*. 2nd ed. Moscow, 1903.
Golyšenko, V. S., and Dubrovina, V. F., eds. *Sinajskij Paterik*. Moscow, 1967.

Gorskij, Aleksandr, and Nevostruev, Kapiton. *Opisanie slavjanskix rukopisej Moskovskoj Sinodal'noj Biblioteki*. Pts. 1 and 2. Moscow, 1855, 1857.

Grumel, V., ed. *Les Regestes des actes du Patriarcat de Constantinople*. Vol. 1, fascs. 2–3 (Paris, 1936–1947).

Hamilton, George H. *The Art and Architecture of Russia*. 2nd. ed. London, 1975.

Hasluck, Frederick W. *Athos and its Monasteries*. London, 1924.

Hausherr, Irénée. *Penthos. La doctrine de la componction dans l'Orient chrétien*. Orientalia Christiana Analecta, 132. Rome, 1944.

Heppell, Muriel. "The *Vita Antonii*, a Lost Source of the *Paterikon* of the Monastery of Caves." *Byzantinoslavica* 13, no. 1 (1952): 46–58.

Historia Monachorum in Aegypto. Édition critique du texte grec et traduction annotée. Ed. André-Jean Festugière. Subsidia Hagiographia, 53. Paris, 1971.

Hudzij, Mykola [Gudzy, Nikolaj]. *A History of Early Russian Literature*. Trans. S. Wilbur Jones. New York, 1949.

Hurwitz, Ellen S. *Prince Andrej Bogoljubskij: the Man and the Myth*. Florence, 1980.

Jakovlev, Vladimir. *Pamjatniki russkoj literatury XII i XIII vekov*. St. Petersburg, 1872. [The first critical edition of the *Kievo-Pečerskij Paterik*].

———, ed. *Drevnekievskie religioznye skazanija*. Warsaw, 1875.

Janin, Raymond. *La géographie ecclésiastique de l'Empire byzantin*. Pt. 1, vol. 3, *Les églises et les monastères*. Paris, 1953.

Jacimirskij, A. I. *Slavjanskie i russkie rukopisi rumynskix bibliotek*. St. Petersburg, 1905 (=*Sbornik Otdelenija russkogo jazyka i slovesnosti IAN* 79).

John Climacus, St. Κλῖμαξ θείας ἀνόδου (*Scala Paradisi*). PG 88:596–1210. Reprint, ed. Pietro Trevisan. 2 vols. Corona Patrum Salesiana, ser. Graeca, 8–9. Turin, 1941 (with Italian trans.). Eng. trans., C. Luibheid and N. Russell, *The Ladder of Divine Ascent*. London, 1982.

Kadlubovsky, E., and Palmer, G. E. H., trans. *Writings from the Philocalia on the Prayer of the Heart*. London, 1951.

Karabinov, Ivan. "Namestnaja ikona drevnego Kievo-Pečerskogo monastyrja." *Gosudarstvennaja Akademija istorii material'noj kul'tury, Izvestija* 5 (1927): 102–13.

Kologrivov, Ivan. "Les 'fous pour Christ' dans l'hagiographie russe." *Revue d'ascétique et mystique* 25 (1949): 426–37.

Kopreeva, T. N. "Obraz inoka Polikarpa po pis'mam Simona i Polikarpa (opyt rekonstrukcii)." *Trudy Otdela drevnerusskoj literatury* 24 (1969): 112–16.

Krappe, Alexander H. "L'arroche biblique et le Paterik." *Revue des études slaves* 13 (1933): 244–55.

Kubarev, A. "O Paterike Pečerskom." *Žurnal Ministerstva narodnogo prosveščenija* 20 (1838): 1–34.

―――. "O redakcijax Paterika Pečerskogo voobšče." *Čtenija v Imperatorskom Obščestve istorii i drevnostej rossijskix pri Moskovskom universitete*, 1858, no. 3: 95–128.

Kuz'min, Apollon. "Letopisnye istočniki poslanij Simona i Polikarpa." *Arxeografičeskij ežegodnik za 1968*. Moscow, 1970, 73–92.

―――. *Načal'nye ėtapy drevnerusskogo letopisanija*. Moscow, 1977.

Laškarev, Petr. "Ostatki drevnix zdanij Kievo-Pečerskoj Lavry." *Trudy Kievskoj duxovnoj akademii*, 1883, no. 1: 119–28.

Lavrent'evskaja letopis'. 2nd ed. Vol. 1 of *Polnoe sobranie russkix letopisej*. Leningrad, 1926–1927. Reprint. Moscow, 1962.

Letopisnyj sbornik, imenuemyj Patriaršeju ili Nikonovskoju letopisju. Vols. 9–12 of *Polnoe sobranie russkix letopisej*. St. Petersburg, 1862–1906. Reprint. Moscow, 1965.

Lisicyn, M. *Pervonačal'nyj slavjano-russkij Tipikon. Istoriko-arxeologičeskoe issledovanie*. St. Petersburg, 1911.

Lixačev, Dmitrij. "The Type and Character of Byzantine Influence on Old Russian Literature." *Oxford Slavonic Papers* 13 (1967): 14–32.

Makarij, Metropolitan. "Obzor redakcij Kievo-Pečerskogo Paterika, preimuščestvenno drevnix." *Istoričeskie čtenija o jazyke i slovesnosti v zasedanijax Vtorogo otdelenija IAN*, 5, no. 3 (1856): 126–67.

―――. *Istorija russkoj cerkvi*. 3rd ed. Vol. 3. St. Petersburg, 1888.

Malyševskij, Ivan. "Evrei v južnoj Rusi i Kieve v X–XII vv." *Trudy Kievskoj duxovnoj akademii*, 1878, no. 9: 481–88.

Martinov, Ivan. *Les manuscrits slaves de la bibliotèque impériale de Paris*. Paris, 1858.

Meester, Placide de. *De monachico statu iuxta disciplinam byzantinam*. Vatican City, 1942.

Meyer, Phillip, ed. *Die Haupturkunden für die Geschichte der Athosklöster*. Leipzig, 1894.

Moschus, John. *Pratum Spirituale*, PG 87: 2851–3116. Partial reprint, ed. M. J. Rouet de Journel. Sources Chrétiennes, 12. Paris, 1946 (with French translation).

Mošin, Vladimir. "Russkie na Afone i russko-vizantijskie otnošenija v XI–XII vv." *Byzantinoslavica* 9, no. 1 (1947): 55–85.
Müller, Ludolf, ed. *Des Metropoliten Ilarion Lobrede auf Vladimir den Heiligen und Glaubensbekenntnis*. Wiesbaden, 1962.
Nau, François. *Histoires des solitaires Égyptiens* (= MS *Coislin* 126, fol. 158 ff). See *Revue de l'orient chrétien* 2 (1907), 3 (1908), 4 (1909), 7 (1912), 8 (1913).
Nazarko, Irynej. "Kyjivs'ki monastyri domonhol's'koji doby." *Analecta Ordinis S. Basilii*, ser. 2, 10 (1963): 503–12.
Nedeljković, Olga. "Problem tipologije slavenskoga paterika." *Slovo* 24 (1974): 7–16.
Novgorodskaja pervaja letopis' staršego i mladšego izvodov. Ed. Arsenij Nasonov. Moscow-Leningrad, 1950.
Novgorodskaja vtoraja letopis'. Vol. 3 of *Polnoe sobranie russkix letopisej*. St. Petersburg, 1841, 121–201.
Novgorodskaja tret'ja letopis'. Vol. 3 of *Polnoe sobranie russkix letopisej*. St. Petersburg, 1841, 205–305.
Novgorodskaja četvertaja letopis'. Ed. A. A. Šaxmatov. Vol. 4 of *Polnoe sobranie russkix letopisej*. 2nd. ed. Petrograd, 1915.
Obolensky, Dimitri. "Byzantium, Kiev and Moscow. A Study in Ecclesiastical Relations." *Dumbarton Oaks Papers* 11 (1957): 21–78.
Oesterreich, T. Konstantin. *Possession, Demonical and Other, among Primitive Races, in Antiquity, the Middle Ages and Modern Times*. Trans. I. D. Ibberson. London, 1930.
Orlov, Aleksandr, Adrianova-Peretc, Varvara, and Gudzij, Nikolaj. *Istorija russkoj literatury*. Vol. 1, *Literatura XI–načala XIII veka*. Moscow-Leningrad, 1941.
Palladius. *The Lausiac History of Palladius*. Ed. E. C. Butler. 2 vols. Texts and Studies, 6. Cambridge, 1898–1904. Trans. R. T. Meyer, *The Lausiac History of Palladius*. Washington D. C., 1965.
Parxomenko, Vladimir. "V kakoj mere bylo tendenciozno nesoxranivšeesja drevnejšee Žitie Antonija Pečerskogo?" *Izvestija Otdelenija russkogo jazyka i slovesnosti IAN* 19, no. 1 (1914): 237–41.
Peeters, Paul. "La canonisation des saints dans l'église russe," *Analecta Bollandiana* 33 (1914): 380–420; 38 (1920): 172–76.
Peretc, Volodymyr. "Kievo-Pečerskij Paterik v pol'skom i ukrainskom perevode." *Slavjanskaja filologija* 3 (1968): 174–210.
Podskalsky, Gerhard. *Christentum und theologische Literatur in der Kiever Rus' (988–1237)*. Munich, 1982.

Pomjalovskij, Ivan, ed. *Žitie Svjatogo Savy Osvjaščennogo sostavlennoe Kirillom Skifopol' skim.* St. Petersburg, 1890.

Ponomarev, Aleksandr. *Pamjatniki drevnerusskoj cerkovno-učitel'noj literatury.* Vols. 1-4. St. Petersburg, 1894-1897.

Pope, Richard W. "Drevnejšij otryvok Poslanija Simona k Polikarpu." *Trudy Otdela drevnerusskoj literatury* 24 (1969): 98-100.

——————. "The Literary History of the Kievan Caves Paterikon up to 1500." Ph. D. dissertation, Columbia University, 1970.

——————. "On the Comparative Literary Analysis of the Patericon Story (Translated and Original) in the Pre-Mongol Period." In *Canadian Contributions to the VIII International Congress of Slavists. (Zagreb-Ljubljana, 1978). Tradition and Innovation in Slavic Literatures, Linguistics, and Stylistics,* ed. Z. Folejewski et. al. Ottawa, 1978, 1-23.

Popov, Aleksandr. *Istoriko-literaturnyj obzor drevnerusskix polemičeskix sočinenij protiv Latinjan XI-XV vv.* Moscow, 1875. Reprint. London, 1972.

Poppe, Andrzej. *Państwo i kościół na Rusi w XI wieku.* Warsaw, 1968.

——————. "Le Prince et l'église en Russie de Kiev depuis la fin du X siècle et jusqu'au début du XII siècle." *Acta Poloniae Historica* 20 (1969): 95-119.

——————. "Russkie mitropolii Konstantinopol'skoj patriarxii v XI stoletii." *Vizantijskij vremennik* 28 (1968): 85-108; 29 (1969): 95-104.

——————. "Russko-vizantijskie cerkovno-političeskie otnošenija v seredine XI v." *Istorija SSSR,* 1970, no. 3: 108-24.

——————. "Die Metropoliten und Fürsten der Kiever Rus'." In G. Podskalsky, *Christentum und theologische Literatur in der Kiever Rus' (988-1237).* Munich, 1982, 290-321.

Povest' vremennyx let. Ed. Dmitrij Lixačev and B. A. Romanov. 2 vols. Moscow-Leningrad, 1950.

Pravda russkaja. Ed. Boris Grekov. 3 vols. Moscow-Leningrad, 1940-1963.

Preobraženskij, V. S. *Slavjano-russkij Skitskij Paterik. Opyt istoriko-bibliografičeskogo issledovanija.* Kiev, 1909.

Preuschen, Erwin, ed. *Palladius und Rufinus. Ein Beitrag zur Quellenkunde des ältesten Mönchtums. Texte und Untersuchungen.* Giessen, 1897.

Priselkov, Mixail. "Afon v načal'noj istorii Kievo-Pečerskogo monastyrja." *Izvestija Otdelenija russkogo jazyka i slovesnosti IAN* 17, no. 3 (1912): 186-97.

----------. *Očerki po cerkovno-političeskoj istorii Kievskoj Rusi*. St. Petersburg, 1913.
Pritsak, Omeljan. *The Origin of Rus'*. Vol. 1. Cambridge, Mass., 1981.
Prodolženie letopisi po Voskresenskomu spisku. Vol. 8 of *Polnoe sobranie russkix letopisej*. St. Petersburg, 1859.
Puc'ko, V. "Kievskij xudožnik XI veka Alimpij Pečerskij, po skazaniju Polikarpa i dannym arxeologičeskix issledovanij." *Wiener slavistisches Jahrbuch* 25 (1979): 63–88.
Rafn, Carl C. *Antiquités russes d'après les monuments historiques des Islandais et des anciens Scandinaves*. 2 vols. Copenhagen, 1850–1852.
Reiter, Hans. *Studien zur ersten kyrillischen Drucksausgabe des Kiever Paterikons*. Munich, 1976.
Rouet de Journel, Marie Joseph. *Monachisme et monastères russes*. Paris, 1952.
Rozanov, S. P., ed. *Žitie prepodobnogo Avraamija Smolenskogo i služby emu*. Pamjatniki drevnerusskoj literatury, 1. St. Petersburg, 1912.
----------. "K voprosu o Žitii prepodobnogo Antonija Pečerskogo." *Izvestija Otdelenija russkogo jazyka i slovesnosti IAN* 19, no. 1 (1914): 34–46.
Šaxmatov, Aleksej. "Neskol'ko slov o Nestorovom Žitii Feodosija" *Izvestija Otdelenija russkogo jazyka i slovesnosti IAN* 1 (1896): 46–65.
----------. "Kievo-Pečerskij Paterik i Pečerskaja Letopis'." *Izvestija Otdelenija russkogo jazyka i slovesnosti IAN* 2 (1897): 795–844.
----------. "Žitie Antonija i Pečerskaja Letopis'" *Žurnal Ministerstva narodnogo prosveščenija* 316 (1898): 105–49.
----------. *O tak nazyvaemoj Rostovskoj Letopisi*. Moscow, 1904.
----------. *Razyskanija o drevnejšix russkix letopisnyx svodax*. St. Petersburg, 1908.
----------, ed. *Povest' vremennyx let*. Petrograd, 1916.
----------. *Obozrenie russkix letopisnyx svodov XIV–XVI vv*. Moscow-Leningrad, 1938.
----------. "Povest' vremennyx let i ee istočniki." Ed. M. D. Priselkov. *Trudy Otdela drevnerusskoj literatury* 4 (1940): 9–150.
Schwartz, E., ed. *Kyrillos von Skythopolis*. Texte und Untersuchungen zur Geschichte der altchristlichen Literatur, 49, 2. Leipzig, 1939.
Smolitsch, Igor. *Das altrussische Mönchtum (11.–16. Jahrhundert) Gestalter und Gestalten*. Das östliche Christentum, 11. Würzburg, 1940.

Sobolevskij, Aleksej. "Poslanie Episkopa Simona." *Izvestija Otdelenija russkogo jazyka i slovesnosti IAN* 14, no. 1 (1909): 1–11.
Sreznevskij, Izmail. *Svedenija i zametki o maloizvestnyx i neizvestnyx pamjatnikax.* Vol. 4. St. Petersburg, 1879.
Stökl, Günther. "Zur Geschichte des russischen Mönchtums." *Jahrbücher Geschichte Osteuropas* 2 (1954): 121–35.
Stroev, Pavel. *Spiski ierarxov i nastojatelej monastyrej rossijskoj cerkvi.* St. Petersburg, 1877.
Stupperich, Robert. "Zur Geschichte der russischen hagiographischen Forschung (von Klučevskij bis Fedotov)." *Kyrios* 1 (1936): 47–56.
Syčev, Nikolaj. "Na zare bytija Kievo-Pečerskoj obiteli." In *Sbornik statej v čest' Akademika A. I. Sobolevskogo.* Moscow, 1928 (=*Sbornik Otdelenija russkogo jazyka i slovesnosti Akademii Nauk SSSR* 101, no. [3]), 289–94.
Theodoret of Cyrrhus. *Historia religiosa.* See *Histoire des moines de Syrie.* Ed. and trans. Pierre Canivet and Alice Leroy-Molinghem. 2 vols. Sources chrétiennes, 234, 257. Paris, 1977, 1979.
Toločko, Petro. "Kievskaja zemlja." In *Drevnerusskie knjažestva X–XIII vv.*, ed. L. G. Beskrovnyj et al. Moscow, 1975, 5–56.
Undols'kij, D. V. "Iosif Trizna, redaktor Paterika Pečerskogo." *Čtenija v Imperatorskom Obščestve istorii drevnostej rossijskix pri Moskovskom universitete*, 1846, no. 4: 5–10.
Velikija Minei Četii. Pamjatniki slavjano-russkoj pis'mennosti. St. Petersburg, 1880.
Velykyj, Atanasij. ČSVV. *Pečers'kyj Pateryk abo pravedni Staroji Ukrajiny.* Rome, 1973.
Vernadsky, George V., trans. *Medieval Russian Laws.* New York, 1947.
———. *Kievan Russia.* New Haven, Conn., 1948.
———. *Russia at the Dawn of the Modern Age.* New Haven, Conn., 1959.
Viktorova, Marija. *Kievo-pečerskij Paterik po drevnim rukopisjam v pereloženii na sovremenyj russkij jazyk.* Kiev, 1911.
Viskovatyj, K. "K voprosu ob avtore i vremeni napisanija 'Slova k Izjaslavu o Latinax'." *Slavia* 16 (1938–1939): 535–67.
Vladimir, Archimandrite. *Sistematičeskoe opisanie rukopisej Moskovskoj Sinodal'noj Patriaršej Biblioteki.* Part 1. Moscow, 1894.
Vlasto, Alexis P. *The Entry of the Slavs into Christendom.* Cambridge, Eng., 1970.

Volkova, T. F. "Xudožestvennaja struktura i funkcii obraza besa v Kievo-Pečerskom Paterike." *Trudy Otdela drevnerusskoj literatury* 33 (1979): 228–37.

Voronin, Nikolaj. "Žitie Leontija Rostovskogo i vizantijsko-russkie otnošenija vtoroj poloviny XII v." *Vizantijskij vremennik* 23 (1963): 23–46.

Vostokov, Aleksandr. *Opisanie russkix i slovenskix rukopisej Rumjancevskogo Muzeuma.* St. Petersburg, 1842.

Wijk, Nicolaas van. "Studien zu den altkirchenslavischen Paterika." *Verhandlingen der Koninklijke Akademie van Wetenschappen. Afdeeling Letterkunde*, n.s., 30, 2. Amsterdam, 1931.

———. "Die slavischen Redaktionen des Μέγα Λειμωνάριον." *Byzantinoslavica* 4 (1932): 236–52.

———. "Dva slavjanskix paterika." *Byzantinoslavica* 4 (1932): 22–34.

———. "Was ist ein Paterik Skitskij?" In *Mélanges Mikkola.* Suomalaisen Tieden Akatemian Toimituksia (Annales Academiae Scientiarum Fennicae), series B, 27. Helsinki, 1932, 348–54.

———. "Zu den slavischen Paterika." *Zeitschrift für slavische Philologie* 9 (1932): 357–59.

———. "Das gegenseitige Verhältnis einiger Redaktionen der 'Ανδρῶν ἁγίων βίβλος und die Entwicklungsgeschichte des Μέγα Λειμωνάριον." *Mededeelingen der Koninklijke Akademie van Wetenschappen. Afdeeling Letterkunde*, series A, 75. Amsterdam, 1933, 91–155.

———. "O proisxoždenii Egipetskogo Paterika." In *Sbornik v cest' na Prof. L. Miletič za sedemdesetgodišninata ot roždenieto mu.* Sofia, 1933, 361–69.

———. "Podrobnyj obzor cerkovno–slavjanskogo perevoda Bol'šogo Limonarija." *Byzantinoslavica* 6 (1935–1936): 38–83.

———. "La traduction slave de l''Ανδρῶν ἁγίων βίβλος et son prototype grec." *Byzantion* 13 (1938): 233–44.

———, ed. *The Old Church Slavonic Translation of the* 'Ανδρῶν ἁγίων βίβλος. Eds. D. Armstrong, R. Pope, and C. H. Schooneveld. The Hague, 1975.

INDEX OF BIBLICAL REFERENCES

		Page			Page
Gen.	18:31	122	Ps. (cont.)	54:22	139
	28:16–17	72		68:7–8	194
	39:12–13	164		70:14	138
	41:45	164		75:11	138
				83:10	120
Exod.	13:21	104		91:12	43
	16:9–18	64		113:17–18	205
	17:8–14	104		117:24	124
				118:71	116
Deut.	21:23	124		125:5–6	181
	28:66	124		127:5	5
				132:1	90
1 Kings	2:30	84, 89, 138		144:18–19	35
2 Kings	16:5–12	115	Prov.	3:34	158
				10:7	89
3 Kings	17:8–16	70		29:2	99
4 Kings	2:13–14	134	Eccles.	5:4	139
	5:10–14	195			
			Isa.	5:6	28
Job	1:21	139, 140		6:10	130
	2:8	133		7:23–24	28
	2:10	126		8:18	102, 112
	29:15	101		32:13	28
				53:1	130
Ps.	6:5	205			
	7:15	38	Jer.	15:19	182
	7:16	38, 125			
	10:8	157	Wisd. of Sol.	3:1, 4:7	89
	13:4	172		5:16	85
	21:16	124			
	21:18	124	Matt.	3:15	214
	23:6	17		5:4	180
	23:7–8	17		5:11	54
	24:18	33		5:12	10, 54
	26:4	114		5:14–15	197
	29:5	170		5:16	128
	31:5	194		5:22	141
	32:1–3	192		5:48	82
	33:15	74		6:14	141
	33:16–18	40		6:19–20	154
	36:14–15	187		6:21	62, 154
	39:1	204		6:24	195
	50:17	179		6:26	71, 170, 181

		Page			Page
Matt. (cont.)	6:31–33	44, 181	Matt. (cont.)	27:46	160
	6:34	56, 181	Mark	1:40–44	194
	7:2	157		4:3–4	130
	7:7	195		4:25	204
	8:11	24		5:1–20	186
	8:2–4	195		6:4	152, 224
	8:28–34	186		8:36–37	167
	10:22	203		9:29	70
	10:27	25		10:7–8	164
	10:37	31, 48		10:25	36
	10:38	31		10:27	24
	10:39	48		10:29	165, 183
	10:41	96		10:30	100, 183
	11:28	31		10:31	100
	11:29	31, 53		10:43–44	43
	13:3–4, 7	130		11:17	114
	13:12	204		13:13	203
	13:46	5		14:36	24
	13:57	152, 224		15:34	160
	16:18	11	Luke	4:24	152, 225
	16:26	167		5:12–14	195
	16:27	213		6:22–23	54
	17:20	24		6:27–28	115
	17:21	70		6:37	141
	18:10	157		8:5, 7	130
	18:20	36, 114		8:18	204
	19:5–6	164		8:26–39	186
	19:24	36		9:25	167
	19:26	24		9:62	36, 48
	19:29	100, 165, 183		10:19	186
	19:30	25, 100		10:20	187
	20:1–16	205		11:9	195
	20:26–27	43		12:3	25
	21:13	114		12:19	170
	24:13	203		12:20	62, 170
	25:21	100		12:24	71
	25:21–23	27		12:29–31	44
	25:26–27	25		12:33	154
	25:29	204		12:34	62, 154
	25:34	5, 27		12:48	205
	26:26	30		14:33	181
	26:28	30		13:28–29	24
	26:31	28		13:30	25, 100
	26:52	190			
	27:25	126			

INDEX OF BIBLICAL REFERENCES

		Page			*Page*
Luke (cont.)	14:26	48	Gal.	1:7–8	214
	15:7	153		3:13	123, 124
	16:9	96		6:2	101
	16:13	195		6:7	156, 158, 203
	17:6	24			
	17:33	48			
	18:1–6	157	Eph.	4:26	142
	18:25	36		4:5	214
	18:29	165, 183		6:5	165
	18:30	100, 183			
	19:17	100	Phil.	2:8	115
	19:22–23	25		3:13	101
	19:26	204			
	19:46	114	2 Thess.	3:8	194
	21:19	203, 204			
	22:26	43	1 Tim.	3:1–7	117
	23:34	115		5:14	164
	23:42	5		6:10	181
	23:43	124			
			Heb.	5:4	116
John	7:38	105		12:7–8	204
	9:1–7	195			
	9:15	126	1 Pet.	1:17	213
	12:24	100		2:23	115
	14:23	190			
			Rev.	20:13	213
Acts	12:1–7	113		21:15–17	3
	12:12–14	50		22:12	213
	15:39	41			
	20:34	194			
Rom.	11:33–34	17			
	12:19	157			
	14:8	123			
1 Cor.	2:9	7			
	3:16	191			
	7:32–33	165			
	7:9	164			
	10:31	114			
2 Cor.	6:16	113, 191			
	12:9	133			

INDEX OF GREEK TERMS

ἀνάργυροι, 115n.
ἀχειροποίητος, 197n.
βασιλεύουσα πόλις, 18n.
γέρων, 2n.
διορατικός, 109n.
δομέστικος, 13n.
ἐξώρασον, 201n.
ἐκτένεια, 77n.
ζωστικὸν ῥάσον, 201n.
ἡσυχία, 113n.
θεοπάτωρ, 89n.
κανονάρχης, 52n.
καταπέτασμα, 193n.
κουκκούλιον, 201v.
μανδύας, 201n.
παλλίον, 201n.
παραμανδύας, 135n.
πατρότης σου, 175n.
παρρησία, 4n., 83n.
πρωτοστάτης, 124n.
πρωτοστράτωρ, 125n.

INDEX OF SLAVONIC TERMS

архимандрита всея Русіи
   и начальника, 24n.
безмолвіи, 113n.
безмѣздника, 115n.
богоотьць, 89n.
Богородичину, 6n.
болярина, боляровъ,
   40n., 41n.
братъ, братїе,
   братіи, 6n.; 224
видѣниѥ, 139n.
властелинъ, 31n.
градъ, 98n.
двоивѣрець,
   двоевѣріе, 213n.
деместьвьникъ,
   13n., 52n.
доска, 15n.
дръзновеніе,
   дьрзновениѥ, 4n., 83n.
завѣса, 193n.
запрещалныя молитвы, 153n.
єклиархъ, 52n.
єксиархъ, 52n.
єктенїа, 77n.
исправление, 1
кинаникъ, 126n.
клепало, 110n.
коуколъ, 201n.
лобеда, 170n.
макомь, 67n.
мантия, 201n.
масломь, 67n.
мастери, 6n.
мниха, 91n.

намѣстная икона, 7n., 193n.
неруѫкотворенная, 197n.
область, 75n.
отечеству (къ твоєму), 175n.
палия, 201n.
парамандии, 135n.
подвигъ, 1
подрясникъ, 201n.
прозорливъ, 109n.
ряса, 201n.
служители, 195n.
старѣи пекущимъ, 47n.
страстіе, 158n.
старѣишина, 6n.
судія, 31n.
уродьствовати, уродьство,
   уродьство творити, 208n.
уставникъ, 52n.
уставу отєчєскому, 102n.
царицину, 6n.
царствующаго града, 18n.
черноризци,
   черноризець, 224–26.

INDEX

Abel, 75
Abkhazians, 11
Abraham, 24, 121, 164
Abramovyč, D., xxxii, xxxiii, xxxvi, 81n., 89n., 138n., 141n., 182n., 199n., 231
Account (of why the Caves Monastery is so called) (Discourse 7), xviii, xxxi, xxxiv–xxxvi, xl, xlv, 66n., 218, 220n., 221n.
Adam, 163
Adam of Bremen, xxxi
Afanasij the Solitary, monk of the Caves Monastery, xl, 129–30, 140
Afrikan, xlvi, 1, 2, 95
Agapit the Physician, monk of the Caves Monastery, xxvii–xxviii, xxx, xxxv, xl, 145, 147–51, 224, 226
Akakios, St., 7
Akindin, archimandrite of the Caves Monastery, xix, xxv, xxviii, xxx, xxxv, 116, 140, 142–43, 147, 152–53, 175, 224–26
  Polikarp's epistle to, 142–43, 147, 152–53, 224–226
Aleksej, bishop of Tver', 117
Aleksej of Volyn', elder of the Caves Monastery, 216
Alessandra Olelkowicz (Olel'kovič), 10n.
Alexios the Stoudite, patriarch of Constantinople, 44n., 45n., 200n.
Alfrekr, xlvi
Alimpij the Icon-painter, monk of the Caves Monastery, xxx, xxxii, xxxiv–xxxv, xlix, 117n., 190, 192–99
  tonsured under Nikon, 193
  ordained priest by Nikon, 194
  cures leper, 194
almsgiving, 14, 65, 79, 94, 123, 132, 137, 139–40, 150, 154, 176, 181, 183, 193, 206
Al'ta River, 2, 3, 162
Amalek, 104
Anastasia, see Verxoslava
Anastasij, steward at the Caves Monastery, 56–57
angels, 7, 9, 59, 73, 81, 104–5, 109, 121, 139–40, 141, 144, 180, 198–99
Antonij, bishop of Jur'ev, 16, 17, 92n.
Antonij, bishop of Novgorod, 117
Antonij, founder of the Caves Monastery, xvii–xviii, xxv, xxxiii, xxxv, xxxix–xliv, xlvii, 2–3, 5–8, 11–13, 15, 19, 20–22, 33–39, 42–43, 98, 102, 108, 111, 115, 118, 120–22, 126, 129, 130, 137, 142–43, 147, 152, 159, 166n., 168–69, 174–75, 179, 180, 187–88, 194, 195, 197, 203–7, 209, 216, 217, 218–221, 224–25, 229
  tonsured on Mt. Athos, 18, 218
  appoints Feodosij superior, 22, 221
  prayer of, 4–5
  teaches Feodosij, 100, 101
  receives Feodosij, 32, 220
  converses with Feodosij's mother, 34
  orders Feodosij ordained, 41
  appoints Varlaam superior, 41, 81n., 220
  founds monastery near Černihiv, 206
  death, xxv, 7n., 11n.
  posthumous miracles, 21

Antonij Poros'kij, bishop, 92
Antony, St., 20, 25, 46, 55n., 219
Apostle (Epistles of St. Paul), see also
   Paul, St., 145, 213
Arabs, 148n.
Arefa, monk of the Caves Monastery,
   xxxiv, xlix, 139–40
Arethas, St., 7
Aristarx, xxvi
Armenia, 132n., 148n.
Armenian(s), xlv
   physician, 148–52, 226n.
Arsenij, bishop of Tver', xxix
Arsenios, St., 154n., 179n.
Artemios, St., 7
Athanasios, St., xxii, 20n.
Athos, Mt., xvii, xxxiii, xl, 18, 20–
   22, 37, 44, 166, 218, 219–21
bakehouse, 52, 70, 191
baker, 70, 190–91
baptism/conversion, 199n., 212
   of Šimon the Varangian, 3, 5
   of Jews, 125, 127
   of Cumans, 127
   of Vjatičians, 128
   of Armenian physician, 151
Barnabas, St., 40
Batu, xxx, 9n.
Berestovo, 19–20, 219
Bilhorod (Bělgorod), 16, 119
Blachernai, 6–7, 10, 13, 87
"blessed one", see Feodosij
Bogoljub Monastery, xxvi
Boldiny Hills (Černihiv), 207
Bolesław I the Brave, king of Poland,
   162, 166–68
Bolesław II, king of Poland, 38,
   132n.
books, 62n., 95, 132, 153–55, 191
   Greek, 12
   divine, 27
   reading of, 52, 144–45

   binding of, 53
   writing of, 56
   of rites, 202
Book of Holy Men, xx–xxi, 25n.,
   101n., 114, 129n., 170n., 181n.,
   192, 201n.
Book of Life, 10, 147
Boris Svjatoslavič, prince, 68n.
Boris Vjačeslavič, prince, 68n.
Boris Volodimerovič, St., prince of
   Rostov, xxii, xxiv, 19, 24, 162n.,
   215, 219
boyar(s), 10, 22, 49, 54, 60, 75–76,
   79, 84, 85, 87, 98, 113, 117n.,
   132, 133, 135, 144, 150, 162,
   188, 221
   Polish, 168
Bulgaria, 149n.
Bulgarian, the, 40, 41
burial, 59, 82, 84, 86, 109, 112, 141,
   157, 174, 189–90, 199, 204,
   209, 212, 215
   special status in the Caves
   Monastery, 3, 10, 51, 63n., 83n.,
   105, 121–22, 127, 129, 147,
   176–78, 180
Byzantine(s), 125
   craftsmen, xlii
   churches, xliii, 193n.
   polemical literature, 211n.
   monasticism, xlix, xli, 74–75n.,
   228
   chant, 145n.
Byzantium, Byzantine Empire, 14n.,
   171n., 228
Cain, 75
Cassian, editor of the *Paterik*, xxx,
   xxxvi, 81n., 222n.
Catherine, wife of Svjatoslav
   Ol'govič, 111n.
cellarer, 35, 53, 62, 64, 66, 67, 69,
   185–86

INDEX

Čern, merchant of Toropec, see Isaakij the Cave-dweller
Černihiv (Černigov), xxxii, xl, 16, 26n., 38, 51n., 74n., 92, 96, 111n., 119, 131, 136n., 145, 149, 207
chains, 31, 125–27, 159–60, 162, 163, 164, 167
charter, 13
Cherson, 125
chiliarch, xlvi, 5, 97
choirmaster, 13, 52n., 171
Climacus, see John
communion bread, 29, 30, 170, 190, 191, 207, 212
Constantine, metropolitan, 111
Constantinople, xxxi, xxxviii, xlvii, xlxi, 6–7, 11, 18, 41, 44, 50–51, 87, 111, 125n., 182, 192, 214n., 218, 223
Cosmas and Damian, SS., 115n.
Cossacks, xxx
cowl, 45, 200, 205
craftsmen, 6, 9, 10–13
Crimean Horde, xxvii
Cumans, xlix, 2, 72n., 98, 123n., 126–27, 156, 157n., 169, 186n.
Cyril of Scythopolis, St., xxii, 40, 134n.
Damian, monk of the Caves Monastery, xix, xxiii, xxx–xxxii, xxxv, xlix, 57–59, 108–9, 152, 109, 152, 205n., 225
David, 89, 113, 115, 124, 191, 194
David Igorevič, prince of Volodymyr, 171, 172n., 190
David Svjatoslavič, prince of Smolensk and Černihiv, 131, 133
deacon, 79, 140
Demetrios, St., 66, 99, 146
demons, 15, 46–47, 55, 56, 69–70, 85, 105, 109, 110, 128, 139–40, 141, 146, 153, 182–89, 206–7, 209
Desert Fathers, 53n., 101n., 193n.
Desna River, 26, 103n.
devil, the enemy, 14, 59, 74, 77, 81, 82, 85, 87, 88, 95, 101, 109, 137, 139, 140, 143–44, 153, 159, 160, 163, 181, 182, 188, 195, 208, 214
Dionisij Ščepa, monk of the Caves Monastery, 216
discernment, gift of, 104, 109, 120
Dnieper, xvii, 19, 42n., 97, 156, 157n., 166n., 187, 219
Dormition of the Theotokos, Church of (Caves Monastery), xxix–xxx, xxxi, xxxix, xl, xlv, xlvi–xlviii, 1, 4, 6, 13, 21, 42, 44, 76, 78, 79, 84, 91, 92, 94, 96, 98, 102, 103–4, 105–6, 107, 109, 110, 112, 126, 137, 138, 176, 192, 193, 204, 220–221
  dimensions miraculously revealed, 3, 8, 9, 10
  name miraculously revealed, 7
  site miraculously indicated, 8, 10, 78
  founding date, 9
  date of consecration, xviii, 15
  miraculous nature of, 10–11
  miraculous appearance of the holy table in, 15–16
  miraculous consecration of, 16–17
  object of robbery, 59
  raised in the air, 60
  completion of, 86
  burned and rebuilt, 186–87
  decoration of, 192–93
Dormition of the Theotokos, Church of (Moscow), xxxvii
Dormition of the Theotokos, Church of (Rostov), 13, 197

Dormition of the Theotokos,
  Church of (Smolensk), 13
Dormition of the Theotokos,
  Church of (Suzdal'), xxviii, 13, 119.
Dormition of the Theotokos,
  Church of (Tmutorokan'), 41
Dormition of the Theotokos,
  Cathedral of (Vladimir), xxiv, xxvi,
  119
Dormition of the Theotokos,
  Monastery of (Černihiv), 207
double faith, 213
Efrem, metropolitan of Kiev, 20, 76n.
Efrem, monk of the Caves Monastery,
  bishop of Perejaslav, xxxiv, xxxv,
  xliii, 23n., 33n., 35n., 37, 40n.,
  41, 44, 92, 99n., 118, 169
Efrem, bishop of Suzdal', 119
Egipetskij Paterik, xix
Egypt, xxi, 72n., 104n., 164n., 165,
  228
elder, 2, 62, 68, 80, 109–10, 114,
  120, 127, 138, 139,
  140, 141, 147
  Jewish, 125
Elijah, 124n., 134
Elisha, 134, 195
Eliu, 70
Emperor of Constantinople, 125
eparch, 125
Ephraim the Syrian, 113n., 141
  Paraenesis, 113n., 141n.
Erazm, monk of the Caves Monastery,
  xlix, 137–38
Ermolin Chronicle, 119n.
Esphigmenou Monastery, 18, 69n.
eunuch(s), 6, 7
Evagrij, deacon of the Caves
  Monastery, 140–41
Evagrios of Pontus, St., 136

Evstratij the Faster, monk of the
  Caves Monastery, xxxix, xlix,
  123–25, 126n.
exorcism, 69–70, 128, 145, 146, 147,
  153, 185
fasting, 23, 47, 55, 67, 70, 72, 73,
  80, 94, 102, 108, 116, 120, 123,
  132, 151, 159, 164, 178, 209,
  212, 215n., 222
Feodor, cellarer at the Caves
  Monastery, xxix, xxxv, xl,
  xliii, xlix, l, 35, 53, 58n.,
  181–86, 188–90
  and the "Varangian Cave", 181, 183,
    188–89
  and Vasilij, 182, 184–90
  commands demons, 186–87
  martyred, 189
Feodor Glebovič Pronskij, *voevoda* of
  Kiev, 216
Feodor Jaroslavič, prince of Pinsk,
  10, 33n.
Feodosij, monk of the Caves
  Monastery, xviii–xx, xxii–xxiv,
  xxx, xxxi, xxxii–xlv, l–li, 2–7,
  9, 11, 12, 13,15, 24–88, 89–107,
  108–12, 115, 120,121n., 122,
  126, 129, 130, 131n., 135, 137,
  139n., 142, 143, 147, 148, 152,
  153, 156, 169, 174, 179, 180,
  187, 194, 195, 197, 199n., 205,
  207–10, 215–17, 218, 221n.,
  222, 224, 225
  birthplace of, 26
  named Feodosij, 26
  death of father, 27
  childhood education of, 27, 100
  attempted pilgrimage of, 28
  beatings by mother, 28, 30, 100
  departure for Kiev, 32, 101
  tonsured, 21, 33, 219
  received by Antonij, 32, 101

confronts mother, 35
ordained priest, 41
obtains Stoudite Rule, 44, 222
edifies Prince Izjaslav, 50, 61–62, 211–14
expels demons,
preaches to Jews, 73
becomes superior, 19n., 23, 43, 102, 222
confronts Prince Svjatoslav, 74–76
builds Dormition church, 78
final days of, 80–83, 102
death of, 11n., 37, 208
first burial of, 84–85
posthumous miracles attributed to, 85–86, 96–97, 103
translations of relics, 89–93, 176
burial in Church of Theotokos, 92–93
entered into *sinodik*, 93
prophecy of, 93–94
decoration of coffin of, 95–99
heals Georgij Simonovič, 98
encomium to, 99–107
sacred tomb of, 175, 200, 201
miraculous well of, 194
saves Isaakij the Cave-dweller, 207–8, 229
Feodosij the Greek, 210n.
Feofil, monk of the Caves Monastery, 177–81
Feoktist, superior of the Caves Monastery, bishop of Černihiv, 15n., 93, 119, 145
Fletcher, Giles, 229n.
Florence, Church Council of, xix, xxxviii, 81n.
folly for Christ's sake, see *jurodstvo*
Friand, 1
Gennadij Bible, 114n.

George, metropolitan of Kiev, 23, 44n., 222
George, St., xvii
Georgij, brother of Moisej the Hungarian, 162
Georgij Simonovič, chiliarch, xix, xlvi, 4–5, 95–98
letter of, 97–98
Georgij Volodimerovič (Jurij Dolgorukij), prince of Suzdal' and Kiev, 5, 13, 97, 98n., 111n.
Georgij Vsevolodovič, prince of Vladimir/Suzdal', xxiv, xxvi, 118, 119n.
Gerasim, monk of the Caves Monastery, 126, 127
German, bishop of Novgorod, 110n., 118
Gertrude, wife of Prince Izjaslav Jaroslavič, 38n., 211n.
gifts to the Caves Monastery, 4, 60, 98, 221
of food, 64, 67
of gold belt and crown, 3–4
of gold for icon, 60–61
for Feodosij's coffin, 95
for holy table, 195
of gospel, 61
of *grivna*, 9, 57, 97, 135
of lamp oil, 68
of land, 22, 221
of wine, 65–66
Glěb Svjatopolčič,
prince of Tmutorokan', 51n., 144
Glěb Volodimerovič, St., prince of Murom, xxii, xxiv, 19, 24, 52, 162, 215, 218
Gospel, 145, 157, 164, 197, 201, 203
Greece, xxxi, xlvi, xlvii, 145n., 218
Greek(s), xlii, 6–8, 11, 12, 18, 23, 51, 169n., 124, 192, 222

Gregory, metropolitan of Kiev, xxxviii, 81n.
Gregory VII, Pope, 211n.
Grigorij, monk of the Caves Monastery, 145
Grigorij the Miracle-worker, monk of the Caves Monastery, xxv, xlii, xlix, 145, 153–57, 226n.
grivna, 2, 3, 9, 14, 15, 16, 54n., 57, 60, 95, 97, 135, 163
habit (Great Angelic Habit), 45, 89, 138, 166, 199n., 200, 201, 202, 204–6, 218
Hagarenes, 123, 174
Hákon jarl Eriksson, xlvi, 1
Hakon the Blind, 1, 3
Halyč (Galič), xli, xlviii, 172, 216
healing, 2, 86, 98, 108–9, 127, 128, 130, 133–34, 135, 146, 147–50, 194–95, 199, 202, 203
herbs, 133, 147, 148, 149, 150–51
heresies, 212, 213
  monophysite, 149, 151
  Sabellianism, 211–13
Herod, 113, 163
Hesychius the Horebite, 129n.
Historia monachorum in Aegypto, see Rufinus
Holy Apostles, Church of (Berestovo), 19, 219
Holy Mountain, Monastery of (Volodymyr), 50–51
Holy Mountain, see Athos, Mt.
Holy Synod (Moscow), xxxvi
Hungarian(s), 162–69
Hustyn' Chronicle, 9, 33n.
Hypatian Chronicle, xvii, xxxi, xli, xliv, xlvi, 197n.
icons(s), 22, 51, 137–38, 193, 195, 196, 197, 212, 213, 221
  of Antonij, 11
  of Feodosij, 11

of Theotokos, 7–9, 11, 12, 13, 14–15, 60–61, 73, 147, 175, 192, 193, 197
  of the Savior, 193
  Deisis, 195
  naměstnaja, xlvii, 7, 12, 192, 195, 197, 198–99
icon painter(s), 11, 190, 192–99
icon painting, 192, 193, 198
Ieremej, elder of the Caves Monastery, xix, xxx–xxxii, xxxv, 109, 110n., 152, 205n., 225
Ierusalemskij Paterik, xxi
Ilarion, archimandrite of the Caves Monastery, 216
Ilarion, bishop of Merlin, 149n.
Ilarion, metropolitan of Kiev, xxxix, 19, 20, 32n., 118, 219
Ilarion, monk of the Caves Monastery, xliii, 55–56
Ingigerd, 35
Inquiry concerning the Latins (Discourse 37), xx, xxvi, xxxii, 211–14
Ioann, archimandrite of the Caves Monastery, 10, 33n.
Ioann, bishop of Černihiv, 16, 92
Ioann, boyar (father of Zaxarija), 14, 15
Ioann, boyar (father of Varlaam), 36, 39, 41, 50, 64
Ioann the Solitary, monk of the Caves Monastery, xxxv, xxxxi, xlix, 158–62, 169
Ioann, superior of the Caves Monastery, 15, 89–91, 127n., 145, 149–51, 170, 171, 173, 180, 196n., 209
Irene, St., xvii
Isaac, 24, 164
Isaia, bishop of Rostov, xxxiv, xxxv, 16, 51, 66n., 118, 145

Isaiah, 130
Isaakij, cook at the Caves Monastery, 208
Isaakij the Cave-dweller, xx, xxxii, xxxiii, xxxv, li, 143, 144n., 145, 152, 205–9, 225, 228–30
    tonsured by Antonij, 205
    driven mad by demons, 206
    saved by Feodosij, 207
    acts like an idiot, 207–8, 228–30
Isidore, metropolitan of Kiev xxxviii, 81n.
Islam, 107n.
ispravlenie, 1
Israel, 104, 154n.
Israelites, 72n., 104n.
Izjaslav III Davidovič, prince of Kiev, 131–36
Izjaslav I Jaroslavič, prince of Kiev, xviii, xxii, xxxii, xliii, xliv, 2, 20, 22, 35n., 38, 39, 40n., 49, 50, 51, 54, 60, 61, 66n., 68, 69, 74–76, 102, 109n., 144, 146, 169, 207, 211, 214n., 220–21
    donates land to monastery, 22, 60, 221
    expels Antonij, 38, 169
    founds Monastery of St. Demetrios, 50, 51, 146
    expelled from Kiev, 74
    "Inquiry concerning the Latins", 211–14
Izjaslav II M'stislavič, prince of Kiev, 98, 11, 211n., 214n.
Jacob, 72, 95, 164
Jagiełło, see Jogaila
Jakov, monk of the Caves Monastery, xliv, 82n.
James, St., 7
Jan, magnate, 93–94
Jaropolk Izjaslavič, prince of Volodymyr, 174n., 211n.

Jaroslav Volodimerovič, prince of Kiev, xvii, 1, 2, 9, 19, 20, 32n., 33, 36n., 51n., 74n., 77, 148n., 162, 171n., 211, 219
Jereboam, 154n.
Jerusalem, 5, 25, 50, 175
Jesus prayer, 132
Jew(s), 73, 105, 123–25, 126, 127, 136, 213
Job, 101, 133, 139, 140
Jogaila, grand duke of Lithuania, 107n.
John II, metropolitan of Kiev, 15–17
John IV, metropolitan of Kiev, 81n.
John the Baptist, St., 163, 195n.
John Climacus, St., 114n., 116n., 118n., 136, 181
    Ladder of Divine Ascent, 129n., 136, 181n.
John the Deacon, xx
John Moschos, 138n.
    Pratum Spirituale, xxi, 138n.
Jordan River, 134n., 195n.
Joseph, 161, 164, 165
Judas, 126
jurodstvo, 188n., 228–30
Jur'ev, 16, 17, 92, 117, 119
Kallistos, bishop, see Ware, T.
Kaniv (Kanev), 12
keybearer, 69
Kiev, xvii, xviii, xxi, xxiv, xxix, xxx, xxxi, xxxiii, xxxiv, xxxvii, xxxviii, xxxix, xli, xlii, xliv–xlvii, xlviii, 5, 6, 16n., 19, 26, 31, 32, 33, 38n., 40n., 73n., 74, 81n., 87n., 95, 96, 98n., 99, 101, 107n., 109n., 11, 112n., 123, 125, 127, 128n., 131n., 132, 144n., 146–49, 150, 151n., 156n., 157, 162, 166n., 168n., 169, 171–72n., 174n., 186n.,

194, 195, 197, 207n., 211n., 215n., 216, 219, 222n.
Kievo–Pečerskja letopis', xxxiii, xli, xlii, 152n.
kinanik, 126
Kiprian, metropolitan of Kiev, xxix
Klim, metropolitan of Kiev, 111, 223
Kliment, boyar of Prince Izjaslav, 60–62
Kliment, superior of monastery at Klov, 91
Klov, 13, 87, 91
Konon, monk of the Caves Monastery, 85
Kosov, Syl'vestr, metropolitan of Kiev, xxxiv
Krevo, Union of (1386), xxxi
Kubarev, A., xxxvi, xxxviii, 81n.
Kukša, monk of the Caves Monastery, 128, 145
kuna, 54, 172
Kursk, 26
Ladder of Divine Ascent, see John Climacus
"Latins", 2, 5, 81n., 107n., 188, 211–14
Laurentian Chronicle, xvii, xxv, xvi, 112n., 197n.
Lausiac History, see Palladius
lavra, xvii, xxv, 1, 89, 104, 105, 106, 120, 216
Lavrentij, bishop of Turov, 119, 216
Lavrentij the Solitary, monk of the Caves Monastery, xxxiii, 22n., 146–47
Lazar, bishop of Smolensk, 117
Lent, 45, 64n., 67, 69n., 73, 82, 102, 151n., 160, 212, 215n.
Leontij, bishop of Rostov, 118
Leontios, bishop of Neapolis, 227
leprosy, 194, 195

Life of Antonij, xxv, xxviii, xxxiv, xxxv, xxxix, xl, xli, xlii, 2n., 9, 18n., 19n., 118, 130, 152, 168, 169n., 175., 188, 218, 221n., 222n., 225
Life of Feodosij, xviii, xx, xxii–xxiii, xxiv, xxx, xxxiv, xxxvi, xxxviii, xl–xliv, xlv, 9, 20n., 22n., 23n., 26n., 89n., 91, 130, 131n., 169, 210n., 217, 220n., 221n.
Life of Leontij the Martyr, 118n.
Life of St. Antony, xxii
Life of St. Euthymios, xxii
Life of St. Sabbas, xxii, 40n., 72n.
Life of St. Symeon of Emesa, 228
Lives of SS. Boris and Glěb, xxii, xxiv, 19n., 24
Lithuania
  Grand Duchy of, 107n.
  grand dukes of, xxx, xxxi, 215n.
liturgy, 41, 42, 65, 77n., 79, 86, 111, 126n., 138, 149n., 212, 213, 214, 223
Ljubeč, 18, 171n., 218
Luka, bishop of Bilhorod, 16, 119
Lukjan, 217
Macarius, 43
magicians, 194
magnates, 76, 96, 104
Makarij, metropolitan of Kiev, 136n., 215
mantle, 39, 191, 200
Maria, wife of Jan, 93–94
Marin, bishop of Jur'ev, 92, 119
Marko the Cave-dweller, monk of the Caves Monastery, xxxiv, xli, 175–80
  raises the dead, 176, 177, 178
martyr(s), 7, 9, 118, 128, 168, 189–90

Matfej, elder of the Caves Monastery, xix, xxxi, xxxii, xxxv, 109–10, 145, 152, 205n., 224
merchants, 11, 56, 172, 205
Merlin, 149n.
Michael, monk of the Stoudios Monastery, 23, 44n., 221
Mina, bishop of Polack, 119
miracles, 6, 9, 11, 12, 17, 72, 85, 104, 108, 120, 127, 128, 140, 142, 147, 152, 153, 157, 174, 175, 189, 197, 208, 220, 225, 226
    of the foundation of the Church of the Theotokos, 6–9, 13
    of the boats, 12
    of the icon of the Theotokos, 14–15
    of the holy table, 15–16
    in the church, 59
    church raised in the air, 59–60
    of the mead, 69
    of the flour, 70
    of the angels, 9, 72
    of fire, 9
    of recovered silver, 85
    of the decaying body, 122
    of commanding demons, 186–87
    of raising the dead, 176–78
    of invisible travel, 126
    of sleeping thieves, 154
    worked by Grigorij, 154–57
    of Proxor's bread, 171, 173
    of salt from ashes, 172–73
    of the dove, 192–93
    Alimpij cures a leper, 194–95
    of the icons, 196–98
    of tonsuring, 200–1
    at Obščina, 215
Mixail, bishop of Jur'ev, 16n.
Mixail Aleksandrovič, prince, 216
Mixail Tobol'kovič, monk of the Caves Monastery, 110

Moisej the Hungarian, monk of the Caves Monastery, xxv, xxxi, xl, xli, xlix, 38n., 161, 162–69
    captured by Poles, 162
    tonsured, 166
    castrated, 168
    enters Caves Monastery, 168
    appears in a vision, 161
    relics of, 161
Mongols, xviii, xxix, xxx, 107n., 118n.
mosaic, 11, 192
Moscow, xxix, xxxvii, xxviii
Moses, 102, 104, 124
Mother of God, see Theotokos
M'stislav Svjatopolčič, prince of Volodymyr, xxvii, 188–90
M'stislav Volodimerovič, prince of Černihiv, 1, 97n.
Murom, 162n.
Muscovy, li, 119n., 154n., 227, 228n.
musicians, 77
Naaman the Syrian, 195
naměstnaja ikona ("special icon"), see icon(s)
Nativity of the Theotokos, Monastery of, xxiv
Neapolis (Cyprus), 228
Nesterec, deacon at the Caves Monastery, 216, 217
Nestor, chronicler, xxiii, 145, 152
Nestor, hagiographer, monk of the Caves Monastery, xviii, xxii, xxiii, xxxi, xxxiv–xxxviii, xl, xlii, xliv, xlv, li, 19n., 24, 25n., 40n., 42n., 68, 72n., 78n., 81n., 87n., 88, 109n., 114n., 131n., 211n., 218, 220, 221n., 222, 225
    tonsured by Feodosij, 23, 88
Nestor, author of Discourse 9, xxxvi, 89, 94, 95

and translation of Feodosij's relics, 90–92
New Testament, 9
Nicholas IV Mouzalon, patriarch of Constantinople, 223
Nifont, monk of the Caves Monastery, bishop of Novgorod, xix, xxx, xxxiii, xxxv, 110–12, 119, 223
Nikephoros II, metropolitan of Kiev, 93, 216
Nikita the Solitary, monk of the Caves Monastery, bishop of Novgorod, xxxv, 110n., 143–46
Nikodim, monk of the Caves Monastery, 191
Nikola, see Svjatoša
Nikola, archimandrite of the Caves Monastery, 216
Nikola, bishop of Tmutorokan', 119, 145
Nikola, bishop of Polack, 216
Nikolaj, monk of the Caves of Monastery, bishop of Perejaslav, 85, 118
Nikon, superior of the Caves Monastery, xxii–xxxv, xliii, li, 11, 14, 20n., 22n., 33, 36, 37, 38, 40, 51–52, 53, 67, 74–75n., 78, 110, 127n., 143–45, 149n., 192, 193, 194, 196, 209
  appointed superior, 87
Nikon "the Dry," monk of the Caves Monastery, xlvii, 125–27
Nikonian Chronicle, 149n.
Non-possessors, li
Novgorod, 16n., 110, 111, 117, 119, 144, 146, 174n., 223
Novgorod Fourth Chronicle, xlii, 145n.
Obščina, 216
Olaf, king of Sweden, 121
Old Testament, 9, 144–45

Oleg Svjatoslavič, prince of Černihiv, 68n., 149n.
Ol'ga, princess of Kiev, xxxiv
On, 164n.
Onisifor, presbyter of the Caves Monastery, 120–22, 145
Orthodox faith, xx, xxi, xxxiv, xxxv, li, 10, 77n., 80, 94, 107, 111, 212–14, 223
Our Lady of Blachernai, Church of (Constantinople), 6n., 87n.
Our Lady of Blachernai, Church of (at Klov), 13, 87
Ovruč, 117n.
pagans, 169, 212
Palestine, xxi, 89n., 95n.
Palladius, xx, xl
  Lausiac History, xx, xxi, xl
Palm Sunday, 45, 73
Pantocrator, 193n.
paramandyas, 135
passions (lust), 94, 120, 158–61, 162–68
Paterik, xviii–xxvi, xviii, xix–xxxiv, xxxvi, xxxvii, xxxviii, xxxix, xliv–li, 83n., 89n., 110n., 121n., 132n., 161n., 175, 199n., 205n., 216, 224, 226
  Arsenian redaction of, xxix–xxx, xxxii, xxxvii, xlviii, 226
  First Cassian redaction of (Cas. I), xxix–xxxi, xxxiv, xxxv, xxxvii, xxxviii
  Second Cassian redaction of (Cas. II), xviii, xxi, xxix, xxx, xxxii–xxxv, xxxvii, xxxviii, 132n., 224
  "Printed" edition, xxxiv, xxxv, xxxiv–xxxvi
  Theodosian redaction of, xxxiii
  Josif Trizna redaction of, xxxiii–xxxiv, xxxvi

Jakovlev, V. A., edition of, xxxvi, xxxviii
Paterikon, xl, 140, 193n.
patriarch, ecumenical, of Constantinople, 111
Paul, St., 40, 93, 101, 114, 116, 117, 164, 164, 190, 193, 204, 214
Paul, superior of a monastery in Černihiv, 76
Pečenegs, 162n.
Pelagius, xx
Peredslava, sister of Jaroslav Volodimerovič, 162
Perejaslav (Perejaslavl'), 2n., 13, 66n., 74n., 92, 99n., 118, 149n.
Peremyšl' (Przemyśl), 171n., 172
Peter, physician of Svjatoša, 132–35
Peter, St., 50, 113
Pharaoh, 164n.
Photios, patriarch of Constantinople, xx
physician(s), 132–34, 147–51, 194
Pimin the Faster, monk of the Caves Monastery, 128, 145, 191n., 199n.
Pimin the Long-suffering, monk of the Caves Monastery, xxxv, xlviii, 45n., 145n., 191n., 199–204
  miraculously tonsured, 200–1
  heals the sick, 202–3
Pimin, superior of the Caves Monastery, 120–22
Pinsk, 10n.
Podil, 197
podvig, 1
Polack (Polock), 119, 139, 206n., 215
Poland, xxviii, 107n., 162–65, 168, 169n., 171n., 207, 216n.
Pole(s), 109, 162, 211n.
Polikarp, archimandrite of the Caves Monastery, xxxii, xxxvi, xxxvii, xlii, 81n., 24, 120n., 215

Polikarp, monk of the Caves Monastery, xix, xx, xxi, xxiii, xxvi–xxxiii, xxxv, xxxvi, xxxvii, xxxix–xliii, xlviii, l, li, 2n., 6n., 9n., 20n., 83n., 117, 120, 127, 128, 130, 136, 138, 140, 142–43, 147, 151n., 152–53, 158n., 164n., 166n., 169n., 175n., 178n., 179n., 190n., 193n., 195n., 197n., 224–27
  Bishop Simon's epistle to, 113–20
  Bishop Simon's notes to, 127–28 130, 136–37, 138–39, 140, 142
  epistle of, to Archimandrite Akindin, 142–43, 147, 152–53, 224–27
Polock, see Polack
Polyeuktos, St., 7
poprišče, 26, 60n.
porter, 49, 50, 57, 60
Possessors, li
Potiphar, 161n., 164n., 165
Potiphera, 164n.
Povĕst vremennyx lĕt (PVL), xvii, xxi, xxiv, xxxviii, xl–xliv, 18n., 66n., 74n., 82n., 83n., 93n., 110n., 123n., 128n., 145n., 152, 162n., 168, 169n., 171n., 175n., 190n., 204n., 205n., 207n., 222n.
Pratum Spirituale, see John Moschos
presbyter, 108, 120
Prolog, 136n., 182n.
prophecy, 93–94, 104, 106, 108, 109n., 128, 144, 152, 156, 167, 174, 199n., 225
  of Antonij, 2, 32–33
  of Feodosij, 93–94, 106
  of Pimin the Faster, 128
  of Nikita the Solitary, 144
  of Grigorij the Miracle-worker, 156
  of Moisej the Hungarian, 167

of Proxor Lobednik, 174
of Marko the Cave-dweller, 179–80
of Vasilij, 189–90
of Pimin the Long-suffering, 202
Protostrator, 124
Proxor Lobednik, monk of the Caves Monastery, xxxv, xlviii, 93n., 169–75
   tonsured by Ioann, 170
   makes bread from pigweed, 170–71
   makes salt from ashes, 172–73
   and Prince Svjatopolk, 173–75
Przemyśl, see Peremyšl'
Psalter, 20, 42, 46, 47, 56, 113, 185, 191, 219
refectory, 72n., 131, 204, 207
relics, 7, 9, 212
   of Feodosij, 89–93
   of Evstratij, 125
   of Svjatoša, 135
   of Moisej the Hungarian, 161
   of Antonij, 219
repentance
   of the Greek painters, 11–12
   of robbers, 60, 154, 155, 156
   of Prince Svjatopolk, 174
   of the sinful leper, 194
robbers, thieves, 59–60, 64, 74, 96, 139, 140, 153–56
Royal Doors, 7n., 192n.
Rogněda, wife of Volodimer I Svjatoslavič, 162
Rome, xxxv
Ros' River, 12n.
Rostislav Rurikovič, prince of Ovruč, 117
Rostislav Volodimerovič, prince of Tmutorokan', 51
Rostislav Vsevolodovič, prince of Perejaslav, xl, 156, 157

Rostov, xxiv, xlvi, 13n., 16, 51, 66n., 117n., 118, 145, 162n., 197
"Rostov chronicle", xli, 119
Royal Doors, 192n.
Rufinus, xx
   Historia monachorum in Aegypto, xx, xxi
Rurikids, 95n., 111n.
Rus', xvii, xviii, xix, xxiii, xxiv, xxvii, xxviii–xxxi, xxxviii, xxxvii, xlii, xlvi, xlxi, 1n., 2n., 3n., 4, 5, 6, 13, 18, 19, 20, 22, 23, 24, 32, 40n., 61n., 69n., 72n., 74–75n., 81n., 94, 99, 100, 103, 107n., 108, 109, 110n., 111, 118, 119n., 123n., 130, 136, 142, 143, 144n., 145n., 154n., 157n., 165, 169, 170n., 171n., 172, 174, 193n., 215n., 216, 218, 219, 220, 222, 223, 224, 225, 230
Russia, Russian, 228, 230
Sabbas, St., xxii, 40n., 72
Sabellius, 211n., 213
sacramental bread, loaves, see communion bread
Saemingar dynasty, 1
Sahajdačnyj, Petro Konaševyč, hetman, xxxiv
St. Demetrios, Church of (Suzdal'), 99n.
St. Demetrios, Monastery of (Kiev), 22, 40n., 43, 50, 51, 66, 116, 146, 221
St. George, Monastery of, xvii, 32n.
St. Irene, Monastery of, xvii, 32n.
St. John the Forerunner, church of, 15
St. Menas, Monastery of, 40
St. Michael, Monastery of, 48
St. Nicholas, Monastery of, 35

St. Sophia, Church of (Kiev), 20, 81, 86, 219
St. Steven, Church of (Kiev), 65
SS. Boris and Glĕb, Church of (Černihiv), 136n.
SS. Cosmas and Damian, Monastery of, 115
Samson, 163
San River, 171n.
Saracens, 213
Saruia, 115
Šaxmatov, A. A., xxxii, xxxiii, xxxvi, xliii, xlv, 74n., 89n., 119n., 124n., 152n., 168n., 190n., 218, 222n.
Scandinavia, xlvi, 1n., 3n.
Šč'kovica, 215
Scriptures, 58, 76, 84
seclusion, 131, 143–44, 146, 158, 159, 185, 206, 207n.
Sejm River, 26n.
Semei, 115
Serapion, 170n.
Sergij, resident of Kiev, xlvii, 14
Sergej, Armenian heresiarch, 149n.
sextons, 202
Sigmundr, xlvi, 3n.
Simeon (Semen) Olel'kovic (Aleksandrovič), prince of Kiev, 9n., 216
Simon (Šimon), the Varangian, xlvi, xlvii, 1–5, 95, 97, 98
Simon, bishop of Vladimir and Suzdal', xviii, xix, xxi, xxiv, xxvi, xxvii, xxviii–xxxii, xxxiv, xxxv, xxxvi, xxxix–xliii, xlvii, xlix, li, 2n., 5n., 9n., 13n., 16n., 20n., 47n., 51n., 78n., 83n., 110n., 113, 114n., 115n, 117, 119, 120, 122, 123n., 124n., 127, 128, 130, 136–37, 138–39, 140, 142, 152, 175, 192, 197n, 225, 226
  epistle of, to Polikarp, 113–20
  notes of, to Polikarp, 127–28, 130, 136–37, 138–39, 140, 142
Sinai, Mt., 102, 175
Sinajskij Paterik, xxi, 138n.
sinodik, 93
Sit' River, 118n.
Sluck, 10n.
Smolensk, 13n., 117, 131n., 170
Sofronij, superior of the Monastery of St. Michael, 48
Sokal', 217
Solomon, 89, 163
Spiridon the Wafer-baker, monk of the Caves Monastery, xxxiv, 190–91
spiritual father, xxvii, li, 87, 118n., 121, 196n.
spiritual child, xxvii, 87, 93, 120, 130, 196
Stefan, superior of the Caves Monastery, bishop of Volodymyr, xxiii, xxxiv, xxxv, xliii, xliv, li, 13, 21n., 52, 79, 86, 91, 92, 110, 119, 208, 209, 222n.
  declared superior, 82
  expulsion of, 67, 68n., 87
  founds monastery at Klov, 87
Stephen, St., 65
steward, 56–57, 65, 68, 80, 117
Stoglav, 77n.
stone church, see Dormition of the Theotokos, Church of (Caves Monastery)
Stoudios Monastery, li, 16n., 23, 41n., 44, 222
Stoudite Rule (typikon), li, 16n., 23, 41n., 44, 61–62, 64n., 69n., 87n., 100n., 120n., 139n., 176n., 193n., 199n., 222
Stuhna River, 12n., 26n., 157n.
Superior(s), 18, 20, 22, 43, 67, 76, 216, 218, 219, 221

of the Caves Monastery, 15, 21, 67,
  79–80, 81, 82, 89, 90, 91, 92,
  97, 110, 116, 117, 118, 119,120,
  127, 129, 130, 131, 135, 143,
  146, 175n., 181, 184, 198, 200,
  201
 appointment of Varlaam as, 21, 41,
  81n., 220
 appointment of Feodosij as, 22–23,
  43, 102, 221
 appointment of Stefan as, 81–82, 86
 appointment of Nikon as, 87
 appointment of Ioann as, 15
 appointment of Vasilij as, 215–16
Suzdal', Suzdalia, xxviii, xxiv, xxxv,
  xxvi, 5, 13, 95, 99n., 113, 117n.,
  118, 119, 120, 142, 225
Svjatopolk II Izjaslavič, prince of
  Kiev, xlix, 93,144, 156n., 169,
  171–75, 188
Svjatopolk Volodimerovič, prince of
  Kiev, 19, 162, 219
Svjatoša (Svjatoslav Davidovič) prince
  of Černihiv, monk of the Caves
  Monastery, xxxii, xli, 1, 47n., 58n.,
  112, 131–36
 becomes monk, 131
 posthumous miracles of, 135
Svjatoslav Jaroslavič, prince of
  Černihiv and Kiev, xxvii, xxxviii,
  2, 9, 38n., 51, 74–78, 80, 84,
  87n., 111n., 131, 133, 207,
  211n.
Svjatoslav Ol'govič, prince of
  Novgorod and Černihiv, 111
Svjatoslav I, prince of Kiev, 128n.
Svjatoslav Volodimerovič, prince of
  the Drevljanians, 19n.
Symeon of Emesa, St., 228, 229
Symeon the New Theologian, 161n.
Syria, 132, 148n.
Tatar(s), xxx, xxxi, 107n.

tears, 23, 47, 179n., 180–81, 206,
  222
Terebovlja, xli, xlviii, 171n.
Theodore, St., 7.
Theodore, superior of the Stoudios
  Monastery, 44n., 48n., 119n.
Theodosios the Cenobiarch, St.,
  xxxvii, 25, 95
Theotokos, 1, 7, 11, 15, 17, 21, 25,
  50, 53, 60, 68, 81, 83, 87, 90,
  97, 105, 107, 111, 112, 137–38,
  147, 156, 168, 174, 195n.,
  216, 220, 221
 Virgin, 106, 210
 Mother of God, 2, 3, 4, 12, 103,
  105, 108; 192, 209, 225
 Mary, 7
Theotokos, Church of, see Dormition
Theotokos, Monastery of (Černihiv),
  see Dormition of the Theotokos,
  Monastery of,
Timofej, superior of the Caves
  Monastery, 97
Timothy, 117
Tit, priest of the Caves Monastery,
  140–41
tithes, 65, 119
Tmutorokan', 41, 51, 78, 87n., 119,
  114n., 145
tonsuring, 18, 21, 23, 32–33, 36–38,
  45, 87, 88, 118, 134, 135, 138,
  147, 152, 166n., 168, 169, 170,
  193, 199–205, 216, 218, 219,
  220, 226n.
Toropec, 206
Trypillja (Trepol'), 12, 157
Trubež River, 2n.
Turov, 119, 174, 188, 215
typikon, see Stoudite rule
Ukraine, xxxiv
Uspenskij sbornik, xxxvii, 24n., 26,
  100

Varangian(s), xlvi, xlvii, 2, 3, 5, 8, 9, 118, 181, 183, 188, 211–14
land, 1
Varangian cave, xl 19, 181, 183, 188, 189, 219
Varlaam, superior of the Caves Monastery, xxxiv, xxxv, xliii, 21, 22, 33n., 35n., 36, 37, 39, 40n., 41, 42, 43, 50, 51, 64n., 66n., 81n., 102, 133, 169, 220, 221
  appointed superior of the Caves Monastery, 21, 41, 81n., 220
  appointed superior of St. Demetrios Monastery, 22, 43, 221
Vasilij, boyar of Georgij Simonovič, 95–97
Vasilij, monk of the Caves Monastery, xxxv, xlii, xlix, 181–82, 184–90
  and Feodor, 182, 184–90
  exorcises demons, 185
  martyred, 189
Vasilij, superior of the Caves Monastery, xx, xl, 116n., 215–16
  tonsured by Nikephoros, 216
Vasil'ko, prince of Terebovlja, xli, xlvi, 131n., 171, 190n.
Vasyl'kiv (Vasil'ev), xxxvii, 26
Vavila, monk of the Caves Monastery, 130
Velikij Čet'i Minei (Great Menologion), xxxii, 136n.
Verxoslava, wife of Rostislav Rurikovič, xxvii, 117
vigils, 47, 72, 73, 108, 154, 209
vision(s), 71, 83, 122, 124, 160–61
  of other monks, 130
  of the church of the Theotokos, 2, 3, 60
  of Antonij, 11, 121, 137
  of Christ, 3
  demonic, 55, 109, 110, 139–40, 143–44, 182–85, 188, 205–6
  of Feodosij, 11, 58, 71, 85, 86, 96–97, 109, 111–12, 137
  of the icon of the Theotokos, 9, 12, 60–61
  of fire, 9, 72, 84, 91, 203
  of a wall, 74
  of light, 91–92
  of a town, 98
  of angels, 6–7, 104, 109, 121, 139–40, 141, 180
  of the Theotokos, 6–8, 13, 137–38
  of Moisej the Hungarian, 161
Vitae Patrum, xx
Vjatičians, 128
Vladimir, xviii, xxiv, xxv, xxvi, 113, 118, 119, 120, 142, 225
Volodar', prince of Peremyšl', 171
Volodimer Davidovič, prince of Černihiv, 131–35
Volodimer Jaroslavič, prince of Novgorod, 51n.
Volodimer Ol'gerdovič, prince of Sluck, 10n.
Volodimer I Svjatoslavič, St., prince of Kiev, xxxiii, xxxiv, 16n., 18, 19, 26n., 100, 109n., 128n., 162n., 211, 218, 219
Volodimer Vsevolodovič Monomax, prince of Perejaslav and Kiev, xxxix, 5, 13, 95n., 97n., 117n., 149, 156, 157, 174, 197
Volodymyr (Volodimer'), 50, 52, 91, 92, 119, 190
Volyn', 216
Vseslav Brjačeslavič, prince of Polack, 38n., 207
Vsevolod III "Great-Nest" Georgievič, prince of Vladimir/Suzdal' and Kiev, xxiv, 117n., 118n., 119n.

Vsevolod I Jaroslavič, prince of
  Perejaslàv and Kiev, 1, 2, 3, 13, 65,
  66n., 74–75, 95n., 148, 149n.,
  156n., 174n., 192, 207n.
Vytautas, grand duke, xxxi
Ware, T. 228, 229n.
Wijk, N. van, xxi
Zavoloč'e, 144
Zaxarija, 14, 15
Zdeislav Ggeuevič, see Kliment, boyar
Zygmunt August, king of Poland, 216

www.ingramcontent.com/pod-product-compliance
Lightning Source LLC
Chambersburg PA
CBHW030305080526
44584CB00012B/446